HOLLYWOOD SCREENWRITING DIRECTORY

SPRING/SUMMER • VOLUME 4

fw
media
BURBANK, CALIFORNIA

Published by F+W Media, Inc.
3510 West Magnolia Boulevard
Burbank, California 91505
www.fwmedia.com

Disclaimer

Every reasonable effort has been made to ensure the accuracy of the information contained in the *Hollywood Screenwriting Directory*. F+W Media, Inc. cannot be held responsible for any inaccuracies, or the misrepresentation of those listed in the Hollywood Screenwriting Directory.

Updates/Change Listing

Please submit corrections and updates to corrections@screenwritingdirectory.com

Print ISBN 13: 978-1-59963-832-4
Print ISBN 10: 1-59963-832-0
ePub ISBN 13: 978-1-59963-836-2
ePub ISBN 10: 1-59963-836-3
PDF ISBN 13: 978-1-59963-834-8
PDF ISBN 10: 1-59963-834-7

Contents

How to Use the *Hollywood Screenwriting Directory* 4

What is a Screenplay? 7

Query Letters 14

Treatments and Log Lines 17

The Legal 411 for Screenwriters 24

The Directory 51

Indexes

    Index by Company Name 281

    Index of Company Websites 292

    Index by Contact Name 308

    Index by Submission Policy 324

        Accepts query letter from produced or represented writers 324

        Accepts query letter from unproduced, unrepresented writers 324

        Accepts query letter from unproduced, unrepresented writers via email 326

        Accepts scripts from produced or represented writers 328

        Accepts scripts from unproduced, unrepresented writers 329

        Accepts scripts from unproduced, unrepresented writers via email 329

        Does not accept any unsolicited material 329

How to Use the *Hollywood Screenwriting Directory*

Dear Fellow Screenwriter,

Congratulations! You've made an investment in your screenwriting career that's sure to reap significant benefits. The *Hollywood Screenwriting Directory* is an essential reference guide that takes the mystery out of the script submission process, and literally puts the contact information of the Industry's top players right at your fingertips. Many of our loyal readers have secured representation and found script-selling success using it. And now, it's your turn.

This Spring/Summer Volume 4 edition brings you current contact information for more than 2,500 Industry insiders, along with updates on hundreds of our listings. It also features a new **Legal 411 for Screenwriters** section, which contains invaluable information from practicing Entertainment Attorney Dinah Perez. From script copyrights to writing collaborations through to public domain and derivative works, Dinah gives you the download on topics you'd have to pay over $400 an hour for in Hollywood.

Plus, the *Hollywood Screenwriting Directory* is now online as an active marketplace that allows you to post your project for purchase consideration in an area accessible only to verified Industry execs looking for new writers and fresh material. Visit screenwritingdirectory.com/c/HSDV4J now for a **free 90-day subscription**. You can also use our handy one-sheet template and screenwriter experience Q&A fields to present your work and yourself as a screenwriter in a way that will catch an exec's attention. You also have the option to have your logline included in our monthly screenplay report sent out to Industry professionals.

The *HSD* is a very specialized directory created by The Writers Store based on our extensive experience serving the screenwriting community since 1982. It contains a range of people to contact regarding your script, from ambitious upstarts to established studio execs, along with management companies who package production deals and independent financiers/distributors with a production wing. For each listing, you'll find the kind of useable information you need: Street and email addresses, whether or not they accept unsolicited material, and how they prefer to receive submissions.

While having access to this data is crucial, just as essential is an understanding of the right way to use it. These insiders are flooded with submissions daily. Any indication of incorrect format or other amateur flubs in the first few pages will quickly send your script to the trash.

We can't emphasize enough how important it is that your submission is polished and professional before you send it out for consideration. Screenwriting software makes producing an Industry-standard screenplay simple and straightforward. Programs like Final Draft and Movie Magic Screenwriter put your words into proper format as you type, letting you focus on a well-told story rather than the chore of margins and spacing. In these pages, we've also included a guide to proper screenplay format, along with sample title and first pages to help you send out a professional script.

Besides a properly packaged submission, it's also wise to know your audience before you send out any materials. If your script is an action thriller with a strong female lead, don't send it to Paul Giamatti's production company. Actors establish their own companies so that they're not reliant on studios for roles. Pad an actor's vanity (and his pipeline) by submitting materials catered specifically to him.

You may find that a good number of companies do not want unsolicited submissions. It's not that they're not open to new ideas; they're not open to liability. A script is property, and with it, come ramifications if not handled properly. If you choose to disregard "no unsolicited submissions," sending your script with a submission release form gives it a better chance of getting read. Consult with an entertainment attorney to draft an appropriate form, or consult a guide like *Clearance and Copyright* by Michael C. Donaldson, which has submission release form templates. It's also prudent to protect your work. We recommend registering your script with the WGA (Writers Guild of America, West) or the ProtectRite registration service.

A benefit of the digital age is that the same companies that are not open to receiving unsolicited submissions will gladly accept a query letter by email. Take advantage of this opportunity. Craft a well-written and dynamic query letter email that sells you and your script. We have included a sample query, and some tips and guidelines on how to write great query letters.

While Hollywood is a creative town it is, above all, professional. Do a service to yourself and the potential buyer by being courteous. If you choose to follow up by phone, don't be demanding and frustrated. These people are overworked and do not owe you anything. It's okay to follow up, but be sure to do so with respect. And if you pique a buyer's interest and she asks for a treatment, you must be ready to send off this vital selling tool at once! That's why we've also included a handy guide to writing treatments in this volume.

While it may oftentimes feel like the opposite, the Entertainment Industry *is* looking for new writers and fresh material. BUT (and this is important) they're also looking for those aspiring scribes to take the time to workshop their scripts with an experienced professional and get them to a marketable level. The Writers Store can help you get ready for the big leagues through our slate of screenwriting courses, personalized coaching and Development Notes service, which works in a format that mirrors the same process occurring in the studio ranks.

Hollywood is the pinnacle of competition and ambition. But that's not to say that dreams can't happen—they can, and they do. By keeping to these professional guidelines and working on your craft daily, you can find the kind of screenwriting success you seek.

Wishing you the best of luck,

Jesse Douma
Editor

What is a Screenplay?

In the most basic terms, a screenplay is a 90-120 page document written in Courier 12pt font on 8.5" x 11" bright white three-hole punched paper. Wondering why Courier font is used? It's a timing issue. One formatted script page in Courier font equals roughly one minute of screen time. That's why the average page count of a screenplay should come in between 90 and 120 pages. Comedies tend to be on the shorter side (90 pages, or 1 ½ hours) while Dramas run longer (120 pages, or 2 hours).

A screenplay can be an original piece, or based on a true story or previously written piece, like a novel, stage play or newspaper article. At its heart, a screenplay is a blueprint for the film it will one day become. Professionals on the set including the producer, director, set designer and actors all translate the screenwriter's vision using their individual talents. Since the creation of a film is ultimately a collaborative art, the screenwriter must be aware of each person's role and as such, the script should reflect the writer's knowledge.

For example, it's crucial to remember that film is primarily a visual medium. As a screenwriter, you must show what's happening in a story, rather than tell. A 2-page inner monologue may work well for a novel, but is the kiss of death in a script. The very nature of screenwriting is based on how to show a story on a screen, and pivotal moments can be conveyed through something as simple as a look on an actor's face. Let's take a look at what a screenplay's structure looks like.

The First Page of a Screenplay

Screenwriting software makes producing an Industry-standard script simple and straightforward. While screenplay formatting software such as Final Draft, Movie Magic Screenwriter, Movie Outline, Montage and Scriptly for the iPad frees you from having to learn the nitty-gritty of margins and indents, it's good to have a grasp of the general spacing standards.

The top, bottom and right margins of a screenplay are 1". The left margin is 1.5". The extra half-inch of white space to the left of a script page allows for binding with brads, yet still imparts a feeling of vertical balance of the text on the page. The entire document should be single-spaced.

Screenplay Elements

Following is a list of items that make up the screenplay format, along with indenting information. Again, screenplay software will automatically format all these elements, but a screenwriter must have a working knowledge of the definitions to know when to use each one.

Ⓐ Fade In

The very first item on the first page should be the words FADE IN:.

Ⓑ Page Numbers

The first page is never numbered. Subsequent page numbers appear in the upper right hand corner, 0.5" from the top of the page, flush right to the margin.

Ⓒ Mores and Continueds

Use mores and continueds between pages to indicate the same character is still speaking.

Ⓓ Scene Heading

Left Indent: 0"   Right Indent: 0"   Width: 6"

A scene heading is a one-line description of the location and time of day of a scene, also known as a "slugline." It should always be in CAPS. Example: EXT. WRITERS STORE - DAY reveals that the action takes place outside The Writers Store during the daytime.

Ⓔ Subheader

Left Indent: 0"   Right Indent: 0"   Width: 6"

When a new scene heading is not necessary, but some distinction needs to be made in the action, you can use a subheader. But be sure to use these sparingly, as a script full of subheaders is generally frowned upon. A good example is when there are a series of quick cuts between two locations, you would use the term INTERCUT and the scene locations.

Ⓕ Action

Left Indent: 0"   Right Indent: 0"   Width: 6"

The narrative description of the events of a scene, written in the present tense. Also less commonly known as direction, visual exposition, blackstuff, description or scene direction. Remember—only things that can be seen and heard should be included in the action.

Sample Screenplay Page

 FADE IN:

 EXT. WRITERS STORE - DAY

 In the heart of West Los Angeles, a boutique shop's large OPEN sign glows like a beacon.

 DISSOLVE TO:

INT. WRITERS STORE - SALES FLOOR - DAY

Writers browse the many scripts in the screenplay section.

ANTHONY, Canadian-Italian Story Specialist extraordinaire, 30s and not getting any younger, ambles over.

 ANTHONY
 Hey, how's everyone doin' here?

A WRITING ENTHUSIAST, 45, reads the first page of "The Aviator" by John Logan.

                    ENTHUSIAST
          Can John Logan write a killer first
          page or what?

                    ANTHONY
          You, sir, are a gentleman of
          refined taste. John Logan is my
          non-Canadian idol.

The phone RINGS. Anthony goes to--

THE SALES COUNTER

And answers the phone.

                    ANTHONY (CONT'D)
          Writers Store, Anthony speaking.

                    VOICE
               (over phone)
          Do you have Chinatown in stock?

I/E LUXURIOUS MALIBU MANSION - DAY

A FIGURE roams his estate, cell phone pressed to his ear.

                    ANTHONY (O.S.)
          'Course we have Chinatown!
          Robert Towne's masterpeice is
          arguably the Great American
          Screenplay...
               (MORE)

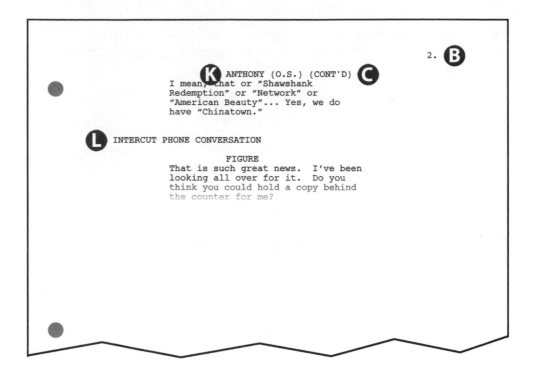

2. **B**

K ANTHONY (O.S.) (CONT'D) **C**
I mean, that or "Shawshank
Redemption" or "Network" or
"American Beauty"... Yes, we do
have "Chinatown."

L INTERCUT PHONE CONVERSATION

FIGURE
That is such great news. I've been
looking all over for it. Do you
think you could hold a copy behind
the counter for me?

Character

Left Indent: 2"   Right Indent: 0"   Width: 4"

G When a character is introduced, his name should be capitalized within the action. For example: The door opens and in walks LIAM, a thirty-something hipster with attitude to spare.

H A character's name is CAPPED and always listed above his lines of dialogue. Minor characters may be listed without names, for example TAXI DRIVER or CUSTOMER.

I Dialogue

Left Indent: 1"   Right Indent: 1.5"   Width: 3.5"

Lines of speech for each character. Dialogue format is used anytime a character is heard speaking, even for off-screen and voice-overs.

J Parenthetical

Left Indent: 1.5"   Right Indent: 2"   Width: 2.5"

A parenthetical is direction for the character, that is either attitude or action-oriented. Parentheticals are used very rarely, and only if absolutely necessary. Why? First, if you need to use a parenthetical to convey what's going on with your dialogue, then it probably needs a good re-write. Second, it's the director's job to instruct an actor, and everyone knows not to encroach on the director's turf!

(K) Extension

Placed after the character's name, in parentheses

An abbreviated technical note placed after the character's name to indicate how the voice will be heard onscreen, for example, if the character is speaking as a voice-over, it would appear as LIAM (V.O.).

(L) Intercut

Intercuts are instructions for a series of quick cuts between two scene locations.

(M) Transition

Left Indent: 4"   Right Indent: 0"   Width: 2"

Transitions are film editing instructions, and generally only appear in a shooting script. Transition verbiage includes:

```
CUT TO:
DISSOLVE TO:
SMASH CUT:
QUICK CUT:
FADE TO:
```

As a spec script writer, you should avoid using a transition unless there is no other way to indicate a story element. For example, you might need to use DISSOLVE TO: to indicate that a large amount of time has passed.

Shot

Left Indent: 0"   Right Indent: 0"   Width: 6"

A shot tells the reader the focal point within a scene has changed. Like a transition, there's rarely a time when a spec screenwriter should insert shot directions. Examples of Shots:

```
ANGLE ON --
EXTREME CLOSE UP --
LIAM'S POV --
```

Spec Script vs. Shooting Script

A "spec script" literally means that you are writing a screenplay on speculation. That is, no one is paying you to write the script. You are penning it in hopes of selling the script to a buyer. Spec scripts should stick stringently to established screenwriting rules. Once a script is purchased, it becomes a shooting script, also called a production script. This is a version of the screenplay created for film production. It will include technical instructions, like film editing notes, shots, cuts and the like. All the scenes are numbered, and revisions are marked with a color-coded system. This is done so that the production assistants and director can then arrange the order in which the scenes will be shot for the most efficient use of stage, cast, and location resources.

A spec script should never contain the elements of shooting script. The biggest mistake any new screenwriter can make is to submit a script full of production language, including camera angles and editing transitions.

It can be very difficult to resist putting this type of language in your script. After all, it's your story and you see it in a very specific way. However, facts are facts. If you want to direct your script, then try to go the independent filmmaker route. But if you want to sell your script, then stick to the accepted spec screenplay format.

Script Presentaction and Binding

Just like the format of a script, there are very specific rules for binding and presenting your script. The first page is the title page, which should also be written in Courier 12pt font. No graphics, no fancy pictures, only the title of your script, with "written by" and your name in the center of the page. In the lower left-hand or right-hand corner, enter your contact information.

In the lower left-hand or right-hand corner you can put Registered, WGA or a copyright notification, though this is generally not a requirement.

Sample Screenplay Title Page

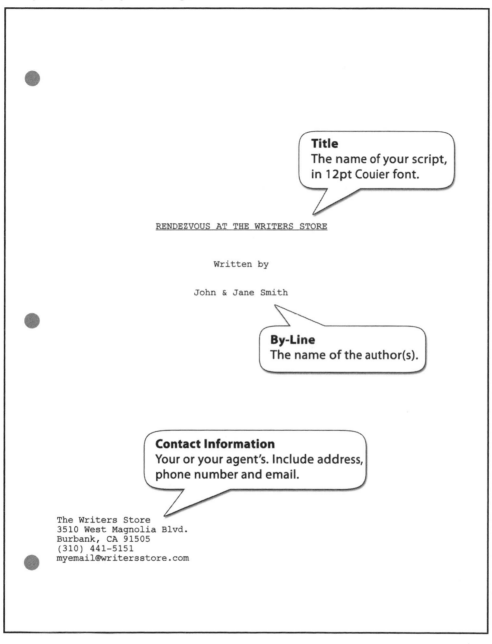

RENDEZVOUS AT THE WRITERS STORE

Title
The name of your script, in 12pt Couier font.

Written by

John & Jane Smith

By-Line
The name of the author(s).

Contact Information
Your or your agent's. Include address, phone number and email.

The Writers Store
3510 West Magnolia Blvd.
Burbank, CA 91505
(310) 441-5151
myemail@writersstore.com

Query Letters

A query is a one-page, single-spaced letter that quickly tells who you are, what the work is, and why the work is appropriate for the market in question. Just as queries are used as the first means of contact for pitching magazine articles and novels, they work just the same for scripts.

A well-written query is broken down into three parts.

Part I: Your Reason for Contacting/Script Details

Before even looking at the few sentences describing your story, a producer wants to see two other things:

1. **What is it?** State the title, genre, and whether it's a full-length script or a shorter one.
2. **Why are you contacting this market/person in particular?** There are thousands of individuals who receive scripts. Why have you chosen this person to review the material? Is it because you met them in person and they requested to see your work? Have they represented writers similar to yourself? Did you read that they were actively looking for zombie comedies? Spelling out your reason upfront shows that you've done your research, and that you're a professional.

Part II: The Elevator Pitch

If you wrote the first paragraph correctly, you've got their attention, so pitch away. Explain what your story is in about 3-6 sentences. The point here is to intrigue and pique only. Don't get into nitty-gritty details of any kind. Hesitate using a whole lot of character names or backstory. Don't say how it ends or who dies during the climax or that the hero's father betrays him in Act II. Introduce us to the main character and his situation, then get to the key part of the pitch: the conflict.

Try to include tidbits here and there that make your story unique. If it's about a cop nearing retirement, that's nothing new. But if the story is about a retiring cop considering a sex change operation in his bid to completely start over, while the police union is threatening to take away his pension should he do this, then you've got something different that readers may want to see.

Sample Query Letter

 **John. Q. Writer**
123 Main St.
Writerville, USA
(212) 555-1234
johnqwriter@email.com

Agent
JQA & Associates
678 Hollywood St.
Hollywood, CA 90210

Dear Mr./Ms (Last Name):

My name is John Q. Writer and we crossed paths at the Screenwriters World Conference in Los Angeles in October 2012. After hearing the pitch for my feature-length thriller, October Surprise, you requested that I submit a query, synopsis and the first 10 pages of the script. All requested materials are enclosed. This is an exclusive submission, as you requested.

U.S. Senator Michael Hargrove is breaking ranks with his own political party to endorse another candidate for President of the United States. At the National Convention, he's treated like a rock star V.I.P. -- that is, until, he's abducted by a fringe political group and given a grim ultimatum: Use your speech on live TV to sabotage and derail the presidential campaign you're now supporting, or your family back home will not live though the night.

The script was co-written with my scriptwriting partner, Joe Aloysius. I am a produced playwright and award-winning journalist. Thank you for considering October Surprise. I will be happy to sign any release forms that you request. May I send the rest of the screenplay?

Best,
John Q. Writer

Part III: The Wrap Up

Your pitch is complete. The last paragraph is where you get to talk about yourself and your accomplishments. If the script has won any awards or been a finalist in a prominent competition, this is the place to say so. Mention your writing credentials and experience. Obviously, any paid screenwriting experience is most valuable, but feel free to include other tidbits such as if you're a magazine freelancer or a published novelist.

Sometimes, there won't be much to say at the end of a query letter because the writer has no credits, no contacts and nothing to brag about. As your mother would tell you: If you don't have anything nice to say, don't say anything at all. Keep the last section brief if you must, rather than going on and on about being an "active blogger" or having one poem published in your college literary magazine.

Following some information about yourself, it's time to wrap up the query and propose sending more material. A simple way to do this is by saying "The script is complete. May I send you the treatment and full screenplay?"

Here are the elements of a query letter in the example on the facing page:

(A) Include all of your contact information—including phone and e-mail—as centered information at the top.

(B) Use proper greetings and last names.

(C) Include a reason for contacting the reader.

(D) Try and keep the pitch to one paragraph.

(E) Regarding your credentials, be concise and honest.

Treatments and Log Lines

Introduction to the Treatment

Nobody reads a full script in Hollywood anymore. Execs don't want to put in the time to read a 90-page comedy script, much less a 180-page epic. They want to know if the goods are there before they invest their precious time, and this is where the treatment comes in. Think of it as reading the back cover of a book before you invest in buying it. You'd never just pay for a book without knowing what type of story to expect. So it is with the movie industry. The treatment is the essential selling tool that can make or break your script.

What is a Treatment

A treatment is a short document written in prose form and in the present tense that emphasizes, with vivid description, the major elements of a screenplay.

That's a very broad definition, to be sure. And while the main purpose of a treatment is as a selling tool, there are variations of the definition to consider.

1. A treatment could be your first attempt toward selling your screenplay to a producer, your first try at getting someone to pay you to write the script.
2. A treatment could be a sales tool for a script that you've already written—a shorter, prose version of the screenplay's story for producers to read, to pique their interest in your project and entice them to read your screenplay.
3. A treatment could describe how you intend to attack a rewrite, either of your own script or of another writer's script. Often when a producer hires a writer to do a rewrite, they'll ask for a treatment first.
4. A treatment could be the first step toward writing your screenplay—it could be one of the first steps toward getting your story down on paper. Maybe you don't have time to write the screenplay yet—a treatment can help cement the story in your mind (and on paper) so that you can work on it later.

Why Write a Treatment?

Ultimately, the best reason to write a treatment is that the process of writing your treatment can help you write a better script. It can be easier to find and solve structural challenges, plot incongruities, lapses in logic, etc. in the prose treatment format than it is to find and solve those challenges in the screenplay format.

Writing a screenplay is a step-by-step process, and some steps are more involved than others. Writing a treatment is a very achievable step in the screenwriting process, and taking that step from beginning to end can be a rewarding boost for your writing ego.

Writing a treatment helps give tangible shape to your story, and makes sharing your story with others simpler and more precise. If you can share your story with others, you can get feedback, which may open up more channels in your brain and help your story to grow. The treatment format is much easier to read and comprehend for people who aren't familiar with the screenplay format.

You might not be ready to write your complete screenplay yet—you might not have time, you might not be fully committed to the idea. Writing a treatment is a good stopgap measure, so that an idea doesn't just exist as an idea—it may exist as something you can sell, share with a collaborator, or simply file away for a rainy day.

When is a Treatment Used

A treatment is usually used when you begin the process of selling your script. When you pitch your script to a producer and he shows interest in your script, he will most likely ask you to send over the treatment. This way, he can review the story and see if he is interested in reading the full script.

Think of the treatment as your business card—the thing you leave behind after you've pitched your story.

You may have heard of writers who sell a script based only a treatment. Yes, this happens, but this happens only for established writers with a track record of produced scripts. They have proven to Hollywood that they can write a blockbuster script, so buyers know that if they like the treatment, they will most likely love the script.

The treatment can also be used as an outline for the writer before he begins his script. It's smart to either outline or summarize a script before you begin writing. If you can complete the story in a smaller form, you know that you'll be able to sustain it in the longer script format. Architects don't erect a building without first designing a blueprint and then creating a model of the structure. The outline is your blueprint and the treatment is your model.

Treatment vs. Synopsis, Coverage, Beat Sheet and Outline

The term treatment is thrown around loosely in Hollywood, and you can be sure that you'll hear a different definition each time you ask. Some buyers will request a treatment when they really want a synopsis, an outline or a beat sheet. So what are the definitions of the other items?

Synopsis

A Synopsis is a brief description of a story's plot or a straightforward presentation of the scenes and events in a story. It is not a selling tool, but rather a summation of the story, and is typically no more than 2 pages long. It's generally used by professional script readers when writing coverage on a script.

Coverage

Coverage is the name of the document generated by the buyer's in house script readers. The main purpose of this document is to assess the commercial viability of the script. The reader supplies the buyer with the basic identifying information of the script, a synopsis, their comments on the script and a rating chart on all of the elements of the script, including characters, dialogue, action, setting, and commercial appeal. The reader then rates the script "pass" (no, thanks. Don't call us, cause we're certainly not gonna call you) "consider" (maybe someone we know can rewrite this puppy into something marketable) or "recommend" (this is the script that will move me from script reader hell to producing heaven!).

Beat Sheet

A Beat Sheet lists the sequence of major events that takes place in a script. It shows what will happen to the main character, and the order in which the events will occur. It can be anywhere from a short paragraph to three pages. Each beat is described in only 1-2 sentences.

Here is an extremely short example from "Die Hard."

1. New York Detective John McClane flies to Los Angeles to reconcile with his wife Holly at her company Christmas party.
2. When he arrives at Holly's high-rise office building, they argue and Holly leaves McClane alone in her executive bathroom.
3. From the bathroom, McClane hears terrorists, lead by Hans Gruber, break in and take over the building.
4. McClane witnesses the murder of Takagi, the CEO of the company, by Gruber and decides to take action.
5. McClane kills the brother of the lead henchman, Karl, and many other terrorists. He greatly angers Hans and Karl in the process.
6. McClane battles the terrorists with the help of a lone police officer.
7. The other police are against McClane and he feels alone in his fight. The police approach fails, so McClane is totally alone.
8. McClane fights Karl, kills him and prepares to go save Holly from Gruber.
9. Seemingly outnumbered, McClane appears to give up.
10. Using his New York wits, McClane kills Gruber and saves Holly.

Outline

An outline is a list of the scenes that make up a screenplay, from FADE IN to FADE OUT. Every writer has a different method of outlining—some are very detailed, while some list only a sentence or even just a word for each scene.

A good way to start a screenplay is to write a beat sheet, an outline and then a treatment. If you work out the story problems with these three tools, you will find that writing the actual script is a breeze.

Why Do I Need a Treatment

Besides being an important selling tool, a treatment allows you to see if your idea can sustain a feature-length film. Many writers take an idea straight to screenplay form, and then find 30 pages in that there is not enough story to continue the script. In this short summary form, you will also be able to identify any weaknesses in your plot, theme and characters.

It is much easier to find and solve these challenges in the prose treatment form than it is to locate them in the screenplay format.

How Long Should It Be?

Sadly, there is no cut and dry length for a treatment. Generally, treatments vary in length from 1-25 pages.

A general rule—the more power the executive holds, the shorter the treatment you should send them. It is recommended to have a few different versions of your treatment. Besides a lengthy summary of the story, have a quick one pager on hand.

What Is the Format?

Your treatment should be written in prose form, and in 12 point Courier font. In essence, the treatment looks like a short story. There should be one line of space between each paragraph, and no indenting.

DON'T insert dialogue, slug lines, or anything else in screenplay format.

DO use standard punctuation for dialogue.

However, be careful not to rely on much dialogue in your treatment in order to effectively tell the story in 10 pages or less. A few carefully chosen thematic lines will suffice. For instance, the treatment for "Forrest Gump" would likely use the line, "Life is like a box of chocolates. You never know what you're gonna get," because it is used throughout the script as a thematic tag line.

What Should I Aspire to Do with the Treatment?

The treatment should not look, sound or read like an outline, a beat sheet or a screenplay. The essence of the story and the characters should be evoked through exhilarating language and imagery. It should sound like an excited moviegoer recanting the details of a film he just saw that was thought provoking, exhilarating and made him feel like he just had to share all the details with his friends. The prose you use in a treatment should be different than the narrative lines of a screenplay.

The beginning of the treatment has to grab the reader and not let go until the very end. Your reader should be able to see the script play out on the silver screen in front of his or her very eyes. After reading the treatment, the reader should be on fire to get this script to her boss, pronto!

The Log Line

A Log Line is a one sentence description of your film. It's really that simple. You've seen log lines, even if you're not aware of it. In essence, TV Guide descriptions of films are log lines. A log line may describe the following elements:

- Genre—comedy, drama, thriller, love story, etc.
- Setting—time and place, locale, other pertinent information
- Plot—the main narrative thrust of the story
- Character—the lead character or group of characters
- Theme—the main subject of the movie

A log line need not contain the following elements:

- Character names (unless the characters are historical figures)
- Back story
- Qualitative judgments—"A hilarious story..." "A fascinating tale..."
- Comparisons to other films—"It's 'Jaws' meets 'Mary Poppins'..."

Here are a few examples of log lines for well-known films. See if you can guess the film being described (the answers are right below, so don't cheat!):

1. A throwback to the serial adventure films of the 1930s, this film is the story of a heroic archeologist who races against the Nazis to find a powerful artifact that can change the course of history.
2. Set at a small American college in the early 1960s, this broad comedy follows a fraternity full of misfits through a year of parties, mishaps and food fights.
3. An illiterate boy looks to become a contestant on the Hindi version of "Who Wants to be A Millionaire" in order to re-establish contact with the girl he loves, who is an ardent fan of the show.

4. A man decides to change his life by saying 'yes' to everything that comes his way. On his journey, he wins $45,000, meets a hypnotic dog, obtains a nursing degree, travels the globe, and finds romance.

5. A behind-the-scenes view of the 2000 presidential election and the scandal that ensued in the weeks following.

Get the idea? The log line is designed to describe and to tease, like a line of advertising copy for your film. It has to be accurate, it can't be misleading. It's the first sentence a producer or executive is going to read, and you've got to make sure it isn't the last. Make it count.

By the way, the log lines above are for:

1. "Raiders of the Lost Ark"
2. "Animal House"
3. "Slumdog Millionaire"
4. "Yes Man"
5. "Recount"

Why Is the Log Line Important in a Treatment?

The log line is the first sentence an executive will ever read from your hand. It's also the shorthand that executives will use to discuss your project with each other. If a junior executive reads your treatment and likes it, she'll need to tell her boss about the project in order to move it to the next step (probably a meeting between you and the boss).

The boss will ask the junior executive "What's it about?" The junior executive will respond with your log line, if you've written it well and accurately. You are helping to provide the junior executive with the tools she needs to help move your project forward. If you don't provide a log line at the beginning of your treatment, you rely on the junior executive's ability to digest your treatment and come up with a good log line of her own. Even in a collaborative art form like filmmaking, it's never a good idea to leave a job undone for someone else to do if you are more capable of doing it yourself. And who knows your story better than you do? Write a great log line for your treatment, and you'll know that your treatment is being discussed in your own words.

Who Is the Log Line For

The log line is for the buyer: the executive, the producer, the agent. By writing a log line for your treatment, you are helping them to process your material more efficiently. Getting a movie made is a sales process, a constant, revolving door sales process. You sell your work to an agent, who then sells your work to a producer, who then sells it to a director, who then sells it to actors and key crew members.

Once the movie is made, the sales process starts all over again, as the producer has to sell the movie to distributors and marketing executives, who have to sell the film to theater owners who have to sell the film to audiences. A good log line can ride the film all the way from start to finish, helping to sell it at each step.

Should the Log Line Refer to Other Movies?

No. It used to be popular to write log lines that were entirely film references. This practice became so prevalent that it became a cliché, and should be avoided if at all possible. Nothing says "schlock" as quickly as a "Die Hard" reference—the classic action movie reference that every movie strived for in the early 1990s. "Speed" was called "Die Hard" on a bus. "Passenger 57" was called "Die Hard" on a plane. Descriptive as these log lines may be, they read as lazy writing, and if your writing isn't even original in the log line, who will be interested in reading your treatment or your script? Avoid hucksterism, overselling and hype. It's a turnoff.

How Long Should the Log Line Be

Your log line should be one sentence long. Pare it down to its essence, and don't let your sentence become a run-on. Try it out loud, see if it works. You don't have to follow every twist and turn of the plot in your log line, you only have to convey the flavor of the script. One sentence will do it.

What Is the Difference Between the Log Line and the Theme?

Your log line is a sales tool that is a teaser and an invitation to read your script. The theme may be contained in the log line, but not necessarily. Theme is the real answer to "What is your script about?" and Theme need not be confined to a one sentence answer. Theme is often related to the discovery that your main character makes during the course of the film. For instance, in "Raiders of the Lost Ark," Indiana Jones discovers that people are actually more important to him than historical artifacts. In "Animal House," the Deltas discover that the camaraderie that they've discovered in their fraternity is the real lasting value of their college experience, not their class work or their social status on campus.

In Closing

You've spent months or years (or even decades) on your script, and so it may be frustrating to jump through the hoops of the submission process—but it's important. Don't give readers an excuse to ignore your work. You must craft a killer query, treatment and log line before the script gets its big shot. Compose them well, and you're on your way to selling that screenplay.

The Legal 411 for Screenwriters

By Dinah Perez

As a practicing entertainment attorney for nearly two decades, I have represented many writers. I have counseled them on the legal issues related to their writing endeavors, negotiated their agreements with agents and managers, helped them sell their screenplays, and settled their disputes with other writers and producers.

You need to be diligent when it comes to dealing with the legal issues that may arise while you are writing and selling your screenplay, including hiring an agent and manager. Otherwise, you may end up jointly owning your screenplay with another writer, though it was not your intention; may be sued for copyright infringement for incorporating copyright protected material into your screenplay that you thought was in the public domain; could waste your time writing a derivative work based on an original whose rights you cannot acquire; may not be paid compensation and rights you're entitled to when you sell your screenplay; may not be able to shop or sell your screenplay; and may find it impossible to replace your current agent or manager. Overall, consulting with an entertainment attorney up front is much more cost efficient that attempting to fix mistakes and settle disputes that could have been avoided. Whenever I say "attorney" herein, I mean "entertainment attorney."

This chapter endeavors to inform you of the legal issues that exist as you navigate through the process of writing, shopping, selling your screenplay, and hiring an agent, manager, and attorney. This is not a full exploration of the law, nor is it intended to make you an expert in the field. Rather, it is meant to help you spot the issues that may require legal counsel and the important deal terms of the agreements into which you may enter into as a screenwriter. There is a primer on the basics of copyright law up front. Thereafter, I have organized the information in a sequential manner that guides you on your journey, start to finish.

Copyright

A "copyright" is a form of protection for the authors of original content which, with few exceptions, bestows upon authors of intellectual property, such as a book, play, magazine article, news story, video game, screenplay, motion pictures, etc., the exclusive right to reproduce, distribute, perform, prepare and sell their creations.[1] Copyright protection does not extend to ideas—only to their expression. The current term of copyright is the life of the author plus 70 years.[2] Copyright is automatic the moment the work is fixed in a tangible medium, like a printed page, a hard drive, a flash drive, digital recording, film, etc.[3] Copyright law may impact your use of any of the source material you incorporate into your screenplay, and the ownership of your screenplay if you collaborate with another writer.

Copyright protection means that you own the object of your creation and that anyone who wants to use it needs to acquire the right to do so from you. In fact, absent an exception, anyone who uses your copyright protected work without your assent is infringing on your copyright. Likewise, you cannot use another's work without permission unless said work is in the public domain, or you are claiming your use is a "Fair Use." This exception to the Copyright Act allows you to utilize another's work without permission for the purpose of "criticism, comment, news reporting, teaching (including multiple copies for classroom use), scholarship, or research" without infringing copyright.[4] I advise that you proceed with caution and consult with an attorney if you are claiming a Fair Use exception to the Copyright Act, since the exception is far narrower than most people realize.

Though copyright protection is automatic, I strongly urge you to spend the $35 it costs to formally register a copyright for your treatment (if you are going to be pitching it prior to writing the screenplay) and screenplay, once you have completed them. You can register a copyright at any time, but I recommend you do so before you start shopping and submitting your treatment and/or screenplay. The benefits that you gain from the registration far outweigh the cost and time it takes to complete the registration form online. Copyright registration within five years of first publication provides proof of ownership and affords you the opportunity to litigate against infringers, since registration is a prerequisite to filing a legal claim. Registration within three month of first publication and prior to an infringement allows a court to award you statutory damages of up to $150,0000 (or actual damages and profits, if they are more than the statutory damages) as well as attorneys' fees. You may only be awarded actual damages and profits if you do not register within the first three months of publication or prior to an infringement.[5]

Registration of your copyright with the U.S. Copyright Office is the only registration that affords the benefits in the preceding paragraph. The "poor man's copyright," which entails you mailing your screenplay (or other creation) to yourself and you saving the unopened package, provides no more protection than the unregistered copyright. The Writers Guild of America ("WGA") script registration service, which allows you to register ideas, treatments, screenplays, and teleplays, may serve to potentially provide proof as to the day of existence of your registered material. I recommend registering with WGA when a production company requests it, or when what you have created is not entitled to copyright protection, e.g., an idea. WGA registration costs $20 for non-members and $10 for members. Note that WGA script registration does not trump the Copyright Act.

Note that in order for anyone to infringe on your screenplay's copyright they actually have to copy it. There is no infringement unless the party you are accusing had access to your screenplay and there is substantial similarity of the copyright protected elements in your screenplay and the screenplay or picture you are claiming is infringing on yours. You have no copyright infringement claim if someone independently creates a screenplay that is similar to yours.

Ready, Set ... Pause

You have come up with an idea for a screenplay which you want to begin writing. I suggest that you stop and ponder what you intend to write and the potential legal issues that may exist at this juncture. Pausing long enough to consider what may be required legally of you at the start of every writing endeavor will help you avoid legal errors and costly mistakes that may undermine your goals.

Ask yourself the questions that follow in order to determine if you need to consult with and/or hire an attorney. Are you writing by yourself or with a writing partner? Is the story you want to tell completely fictional and original to you? Is your screenplay based on, or inspired by, outside source material, like a book, play, news article, magazine article, or trial transcript? Are you writing about a living person? It is important that you ask yourself these questions at the outset so that you do not waste time writing something you cannot sell.

Resist the temptation to use a boilerplate agreement not specifically drafted for you by an attorney. Chances are you do not know enough about the law, or crafting an agreement, to revise the agreement without creating a litigation worthy mistake, or one that forces you to shelve your screenplay. The time that you are investing writing warrants the cost of hiring an attorney to do things right.

Writing the Screenplay

Collaborations

A "collaboration" occurs when you write with another writer. You have to consider the long-term implications of any writing partnership because the term of copyright, in the proceeds of your collaboration, is your life plus 70 years. As such, it is important that your writing partner and you share a similar vision for the screenplay you intend to write, that you agree on the deal terms of your partnership, and that you assess the relationship and its long term viability. Note that your writing partner and you will equally co-own the screenplay you write together the moment you fix it in a tangible medium, since copyright automatically attaches regardless of oral agreements or intention to the contrary.

I strongly urge that you retain an attorney, if you do not already have one, and that you enter into a "Collaboration Agreement," a three to four page agreement that addresses all of the pertinent terms of your writing partnership, e.g., split of copyright and revenues, who gets the first position credit, who gets to make the final decision if you disagree on a creative or business issue, who will be responsible for shopping the screenplay, who approves the sale, etc.

Your attorney will help you compromise when your writing partner and you cannot seem to agree on a deal term so that you both feel fairly treated. When a client and collaborator cannot agree on the credit, I suggest that one take the first position credit on screen and the other in ads. When both want final approval, I suggest that one have it on business decisions and the other on creative ones. You can start writing once you have executed the Collaboration Agreement. If you cannot agree, despite the attorney's efforts, then you both just walk away, only having expended the legal fees. This is a small price to pay to avoid a time-intensive and potentially costly dispute down the line.

What happens if you started writing without a Collaboration Agreement and now realize that you do not want to complete the screenplay with your writing partner? You may not have to shelve what you have written thus far if your writing partner is willing to assign it to you. To "assign" means to transfer an asset. You want the other writer to transfer his/her interest in the screenplay to you. This is done via an "Assignment," since copyright law requires that a transfer of a copyright interest be affected by a written document signed by the party assigning rights.[6] I suggest that you execute an Assignment, even if what you have written does not qualify for copyright protection. In addition to drafting the Assignment, an attorney can motivate a recalcitrant collaborator by negotiating terms whereby he/she is paid a portion of the screenplay's sale price. Unfortunately, you may have to chalk this experience up to a lesson learned if your collaborator and you are at an impasse. The alternative, in such a circumstance, is that you assign the results and proceeds of your collaboration to the other writer.

Original Fictional Screenplays

You can proceed to write without regard to any legal issues if you are writing a completely original screenplay either on your own or with a writing partner, as long as you have entered into a Collaboration Agreement. For the purposes of this chapter, "completely original to you" means that you are writing a work of fiction that is not based on outside material, be it a book, play, magazine article, life story, video game, etc. If you are doing research, then it is best that you determine if any of the other sections of this chapter apply to your use of the source materials you may be incorporating into your screenplay.

Screenplays Based on Public Domain Material

You may write a screenplay that is an adaptation of, or based upon, a work that is in the public domain without infringing its copyright. A work is in "Public Domain" when no one owns that work's copyright or if the work never qualified for copyright protection. A work is in the public domain because it was not registered for copyright at a time when an actual registration was mandatory, did not comply with the formalities of the Copyright Act, or the copyright term has expired. You can use a work that is in public domain without securing permission to do so from the author. Works in the public domain include the following: Works published between 1923 and 1977 that were never registered for copyright; works published prior to 1923; works published between 1923 and 1963 that were registered for copyright but published without a copyright notice; works published between 1978 and March 1, 1989 without a copyright notice and without a subsequent registration (within 5 years); unpublished works from authors who died prior to 1944; unpublished anonymous or pseudonymous works created prior to 1894; unpublished works created prior to 1894 when the author's date of death is unknown; and, foreign works that are in the public domain in their country of origin.[7]

Facts, numbers, events, government works (written by government employees), and ideas do not qualify for copyright protection and are, therefore, also in the public domain. Keep in mind that though the aforementioned are in the public domain, their expression and any theories that are original to the author may be protected by copyright. Be extremely careful when using material in historical biographies. Do extensive research in order to separate the historical facts from the author's theories and expression thereof.

Keep your notes and research and annotate your screenplay if you are including any public domain works or information in your screenplay; this may seem burdensome, but you will be grateful you did it if you are ever accused of copyright infringement, since you may have to provide it to prove your innocence. Furthermore, whoever produces your screenplay is going to purchase Errors and Omissions Insurance which, among other things, insures producers against copyright infringement law suits. The insurance carrier may require an opinion letter from an attorney, who may request the annotated script from you. It is far easier to annotate a script as you write than to try to piece it together after the fact.

You are not required to credit the source of your public domain materials. Notwithstanding, I recommend that you credit the author and work if your screenplay is an adaptation of it, or if your screenplay is based upon the work. You do not need to credit your research sources for facts, numbers and such.

Derivative Works

You need to secure the author's or publisher's ("author/publisher") permission if you want to adapt or write a screenplay based upon or inspired by another literary work, such as a book, play, magazine article, essay, etc. Do not take the risk of writing first and attempting to acquire rights afterwards. You are not only infringing copyright when you do this—you are also potentially wasting your time because the author/publisher of the literary work may refuse to let you acquire the rights you need to proceed. They do not always want to have their literary works adapted to the big screen and, even if they do, may prefer to do business with a studio, which is more likely to pay them hefty option fees and purchase prices. If that is the case, it is best that you discover it up front before you invest your time.

Copyright protection applies to that portion of a derivative work created by you, but not to the original work itself. If you adapt a book, your adaptation is protected by copyright, but you acquire no rights in the original materials from the underlying book. In other words, the characters, locations, dialogue, storyline and other elements from the book belong to its author/publisher. The same goes any for public domain facts you incorporate into your screenplay; they remain in the public domain while your expression of those facts is subject to copyright protection.

You acquire the rights to a literary work by entering into an "Option/Purchase Agreement" whereby you have the exclusive option to buy said literary work for a determined period of time. The Option/Purchase Agreement has two components: the Option Agreement ("Option") itself states how much time you have to buy the literary work, and the purchase agreement includes the sale price and rights to be granted. You purchase the literary work by exercising the Option and paying the purchase price prior to the Option's expiration date. You do not actually purchase the literary work until the commencement of principal photography—when you know that the picture is being produced.

Options usually run in one year increments ("option period(s)") and can have one or more extensions. I recommend a one year initial option period with a minimum of two one year extension periods. You pay an "option fee" at the commencement of each option period. Option fees are considered advances and, therefore, may be applicable against the purchase price. If you have paid $20,000 in applicable option fees, when you exercise the Option, you pay $80,000 of the total $100,000 purchase price. If you do not make the option fees applicable, then you would pay the full purchase price irrespective of the option fees paid. The Option expires if you let it lapse due to non-payment of the applicable option fee, so be sure to extend the Option one week prior to its expiration; to avoid any mishaps mail the option fee and notice of extension via registered mail return receipt requested.

My clients have paid option fees as low as $1 and as high as $25,000 per option period. Expect to deplete your bank account if you are entering into an Option/Purchase Agreement on behalf of a best-selling book or play, or a magazine article or news story from a well known publication. Authors/publishers in the know expect an option fee equal to 10% of the purchase price. Some may consider this an industry standard—I do not because this is a point of negotiation versus a hard and fast rule. If you cannot afford to pay an option fee equal to 10% of the purchase price, then offer what you can pay, keeping in mind that you do not want to insult the author/publisher. Among other things, I may offer to make one or more of the option fees non-applicable if they are on the low end and it seems like they may be keeping the author/publisher from agreeing to the Option/Purchase Agreement. A "free" Option may be possible if you are acquiring a self-published or obscure book or play, or an article published in a relatively unknown publication. Notwithstanding that the Option is free, you should pay at least one dollar per option period so that the Option/Purchase Agreement does not fail for lack of consideration of some kind. "Consideration" is necessary for the formation of a binding contract—each party to the transaction needs to get a benefit.

The Option/Purchase Agreement for the literary work upon which you are basing your screenplay will determine whether you can sell your creation upon its completion. You will not be able to sell your screenplay if you go about it incorrectly or offer too high a purchase price. I advise that you hire an attorney to help you negotiate and draft an Option/Purchase Agreement that provides you with all the rights you need to deliver to your screenplay's buyer.

Remakes and Sequels Based on Pre-Existing Pictures

Do not write a screenplay based on a previously released motion picture or television show. This is not only copyright infringement—it is a monumental waste of your time! Under no uncertain terms will the motion picture studio or television network ("studio/network") which produced the original ever give you permission to write a sequel or remake based on their original motion picture or television show; they do not let third parties acquire an interest in their library. When the studio/network is ready, it will develop the remake or sequel in-house, with writers of their own choosing. Delete the screenplay if you have already written it, since you cannot use it as a writing sample or share it with anyone due to copyright infringement. Do not waste your money hiring an attorney to attempt to make a submission for you since the studio/network always responds with a resounding, "no." They do not want to read your screenplay because they do not want to risk you filing a copyright infringement, unjust enrichment, and/or breach of implied contract law suit against them, when they produce a remake or sequel that contains elements that were in your submitted screenplay. This happened to MGM and Sylvester Stallone when a writer submitted his version of "Rocky IV" to them. MGM and Sylvester Stallone prevailed over the writer because the "Rocky" characters were entitled to copyright protection.

Life Stories

"Private Persons"

Every living person has the "right of privacy"—the right to be left alone and the right to keep private facts from the public. As a consequence thereof, you need to enter into a Life Story Agreement if the subject of your screenplay is a "private person" whose story has not been in the national news and, hence, is not known by the general public. Do not commence writing until you have entered into a Life Story Agreement. The only exception here is if you are writing about a deceased person, since the right of privacy terminates upon death.

A Life Story Agreement is an agreement whereby the person whose life story you are writing (the "subject" of your screenplay) gives you permission to base your screenplay on his/her life story. It also allows your screenplay's buyer to produce and distribute the picture based on your screenplay. The Life Story Agreement is an Option/Purchase Agreement which takes into account the personal nature of the rights being acquired. The option fee and purchase price for a private person's Life Story Agreement are generally on the low end, because the life story is arguably not in big demand. Both tend to be far lower than the subject usually expects. It is more likely that the purchase price will be in the $80,000 range than the $1 million—the sum a subject asked of a client of mine a couple of years ago. You will not be able to find a buyer for your screenplay if you overpay for the rights, so that is something to always keep in mind.

The Life Story Agreement will give you access to the subject's life story via any news clippings, journals, and interviews. Do not be surprised if the subject wants "final approval" of the screenplay. You can grant the subject the right to comment on a draft of your screenplay, but never final approval. The former is just feedback, the latter means that the subject can stop you from producing any version of the screenplay he/she does not like. Needless-to-say, you never give a subject final approval of the screenplay.

The Life Story Agreement conveys upon you the right to write the screenplay, but it does not give you permission to defame or portray the subject of your screenplay in a false light without legal repercussions. You can take certain dramatic license with the story, but cannot depict the subject in an untrue and in an inaccurate manner—especially one that would be offensive or damaging to him/her. Let the subject comment on the screenplay so that you know where you have potential issues. It is much easier and cost efficient to fix the issues during the writing process than to address them in a court of law. Note that defamation and false light are not the same thing: the former is making false statements that harm a person's reputation and the latter is making untrue statements that depict a person in a false light and are offensive or cause the person embarrassment.

"Public Persons"

Celebrities, politicians, and other persons in whom the general public has great interest are all considered "public persons" because they have disclosed their private facts and live so much of their lives out in the public. As a consequence, public persons have a more limited right of privacy than the private person, and have a lesser expectation of it.

You have a lot of leeway to write about a politician because of the First Amendment and the public's right and need to know about any individual running for, or in, political office.[8] You may disclose truthful facts about politicians, e.g., that a politician is taking bribes, is an alcoholic or drug addict, has cancer, etc. Limit disclosure to facts that impact the politician's ability to do his/her job or how he/she carries out the responsibilities of office. You do not have the same berth where a living celebrity is concerned. If you want to avoid a costly judgment in favor of a celebrity, use facts that are already in the public consciousness, garnered from the likes of a trial transcript, news story, magazine article, biography, autobiography, television interviews, etc.

In the category of public persons are criminals whose crimes have catapulted them to celebrity status. Casey Anthony, Amy Fisher, Ted Bundy, and David Berkowitz aka the Son of Sam are what I call "celebrity criminals." The aforementioned have all had pictures produced about them, but not all entered into Life Story Agreements with the television networks that produced movies about them. In fact, two of the three networks that produced pictures about

Amy Fisher, the "Long Island Lolita," did so without a Life Story Agreement. You can write about a celebrity criminal as long as you stick to the facts disclosed in court during a trial and/ or are in the public domain.

Notwithstanding, since the public person has a right to privacy, limited though it may be, I always recommend that you consult with an attorney and that you enter into a Life Story Agreement rather than proceed without one. In order to sell your screenplay, you are going to have to warrant and represent that you have not invaded anyone's right of privacy, and will be required to agree to indemnify and hold harmless the producer if you breach that warranty and representation. This means that you have to reimburse the producer for any damages the producer suffers due to your breach of the right of privacy via your screenplay. The Life Story Agreement greatly eliminates the risk of litigation and a costly judgment, as long as you do not defame or portray your subject in a false light (there has to be an element of maliciousness where celebrities are concerned). The producer and distributor may want the assurances and rights granted via the Life Story Agreement and may make it a condition of financing and distribution. Also, you may want the public person's cooperation either because you may want to interview him/her to gain access to information that was not previously disclosed and/or need his/her help in securing any releases from other individuals integral to the life story.

The Right of Publicity

Every person, be they private or public, also has the "right of publicity," which gives everyone the right to control the commercial exploitation of their name, likeness, voice, and any other identifying aspect of their persona. In other words, your screenplay's producer cannot advertise and distribute a picture based on your screenplay unless you acquired the subject's right of publicity. This is best done via a Life Story Agreement, which grants the buyer the right to use the subject's, name, voice and likeness to produce, advertise, and distribute the picture.

Also, though the right of privacy terminates at death, the right of publicity does not always because state law determines whether the right dies or survives. For example, in New York, the right of publicity is extinguished at death for persons domiciled there[9] and, as per California statute, the right of publicity is a descendible property right that currently survives death by 70 years (for persons who died there prior to 1985).[10] You need to know where the subject of your screenplay died in order to ascertain whether the right of publicity ended with, or outlived, your subject's life.

Representation: Signing with an Agent or Manager

You are going to need representation via an agent or manager once you are done writing your screenplay. The California Talent Agency Act ("TAA") says that only licensed "agents" may procure, offer, promise, or attempt to procure employment or engagements for you. Agents must limit their commissions to 10% of what you earn, post a $50,000 surety bond with the Labor Commissioner, submit their artist agreement for approval by the Labor Commissioner, and segregate client monies from agency monies in a client trust fund.[11] In addition, agents are not supposed to have a conflict of interest with their clients, which means that they do not attach themselves to produce their clients' screenplays.

Managers are not licensed agents and, therefore, are not supposed to engage in agent type activities, such as pitching, shopping screenplays, and attempting to secure writing assignments. Because of the TAA, managers are limited to advising their clients on matters related to their careers, helping their clients secure agency representation, and assisting in the development of their clients' screenplays. They cannot procure, promise to procure or attempt to procure work. Since managers are not agents, they are not required to post a surety bond or maintain a client trust account, and have no limit on their commissions—though the industry standard is 10%. Notwithstanding the TAA, most literary managers do engage in agent type activities on behalf of their clients when their clients lack agency representation. Managers risk rescission of the management agreement with you, and forfeiture of past and future commissions from you, if you file a complaint against them with the California Labor Commissioner alleging that the manager engaged in activities in violation of the TAA, and the California Labor Commissioner determines your allegations to be true.

I am grateful for every reputable manager who works to create and improve the career of any writer—more so when the writer is not represented by an agent. I believe managers should be paid for the value of services they render regardless of the TAA. They should get to collect commissions if their services contributed to your success and earnings. The only problem I have with managers is that their interests are very often in conflict with those of their clients. This occurs when managers attempt to attach themselves to produce their clients' screenplays. A manager friend tells me that she should be credited and paid as a producer because the development work that she does with her clients is actually a producer's job. I disagree.

My biggest concern with managers attaching themselves to produce is that it might deter a producer from going forward—especially if the manager has not produced before. It's best to have an agreement with the manager whereby the manager does not insist on being attached, or will step aside if his/her attachment negatively impacts the negotiation. If necessary, I would offer the manager a higher commission (up to 20% total) to compensate him/her for development services.

Notwithstanding the possible drawbacks, there are a couple of advantages when a manager produces: you have someone advocating on your behalf and you pay a lower commission because the manager's producing fee is credited against the commission you owe. (A commission of $100,000 gets reduced to $20,000 if the manager's producing fee is $80,000.) Whether you want a manager/producer representing you is something that you need to consider prior to entering into the management agreement. Very often, managers will decline representation if they cannot produce the material they develop.

Standard agency and management agreements include a variety of clauses related to your relationship with the agent and/or manager, their duties, compensation, the term of the agreement, how you may be able to terminate the agreement do to non-performance, etc. The agreement you sign most likely will not contain a "sunset clause" unless your attorney makes it a requirement.

A "sunset clause" reduces and eventually terminates continuing commissions owed to the agent and/or manager once the agreement terminates. The need for a sunset clause most often arises when your agent and/or manager secures you a position as a staff writer on a television series, sells your screenplay and it spins off into a series, or your screenplay becomes a studio franchise. The agent or manager wants to receive his/her commission on any monies earned by you, in perpetuity, from agreements you entered into during the term of their representation—even after their agreement with you terminates. The problem with this is that whoever represents you next is going to want to commission *all* your earnings as payment for the services they are rendering in the present. Since agents individually or jointly cannot charge you in excess of 10%, you are in the position of not being able to hire any agent that wants to commission the pre-existing deal, which is likely most of them. You could end up paying a double commission to your managers, since there is no restriction as to how much they can charge.

The alternative is the sunset clause whereby the commission to the previous agent and/or manager is reduced by 33 ⅓% per year until it zeroes out—you pay the new agent or manager that commission on an escalating basis until he/she is receiving 100% of the commission on those earnings. You will only reap the benefit of the sunset clause if it is negotiated into your agreement up front, since the agent will not incorporate it after the fact; it impacts them negatively.

Whether you need both an agent and manager depends on where you are in your career. As I said above, the agent's job is to sell you while the manager's job is to develop you. You are more likely to need a manager earlier in your career, when you do not have an agent, need help getting your career off the ground, and need help developing your talent. You always need an agent. It is highly unlikely that you are going to be able to secure an agent or manager with the top five companies early in your career—unless you are introduced by someone whose opinion they value or you have been extremely successful in another medium, e.g., you have a best-selling novel, graphic novel or video game. Sign with the agent and/or manager you can at this time. You can upgrade later if the opportunity presents itself.

Your relationship with your agent or manager, how much money you get to keep, what expenses you are reimbursing the manager for, how much help you get from both, and how long you are tied to them is going to be dictated by the agreement you sign. You will regret not having hired an attorney to advise you where this agreement is concerned when you realize that you could have made a better deal and/or that the deal you made has drawbacks.

As far as your attorney goes, be sure to keep him/her in the loop at all times. My clients always end up with a better deal when their representatives and I work together. I always improve the financial terms, credit, make sure that my client reaps the benefits of a box office success, and/or include clauses that protect my client and maintain my client's involvement if the picture or series has a life beyond the original production.

Shopping and Submissions

Shopping

Your agent (or manager if you do not have an agent) will shop and submit your screenplay once you have completed it. "Shopping" is defined in the industry to mean marketing your screenplay in an effort to entering into an Option/Purchase Agreement. A "pitch" is a three to four minute oral summary of your screenplay. The producer and your agent will negotiate the terms of the Option/Purchase Agreement if the producer wants to develop and potentially produce a picture based on your screenplay. Again, I strongly recommend that you insist that your agent work jointly with your attorney to get you the best option fee, purchase price, and overall terms. Whatever additional monies you have to pay your attorney will be justified by the end result.

You can shop your screenplay directly to producers if you do not have an agent or manager. This directory includes within it the information you need to contact producers. When dealing with a producer that has a development department, contact a development executive, unless you have a pre-existing relationship with the producer. You will pitch your screenplay on that first call if you make contact, so be sure to have a prepared pitch and logline. A "logline" is a sentence summary of your script.

Protecting Your Ideas

You have to be careful not to "blurt out" the idea for your screenplay, since ideas are not protected by copyright law. A "blurt out" most often occurs when a writer meets a producer by chance, like at a party, restaurant, or in an elevator, and takes advantage of the moment by sharing the idea without asking for permission to do so. Producers do not want to be liable for hearing an unsolicited idea, nor should they be. Since it is not entitled to copyright protection, your idea is in the public domain and is up for grabs once you blurt it out. For the reasons stated below, I prefer that you pitch in a formal setting even if the producer grants you permission to pitch during the chance encounter.

Pitching your idea and/or screenplay in a business meeting goes a long way in protecting it because contract law fills the void that exists in copyright law. You can protect your idea by setting up an oral agreement or an implied-in-fact contract. Both require that you work smart and be patient enough to pitch in formal settings only.

An oral agreement is a spoken versus written contract. You protect your idea by creating an oral agreement with the producer for that purpose. You create the oral agreement during your pitch meeting by making disclosure of the idea contingent on the producer's agreement to your terms. Prior to pitching say, "As you know, I'm here to pitch my screenplay (or the idea for a screenplay), but before I do, I just want to make sure you are willing to credit me and purchase my screenplay for no less than WGA minimum if you use it. Can we agree to that?" Oral agreements are difficult to prove so be sure to create a paper trail to substantiate its existence. You do this by sending an email to confirm the scheduled meeting and its purpose beforehand. Afterwards, send the producer an email thanking him/her for the meeting, the purpose of the meeting, and reiterate the agreed upon oral agreement.

You can also protect an idea via an implied-in-fact contract, which is formed when you pitch in a formal setting and it is clear from the conduct that you met with the producer for the purpose of selling your idea and, hence expect payment for its use. The idea can even be based on material that is in the public domain, like a Shakespearean play, as was the case with *Blaustein v. Burton*.

Julian Blaustein, came up with the idea to produce "The Taming of the Shrew", starring Elizabeth Taylor and Richard Burton. He pitched the idea to Richard Burton's agent. Blaustein conditioned the disclosure on the agent being interested in his idea and Burton and Taylor being available to star in it. The agent confirmed both. Blaustein went ahead with the pitch. The agent responded positively and confirmed that it was something Burton and Taylor had not previously considered. Burton and Taylor went ahead and produced the picture without Blaustein's involvement. Blaustein sued for breach of an implied-in-fact contract and prevailed even though the idea was for material in the public domain.[12]

You see here why the conduct and circumstances under which the idea is pitched are so important. Blaustein would not have prevailed if the agent had informed him that Burton and Taylor were already developing the idea, had previously considered it, if they had produced the picture based on a screenplay they had received from an independent source, or if Blaustein had blurted out the idea in an informal setting. As with the oral agreement, I recommend that you create a paper trail as evidence of your meeting and your intentions. Send an email confirming the meeting and its purpose. Send another afterward to evidence the fact that the meeting took place, what you pitched, and why.

Notwithstanding, the above, be aware that idea theft is rather rampant and difficult to prove. The trend is for courts tend to side with the studios/networks and producers versus the writers. The conundrum is that you risk theft when you pitch, but that you can never sell anything unless you do. In light of that, do everything you can to protect your idea. Never pitch without permission to do so, only do so in a formal setting, and create a paper trail. Do not pitch the idea for your completed screenplay until you have registered it with the U.S. Copyright Office since, among other things, it is prima facie evidence as to the date of your screenplay's existence. If you are pitching an idea for a screenplay that you have yet to write, at least write up a summary and register it with the WGA; this does not provide copyright protection, but you at least have proof as to the date of your idea's existence.

Submission Releases

If you are not represented by an agent or manager, it is likely that you will be required to sign a "Submission Release" when you ask to submit your screenplay to a producer or studio/network. A "Submission Release" is a written agreement whereby you relieve the recipient of your screenplay from liability should he/she use any of the content in your screenplay that is not protected by copyright, such as your idea or the public domain material incorporated therein. It also relieves the producer and studio/network of the obligation to pay you if it independently creates material similar to yours, or comes by it from an independent source. Furthermore, the Submission Release also states that the recipient will pay you fair market value if they use of your screenplay, or any portion thereof that is protected by copyright. The Submission Release is going to override any oral agreement you have made to the contrary with the producer once you sign it.

As onerous as Submission Releases are, I understand that producers and studios/networks require them as a form of protection against lawsuits that may or may not be warranted. You can pay an attorney to explain the Submission Release to you, but it is unlikely that the attorney will be able to convince the producer to revise it. You might be tempted to throw caution to the wind and sign the Submission Release if you are unrepresented by an agent or manager. I recommend that you ask the producer if he/she will accept an attorney submission instead. Your lawyer can make the submission for you if the producer agrees to accept it. If not, then I suggest that you continue pounding doors until you do find an agent or manager willing to represent you. I know that it is difficult to walk away from what you may think is your only opportunity, but you have to be patient unless you are willing to risk your screenplay.

Note that agents will also require that you sign a Submission Release as a condition to reading your screenplay. You cannot submit otherwise. Be aware that agents can share your screenplay with other agents and the agency's clients with impunity once you sign the Submission Release. You might try having your manager make the submission, or asking if the agent will accept an attorney submission. Otherwise, you will have to take the risk if you want to the agent to consider representing you.

Selling Your Screenplay: The Option/Purchase Agreement

The Option

Any producer who is serious about producing a picture based on your screenplay will offer to Option it. The "Option/Purchase Agreement," in this instance, is a written agreement whereby a producer acquires the exclusive right to develop, produce and distribute a picture based on your screenplay. The Option automatically expires at the end of each option term unless the producer renews it (if it has any remaining terms), or the producer exercises it and purchases the screenplay. The producer will not buy your screenplay until the commencement of principal photography.

Typically, producers want a minimum one year option term with a one year extension. This is not excessive considering that it takes an average of seven years to get a picture produced. You need to give the producer a realistic amount of time to develop the screenplay with you, to attach talent and a director, and to shop it for financing. In fact, do not be surprised if the producer wants an extension at the end of the second option term. I advise my clients to extend if the producer is paying a decent option fee, or has made good use of the time, e.g., talent or a director capable of attracting funding are attached.

The option fee that the producer offers to pay you is influenced by a number of factors: your track record, the producer's track record, the heat generated by your screenplay (if any), the subject's notoriety if the screenplay is based on a true life story, whether you are a WGA member, the screenplay's purchase price, the option term, and whether the producer is a studio or independent producer. Due to the foregoing, I disagree with the notion that the industry standard option fee is 10% of the purchase price. I always try to negotiate the highest option fee possible; in my experience, they generally tend to be under 10% for unproduced writers unless the purchase price is less than WGA low budget minimum. They are in the 10% range for writers with a successful track record.

Whether a writer is a WGA member will influence the option fee because the WGA requires that its members be paid an option fee equal to no less than 10% of the applicable WGA minimum purchase price (for a term not to exceed 18 months). As of May 2014, the WGA minimums for a low budget and high budget completed screenplay are $44,445 and $90,982 respectively. The option fee required for a purchase price of $250,000 is only $9,098. The producer can offer a higher option fee, but he/she is not required to do so by the WGA. If the producer does so, it will depend on the above factors.

When considering option fees, you have to take into account the fact that most independent producers lack development funds. As such, be flexible and consider the entirety of the circumstances, e.g., the producer's track record, connections, and ability to raise financing. I do recommend that you consider an earnest and reasonable offer. I consider a reasonable offer to be one that takes into consideration the benefit the producer gets by having your screenplay available to develop and produce and the legal fees you will incur to enter into the Option/Purchase Agreement. I appreciate the time, effort and money that the producer is going to invest in getting your screenplay made; I also believe you should not be out-of-pocket on the legal fees.

Options fees are technically advances against the purchase price, but whether they are applied against the purchase price is up to negotiation. Most often, the end result is that the first option fee is applicable against the purchase price and the subsequent ones are not.

I advise you against entering into "free" Options. Free Options usually result in a waste of time, money and opportunity, since you are out-of-pocket on legal fees, cannot shop the screenplay while it is under Option, and producers tend to be less productive when they have no money at stake. An alternative to the free Option is a "Shopping Agreement" wherein you allow the producer to shop the screenplay without acquiring the right to purchase it from you. This arrangement usually works well when you are dealing with a proven producer, who has studio or production company connections, and who could potentially enter into an Option/Purchase Agreement directly with you and pay you an option fee. Shopping Agreements are usually in the 60-90 day range and get extended if you are in the midst of negotiations with a studio/network or production company interested in entering into an Option/Purchase Agreement with you. The producer does not negotiate the terms of the Option/Purchase Agreement on your behalf. He/she only gets the ball rolling so that your agent and attorney can step in and negotiate for you. Keep in mind that if the producer is not successful, that you will not be able to shop your screenplay where he/she shopped it for at least a year—or until there are new executives working there. Other producers may not be interested in paying you for an Option if the previous producer has limited his/her opportunities for success, so this is something to keep in mind.

Purchase Price

There is no such thing as a "standard" purchase price for a screenplay. WGA members cannot accept less than the sum prescribed in the WGA Schedule of Minimums, but can exceed the minimum, and non-WGA members can sell their screenplays for any price they are able to negotiate. Sale prices typically range between 1% and 3% of the cash production budget of the picture. How much you are offered for your screenplay depends on who you are and what you bring to the table. Producers consider your track record; whether there is a bidding war for your screenplay; whether the screenplay is based on a best-selling novel; whether it is about a salacious, interesting or well publicized person or event; the screenplay's genre; and, if known ahead of time, the picture's potential production budget. If the production budget is not known going into the negotiations, I suggest a purchase price based on a sliding scale, e.g., "for a picture not to exceed $15,000,000 dollars, the purchase price shall be 2 ½% of the cash budget of the picture, but in no event less than WGA low budget minimum and no more than $250,000. The purchase price will be increased by $10,000 for every $1 million increase in the picture's production above $15,000,000 not to exceed a total purchase price equal to $500,000." The attorney attempts to secure the highest ceiling possible while the producer tries to limit it.

Additional Compensation

If the purchase price is on the lower end due to limited financing, I ask for additional compensation in the form of a deferment. "Deferred compensation" is a sum of money that is paid at a future date, from first revenues on a pari passu basis with the other parties being paid on a deferred basis. "Pari passu" means dollar for dollar. For example, if you and four cast members are entitled to deferred monies, where you are due $100,000 and each cast member $25,000, and the production company receives $100,000 in revenues, then you each receive $20,000 from the $100,000. Monies received by the production company will be distributed this way until each deferral is satisfied. Deferred compensation is usually paid prior to investor recoupment, since it is considered part of the screenplay's purchase price and is a production cost.

Whenever possible, I negotiate for my clients to receive a "Box Office Bonus," which is not guaranteed and only gets paid when, and if, the picture reaches a specific and pre-determined sales goal. Box Office Bonus compensation may be expressed as follows: "Writer shall be entitled to a Box Office Bonus of $50,000 when, and if, the picture's domestic and international gross box office, as reported in Variety, exceeds three times the picture's production budget." The bonus is only paid if you are a credited writer. I also negotiate for Nomination/Award Bonus that is paid for award nominations and wins, e.g., Golden Globes and Academy Awards.

Sequels, Remakes…

It is standard for a producer to pay the writer of an original screenplay additional monies if he/she produces a sequel, remake, or television series based on the writer's original screenplay. These additional monies are passive payments, which means that the writer does not have to render additional writing services in order receive them. As per industry standard, if a sequel based on your original screenplay is produced, you are paid 50% of the original screenplay's purchase price and 50% of the profit participation allocated to you for the original screenplay. The passive payment drops from 50% to 33 ⅓% on behalf of remakes based on your original screenplay. As such, if you were paid a $100,000 purchase price and 5% of picture's net profits for your original screenplay, you will be paid $50,000 plus 2 ½% of picture's net profits for any sequels and $33,333 plus 1 ⅔% of picture's net profits for any remakes produced. For any television series based on your screenplay, you will receive passive payments based on the running time of each episode, on its first airing and a portion thereof up to the sixth rerun. I usually refer to the WGA schedule of minimums to calculate the television payments even if my client is not a WGA member.

I always negotiate for my clients to have the Right of First Refusal to write any subsequent versions of their original screenplay, be it a sequel, remake, prequel, television series, or television motion picture. How much you are paid to write any of the aforementioned may depend on whether you are a WGA member, the success of your original screenplay, whether you were credited on your original screenplay (sometimes requires sole credit), and whether you are a working writer at the time of the subsequent version's negotiation. The terms for these writing services will not be negotiated until your services are required, and whether you are engaged to write is contingent upon the producer and you coming to an agreement for your services, since this is just a "Right of First Refusal." Passive payments are generally offered in lieu of writing fees.

Separated Rights

The WGA may determine that you are entitled to "Separated Rights" if you are a WGA member: these are a bundle of rights that the WGA has determined belong to writers of original screenplays. Dramatic stage and publication rights are both included in Separated Rights, as is the mandatory first rewrite of your original screenplay for WGA minimum; the right to meet with a senior production executive if the producer wants to replace you with another writer; the right to reacquire the screenplay if it has not been produced within five years; and, WGA minimum payment for sequel theatrical motion pictures, television movies, and television series.

As far as the dramatic stage rights are concerned, you will be entitled to a royalty free license to produce the screenplay as a dramatic stage play after the producer's holdback period of two years from the picture's general release or five years from the purchase agreement. A "holdback period" is a period of time during which the producer has exclusivity to exploit the right. If the producer exploits the dramatic stage rights prior to expiration of the holdback period, then you shall be paid 50% of the minimum sum paid to authors under the Minimum Basic Contract of the Dramatist Guild of the Author's League of America, Inc. Regarding publishing, you will be able to publish the script or novelization of the script subject to a holdback period equal to six months from the picture's general release or three years from date of the purchase agreement. The producer has to give you the opportunity to negotiate directly with the publisher to write a novel based on your screenplay, if the producer publishes it during the holdback period. The producer has to pay you WGA minimum if you do not write the novel and it is published.

Remember, the compensation and the rights guaranteed via the WGA Basic Agreement are the bare minimum to which you are entitled as a WGA member. Sometimes industry standards are higher, as is the case for passive payments for sequels and remakes. Your attorney can always negotiate for more rights and compensation than that required by the WGA.

Profit Participation

"Net Profits," an additional form of remuneration, are paid when, and if, the Picture based on your screenplay reaches a profit position. Net profits are usually calculated by subtracting all of the costs incurred in the making, marketing and distributing the Picture; this calculation includes the production budget, all financing costs, legal fees, bank interest, production company overhead, collection costs, prints, ads, distribution fees, residuals paid to any union, etc. I negotiate for my clients to have net profits allocated, knowing that it is unlikely that they will ever receive them due to the industry's accounting practices and distribution expenses. In other words, it would be nice if you received net profits—just do not count on it.

It is standard to allocate writers 5% of the picture's net profits, though independent producers tend to offer 5% of producer's net profits instead. It is important for you to understand the difference between the two calculations: "Picture's net profits" refers to 100% of the net profits of the picture whereas "producer's net profits" accounts for only 50% of the net profits. Independent producers prefer the latter formula because they generally only retain 50% of the picture's net profits themselves. Rather than push for 5% of Picture's Net Profits, my clients prefer for me to negotiate a Box Office Bonus instead.

Credit

You are entitled to a "Written by" credit if the screenplay was completely original to you, or "Screenplay by" credit if the screenplay is derived from another work, e.g., a book or play. Your credit should appear in the main credits of the picture, on a single card, in a size and type equal to the size and type of the director's credit. The credit should also appear on screen, in the position prior to the director's credit, and in paid ads whenever the director or producers are credited (excepting paid ads which are award/congratulatory type ads). If you are not the only credited writer, as happens so often, then you will have to share the writing credit on the same card with the other credited writer(s).

The WGA has a credit determination process[13] whereby it decides who gets credited (and how) when there are multiple writers on any one screenplay. The WGA compares the written drafts against the produced draft and then determines who gets the credit and in what order, and who does not. The basic credit determination rule is this: Any writer whose work equals 33% of a non-original screenplay, e.g., an adaptation, or 50% an original screenplay will be credited. Credits are limited to two writers unless the credit determination rules otherwise.

Non-members of the WGA do not get the benefit of the WGA's credit determination process. Notwithstanding, I always negotiate into my client's agreements that the producer will apply the WGA rules to determine my client's credit if he/she is not the only writer who worked on the screenplay. This way the subsequent writer only receives a credit if his/her contribution to the screenplay is substantial. I avoid credit provisions whereby the producer is given sole discretion over all aspects of your credit.

If the writer is not a member of the WGA and is entering into an Option/Purchase Agreement with a producer, who is not a WGA signatory, it is a good idea to include language in the credits clause that states that the writer will be "upgraded" (and become a WGA member) if the production company becomes a WGA signatory, or finances the Picture through a WGA signatory company, such as a studio/network. I suggest this additional terminology because a writer, who is not WGA member, will not get the benefit of a WGA credit determination or the credit he/she agreed to in the Option/Purchase Agreement, if the screenplay is rewritten by a WGA member.

Rewrites

You always want the opportunity to do the first paid rewrite of your screenplays, since whether you are credited or share credit hinges on how much of your writing ends up in the final screenplay. I attempt to secure this right for my client regardless of their WGA membership status. I always ask for the rewrite fee to be no less than WGA minimum—more if the writer has a track record. Sometimes producers attempt to credit the rewrite fee against the purchase price—whether it is will depend on your bargaining power. Either way, the goal is to not only do the first rewrite but all of them. The better you rewrite and collaborate with the producer, the more likely it is that you will be the only credited writer. I had a client who Optioned her screenplay to a major studio, refused to do the rewrite that the development executive wanted, breached her contract with the studio, and gave up the career she could have had. You may not believe in the rewrite the producer wants of you, but you have to do it if you want to stay on board and get that credit.

Occasionally, an independent producer without development funding may ask you to do a free rewrite if you are not a WGA member. Whether or not you should do it is contingent on the circumstances. I would not advise you to undertake writing for free for a producer without a good track record, since you will likely be wasting your time. If you are unproduced or need to get a screenplay produced, and a producer asks you to rewrite for free, then I might advise you to do it if the producer lacks development funding, has a very good track record, has the ability to help you develop a production worthy screenplay, and has the connections and capacity to get your screenplay produced. The caveat here is that you have to own the rewrite.

Warranties & Representations

The Option/Purchase Agreement will include a paragraph whereby you will have to make certain representations and warranties in order to sell the screenplay. You will have to warrant and represent the following: that your screenplay is original; that if any material in the screenplay is not original, that said material came from the public domain; that if any material in the screenplay is not original or in the public domain, that it is included with the permission of the original material's author; that your screenplay does not defame anyone; that it does not infringe on another person's right to privacy, and that you are the screenplay's sole and exclusive proprietor and, hence, have the authority to enter into the Option/Purchase Agreement. You cannot enter into the Option/Purchase Agreement knowing that you will be in breach of this clause the moment you sign it because the repercussions are great: you are going to be liable for whatever damages are caused to the producer via an indemnification and hold harmless clause whereby you have to reimburse the producer for any and all damages and legal fees. You need for there to be a reciprocal indemnity and hold harmless clause from the producer to you for damages incurred by you as a consequence of the production and distribution of the picture.

Rights Sold

The Option/Purchase Agreement will, at the very least, require that you sell exclusively and forever all motion picture rights, all television motion picture, all television series and all television spin-off rights and all allied and ancillary rights for the term of the copyright and all renewals and extensions thereof. The allied and ancillary rights include the right to create and sell the picture's soundtrack, merchandise, video games, etc.

In the end, what rights you get to reserve for yourself will depends on your bargaining position and the buyer. For example, studios/networks want to acquire any and all rights in and to your screenplay, whether now in existence or yet to be invented, because in addition to creating filmed entertainment, they may want the right to sell books, create theme parks or theme park rides, stage plays, etc. I try to reserve dramatic, publishing and radio rights. It is next to impossible to reserve them if you are an unproduced writer entering into an Option/Purchase Agreement with a studio/network and more likely with an independent producer. Notwithstanding, you may be entitled to Separated Rights as a WGA member.

Option Reversion

The Option on your screenplay expires if the producer does not renew or exercise the Option prior to its termination date. All rights in and to the screenplay automatically revert to you when the Option expires. You retain any and all option and writing fees paid to you by the producer without the obligation of repayment.

Turnaround Right

You will have a "turnaround right" that provides you with the opportunity to buy back your screenplay if the producer purchased the screenplay, but did not produce it within the time specified in the Option/Purchase Agreement—usually five years. You will have an 18 to 24 month window to reacquire the screenplay. You, or whoever is buying your screenplay, will have to reimburse the producer's direct out-of-pocket cost to purchase and develop the screenplay.

Works-For-Hire: Getting Paid to Write

Most working writers in the film industry work on a for hire basis. A "work-for-hire", as it is known, means that the writer is specifically hired and paid to write on behalf of someone who employs his/her services. In the film industry, this usually occurs when a producer hires you to write a treatment, outline, or screenplay either based on the producer's idea or assigned material, such as a book, news story, or life story. I strongly recommend that you engage an attorney to negotiate and review the producer's draft of the Work-for-Hire Agreement.

Copyright in the Work-For-Hire

Although copyright normally vests in the author of an original work, copyright to your work vests in the producer if the producer and you entered into a written Work-for-Hire Agreement prior to the commencement of services. The Work-for-Hire Agreement will, among other things, clearly state that you are working on a for-hire basis and, therefore, that all results and proceeds of your labor and the copyright to your work are the property of the producer. It is imperative that the producer and you enter into the Work-for-Hire Agreement beforehand so that the copyright vests in the producer versus you. Otherwise, you will have to assign the results and proceeds of your labor and the copyright to the producer.

Compensation

Any producer who asks you to write for "free" is not treating you with respect and, is likely, a producer without the power and ability to get the screenplay he/she expects you to write produced. You have to value yourself and your talent if you expect anyone else to do the same. Whether I advise my client to write depends on the reasonableness of the compensation and terms offered by the producer.

Work-for-Hire Agreements are done on a "flat deal" or "step deal" basis. "Flat deal" means that the producer is going to pay you a lump sum to write the treatment, outline, first draft, second draft, final draft, polish, etc. It is important that the flat deal be well defined in the agreement, so that you know exactly how many steps you need to write for that flat deal payment. Otherwise, you could end up writing an infinite number of steps until the producer is satisfied, if ever. Payments pursuant to the Work-for-Hire Agreement occur at commencement and delivery of each step, e.g., treatment/outline, first draft, second draft, and final draft. A "step deal" means that the producer is hiring you on a step-by-step basis, so that he/she has the discretion to order the next step in the writing process, or not, and only paying for the steps ordered.

The compensation the producer offers you will take into account your track record, whether you are a member of the WGA, and whether the producer has a development deal or financing. "Development deal" refers to an arrangement between a studio/network and producer whereby the studio/network funds the producer's overhead and development expenses. It is unlikely that the producer will offer you WGA minimum compensation if you are not a WGA member, and not much beyond it if you are, but do not have track record that warrants more.

Additional Compensation

I ask the producer for deferred compensation if you are being offered a less than competitive flat deal or step deal. In addition, I negotiate for a Set Up Bonus, Box Office Bonus and a Nomination/Award Bonus. A "Set Up Bonus" gets paid when, and if, the producer sets up the screenplay at a studio/network.

Profit Participation

The producer should agree to allocate you a portion of net profits as part of your overall compensation, which as per industry standard is five percent (5%) of the net profits of the picture or producer's net profits. If I have to choose between net profits and actual money, I always chose the latter. Whether you are paid net profits, even assuming the picture is profitable, is going to depend on whether you are a credited writer (more on credits below). Your five percent (5%) will get cut in half if you share the credit. Uncredited writers get zero net profits unless the Work-for-Hire Agreement specifically states otherwise.

Credit

Your credit is not eliminated because the copyright is vesting in the producer. You are the screenplay's writer irrespective of copyright law because you wrote it. How, when, and if you are credited is more a function of the WGA or the Work-for-Hire Agreement. There is nothing you can do about your credit if the producer is a WGA signatory, you are WGA member, and you are not the screenplay's only writer due to the WGA's credit determination process. Your credit is completely up to the terms of the Work-For-Hire Agreement if you are not a WGA writer and the producer is not a WGA signatory. Notwithstanding, I try to make the producer follow the WGA's rules for credit determination, so that you are treated fairly should another writer be engaged after you.

Sequels, Remakes...

You may be entitled to passive payments if you are not a WGA member and your attorney was successful in negotiating for them. Whether you need to be the sole writer in order to get paid passive payments will be a function of the Work-for-Hire Agreement. The WGA will determine whether you are entitled to Separated Rights if you are WGA member; this is possible even though you worked on assigned material if your screenplay is substantially different from what was assigned to you, or the assigned material was not available to you, i.e., you adapt a book without referring to it.

Right of First Refusal

You may have the ability to write subsequent versions of your original screenplay, e.g., sequel, remakes, television series, if you are granted the Right of First Refusal in your Work-for-Hire Agreement and are a credited writer. I find that it is always worth asking for this right, since you should benefit if your work resulted in a screenplay with a life beyond the original. As I previously mentioned, how much you are paid to write any of the aforementioned will depend on whether you are a WGA member, the success of your original screenplay, and whether you are a working writer. Whether you get to write the subsequent version will depend on whether the producer and you are able to reach an agreement for your engagement to do so.

Warranties and Representations

As with the Option/Purchase Agreement, you will have to warrant and represent that whatever you write is original to you with the exception of any material assigned to you. You will have to indemnify and hold harmless the producer should you breach this warranty and representation. You need for there to be a reciprocal indemnity and hold harmless clause for any of the assigned materials provided by the producer and producer's production and distribution of the picture, since you do not want to be legally and financially liable for the producer's actions.

Becoming a WGA Member

Joining the WGA requires that you earn 24 units in the three years preceding the application and payment of a $2,500 initiation fee. You accumulate units by writing for, selling, or by entering into an Option/Purchase Agreement on behalf your screenplay with a WGA signatory producer. Below is the WGA Schedule of Units that applies to screenplays:

- 8 units for a short subject theatrical screenplay.
- 12 units for story for a feature-length theatrical screenplay.
- 24 units for a feature-length theatrical screenplay.

A rewrite will earn you half of the units applicable to the category, e.g., you get four units for rewriting a short subject theatrical screenplay.

A polish will earn you one-quarter of the units applicable to the category, e.g., you get two units for polishing a short subject theatrical screenplay.

An Option will earn one-half of the units you would be entitled to on the purchase up to a maximum of eight units per year, e.g., you are allocated four units if you Option a short subject theatrical screenplay. You are only entitled to units for the initial option period. You receive no units for extensions and renewals.

You can refer to WGA's website for the Schedule of Units available for television, radio, and New Media.[14]

Hiring an Attorney

I have discussed above the reasons why and when you may need to retain an attorney. Now the issue is, how do you find the attorney that is right for you? I suggest you do a little research: ask friends and colleagues for referrals, read legal articles and books written by attorneys, and refer to the posts by attorneys you have read and liked on Linkedin.com or another social forum. Narrow your list down to five attorneys and then interview them. Most attorneys offer a free half hour initial consultation, which is for both your benefit and the attorney's. Take advantage of it. I use the consultation to get to know the potential client, his/her needs and expectations, the likelihood that I can be of service, and to determine if our personalities are compatible. My advice to you is that you retain an attorney that you feel comfortable asking questions, who respects you, who tells you the truth—even if you do not want to hear it—and who you feel is going to be a good advocate for you. If you want an attorney for the long term, which I recommend, steer clear of attorneys that intimidate you or are arrogant. Use the free consultation to shop for an attorney—not for the purpose of picking the attorney's brain when you have no intention of retaining legal counsel.

Attorneys most often get paid an hourly fee, a flat fee, or a percent of the gross monies earned by you. Hourly rates run the gamut. How much you pay by the hour is going to depend on the attorney's experience and whether the attorney is with a large law firm. The average hourly rate is in the $300-$500 range. When billing on an hourly basis, the attorney charges for all the time spent on your behalf: negotiating, drafting, redlining (revising agreements presented to you), phone calls on your behalf or with you, copies, messenger, etc. You might be able to convince an attorney to represent you on a flat fee basis if your financial resources are limited. A flat fee entails the attorney quoting you a price that is inclusive of all the phone calls and work to be done by the attorney on your behalf. The attorney gets no more than the flat fee quoted regardless of how long it takes to conclude the task. Flat fees are on a task by task basis. Either way, you are going to have to provide an up-front deposit based on the attorney's guesstimate or flat fee quote. Whether an attorney will represent you on a percentage basis will depend on whether you are currently making money writing, are represented by a reputable agency or manager, have a track record, or have an offer on the table that will result in a payment to you large enough to compensate the attorney. It is unlikely that an attorney will represent you on a percentage basis otherwise. The average percent is 5%, but it can be as high as 10% if the attorney is representing you on a very low paying matter. Sometimes an attorney will structure a hybrid billing arrangement so that you are paying a portion of your fee up front and the other portion as a percent of the monies earned by you. Attorneys do this sometimes to accommodate a client's limited financial resources.

You will have to sign an engagement agreement with the attorney, which explains the basis of the representation, the fees, deposits (if any), and contains any necessary disclosures. The California State Bar requires one whenever the matter is going to result in payment to the attorney exceeding $1,000 and in contingent fee arrangements. The deposit that you give the attorney will go into an Attorney/Client Trust Account until it is earned by the attorney. Any monies remaining at the end of representation, if any, are returned to you. If you do not understand the engagement agreement have the attorney explain it to you, or consult with another attorney about it.

Is the cost of hiring an attorney worth it if you have an agent or manager? Absolutely, yes! The attorney is an important part of your team who is responsible for not only improving the deal terms but, also, making sure you are protected. I have yet to work on a negotiation with an agent or manager where I did not substantially improve the overall deal. Among other things, I have secured deferrals and bonuses for my clients that were not offered up front and improved my client's credit and the likelihood that he/she would retain it. I always say, "When you think you cannot afford attorney is exactly when you cannot afford to go without one."

Conclusion

As I hope you have realized by reading this chapter, writing is not just about sitting down and creating, it is also about working smart to avoid the types of situations that might detour your writing career. When in doubt, consult with an attorney. Do not rely on advice from "friends," or attorneys who are not familiar with entertainment and intellectual property law. Do not use boilerplates or attempt to draft your own agreements. It is better that you consult and determine that you are in the clear, than discover that you have made a very costly mistake.

This chapter is not a complete review of the subject matter. You should consult with an attorney if you have questions, need additional information, or require legal representation.

About the Author

Dinah Perez graduated from Loyola Law School and has been in the practice of entertainment law since 1996. She practices film, television, theater, music, new media, publishing, copyright, and trademark law. She enjoys her practice because she has great respect for the arts and those who create, and relishes helping her clients attain their professional goals.

Ms. Perez has been published in *Story Board Magazine, Release Print*, and *Script Magazine, The Screenwriter's Guide to Agents and Managers*, and the *Hollywood Screenwriting Directory*. She has been quoted in *Entertainment Weekly, Wired Magazine, Wired.Com*, and *Alone in a Room*.

Ms. Perez has participated in panels and/or spoken at the Black Hollywood Film Festival, the Latin Heat Film Festival, Women in Film, Cinewomen, Independent Feature Project West, American Film Market, the Inktip Pitch Summit, The Writers Store, the Showbiz Store and Cafe, and the Screenwriters World Conference.

She is a member of the Beverly Hills Bar Association (Entertainment Law Section, Executive Committee) and the California State Bar. She was a founding board member of Cinewomen in Los Angeles, CA.

Ms. Perez is available for consultation. She may be reached by phone at (323) 935-7955, via her website at www.dinahperezlaw.com, or email at dinahperezlaw@gmail.com.

[1] 17 U.S.C. §302.

[2] 17 U.S.C. §102

[3] 17 U.S.C. §102.

[4] 17 U.S.C. §107.

[5] U.S. Copyright Office, *Copyright Basics Circular 1*, Library of Congress, May 2012.

[6] 17 U.S.C. §107.

[7] http://www.unc.edu/~unclng/public-d.htm

[8] Michael C. Donaldson, *Clearance & Copyright* (Silman James Press 2008), 332-335.

[9] N.Y. CVR. LAW § 50 and 51.

[10] CAL. CIV. CODE §3344.1

[11] Cal. Labor Code §1700.4.

[12] *Blaustein v. Burton* (1970) 9 Cal.App.3d 161, 88 Cal.Rptr. 319.

[13] http://www.wga.org/subpage_Writersresources.aspx?id=170

[14] http://www.wga.org/

The Directory

100% ENTERTAINMENT

200 N. Larchmont Blvd.
Los Angeles, CA 90004
Phone: 323-461-6360
Fax: 323-871-8203

Email: 100percent@iname.com
Home Page: 100percentent.com
IMDb: imdb.com/company/co0077804

Accepts query letter from unproduced, unrepresented writers via email. Project types include TV. Preferred genres include Drama, Non-Fiction, and Science Fiction. Established in 1998.

Stanley Isaacs
President
Phone: 323-461-6360
Email: sisaacs100@mac.com
IMDb: imdb.com/name/nm0410570

100% TERRYCLOTH

421 Waterview St
Los Angeles, CA 90293
Phone: 310-823-3432
Fax: 310-861-9093

Email: contact@terencemichael.com
Home Page: terencemichael.com
IMDb: imdb.com/company/co0194989
Facebook: facebook.com/pages/100-Percent-Terry-Cloth-Inc/147268518656038

Accepts query letter from unproduced, unrepresented writers via email. Project types include TV. Preferred genres include Comedy and Reality.

Terence Michael
Producer
Phone: 310-823-3432
Email: tm@terencemichael.com
IMDb: imdb.com/name/nm0006709

Erik Adams
Development

1019 ENTERTAINMENT

1680 N Vine St, Suite 600
Hollywood, CA 90028

Phone: 323-645-6840
Fax: 323-645-6841

Email: info@1019ent.com
Home Page: 1019ent.com
IMDb: imdb.com/company/co0263748
Facebook: facebook.com/pages/1019-Entertainment/339985172752485

Does not accept any unsolicited material. Project types include TV. Preferred genres include Comedy, Drama, and Non-Fiction.

Terry Botwick
Partner
Phone: 323-645-6840
Email: terry@1019ent.com
IMDb: imdb.com/company/co0263748

Ralph Winter
Principle
Phone: 323-645-6840
Email: ralph@1019ent.com
IMDb: imdb.com/name/nm0003515

10 BY 10 ENTERTAINMENT

1950 Sawtelle Blvd.
Suite 200
Los Angeles, CA 90025
Phone: 310-575-1235
Fax: 310-575-1237

IMDb: imdb.com/company/co0112253
Facebook: facebook.com/pages/10x10-Entertainment/114948301852714

Accepts query letter from unproduced, unrepresented writers. Project types include TV. Preferred genres include Comedy, Drama, and Non-Fiction.

Brad Austin
Director of Development
Phone: 310-575-1235
IMDb: imdb.com/name/nm4114614

Ken Mok
Principle
Phone: 310-575-1235
IMDb: imdb.com/name/nm0596298

1821 PICTURES

205 S. Beverly Dr.
Suite 206
Beverly Hills, CA 90212
Phone: 310-860-1121
Fax: 310-860-1123

Email: asst@1821pictures.com
Home Page: 1821pictures.com
IMDb: imdb.com/company/co0237259
Facebook: facebook.com/1821Pictures

Accepts query letter from unproduced, unrepresented writers via email. Project types include TV. Preferred genres include Animation, Comedy, Drama, and Non-Fiction. Established in 2005.

Billy Piché
Director of Development
Phone: 310-860-1121
IMDb: imdb.com/name/nm5046038

Paris Latsis
Phone: 310-860-1121
IMDb: imdb.com/company/co0237259

Terry Douglas
Principle
Phone: 310-860-1121
IMDb: imdb.com/name/nm0234806

19 ENTERTAINMENT

8560 W Sunset Blvd, 9th Floor
West Hollywood, CA 90069
Phone: 310-777-1940
Fax: 310-777-1949

Email: contact@19.co.uk
Home Page: 19.co.uk
IMDb: imdb.com/company/co0085773
Facebook: facebook.com/19EntertainmentLtd

Does not accept any unsolicited material. Project types include TV. Preferred genres include Animation, Comedy, and Drama.

Iain Pirie
President (U.S.)
Phone: 310-777-1940
IMDb: imdb.com/name/nm2227040

21 LAPS ENTERTAINMENT

c/o Twentieth Century Fox
10201 W Pico Blvd
Building 41, Suite 400
Los Angeles, CA 90064
Phone: 310-369-7170
Fax: 310-969-0443

IMDb: imdb.com/company/co0158853
Facebook: facebook.com/pages/21-Laps-Entertainment/185829081580687

Does not accept any unsolicited material. Project types include Feature Films and TV. Preferred genres include Action, Comedy, and Drama.

Dan Levine
President of Production
IMDb: imdb.com/name/nm0505782

Shawn Levy
Principal
Phone: 310-369-4466
IMDb: imdb.com/name/nm0506613

Billy Rosenberg
Senior Vice President Development
Phone: 310-369-7170
IMDb: imdb.com/name/nm1192785

Will Rack
Director of Development
Phone: 310-369-7170
IMDb: imdb.com/name/nm5211280

25/7 PRODUCTIONS

10999 Riverside Dr, Suite 100
North Hollywood, CA 91602
Phone: 818-432-2800
Fax: 818-432-2810

Email: info@257productions.com
Home Page: 257productions.com
IMDb: imdb.com/company/co0200336

Accepts query letter from unproduced, unrepresented writers. Project types include TV. Preferred genres include Animation, Comedy, Drama, and Non-Fiction. Established in 2003.

David Broome
President
Phone: 818-432-2800
IMDb: imdb.com/company/co0200336

26 FILMS

8748 Holloway Dr
Los Angeles, CA, 90069
Phone: 310-205-9922
Fax: 310-206-9926

Email: asst@26films.com
Home Page: 26films.com

Accepts query letter from unproduced, unrepresented writers via email.

Nathalie Marciano
Principal
Phone: 310-205-9922
Email: asst@26films.com
IMDb: imdb.com/name/nm0545695

Elena Brooks
Director of Development
Phone: 310-205-9922
Email: asst@26films.com
IMDb: imdb.com/name/nm4542983

2929 PRODUCTIONS

1437 Seventh St, Suite 250
Santa Monica, CA 90401
Phone: 310-309-5200
Fax: 310-309-5716

Home Page: 2929entertainment.com

Accepts query letter from unproduced, unrepresented writers. Preferred genres include Action, Drama, and Non-Fiction.

Todd Wagner
Principal
Phone: 310-309-5200
Email: todd@2929entertainment.com
IMDb: imdb.com/company/co0005596

Shay Weiner
Director of Development
Phone: 310-309-5200
Email: sweiner@2929ent.com
IMDb: imdb.com/name/nm1674317

Michael Merlob
Creative Executive

2S FILMS

10390 Santa Monica Blvd
Suite 210
Los Angeles, CA 90025
Phone: 310-789-5450
Fax: 310-789-3060

Email: info@2sfilms.com
IMDb: imdb.com/company/co0238996

Does not accept any unsolicited material. Project types include Feature Films. Preferred genres include Comedy and Romance. Established in 2007.

Allison Rayne
Vice President of Development
Phone: 310-789-5450
Email: info@2sfilms.com
IMDb: imdb.com/name/nm2588349

Molly Smith
Principle
Phone: 310-789-5450
Email: info@2sfilms.com
IMDb: imdb.com/company/co0238996

Jon Schumacher
Development Executive
IMDb: imdb.com/name/nm2749499

2WAYTRAFFIC - A SONY PICTURES ENTERTAINMENT COMPANY

Middenweg 1
PO Box 297
Hilversum 1217 HS
The Netherlands
Phone: +31(0)357508000
Fax: +31(0)357508020

Email: info@2waytraffic.com
Home Page: 2waytraffic.com
IMDb: imdb.com/company/co0211160

Does not accept any unsolicited material. Project types include Feature Films and TV. Established in 2004.

3311 PRODUCTIONS

8938 Keith
West Hollywood, CA 90069
Phone: 323-319-5060
Fax: 323-306-5534

Email: info@3311productions.com
Home Page: 3311productions.com

Accepts query letter from produced or represented writers. Project types include Feature Films. Preferred genres include Comedy and Drama.

Mark Roberts
Executive
IMDb: imdb.com/name/nm4224736

Ross Jacobson
IMDb: imdb.com/name/nm2278951

Eddie Vaisman
IMDb: imdb.com/name/nm4224744

34TH STREET FILMS

8200 Wilshire Blvd, Suite 300
Beverly Hills, CA 90211
Phone: 323-315-7963
Fax: 323-315-7117

Does not accept any unsolicited material. Project types include Feature Films. Preferred genres include Action, Comedy, Family, and Romance.

Matt Moore
Executive Vice President
Phone: 323-315-7963
IMDb: imdb.com/name/nm0601597

Amber Rasberry
Director of Development
Phone: 323-315-7963
IMDb: imdb.com/name/nm2248393

Poppy Hanks
Senior Vice President (Production & Development)
Phone: 323-315-7963
IMDb: imdb.com/name/nm1585325

3 ARTS ENTERTAINMENT

9460 Wilshire Blvd 7th Floor
Beverly Hills, CA 90212
Phone: 310-888-3200
Fax: 310-888-3210

16 W 22nd St
Suite 201
New York, NY 10010

Home Page: 3arts.com
IMDb: imdb.com/company/co0070636

Accepts query letter from unproduced, unrepresented writers. Project types include Feature Films and TV. Preferred genres include Comedy and Drama. Established in 1992.

Howard Klein
Partner
Phone: 310-888-3200
Email: hklein@3arts.com
IMDb: imdb.com/name/nm2232433

Erwin Stoff
Partner (Chairman)
Phone: 310-888-3200
Email: estoff@3arts.com
IMDb: imdb.com/name/nm0831098

3 BALL PRODUCTIONS

3650 Redondo Beach Ave
Redondo Beach, CA 90278
Phone: 424-236-7500
Fax: 424-236-7501

Email: 3ball.reception@eyeworks.tv
Home Page: 3ballproductions.com
IMDb: imdb.com/company/co0100000

Accepts query letter from unproduced, unrepresented writers via email. Project types include TV. Preferred genres include Drama.

J.D. Roth
CEO
Phone: 424-236-7500
IMDb: imdb.com/name/nm0744870

Brandt Pinvidic
President
Phone: 424-236-7500
IMDb: imdb.com/name/nm1803480

40 ACRES & A MULE FILMWORKS, INC.

75 S Elliot Place
Brooklyn, NY 11217
Phone: 718-624-3703
Fax: 718-624-2008

Home Page: 40acres.com
IMDb: imdb.com/company/co0029134

Does not accept any unsolicited material. Project types include TV. Preferred genres include Action, Comedy, Drama, and Non-Fiction.

Spike Lee
Chairman
Phone: 718-624-3703
IMDb: imdb.com/name/nm0000490

44 BLUE PRODUCTIONS, INC.

4040 Vineland Ave, Suite 105
Studio City, CA 11217
Phone: 818-760-4442
Fax: 818-760-1509

Email: reception@44blue.com
Home Page: 44blue.com
IMDb: imdb.com/company/co0012712

Does not accept any unsolicited material. Project types include TV. Preferred genres include Comedy, Drama, and Non-Fiction.

Rasha Drachkovitch
Phone: 818-760-4442
Email: reception@44blue.com
IMDb: imdb.com/name/nm0236624

Stephanie Drachkovitch
Phone: 818-760-4442
Email: reception@44blue.com
IMDb: imdb.com/name/nm1729517

495 PRODUCTIONS

4222 Burbank Blvd, 2nd Floor
Burbank, CA 91505
Phone: 818-840-2750
Fax: 818-840-7083

Email: info@495productions.com
Home Page: 495productions.com
IMDb: imdb.com/company/co0192481

Does not accept any unsolicited material. Project types include TV. Preferred genres include Comedy, Drama, Non-Fiction, and Reality.

SallyAnn Salsano
President
Phone: 818-840-2750
Email: info@495productions.com
IMDb: imdb.com/name/nm1133163

James Bianco
Head (Production)
IMDb: imdb.com/name/nm1291179

4TH ROW FILMS

27 W 20th St, Suite 1006
New York, NY 10011
Phone: 212-974-0082
Fax: 212-627-3090

Email: info@4throwfilms.com
Home Page: 4throwfilms.com
IMDb: imdb.com/company/co0117932

Does not accept any unsolicited material. Project types include TV. Preferred genres include Comedy, Drama, and Non-Fiction.

Douglas Tirola
President / Producer
Phone: 212-974-0082
Email: info@4throwfilms.com
IMDb: imdb.com/name/nm0864263

Susan Bedusa
Vice President, Development
Phone: 212-974-0082
Email: info@4throwfilms.com
IMDb: imdb.com/name/nm1513256

51 MINDS ENTERTAINMENT

6565 Sunset Blvd, Suite 301
Los Angeles, CA 90028
Phone: 323-466-9200
Fax: 323-466-9202

Email: info@51minds.com
Home Page: 51minds.com
IMDb: imdb.com/company/co0166565
Facebook: facebook.com/pages/51-Minds-
Entertainment/162815400414419

Accepts query letter from unproduced, unrepresented writers via email. Project types include TV. Preferred genres include Comedy, Drama, and Reality.

Mark Cronin
Co-President
Phone: 323-466-9200
Email: info@51minds.com
IMDb: imdb.com/name/nm0188782

David Caplan
Vice President (Development)
Phone: 323-466-9200
Email: info@51minds.com
IMDb: imdb.com/name/nm4933376

Cris Abrego
Co-President
Phone: 323-466-9200
Email: info@51minds.com
IMDb: imdb.com/name/nm0009312/maindetails

59TH STREET FILMS

101 Destiny Dr
Lafayette, LA 70506
Phone: 337-280-9370

Email: 59thstreetfilms@gmail.com

Accepts scripts from unproduced, unrepresented writers. Project types include TV. Preferred genres include Comedy and Drama.

Sarah Agor
Producer
IMDb: imdb.com/name/nm2706070

Jennifer Jarrett
Producer
IMDb: imdb.com/name/nm1838264

Alfred Rubin Thompson
Producer
IMDb: imdb.com/name/nm0867022

Nicholas Scott
IMDb: imdb.com/name/nm4641966

Steve Sirkis
IMDb: imdb.com/name/nm2401659

5IVE SMOOTH STONES PRODUCTIONS

8500 Wilshire Blvd, Suite #527
Beverly Hills, CA 90211

Home Page: 5ivesmoothstones.com

Accepts query letter from unproduced, unrepresented writers via email. Project types include Feature Films. Preferred genres include Comedy and Family.

Terry Crews
Actor/CEO
IMDb: imdb.com/name/nm0187719

Robert Wise
President Scripted Development

72ND STREET PRODUCTIONS

1041 N Formosa Ave
Formosa Building, Suite 3
West Hollywood, CA 90046
Phone: 323-850-3139
Fax: 323-850-3179

Email: contact@72ndstreetproductions.com
Home Page: 72ndstreetproductions.com
IMDb: imdb.com/company/co0180596

Accepts query letter from unproduced, unrepresented writers via email. Project types include Feature Films, TV, and Commercials. Preferred genres include Drama.

Tim Harms
Principle
Phone: 323-850-3139
Email: tharms@72ndstreetproductions.com
IMDb: imdb.com/name/nm0363608

Lee Toland Krieger
Principle
Phone: 323-850-3139
Email: lkrieger@72ndstreetproductions.com
IMDb: imdb.com/name/nm1767218

Steven Krieger
Principle
Phone: 323-850-3139
Email: skrieger@72ndstreetproductions.com
IMDb: imdb.com/name/nm2544844

72 PRODUCTIONS

8899 Beverly Suite 716
West Hollywood, CA 90048
Phone: 310-278-1221
Fax: 310-278-1224

Home Page: 72productions.com
IMDb: imdb.com/company/co0196483

Accepts query letter from unproduced, unrepresented writers. Project types include Feature Films. Preferred genres include Science Fiction and Thriller.

Jennifer Chaiken
Principle
Phone: 310-278-1221
IMDb: imdb.com/name/nm0149671

Sebastian Dungan
Principle
Phone: 310-278-1221
IMDb: imdb.com/name/nm0242253

777 GROUP

1015 Gayley Ave, Suite 1128
Los Angeles, CA 90024
Phone: 312-834-7770

Email: 777group@gmail.com
Home Page: the777group.com
IMDb: imdb.com/company/co0133127

Accepts query letter from unproduced, unrepresented writers via email. Project types include TV. Preferred genres include Animation, Comedy, Drama, and Non-Fiction.

Marcello Robinson
CEO
Phone: 312-834-7770
Email: info@the777group.com
IMDb: imdb.com/name/nm0732883

7ATE9 ENTERTAINMENT

740 N. La Brea Ave
Los Angeles, CA 90038
Phone: 323-936-6789
Fax: 323-937-6713

Email: info@7ate9.com
Home Page: 7ate9.com
IMDb: imdb.com/company/co0171281

Does not accept any unsolicited material. Project types include TV.

Artur Spigel
Creative Director
IMDb: imdb.com/name/nm1742493

8:38 PRODUCTIONS

10390 Santa Monica Blvd.
Suite 200
Los Angeles, CA 90064
Phone: 310-789-3056
Fax: 310-789-3077

IMDb: imdb.com/company/co0252672

Does not accept any unsolicited material. Preferred genres include Family and Romance.

Kira Davis
Principle
Phone: 310-789-3056
IMDb: imdb.com/name/nm0204987

8790 PICTURES, INC.

11400 W Olympic Blvd, Suite 590
Los Angeles, CA 90064
Phone: 310-471-9983
Fax: 310-471-6366

Email: 8790pictures@gmail.com
IMDb: imdb.com/company/co0159892

Accepts query letter from unproduced, unrepresented writers via email. Project types include Feature Films and TV. Preferred genres include Action, Animation, Comedy, Drama, and Romance.

Joan Singleton

Phone: 310-471-9983
Email: 8790pictures@gmail.com
IMDb: imdb.com/name/nm0802306

Ralph Singleton

Phone: 310-471-9983
Email: 8790pictures@gmail.com
IMDb: imdb.com/name/nm0802326

8TH WONDER ENTERTAINMENT

7961 W 3rd St
Los Angeles, CA 90048

Email: info@8thwonderent.com
IMDb: imdb.com/company/co0226729

Accepts query letter from unproduced, unrepresented writers via email.

David Luong

Director of Development
Email: info@8thwonderent.com

Michael McQuarn

Email: mcq@8thwonderent.com

900 FILMS

1611A South Melrose Dr
Vista, CA 92081
Phone: 760-477-2470
Fax: 760-477-2478

Email: asst@900films.com
Home Page: 900films.com
IMDb: imdb.com/company/co0086829

Accepts query letter from unproduced, unrepresented writers via email. Project types include Feature Films, TV, and Commercials. Preferred genres include Non-Fiction and Reality.

Tony Hawk

Skateboarder/Principle
IMDb: imdb.com/name/nm0005000

Angela Rhodehamel

Production Manager/ Producer

9.14 PICTURES

1804 Chestnut St, Suite 2
Philadelphia, PA 19103
Phone: 215-238-0707
Fax: 215-238-0663

Email: info@914pictures.com
Home Page: 914pictures.com
IMDb: imdb.com/company/co0145535

Accepts query letter from unproduced, unrepresented writers via email. Established in 2002.

Sheena Joyce

Owner
Phone: 215-238-0707 ext. 11#
Email: info@914pictures.com
IMDb: imdb.com/name/nm1852224

Don Argott

Phone: 215-238-0707 ext. 12#
Email: info@914pictures.com
IMDb: imdb.com/name/nm0034531

AARDMAN ANIMATIONS

Gas Ferry Rd
Bristol BS1 6UN
United Kingdom
Phone: +44117-984-8485
Fax: +44117-984-8486

Email: mail@aardman.com
Home Page: aardman.com
IMDb: imdb.com/company/co0103531

Does not accept any unsolicited material. Preferred genres include Animation.

Alicia Gold

Head (Feature Development)
Phone: +44117-984-8485
Email: mail@aardman.com
IMDb: imdb.com/name/nm1664759imdb.com/name/nm4211100

ABANDON INTERACTIVE ENTERTAINMENT

711 Route 302
Pine Bush, NY 12566
Phone: 845-361-9317
Fax: 845-361-9150

Email: info@abandoninteractive.com
Home Page: abandoninteractive.com
IMDb: imdb.com/company/co0025591

Does not accept any unsolicited material.

Karen Lauder
Phone: 845-361-9317
Email: info@abandoninteractive.com
IMDb: imdb.com/name/nm0490746

ABC STUDIOS

500 S Buena Vista St
Burbank, CA 91505
Phone: 818-460-7777

Does not accept any unsolicited material. Project types include TV and Commercials. Preferred genres include Comedy and Drama.

Gary French
Senior Vice President (Production)
IMDb: imdb.com/name/nm2380686

Brenda Kyle
Vice President (Television Production)
IMDb: imdb.com/name/nm0477368

Patrick Moran
Executive Vice President (Creative & Production)
IMDb: imdb.com/name/nm3988896

ABERRATION FILMS

1425 N Crescent Heights Blvd, #203
West Hollywood, CA 90046
Phone: 323-656-1830

Email: aberrationfilms@yahoo.com
Home Page: aberrationfilms.com
IMDb: imdb.com/company/co0164476

Accepts query letter from unproduced, unrepresented writers. Project types include Feature Films. Preferred genres include Drama.

Susan Dynner
Phone: 323-656-1830
Email: aberrationfilms@yahoo.com
IMDb: imdb.com/name/nm1309839

ACAPPELLA PICTURES

8271 Melrose Ave, Suite 101
Los Angeles, CA 90046
Phone: 323-782-8200
Fax: 323-782-8210

Email: charmaine@acappellapictures.com
Home Page: acappellapictures.com
IMDb: imdb.com/company/co0055414

Accepts query letter from unproduced, unrepresented writers via email.

Charles Evans
President
Phone: 323-782-8200
Email: charmaine@acappellapictures.com
IMDb: imdb.com/name/nm0262509

Charmaine Parcero
Development Executive
Phone: 323-782-8200
Email: charmaine@acappellapictures.com
IMDb: imdb.com/name/nm0661019

ACCELERATED ENTERTAINMENT LLC

10201 W Pico Blvd, Building 6
Los Angeles, CA 90064

Email: cleestorm@acceleratedent.com
Home Page: acceleratedent.com
IMDb: imdb.com/company/co0208920

Accepts query letter from unproduced, unrepresented writers via email. Project types include Feature Films. Preferred genres include Drama and Non-Fiction.

Christina Lee Storm
Email: cleestorm@acceleratedent.com
IMDb: imdb.com/name/nm0497028

Jason Perr
Email: jperr@acceleratedent.com
IMDb: imdb.com/name/nm1280790

A.C. LYLES PRODUCTIONS, INC.

5555 Melrose Ave, Hart Building 409
Hollywood, CA 90038-3197
Phone: 323-956-5819

IMDb: imdb.com/company/co0074718

Accepts query letter from unproduced, unrepresented writers via email.

ACT III PRODUCTIONS

100 N Crescent Dr, Suite 250
Beverly Hills, CA 90210
Phone: 310-385-4111
Fax: 310-385-4148

Home Page: normanlear.com/act_iii.html
IMDb: imdb.com/company/co0030401

Accepts query letter from unproduced, unrepresented writers.

Norman Lear
Phone: 310-385-4111
Email: normanl@actiii.com
IMDb: imdb.com/name/nm0005131

Lara Bergthold
Director of Development
Phone: 310-385-4111
IMDb: imdb.com/name/nm2401887

ACTUAL REALITY PICTURES

Phone: 310-202-1272
Fax: 310-202-1502

Email: questions@arp.tv
Home Page: actualreality.tv
IMDb: imdb.com/company/co0004087

Does not accept any unsolicited material.

R.J. Cutler
President
Phone: 310-202-1272
IMDb: imdb.com/name/nm0191712

ADAM FIELDS PRODUCTIONS

1601 Cloverfield Suite 2000 North
Santa Monica, CA 90404

Phone: 310-745-5454
Fax: 310-859-4795

IMDb: imdb.com/company/co0064962

Accepts query letter from unproduced, unrepresented writers.

Adam Fields
President
Phone: 310-859-9300
IMDb: imdb.com/name/nm0276178

ADELSTEIN PRODUCTIONS

144 S Beverly Dr, Suite 500
Beverly Hills, CA 90212
Phone: 310-860-5502

Does not accept any unsolicited material.

Marty Adelstein
Producer
Phone: 310-270-4570
IMDb: imdb.com/name/nm1374351

AD HOMINEM ENTERPRISES

506 Santa Monica Blvd
Suite 400
Santa Monica, CA 90401
Phone: 310-394-1444
Fax: 310-394-5401

IMDb: imdb.com/company/co0171502

Does not accept any unsolicited material. Project types include Feature Films.

Jim Burke
Partner
Phone: 310-394-1444
Email: jwb@adhominem.us
IMDb: imdb.com/name/nm0121724
Assistant: Adam Wagner

Adam Wagner
Director of Development
Phone: 310-394-1444

Alexander Payne
Partner
Phone: 310-394-1444
IMDb: imdb.com/name/nm0668247

ADULT SWIM

1065 Williams St NW
Atlanta, GA 30309
Phone: 404-827-1500

Home Page: adultswim.com
IMDb: imdb.com/company/co0153115

Does not accept any unsolicited material.

Keith Crofford
IMDb: imdb.com/name/nm0188443

AEGIS FILM GROUP

7510 Sunset Blvd
Ste 275
Los Angeles, CA 90046
Phone: 818-588-3545
Fax: 323-650-9954

Email: aegisfilmgroup@ca.rr.com
Home Page: aegisfilmgroup.com

Project types include Feature Films. Preferred genres include Documentary.

Arianna Eisenberg
CEO
Phone: 323-848-7977
IMDb: imdb.com/name/nm1985255

Steven Shultz
President (Production)
Phone: 323-848-7977
IMDb: imdb.com/name/nm0795789

AEI - ATCHITY ENTERTAINMENT INTERNATIONAL, INC.

9601 Wilshire Blvd, #1202
Beverly Hills, CA 90210
Phone: 323-932-0407
Fax: 323-932-0321

Email: submissions@aeionline.com
Email: bl@aeionline.com
Home Page: aeionline.com
IMDb: wwwimdb.com/company/co0010944

Accepts query letter from unproduced, unrepresented writers.

Jennifer Pope
Submissions Coordinator
Phone: 323-932-0407
Email: jp@aeionline.com
IMDb: imdb.com/name/nm1026413

David Angsten
Development Executive

A&E NETWORK

235 E 45th St
New York, NY 10017
Phone: 212-210-1400
Fax: 212-210-9755

2049 Century Park East Tenth Floor
Los Angeles, CA 90067
Phone: 310-556-7500

Email: feedback@aetv.com
Home Page: aetv.com
IMDb: imdb.com/company/co0056790

Does not accept any unsolicited material.

Thomas Moody
Senior Vice President
Phone: 212-210-1400
Email: feedback@aetv.com
IMDb: imdb.com/name/nm1664759

AFTER DARK FILMS

6350 Santa Monica Blvd.
Suite 117
Hollywood, CA 90038
Phone: 310-270-4260
Fax: 310-270-4262

Email: info@afterdarkfilms.com
Home Page: afterdarkfilms.com
IMDb: imdb.com/company/co0166161

Does not accept any unsolicited material. Preferred genres include Horror.

Stephanie Caleb
Executive Vice President
Phone: 310-270-4260
Email: info@afterdarkfilms.com
IMDb: imdb.com/name/nm2554487

Richard Cardona
Creative Executive

AGAMEMNON FILMS

650 N Bronson Ave, Suite B225
Los Angeles, CA 90004
Phone: 323-960-4066
Fax: 323-960-4067

Home Page: agamemnon.com
IMDb: imdb.com/company/co0004137

Accepts query letter from unproduced, unrepresented writers via email. Project types include TV. Preferred genres include Action, Drama, Family, Non-Fiction, Reality, and Thriller.

Fraser Heston
President
IMDb: imdb.com/name/nm0381699
Assistant: Heather Thomas

Alex Butler
Senior Partner
Phone: 323-960-4066
IMDb: imdb.com/name/nm0124808

AGGREGATE FILMS

100 Universal City Plaza
Bungalow 4144
Universal City, CA 91608
Phone: 818-777-8180

Does not accept any unsolicited material. Project types include Feature Films. Preferred genres include Comedy and Family.

Jim Garavente
President
IMDb: imdb.com/name/nm4814574

Jason Bateman
Principle
IMDb: imdb.com/name/nm0000867

AGILITY STUDIOS

11928 Ventura Blvd
Studio City, CA 91604
Phone: 310-314-1440
Fax: 310-496-3292

Email: info@agilitystudios.com
Home Page: agilitystudios.com
IMDb: imdb.com/company/co0293230

Accepts query letter from unproduced, unrepresented writers via email. Established in 2008.

Scott Ehrlich
Principle
Phone: 310-314-1440
Email: info@agilitystudios.com
IMDb: imdb.com/name/nm3796990

AHIMSA FILMS

6671 Sunset Blvd, Suite 1593
Los Angeles, CA 90028
Phone: 323-464-8500
Fax: 323-464-8535

IMDb: imdb.com/company/co0202538

Accepts query letter from unproduced, unrepresented writers.

Rebecca Yeldham
President
Phone: 323-464-8500
IMDb: imdb.com/name/nm0947344

AHIMSA MEDIA

8060 Colonial Dr, Suite 204
Richmond, BC V7C 4V1
Canada
Phone: 604-785-3602

Email: info@ahimsamedia.com
Home Page: ahimsamedia.com
IMDb: imdb.com/company/co0222513
Facebook: facebook.com/ahimsamedia

Accepts query letter from unproduced, unrepresented writers via email. Project types include Commercials.

Erica Hargreave
President/Head of Creative and Interactive
Phone: 604-785-3602
Email: info@ahimsamedia.com
IMDb: imdb.com/name/nm2988128

AIRMONT PICTURES

344 Mesa Rd
Santa Monica, CA 90402
Phone: 310-985-3896

IMDb: imdb.com/company/co0176167

Accepts query letter from unproduced, unrepresented writers.

Matthew Gannon
Producer
Phone: 310-985-3896
IMDb: imdb.com/name/nm0304478

AKIL PRODUCTIONS

Phone: 212-608-2000

Email: info@akilproductions.com
Home Page: akilproductions.com

Project types include TV. Preferred genres include Drama.

Mara Akil
Principle
IMDb: imdb.com/name/nm0015327

Salim Akil
Principle
IMDb: imdb.com/name/nm0015328

ALAMO DRAFTHOUSE FILMS

Austin, TX

Email: info@drafthousefilms.com
Home Page: drafthousefilms.com
IMDb: imdb.com/company/co0313579
Facebook: facebook.com/drafthousefilms

Does not accept any unsolicited material. Project types include Feature Films. Preferred genres include Action, Comedy, Documentary, Drama, and Thriller.

Tim League
CEO
IMDb: imdb.com/name/nm1382506

James Emanuel Shapiro
COO
IMDb: imdb.com/name/nm4874938

Evan Husney
Creative Director
IMDb: imdb.com/name/nm3432889

ALAN BARNETTE PRODUCTIONS

100 Universal City Plaza
Building 2352, Suite 101
Universal City, CA 91608
Phone: 818-733-0993
Fax: 818-733-3172

Email: dabarnette@aol.com
IMDb: imdb.com/company/co0056462

Does not accept any unsolicited material.

Alan Barnette
Executive Producer
Phone: 818-733-0993
Email: dabarnette@aol.com
IMDb: imdb.com/name/nm0056002

Nancy Mosher Hall
Development Executive
IMDb: imdb.com/name/nm0355945

ALAN DAVID MANAGEMENT

8840 Wilshire Blvd,
Suite 200
Beverly Hills, CA 90211
Phone: 310-358-3155
Fax: 310-358-3256

Email: ad@adgmp.com
IMDb: imdb.com/company/co0097077

Does not accept any unsolicited material.

Alan David
President
Phone: 310-358-3155
Email: ad@adgmp.com
IMDb: imdb.com/name/nm2220960

ALAN SACKS PRODUCTIONS

11684 Ventura Blvd, Suite 809
Studio City, CA 91604
Phone: 818-752-6999
Fax: 818-752-6985

Email: asacks@pacbell.net
IMDb: imdb.com/company/co0013945

Does not accept any unsolicited material.

Alan Sacks
Executive Producer
Phone: 818-752-6999
Email: asacks@pacbell.net
IMDb: imdb.com/name/nm0755286

ALCHEMY ENTERTAINMENT

7024 Melrose Ave, Suite 420
Los Angeles, CA 90038
Phone: 323-937-6100
Fax: 323-937-6102

IMDb: imdb.com/company/co0094892

Does not accept any unsolicited material.

Jason Barrett
Principle (Manager)
Phone: 323-937-6100
IMDb: imdb.com/name/nm2249074

ALCON ENTERTAINMENT, LLC

10390 Santa Monica Blvd, Suite 250
Los Angeles, CA 90025
Phone: 310-789-3040
Fax: 310-789-3060

Email: info@alconent.com
Home Page: alconent.com
IMDb: imdb.com/company/co0054452

Does not accept any unsolicited material. Project types include Feature Films.

Broderick Johnson
Co-CEO/Co-Founder
Phone: 310-789-3040
Email: info@alconent.com
IMDb: imdb.com/name/nm0424663

Steven Wegner
Executive Vice President of Production
Phone: 310-789-3040
Email: info@alconent.com
IMDb: imdb.com/name/nm1176853

ALDAMISA FILMS

15760 Ventura Blvd.
Suite 1450
Encino, CA 91436
Phone: 818-783-4084
Fax: 818-753-2310

Email: sales@aldamisa.com
Email: emin@aldamisa.com
Home Page: aldamisa.com

Accepts query letter from produced or represented writers. Project types include Feature Films. Preferred genres include Action, Comedy, Crime, Drama, Fantasy, Horror, Romance, and Thriller.

Jere Hausfater
COO

Michael Kupisk
Head of Development
IMDb: imdb.com/name/nm3161790
Assistant: Josh Baker

Marina Bespalov
CO-CEO
IMDb: imdb.com/name/nm4208519
Assistant: Kirby Lodin

Sergei Bespalov
Co-CEO
IMDb: imdb.com/name/nm3703488
Assistant: Michelle Faraji

ALEXANDER/MITCHELL PRODUCTIONS

201 Wilshire Blvd Third Floor
Santa Monica, CA 90401
Phone: 310-458-3003
Fax: 310-393-7238

IMDb: imdb.com/company/co0241249

Accepts query letter from unproduced, unrepresented writers via email. Project types include Feature Films and TV. Preferred genres include Drama.

Les Alexander
IMDb: imdb.com/name/nm0018573

Jonathan Mitchell
IMDb: imdb.com/name/nm2927057

ALEX ROSE PRODUCTIONS

8291 Presson Place
Los Angeles, CA 90069
Phone: 323-654-8662
Fax: 323-654-0196

IMDb: imdb.com/company/co0177705

Accepts query letter from unproduced, unrepresented writers.

Alexandra Rose

President
Phone: 323-654-8662
IMDb: imdb.com/name/nm0741228

ALIANZA FILMS INTERNATIONAL

11941 Weddington St, Suite #106
Studio City, CA 91607
Phone: 310-933-6250
Fax: 310-388-0874

Email: shari@alianzafilms.com
Home Page: alianzafilms.com
IMDb: imdb.com/company/co0022267

Accepts query letter from unproduced, unrepresented writers. Established in 1984.

Shari Hamrick

Executive
Phone: 310-933-6250
Email: shari@alianzafilms.com
IMDb: imdb.com/name/nm0359089

A-LINE PICTURES

2231 Broadway #19
New York, NY 10024
Phone: 212-496-9496
Fax: 212-496-9497

Email: info@a-linepictures.com
Home Page: a-linepictures.com
IMDb: imdb.com/company/co0156447

Does not accept any unsolicited material. Established in 2005.

Caroline Baron

Producer
Phone: 212-496-9496
Email: info@a-linepictures.com
IMDb: imdb.com/name/nm0056205

ALLAN MCKEOWN PRESENTS

1534 17th St, #102
Santa Monica, CA 90404
Phone: 310-264-2474
Fax: 310-264-4663

Email: info@ampresents.tv
Home Page: ampresents.tv
IMDb: imdb.com/company/co0206885

Accepts query letter from unproduced, unrepresented writers via email. Established in 2007.

Allan McKeown

Phone: 310-264-2474
Email: info@ampresents.tv
IMDb: imdb.com/name/nm0571647

ALLENTOWN PRODUCTIONS

100 Universal City Plaza
Building 2372B, Suite 114
Universal City, CA 91608
Phone: 818-733-1002
Fax: 818-866-4181

Email: writetous@allentownproductions.com
Home Page: allentownproductions.com
IMDb: imdb.com/company/co0122945

Does not accept any unsolicited material. Preferred genres include Non-Fiction. Established in 1994.

James Moll

Phone: 818-733-1002
Email: writetous@allentownproductions.com
IMDb: imdb.com/name/nm0002224

Chris W. King

Director of Development
Phone: 818-733-1002
Email: writetous@allentownproductions.com
IMDb: imdb.com/name/nm1648242

ALLIANCE FILMS

45 Kings St East Suite 300
Toronto, ON, Canada, M5C2Y7
Phone: 416-309-4200
Fax: 416-309-4290

Email: info@alliancefilms.com
Home Page: alliancefilms.com

Does not accept any unsolicited material. Project types include Feature Films. Preferred genres include Action, Comedy, Crime, Drama, Fantasy, Horror, Romance, Science Fiction, and Thriller.

Xavier Marchand
President
IMDb: imdb.com/name/nm0545421

ALLOY ENTERTAINMENT

4000 Warner Blvd.
Building 146, Room 203
Burbank, CA 91522
Phone: 818-954-3074
Fax: 818-954-3508

151 W. 26th St
11th Floor
New York, NY 10001
Phone: 212-329-8448

Email: LAassistant@alloyentertainment.com
Home Page: alloyentertainment.com
IMDb: imdb.com/company/co0142434

Accepts query letter from unproduced, unrepresented writers via email.

Josh Bank
Executive Vice President
Phone: 212-329-8448
IMDb: imdb.com/name/nm2987370

ALOE ENTERTAINMENT

433 N Camden Dr, Suite 600
Beverly Hills, CA 90210
Phone: 310-288-1886
Fax: 310-288-1801

Email: info@aloeentertainment.com
Home Page: aloeentertainment.com
IMDb: imdb.com/company/co0261920

Does not accept any unsolicited material. Established in 1999.

Mary Aloe
Phone: 310-288-1886
Email: info@aloeentertainment.com
IMDb: imdb.com/name/nm0022053

AL ROKER PRODUCTIONS

250 W 57th St, Suite 1525
New York, NY 10019
Phone: 212-757-8500
Fax: 212-757-8513

Email: info@alroker.com
Home Page: alrokerproductions.com
IMDb: imdb.com/company/co0095131

Does not accept any unsolicited material. Project types include Feature Films. Established in 1994.

Al Roker
CEO
Phone: 212-757-8500
Email: info@alroker.com
IMDb: imdb.com/name/nm0737963

Tracie Brennan
Phone: 212-757-8500
Email: info@alroker.com
IMDb: imdb.com/name/nm2200420

ALTA LOMA ENTERTAINMENT

9346 Civic Center Dr.
Beverly Hills, CA 90210
Phone: 310-424-1800

Home Page: alta-loma.com
IMDb: imdb.com/company/co0008514

Does not accept any unsolicited material.

J.W. Starrett
Director of Development
Phone: 323-276-4211
IMDb: imdb.com/name/nm2852786

ALTURAS FILMS

1617 Broadway Ave. 2nd Floor
Santa Monica, CA 90404

Phone: 310-401-6200
Fax: 310-401-6129

Email: info@alturasfilms.com
Email: reception@alturasfilms.com
Home Page: alturasfilms.com
IMDb: imdb.com/company/co0169508

Does not accept any unsolicited material. Established in 2004.

Marshall Rawlings

CEO (Producer)
Phone: 310-401-6200
Email: reception@alturasfilms.com
IMDb: imdb.com/name/nm1987844

A-MARK ENTERTAINMENT

233 Wilshire Blvd, Suite 200
Santa Monica, CA 90401
Phone: 310-255-0900

Email: info@amarkentertainment.com
Home Page: amarkentertainment.com
IMDb: imdb.com/company/co0135086

Does not accept any unsolicited material. Established in 2004.

Bruce McNall

Co-Chairman
Phone: 310-255-0900
Email: info@amarkentertainment.com
IMDb: imdb.com/name/nm1557652

AMBASSADOR ENTERTAINMENT, INC.

P. O. Box 1522
Pacific Palisades, CA 90272
Phone: 310-862-5200
Fax: 310-496-3140

Email: aspeval@ambassadortv.com
Home Page: ambassadortv.com
IMDb: imdb.com/company/co0175998

Does not accept any unsolicited material. Established in 1999.

Albert Spevak

President
Phone: 310-862-5200
Email: aspeval@ambassadortv.com
IMDb: imdb.com/name/nm0818411

AMBER ENTERTAINMENT

21 Ganton St, 4th Floor
London
United Kingdom
W1F 98N
Phone: +44207-292-7170

Email: info@amberentertainment.com
Home Page: amberentertainment.com
IMDb: imdb.com/company/co0266476

Does not accept any unsolicited material. Project types include Feature Films. Preferred genres include Crime, Drama, Fantasy, Horror, and Thriller. Established in 2010.

Lawrence Elman

Executive Producer
IMDb: imdb.com/name/nm3793846

Ileen Maisel

Executive
Phone: +44207-292-7170
Email: info@amberentertainment.com
IMDb: imdb.com/name/nm0537884

AMBLIN ENTERTAINMENT

100 Universal Plaza
Bldg 477
Universal City, CA 91608
Phone: 818-733-7000
Fax: 818-509-1433

Does not accept any unsolicited material. Project types include Feature Films. Preferred genres include Action, Comedy, Drama, Fantasy, and Science Fiction.

Steven Spielberg

Chairman
Phone: 818-733-7000
IMDb: imdb.com/name/nm0000229

AMBUSH ENTERTAINMENT

360 N. La Cienega Blvd. Third Floor
Los Angeles, CA 90048
Phone: 323-951-9197
Fax: 323-951-9998

Email: info@ambushentertainment.com
Home Page: ambushentertainment.com
IMDb: imdb.com/company/co0091524

Accepts scripts from produced or represented writers.
Established in 2000.

Miranda Bailey

Partner (CEO)
Phone: 323-951-9197
Email: 323-951-9998
IMDb: imdb.com/name/nm0047419

Amanda Marshall

Head (Production)
IMDb: imdb.com/name/nm1622973

AMERICAN MOVING PICTURES

108 W 2nd St.
Suite 1012
Los Angeles, CA 90012

Home Page: americanmovingpictures.com

Accepts query letter from unproduced, unrepresented
writers via email. Project types include Feature Films.
Preferred genres include Comedy and Drama.

Matt D'Elia

Email: matt@americanmovingpictures.com
IMDb: imdb.com/name/nm2532035

Julian King

Email: julian@americanmovingpictures.com
IMDb: imdb.com/name/nm2398047

AMERICAN WORK INC.

7030 Delongpre
Los Angeles, CA 90028
Phone: 323-668-1100
Fax: 323-668-1133

IMDb: imdb.com/company/co0167015

Accepts query letter from unproduced, unrepresented
writers. Preferred genres include Comedy.

Scot Armstrong

IMDb: imdb.com/name/nm0035905

AMERICAN WORLD PICTURES

21700 Oxnard St, Suite 1770
Woodland Hills, CA 91367
Phone: 818-340-9004
Fax: 818-340-9011

Email: info@americanworldpictures.com
Home Page: americanworldpictures.com
IMDb: imdb.com/company/co0054536

Accepts scripts from unproduced, unrepresented
writers. Project types include Feature Films. Preferred
genres include Action, Comedy, Drama, Family,
Horror, Romance, and Thriller.

Mark Lester

Phone: 818-340-9004
Email: mark@americanworldpictures.com
IMDb: imdb.com/name/nm0504495

Dana Dubovsky

Phone: 818-340-9004
Email: dana@americanworldpictures.com
IMDb: imdb.com/name/nm0239541

Dee Camp

Phone: 818-340-9004
Email: dee@americanworldpictures.com
IMDb: imdb.com/name/nm3036636

AMERICAN ZOETROPE

916 Kearny St Sentinel Building
San Francisco, CA 94133
Phone: 415-788-7500
Fax: 415-989-7910

1641 N Ivar Ave
Los Angeles, CA 90028

Email: contests@zoetrope.com
Home Page: zoetrope.com
IMDb: imdb.com/company/co0020958

Accepts scripts from unproduced, unrepresented
writers. Preferred genres include Action, Crime, Non-
Fiction, and Thriller. Established in 1972.

Francis Coppola
Emeritus
Phone: 415-788-7500
IMDb: imdb.com/name/nm0000338

Michael Zakin
Vice President (Production & Acquisitions)
Phone: 323-460-4420
IMDb: imdb.com/name/nm2943902

ANCHOR BAY FILMS

9242 Beverly Blvd Suite 201
Beverly Hills, CA 90210
Phone: 424-204-4166

1699 Stutz Dr.
Troy, MI 48084
Phone: 248-816-0909
Fax: 248-816-3335

Email: questions@anchorbayent.com
Home Page: anchorbayent.com

Accepts query letter from unproduced, unrepresented writers. Preferred genres include Crime, Horror, and Thriller. Established in 1997.

Bill Clark
President
Phone: 424-204-4166
IMDb: imdb.com/name/nm0163694

ANDREA SIMON ENTERTAINMENT

4230 Woodman Ave.
Sherman Oaks, CA 91423
Phone: 818-380-1901
Fax: 818-380-1932

Email: asimon@andreasimonent.com
IMDb: imdb.com/company/co0102747

Accepts query letter from unproduced, unrepresented writers. Project types include Feature Films and TV. Preferred genres include Comedy and Drama.

Andrea Simon
Email: asimon@andreasimonent.com
IMDb: imdb.com/name/nm2231084

ANDREW LAUREN PRODUCTIONS

36 E 23rd St, Suite 6F
New York, NY 10010
Phone: 212-475-1600
Fax: 212-529-1095

Email: asst@andrewlaurenproductions.com
Home Page: andrewlaurenproductions.com
IMDb: imdb.com/company/co0032488

Accepts scripts from unproduced, unrepresented writers. Project types include Feature Films and TV. Preferred genres include Drama.

Andrew Lauren
Principle
Phone: 212-475-1600
Email: asst@andrewlaurenproductions.com
IMDb: imdb.com/name/nm0491054

Dave Platt
Creative Executive
Phone: 212-475-1600
Email: asst@andrewlaurenproductions.com
IMDb: imdb.com/name/nm5255879

ANGELWORLD ENTERTAINMENT LTD.

New Bridge House
30-34 New Bridge St
London
EC4 V6BJ

6 Triq Ta Fuq Il Widien
Mellieha
Malta

Email: asst@angelworldentertainment.com
Home Page: angelworldentertainment.com

Accepts query letter from unproduced, unrepresented writers via email. Project types include Feature Films. Established in 2007.

Darby Angel
CEO/Producer
Email: chris@angelworldentertainment.com
IMDb: imdb.com/name/nm3786007
Assistant: Christopher Tisa

John Michaels
Head of Production

ANIMUS FILMS

914 Hauser Blvd
Los Angeles, CA 90036
Phone: 323-988-5557
Fax: 323-571-3361

Email: info@animusfilms.com
Home Page: animusfilms.com
IMDb: imdb.com/company/co0092860

Accepts query letter from unproduced, unrepresented writers. Preferred genres include Non-Fiction and Thriller. Established in 2003.

Jim Young
Principle
Phone: 323-988-5557
Email: info@animusfilms.com
IMDb: imdb.com/name/nm1209063

ANNAPURNA PICTURES

Phone: 310-724-5678
Fax: 310-724-8111

Home Page: annapurnapics.com
IMDb: imdb.com/company/co0323215

Does not accept any unsolicited material. Project types include Feature Films and TV. Preferred genres include Action, Comedy, Crime, Drama, Non-Fiction, and Thriller.

David Distenfeld
Development Executive
IMDb: imdb.com/name/nm3367048

Megan Ellison
Producer
IMDb: imdb.com/name/nm2691892

AN OLIVE BRANCH PRODUCTIONS, INC.

9100 Wilshire Blvd, Suite 616
East Tower
Beverly Hills, CA 90212
Phone: 310-860-6088
Fax: 310-362-8922

38 Highbridge Place
Toronto, ON M1V4R9

Email: info@anolivebranchmedia.com
Home Page: anolivebranchmedia.com
IMDb: imdb.com/company/co0055694imdb.com/company/co0308344

Accepts scripts from produced or represented writers. Project types include Feature Films. Preferred genres include Drama.

Cybill Lui
Phone: 310-860-6088
Email: info@AnOlivBranchmedia.com
IMDb: imdb.com/name/nm3359236

George Zakk
Phone: 310-860-6088
Email: info@AnOlivBranchmedia.com
IMDb: imdb.com/name/nm0952327

ANOMALY ENTERTAINMENT

10990 Wilshire Blvd
Eighth Floor
Los Angeles, CA 90024

Project types include Feature Films and TV. Preferred genres include Documentary, Drama, Non-Fiction, and Period.

Stephen J. Rivele
IMDb: imdb.com/name/nm0729151

Christopher Wilkinson
IMDb: imdb.com/name/nm0929349

ANONYMOUS CONTENT

3532 Hayden Ave
Culver City, CA 90232
Phone: 310-558-3667
Fax: 310-558-4212

588 Broadway Suite 308
New York, NY 10012
Phone: 212-925-0055
Fax: 212-925-5030

Email: filmtv@anonymouscontent.com
Email: litmanagement@anonymouscontent.com
Home Page: anonymouscontent.com

Accepts query letter from unproduced, unrepresented writers via email. Project types include Feature Films, TV, and Commercials. Preferred genres include

Action, Comedy, Crime, Drama, Family, Non-Fiction, and Thriller. Established in 1999.

Steve Golin
CEO
IMDb: imdb.com/name/nm0326512

Emmeline Yang
Executive (Features)
Phone: 310-558-3667
IMDb: imdb.com/name/nm2534779

Matt DeRoss
Vice President (Features)
Phone: 310-558-3667
Email: mattd@anonymouscontent.com
IMDb: imdb.com/name/nm2249185

ANTIDOTE FILMS

PO Box 150566
Brooklyn, NY 11215-0566
Phone: 646-486-4344

Email: info@antidotefilms.com
Home Page: antidotefilms.com

Does not accept any unsolicited material. Project types include Feature Films. Preferred genres include Documentary. Established in 2000.

Jeffrey Levy-Hinte
President
Phone: 646-486-4344 x301
Email: jeff@antidotefilms.com
IMDb: imdb.com/name/nm0506664

Takeo Hori
Phone: 646-486-4344 x300
IMDb: imdb.com/name/nm0394659

Gerry Kim

James Debbs
Phone: 646-486-4344 x305
IMDb: imdb.com/name/nm0999455

APATOW PRODUCTIONS

11788 W Pico Blvd, Suite 141
Los Angeles, CA 90064
Phone: 310-943-4400
Fax: 310-479-0750

IMDb: imdb.com/company/co0073081

Does not accept any unsolicited material. Project types include Feature Films and TV. Preferred genres include Action, Comedy, Documentary, Drama, and Romance. Established in 2000.

Judd Apatow
IMDb: imdb.com/name/nm0031976
Assistant: Amanda Glaze, Rob Turbovsky, Michael Lewen

APERTURE ENTERTAINMENT

7620 Lexington Ave
West Hollywood, CA 90046
Phone: 323-848-4069

Email: agasst@aperture-ent.com
IMDb: imdb.com/company/co0265611

Accepts scripts from unproduced, unrepresented writers. Project types include Feature Films and TV. Preferred genres include Action, Fantasy, Horror, Science Fiction, and Thriller. Established in 2009.

Adam Goldworm
Principle
Phone: 323-848-4069
Email: adam@aperture-ent.com
IMDb: imdb.com/name/nm0326411

APPLESEED ENTERTAINMENT

7715 Sunset Blvd
Ste 101
Hollywood, CA 90046
Phone: 818-718-6000
Fax: 818-556-5610

Email: queries@appleseedent.com
Email: films@appleseedent.com
Home Page: appleseedent.com
IMDb: imdb.com/company/co0176039

Does not accept any unsolicited material. Project types include Feature Films. Preferred genres include Comedy, Drama, and Family.

Ben Moses
Executive
Email: ben@appleseedent.com
IMDb: imdb.com/name/nm0608558

Lynne Moses
Executive
Email: lynne@appleseedent.com
IMDb: imdb.com/name/nm1030988

ARCLIGHT FILMS

8447 Wilshire Blvd, Suite 101
Beverly Hills, CA 90211
Phone: 310-777-8855
Fax: 310-777-8882

Fox Studios Australia Suite 228 (FSA # 40), Building
61 Drr Ave
Moore Park, NSW, Australia, 2021
Phone: 011-612-83532440

Email: info@arclightfilms.com
Home Page: arclightfilms.com

Accepts query letter from unproduced, unrepresented
writers via email. Project types include Feature Films.

Gary Hamilton
Co-Chairman
Phone: 310-528-5888
Email: gary@arclightfilms.com
IMDb: imdb.com/name/nm0357861

Mike Gabrawy
CCO
Phone: 310-475-2330
Email: info@arclightfilms.com
IMDb: imdb.com/name/nm0300166

ARENAS ENTERTAINMENT

3375 Barham Blvd
Los Angeles, CA 90068
Phone: 323-785-5555
Fax: 323-785-5560

Email: general@arenasgroup.com
Home Page: arenasgroup.com
IMDb: imdb.com/company/co0051527

Does not accept any unsolicited material. Project types
include Feature Films. Established in 1988.

Santiago Pozo
CEO
IMDb: imdb.com/name/nm0694815

ARGONAUT PICTURES

Phone: 310-359-8481

Home Page: argonautpictures.com

Accepts query letter from unproduced, unrepresented
writers. Project types include Feature Films. Preferred
genres include Drama.

Scott Bloom
Owner
IMDb: imdb.com/name/nm0089231

Giovanni Agnelli
Owner
IMDb: imdb.com/name/nm1278301

Karim Mashouf
Owner
IMDb: imdb.com/name/nm3196690

Manny Mashouf
Owner
IMDb: imdb.com/name/nm3196705

Paul Marashlian
Email: Paul@argonautpictures.com
IMDb: imdb.com/name/nm2281671

Carter Hall
Email: carter@argonautpictures.com
IMDb: imdb.com/name/nm3050292

ARIESCOPE PICTURES

10750 Cumpston St
North Hollywood, CA 91601

Email: info@ariescope.com
Home Page: ariescope.com

Does not accept any unsolicited material. Project types
include Feature Films and TV. Preferred genres
include Comedy, Crime, Drama, Fantasy, Horror,
Romance, and Thriller.

Will Barratt
IMDb: .imdb.com/name/nm1701139

Cory Neal
IMDb: imdb.com/name/nm1425628

Adam Green
IMDb: imdb.com/name/nm1697112

ARS NOVA

511 W 54th St
New York, NY 10019
Phone: 212-586-4200
Fax: 212-489-1908

Email: info@arsnovaent.com
Home Page: arsnovaent.com
IMDb: imdb.com/company/co0176042

Accepts scripts from unproduced, unrepresented writers. Preferred genres include Action, Comedy, Fantasy, Myth, and Science Fiction.

Jon Steingart
Producer
Phone: 212-586-4200
Email: japfelbaum@arsnovaent.com
IMDb: imdb.com/name/nm0826050

Jillian Apfelbaum
Producer
Phone: 212-586-4200
Email: japfelbaum@arsnovaent.com
IMDb: imdb.com/name/nm2249752

ARTFIRE FILMS

740 N. La Brea Ave.
Hollywood, CA 90038
Phone: 323-937-7188
Fax: 323-937-6713

Email: contact@artfirefilms.com
Home Page: artfirefilms.com
IMDb: imdb.com/company/co0188290

Does not accept any unsolicited material. Project types include Feature Films. Preferred genres include Action, Comedy, Crime, Documentary, Drama, Horror, Period, Romance, and Science Fiction. Established in 2007.

Jennah Dirksen
Creative Executive
IMDb: imdb.com/name/nm3302694

Ara Katz
Producer
IMDb: imdb.com/name/nm1433420

Andy Spellman
Executive Producer

Arthur Spigel
IMDb: imdb.com/name/nm1742493

Dan Fireman
IMDb: imdb.com/name/nm2379207

ARTICLE19 FILMS

247 Centre St, Suite 7W
New York, NY 10013
Phone: 212-777-1987
Fax: 212-777-2585

Email: info@article19films.com
Home Page: article19films.com
IMDb: imdb.com/company/co0164965

Accepts query letter from unproduced, unrepresented writers. Preferred genres include Non-Fiction.

Filippo Bozotti
Executive
Phone: 212-777-1987
Email: article19films@gmail.com
IMDb: imdb.com/name/nm1828075

ARTISTS PUBLIC DOMAIN

225 W 13th St
New York, NY 10011

Email: info@artistspublicdomain.com
Home Page: artistspublicdomain.com

Accepts query letter from unproduced, unrepresented writers. Project types include Feature Films. Preferred genres include Comedy, Drama, Family, Non-Fiction, Romance, Sociocultural, and Thriller.

Hunter Gray
Producer
IMDb: imdb.com/name/nm0336683

Alex Orlovsky
Producer
IMDb: imdb.com/name/nm0650164

Andrew Adair
IMDb: imdb.com/name/nm4253715

A. SMITH & COMPANY PRODUCTIONS

9911 W Pico Blvd, Suite 250
Los Angeles, CA 90035
Phone: 310-432-4800
Fax: 310-551-3085

Email: info@asmithco.com
Home Page: asmithco.com
IMDb: imdb.com/company/co0095150

Accepts query letter from unproduced, unrepresented writers via email.

Arthur Smith
CEO
Phone: 310-432-4800
Email: info@asmithco.com
IMDb: wwwimdb.com/name/nm0807368

Christmas Rini
Phone: 310-432-4800
Email: info@asmithco.com
IMDb: imdb.com/name/nm2859471

ASYLUM ENTERTAINMENT

15301 Ventura Blvd
Suite 400 Building B
Sherman Oaks, CA 91403
Phone: 310-696-4401
Fax: 310-696-4891

15503 Ventura Blvd.
Suite 240
Encino, CA 91436
Phone: 310-696-4600

Email: info@asylument.com
Home Page: asylument.com

Accepts scripts from unproduced, unrepresented writers. Project types include TV. Preferred genres include Action, Crime, Drama, Fantasy, Horror, Non-Fiction, Science Fiction, and Thriller.

Marielle Skouras
Director of Development
Phone: 310-696-4401
Email: info@asylument.com
IMDb: imdb.com/name/nm4413245

ATLAS ENTERTAINMENT (PRODUCTION BRANCH OF MOSAIC)

9200 Sunset Blvd, 10th Floor
Los Angeles, CA 90069
Phone: 310-786-8900
Fax: 310-777-2185

IMDb: imdb.com/company/co0028338

Does not accept any unsolicited material. Project types include Feature Films and TV.

Alex Gartner
Producer
Phone: 310-786-8105
IMDb: imdb.com/name/nm0308672

Jake Kurily
Vice President (Motion Pictures & Television)
Phone: 310-786-8974
IMDb: imdb.com/name/nm2464228

Andy Horwitz
Vice President (Motion Pictures & Television)
Phone: 310-786-4948
IMDb: imdb.com/name/nm2191045

ATLAS MEDIA CORPORATION

242 W 36th St, 11th Floor
New York, NY, 10018
Phone: 212-714-0222
Fax: 212-714-0240

Email: info@atlasmediacorp.com
Home Page: atlasmediacorp.com
IMDb: imdb.com/company/co0280783

Accepts query letter from produced or represented writers. Preferred genres include Non-Fiction.

Glen Freyer
Phone: 212-714-0222
Email: info@atlasmediacorp.com
IMDb: imdb.com/name/nm0294662

Andrew Jacobs
Phone: 212-714-0222
Email: info@atlasmediacorp.com

ATMOSPHERE ENTERTAINMENT MM, LLC

4751 Wilshire, Blvd, 3rd Floor
Los Angeles, CA, 90010
Phone: 323-549-4350
Fax: 323-549-9832

IMDb: imdb.com/company/co0014103

Accepts scripts from produced or represented writers. Preferred genres include Fantasy, Horror, and Thriller.

David Hopwood

Senior Vice President (Production & Development)
Phone: 323-549-4350
IMDb: imdb.com/name/nm2055027

AUTOMATIC PICTURES

5225 Wilshire Blvd
Suite 525
Los Angeles, CA 90036
Phone: 323-935-1800
Fax: 323-935-8040

Email: automaticstudio@mail.com
Home Page: automaticpictures.net

Accepts query letter from unproduced, unrepresented writers via email. Project types include Video Games. Preferred genres include Fantasy.

Liz Cavalier

Creative Executive
IMDb: imdb.com/name/nm2248983

Frank Beddor

IMDb: imdb.com/name/nm0065980
Assistant: Bo Liebman

Nate Barlow

Email: nate@automaticpictures.net
IMDb: imdb.com/name/nm0055269

BAD HAT HARRY PRODUCTIONS

10201 W Pico Blvd
Building 50
Los Angeles, CA 90064
Phone: 310-369-2080

Email: reception@badhatharry.com
Home Page: badhatharry.com
IMDb: imdb.com/company/co0057712

Accepts scripts from produced or represented writers. Project types include TV. Preferred genres include Action, Drama, Fantasy, Myth, Science Fiction, and Thriller.

Bryan Singer

CEO
Phone: 310-369-2080
IMDb: imdb.com/name/nm0001741

Mark Berliner

Vice President (Development)
Phone: 310-369-2080
IMDb: imdb.com/name/nm2249392

BAD ROBOT

1221 Olympic Blvd
Santa Monica, CA 90404
Phone: 310-664-3456
Fax: 310-664-3457

Home Page: badrobot.com
IMDb: wwwimdb.com/company/co0021593

Does not accept any unsolicited material. Project types include Feature Films and TV. Preferred genres include Action, Drama, Fantasy, and Science Fiction.

J.J. Abrams

CEO
Phone: 310-664-3456
IMDb: imdb.com/name/nm0009190

Jonathan Cohen

Executive (Film)
Assistant: Veronica Baker

Kevin Jarzynski

Executive (Film)
IMDb: imdb.com/name/nm1704653
Assistant: Veronica Baker

Bryan Burk

Partner (Vice President)
IMDb: imdb.com/name/nm1333357
Assistant: Max Taylor

Kathy Lingg

Head (Television)
IMDb: imdb.com/name/nm2489727
Assistant: Matthew Owens

Lindsey Paulson Weber
Head (Film)
IMDb: imdb.com/name/nm1439829
Assistant: Corrine Aquino

David Baronoff
Executive (New Media, Film, & Television)
IMDb: imdb.com/name/nm2343623

Athena Wickham
Executive (Television)
IMDb: imdb.com/name/nm2204043
Assistant: Casey Haver

BALDWIN ENTERTAINMENT GROUP, LTD.

3000 W Olympic Blvd Suite 2510
Santa Monica, CA
Phone: 310-243-6634

Email: info@baldwinent.com
Home Page: baldwinent.com
IMDb: imdb.com/company/co0057712mdb.com/
company/co0145519

Does not accept any unsolicited material. Project types
include Feature Films. Preferred genres include Action,
Comedy, Drama, Non-Fiction, and Romance.
Established in 2009.

Ryan Wuerfel
Creative Executive
Phone: 310-243-6634
Email: ryan@baldwinent.com
IMDb: imdb.com/name/nm3601274

Howard Baldwin
Phone: 310-243-6634
IMDb: imdb.com/name/nm0049920

Karen Baldwin
Phone: 310-243-6634
IMDb: imdb.com/name/nm0049945

BALLYHOO, INC.

6738 Wedgewood Place
Los Angeles, CA 90068
Phone: 323-874-3396

Accepts scripts from unproduced, unrepresented
writers. Project types include Feature Films. Preferred
genres include Action and Comedy.

Michael Besman
Producer
Phone: 323-874-3396
IMDb: imdb.com/name/nm0078698

BALTIMORE PICTURES

8306 Wilshire Blvd
PMB 1012
Beverly Hills, CA 90211
Phone: 310-234-8988

Home Page: levinson.com/index_bsc.htm
IMDb: imdb.com/company/co0038108

Does not accept any unsolicited material. Project types
include Feature Films. Preferred genres include
Comedy, Crime, Drama, Romance, Science Fiction,
and Thriller.

Barry Levinson
IMDb: imdb.com/name/nm0001469

Jason Sosnoff
IMDb: imdb.com/name/nm0815369

BANDITO BROTHERS

3115 S La Cienega Blvd.
Los Angeles, CA 90016
Phone: 310-559-5404
Fax: 310-559-5230

Email: info@banditobrothers.com
Home Page: banditiobrothers.com

Project types include Feature Films. Preferred genres
include Action, Comedy, Drama, Fantasy, Science
Fiction, and Thriller.

Scott Waugh
Founder
IMDb: imdb.com/name/nm0915304

Max Leitman
COO
IMDb: imdb.com/name/nm2649648

Mike McCoy
IMDb: imdb.com/name/nm0566788

Jay Pollak

Suzanne Hargrove
IMDb: imdb.com/name/nm2597628

Jacob Rosenberg
IMDb: imdb.com/name/nm0742230

BARNSTORM FILMS

73 Market St
Venice, CA 90291
Phone: 310-396-5937
Fax: 310-450-4988

Email: tbtb@comcast.net
IMDb: imdb.com/company/co0044065

Accepts query letter from unproduced, unrepresented writers.

Tony Bill
Phone: 310-396-5937
Email: tbtb@comcast.net
IMDb: imdb.com/name/nm0082300

BARRY FILMS

4081 Redwood Ave
Los Angeles, CA 90066
Phone: 310-871-3392

Email: mail@barryfilms.com
Home Page: barryfilms.com
IMDb: imdb.com/company/co0075789

Does not accept any unsolicited material. Project types include Feature Films. Preferred genres include Action, Animation, Detective, Fantasy, and Romance.

Benito Mueller
Producer
Phone: 310-871-3392
Email: benito@barryfilms.com
IMDb: imdb.com/name/nm1762339

BASRA ENTERTAINMENT

68-444 Perez Rd, Suite O
Cathedral City, CA 92234
Phone: 760-324-9855
Fax: 760-324-9035

Email: info@basraentertainment.com
Email: daniela@basraentertainment.com

Home Page: basraentertainment.com
IMDb: imdb.com/company/co0092056

Accepts query letter from unproduced, unrepresented writers. Established in 2002.

Daniela Ryan
Producer
Phone: 760-324-9855
Email: daniela@basraentertainment.com
IMDb: imdb.com/name/nm0752491

Tony Shawkat
President
Email: tony@basraentertainment.com
IMDb: imdb.com/name/nm0790059

Dina Burke
Producer
Email: dina@basraentertainment.com
IMDb: imdb.com/name/nm1318482

BAUER MARTINEZ STUDIOS

601 Cleveland St, Suite 501
Clearwater, FL 33755
Phone: 727-210-1408
Fax: 727-210-1470

Email: cindy@bauermartinez.com
Home Page: bauermartinez.com
IMDb: imdb.com/company/co0025891

Accepts query letter from unproduced, unrepresented writers.

Phillipe Martinez
Phone: 727-210-1408
Email: cindy@cinepropictures.com
IMDb: imdb.com/name/nm0553662

BAY FILMS

631 Colorado Ave
Santa Monica, CA 90401
Phone: 310-319-6565
Fax: 310-319-6570

Does not accept any unsolicited material. Project types include Feature Films. Preferred genres include Action, Comedy, Drama, Fantasy, Science Fiction, and Thriller.

Michael Bay
CEO
IMDb: imdb.com/name/nm0000881
Assistant: Talley Singer

Matthew Cohan
IMDb: www,imdb.com/name/nm0169134

BAYONNE ENTERTAINMENT

6560 W Sunset Blvd Ninth Floor
West Hollywood, CA 90069
Phone: 310-777-1940
Fax: 310-889-9323

Email: assistant@bayonne-ent.com

Accepts query letter from produced or represented
writers. Project types include TV. Preferred genres
include Comedy, Drama, Fantasy, and Science Fiction.

Rob Lee
President
IMDb: imdb.com/name/nm0498098

BAZELEVS PRODUCTIONS

Pudovkina St
6/1
Moscow, Russia, 119285
Moscow 119285
Russia
Phone: +7 495-223-04-00

Email: film@bazelevs.ru
Home Page: bazelevs.ru
IMDb: imdb.com/company/co0042742

Does not accept any unsolicited material. Project types
include Feature Films.

Timur Bekmambetov
Phone: +7 495-223-04-00
Email: film@bazelevs.ru
IMDb: imdb.com/name/nm0067457

BBC FILMS

Room 6023
BBC Television Centre
Wood Ln, London W12 7RJ
UK

Phone: +44 20-8576-7265
Fax: +44 20-8576-7268

Home Page: bbc.co.uk/bbcfilms
IMDb: imdb.com/company/co0103694

Accepts scripts from unproduced, unrepresented
writers. Project types include Feature Films and TV.
Preferred genres include Action, Comedy, Crime,
Detective, Drama, Fantasy, Horror, Myth, Non-
Fiction, Romance, Science Fiction, and Thriller.

Joe Oppenheimer
Phone: +44 20-8576-7265
IMDb: imdb.com/name/nm0649189

BCDF PICTURES

P.O. Box 849
Kerhonkson, NY 12446
Phone: 212-945-8618
Fax: 917-591-7589

Email: submissions@bcdfpictures.com
Email: info@bcdfpictures.com
Home Page: bcdfpictures.com

Accepts query letter from unproduced, unrepresented
writers via email. Project types include Feature Films.
Preferred genres include Comedy, Crime, Drama,
Family, Romance, and Thriller.

Brice Dal Farra
Principal
IMDb: imdb.com/name/nm3894454

Claude Dal Farra
Principal
IMDb: imdb.com/name/nm3894387

Lauren Munsch
Producer
IMDb: imdb.com/name/nm3907323

Paul Prokop
COO (Executive Producer)
IMDb: imdb.com/name/nm2373782

BEACON PICTURES

2900 Olympic Blvd
2nd Floor
Santa Monica, CA 90404
Santa Monica, CA 90404

Phone: 310-260-7000
Fax: 310-260-7096

Email: contactus@beaconpictures.com
Home Page: beaconpictures.com

Does not accept any unsolicited material. Project types include Feature Films and TV. Preferred genres include Action, Comedy, Crime, Detective, Drama, Family, Fantasy, Romance, Science Fiction, and Thriller. Established in 1990.

Armyan Berstein
Chairman
IMDb: imdb.com/name/nm0077000

Suzann Ellis
President
Email: sellis@beaconpictures.com
IMDb: imdb.com/name/nm0255104

Rudy Langlais
Producer

Mark Pennell
Producer
Email: mpennell@beaconpictures.com
IMDb: imdb.com/name/nm0672075

Peter Almond
Producer

Glenn Klekowski
IMDb: imdb.com/name/nm0459192

Joeanna Sayler

Jeffrey Crooks
IMDb: imdb.com/name/nm3715349

BEDFORD FALLS COMPANY

409 Santa Monica Blvd
Penthouse Suite
Santa Monica, CA 90401-2388
Phone: 310-394-5022
Fax: 310-394-2512

Does not accept any unsolicited material. Project types include Feature Films. Preferred genres include Action and Drama.

Troy Putney
Creative Executive
IMDb: imdb.com/name/nm1586726

BEE HOLDER PRODUCTIONS

Phone: 310-860-1005
Fax: 310-860-1007

Email: asst@beeholder.com

Accepts query letter from unproduced, unrepresented writers. Project types include Feature Films. Preferred genres include Comedy, Crime, Detective, Documentary, Drama, and Thriller.

John Hill
IMDb: imdb.com/name/nm4787026

Michelle Jones
Executive
IMDb: imdb.com/name/nm4786947

Steven Lee Jones
President
IMDb: imdb.com/name/nm2831867

Dan Fugardi
Director of Development
Email: dan@beeholder.com
IMDb: imdb.com/name/nm2809882

Chad Hively
Email: chad@beeholder.com
IMDb: imdb.com/name/nm3510973

BEFORE THE DOOR PICTURES

1138 Hyperion Ave
Los Angeles, CA 90029
Phone: 323-644-5525
Fax: 323-644-5528

Email: staff@beforethedoor.com
Home Page: beforethedoor.com
IMDb: imdb.com/company/co0271126

Does not accept any unsolicited material. Project types include Feature Films, TV, and Commercials. Preferred genres include Action, Comedy, Crime, Drama, Science Fiction, and Thriller.

Zachary Quinto
IMDb: imdb.com/name/nm0704270

Corey Moosa
IMDb: imdb.com/name/nm0602161

Neal Dodson
IMDb: imdb.com/name/nm0230306

Sean Akers
IMDb: imdb.com/name/nm3577109

BELISARIUS PRODUCTIONS

1901 Ave of the Stars Second Floor
Los Angeles, CA 90067
Phone: 310-461-1361
Fax: 310-461-1362

Does not accept any unsolicited material. Project types include TV. Preferred genres include Crime, Detective, Drama, and Thriller.

Donald Bellisario
Executive Producer
IMDb: imdb.com/name/nm0069074

David Bellisario
Producer
IMDb: imdb.com/name/nm0069072

Shane Brennan
Producer
IMDb: imdb.com/name/nm0107402

John C. Kelley
IMDb: imdb.com/name/nm0445931

Chas Floyd Johnson
IMDb: imdb.com/name/nm0424759

Mark Horowitz
IMDb: imdb.com/name/nm0395317

BELLADONNA PRODUCTIONS

164 W 25th St 9th Floor
New York, NY 10001
Phone: 212-807-0108
Fax: 212-807-6263

Email: mail@belladonna.bz
Home Page: belladonna.bz
IMDb: imdb.com/company/co0003224
Facebook: facebook.com/belladonnaproductions

Accepts query letter from unproduced, unrepresented writers. Project types include Feature Films and Commercials. Preferred genres include Comedy, Non-Fiction, and Thriller. Established in 1994.

René Bastian
Owner/Producer
Phone: 212-807-0108
Email: mail@belladonna.bz
IMDb: imdb.com/name/nm0060459

BELLWETHER PICTURES

Accepts query letter from unproduced, unrepresented writers via email. Project types include Feature Films and Commercials. Preferred genres include Action, Comedy, Drama, and Science Fiction. Established in 2011.

Joss Whedon
IMDb: imdb.com/name/nm0923736

Kai Cole
IMDb: imdb.com/name/nm4740874

BENAROYA PICTURES

8383 Wilshire Blvd
Suite 310
Beverly Hills, CA 90212
USA
Phone: 323-883-0056
Fax: 866-220-5520

Email: general@benaroyapics.com
Home Page: benaroyapics.com
IMDb: imdb.com/company/co0232586

Accepts query letter from unproduced, unrepresented writers via email. Project types include Feature Films. Preferred genres include Drama. Established in 2006.

Michael Benaroya
Phone: 323-883-0056
IMDb: imdb.com/name/nm2918260

Joe Jenckes
Phone: 323-883-0056
Email: joel@benaroyapics.com
IMDb: imdb.com/name/nm3765270

Clayton Young
Phone: 323-883-0056
Email: clay@benaroyapics.com
IMDb: imdb.com/name/nm4464240

BENDERSPINK

5870 W Jefferson Blvd
Studio E
Los Angeles, CA 90016
Phone: 323-904-1800
Fax: 323-297-2442

Email: info@benderspink.com
Home Page: benderspink.com
IMDb: imdb.com/company/co0044439

Does not accept any unsolicited material. Project types include TV. Preferred genres include Action, Comedy, Crime, Detective, Drama, Fantasy, Horror, Myth, Non-Fiction, Romance, Science Fiction, and Thriller.

Chris Bender
Founder
Phone: 323-904-1800
Email: info@benderspink.com
IMDb: imdb.com/name/nm0818940

J.C. Spink
Founder
Phone: 323-904-1800
Email: info@benderspink.com
IMDb: imdb.com/name/nm0818940

BERK/LANE ENTERTAINMENT

9595 Wilshire Blvd, Suitee 900
Beverly Hills, CA 90212
Phone: 310-300-8410

Email: info@berklane.com
IMDb: wwwimdb.com/company/co0183891

Does not accept any unsolicited material. Preferred genres include Action, Comedy, and Crime.

Jason Berk
Phone: 310-300-8410
Email: info@berklane.com
IMDb: imdb.com/name/nm1357809

Matt Lane
Phone: 310-300-8410
Email: info@berklane.com
IMDb: imdb.com/name/nm2325262

BERLANTI TELEVISION

500 S Buena Vista St
Old Animation Building, 2B-5
Burbank, CA 91521
Phone: 818-560-4536
Fax: 818-560-3931

IMDb: imdb.com/company/co0192672

Accepts query letter from unproduced, unrepresented writers. Project types include TV. Preferred genres include Drama.

Greg Berlanti
IMDb: imdb.com/name/nm0075528

BERMANBRAUN

2900 W Olympic Blvd, 3rd Floor
Sanata Monica, CA, 90404
Phone: 310-255-7272
Fax: 310-255-7058

Email: info@bermanbraun.com
Home Page: bermanbraun.com
IMDb: imdb.com/company/co0199425

Does not accept any unsolicited material.

Chris Cowan
Executive, Head of Unscripted Television
Phone: 310-255-7272
Email: info@bermanbraun.com
IMDb: imdb.com/name/nm0184544

Andrew Mittman
Phone: 310-255-7272
Email: info@bermanbraun.com
IMDb: imdb.com/name/nm3879410

BERNERO PRODUCTIONS

500 S. Buena Vista St, Suite 2D-4
Burbank, CA 91521
Phone: 818-560-1442

Email: info@berneroproductions.com
Home Page: berneroproductions.com
IMDb: imdb.com/company/co0281008

Accepts query letter from unproduced, unrepresented writers via email.

Bob Kim
Producer
IMDb: imdb.com/name/nm2344755

BETH GROSSBARD PRODUCTIONS

5168 Otis Ave
Tarzana, CA 91356
Phone: 818-758-2500
Fax: 818-705-7366

Email: bgpix@sbcglobal.net
IMDb: imdb.com/company/co0037144

Accepts query letter from produced or represented writers. Project types include TV. Preferred genres include Comedy and Drama.

Beth Grossbard
Executive Producer
Email: bgpix@sbcglobal.net
IMDb: imdb.com/name/nm0343526

BET NETWORKS

One BET Plaza
1235 W St NE
Washington, DC 20018-1211
Phone: 202-608-2000
Fax: 206-608-2631

Home Page: bet.com
IMDbı imdb.com/company/co0176390

Does not accept any unsolicited material. Project types include Feature Films and TV. Preferred genres include Comedy, Documentary, and Drama.

Rickey Austyn Biggers
Director of Development
Phone: 310-481-3741
Email: austyn.biggers@bet.net
IMDb: imdb.com/name/nm2056137

Robyn Lattaker-Johnson
IMDb: imdb.com/name/nm0426464

BIG FOOT ENTERTAINMENT, LTD.

1214 Abbot Kinney Blvd
Los Angeles, CA 90291
Phone: 310-593-4646

Email: info@bigfoot.com
Home Page: bigfoot.com
IMDb: imdb.com/company/co0261687

Accepts query letter from unproduced, unrepresented writers via email. Project types include Feature Films and TV. Preferred genres include Action, Animation, Drama, Fantasy, Myth, Science Fiction, and Thriller. Established in 2004.

Ashley Jordan
CEO
Email: ashley@bigfootcorp.com
IMDb: imdb.com/name/nm1248442

BIG TALK PRODUCTIONS

26 Nassau St
London
W1W 7AQ
Phone: +44 (0) 20-7255-1131
Fax: +44 (0) 20-7255-1132

Email: info@bigtalkproductions.com
Home Page: bigtalkproductions.com

Does not accept any unsolicited material. Project types include TV. Preferred genres include Action, Comedy, Crime, Drama, and Science Fiction.

Rachael Prior
Phone: +44 (0) 20-7255-1131
Email: info@bigtalkproductions.com
IMDb: imdb.com/name/nm0975099

BIRCH TREE ENTERTAINMENT

10620 Southern Highlands Parkway
Suite 110-418
Las Vegas, NV 89141
Las Vegas, NV 89141
Phone: 702-858-2782
Fax: 702-583-7928

Email: sales@birchtreefilms.com
Home Page: birchtreeentertainment.com
IMDb: imdb.com/company/co0114722

Accepts scripts from produced or represented writers. Project types include Feature Films. Preferred genres include Action.

Art Birzneck

Phone: 702-858-2782
Email: sales@birchtreefilms.com
IMDb: imdb.com/name/nm1010723

BISCAYNE PICTURES

Los Angeles, CA
Phone: 310-777-2007

Email: info@biscaynepictures.com
Home Page: biscaynepictures.com
IMDb: imdb.com/company/co0152645

Does not accept any unsolicited material. Project types include Feature Films and TV. Preferred genres include Action, Animation, Crime, Detective, Drama, Fantasy, Myth, Science Fiction, and Thriller.

Jeffrey Silver

Principle
Phone: 310-777-2007
Email: info@biscaynepictures.com
IMDb: imdb.com/name/nm0798711

BIX PIX ENTERTAINMENT

3511 W Burbank Blvd
Burbank, CA 91505
Phone: 818-953-7474
Fax: 818-953-9948

Email: info@bixpix.com
Home Page: bixpix.com
IMDb: imdb.com/company/co0187260

Accepts query letter from unproduced, unrepresented writers. Preferred genres include Fantasy. Established in 1998.

Kelli Bixler

Phone: 818-953-7474
Email: info@bixpix.com
IMDb: imdb.com/name/nm1064778

BLACK BEAR PICTURES

185 Franklin St
4th Floor
New York, NY 10013
New York, NY 10013

Phone: 212-931-5714
Fax: 212-966-3311

Email: info@blackbearpictures.com
Home Page: blackbearpictures.com

Accepts query letter from unproduced, unrepresented writers. Project types include Feature Films. Preferred genres include Comedy, Drama, and Romance. Established in 2011.

Ben Stillman

Creative Executive
IMDb: imdb.com/name/nm4212466

Teddy Schwarzman

IMDb: imdb.com/name/nm3267061

Amanda Greenblatt

IMDb: imdb.com/name/nm1716375

BLACKLIGHT TRANSMEDIA

9465 Wilshire Blvd
Beverly Hills, CA 90212
Phone: 310-858-2196

Email: info@blacklighttransmedia.com
Home Page: blacklighttransmedia.com
IMDb: imdb.com/company/co0333337

Accepts scripts from produced or represented writers. Project types include Feature Films.

Zak Kadison

Phone: 310-858-2196
Email: info@blacklighttransmedia.com
IMDb: imdb.com/name/nm1780162

Justin Catron

Creative Executive
Phone: 310-858-2196
Email: info@blacklighttransmedia.com
IMDb: imdb.com/name/nm2031037

BLACK SHEEP ENTERTAINMENT

11271 Ventura Blvd, #447
Studio City, CA 91604
Phone: 310-424-5085
Fax: 310-424-7117

Email: info@blacksheept.com
IMDb: imdb.com/company/co0029807

Accepts query letter from unproduced, unrepresented writers. Established in 2009.

Steven Feder
Phone: 310-424-5085
Email: steven@blacksheepent.com
IMDb: imdb.com/name/nm027009

BLEIBERG ENTERTAINMENT

225 S Clark Dr
Beverly Hills, CA 90211
Phone: 310-273-0003
Fax: 310-273-0007

Email: info@bleibergent.com
Home Page: bleibergent.com
IMDb: imdb.com/company/co0165151

Accepts query letter from unproduced, unrepresented writers via email. Project types include Feature Films and TV.

Ehud Bleiberg
Phone: 310-273-0003
Email: ehud@bleibergent.com
IMDb: imdb.com/name/nm0088173

Nicholas Donnermeyer
Phone: 310-273-0003
Email: nick@bleibergent.com
IMDb: imdb.com/name/nm2223730

BLINDWINK PRODUCTIONS

8 Mills Place 2nd Floor
Pasadena, CA 91105
Phone: 626-600-4100

Email: info@blindwink.com
Home Page: blindwink.com

Does not accept any unsolicited material. Project types include Feature Films. Preferred genres include Action, Comedy, Crime, Drama, Family, Fantasy, Science Fiction, and Thriller.

Gore Verbinski
Principal
IMDb: imdb.com/name/nm0893659

Nils Peyron
Executive Vice President
IMDb: imdb.com/name/nm3741163

Jonathan Krauss
Head of Film Production & Development
IMDb: imdb.com/name/nm0470310

Josh Pincus
Director of Development

BLONDIE GIRL PRODUCTIONS

1040 N Las Palmas
Building 40
Los Angeles, CA 90038
Phone: 323-860-8610
Fax: 323-860-8601

Email: jessica@blondiegirlprod.com
Home Page: blondiegirlproductions.com
IMDb: imdb.com/company/co0261290

Does not accept any unsolicited material. Project types include TV.

Ashley Tisdale
IMDb: imdb.com/name/nm0864308

Jennifer Tisdale
IMDb: imdb.com/name/nm1056279

Jessica Rhodes
IMDb: imdb.com/name/nm1224043

BLUEGRASS FILMS

100 Universal City Plaza
Bungalow 4171
Universal City, CA 91608
Phone: 818-777-3200
Fax: 818-777-0020

IMDb: imdb.com/company/co0376117

Does not accept any unsolicited material. Project types include Feature Films and TV. Preferred genres include Action, Crime, Drama, Fantasy, Romance, Science Fiction, and Thriller.

Scott Stuber
Producer
IMDb: imdb.com/name/nm0835959

Michael Clear
Creative Executive
IMDb: imdb.com/name/nm2752795

Nicholas Nesbitt
Creative Executive
IMDb: imdb.com/name/nm1704779

BLUE PRINT PICTURES

43-45 Charlotte St
London W1T 1RS
United Kingdom
Phone: +44 0207-580-6915
Fax: +44 0207-580-6934

Email: asst@blueprintpictures.com

Does not accept any unsolicited material. Established in 2004.

Graham Broadbent
Producer
Phone: +44 0207-580-6915
Email: asst@blueprintpictures.com
IMDb: imdb.com/name/nm0110357

BLUE SKY STUDIOS

One American Ln
Greenwich, CT 06831
Phone: 203-992-6000
Fax: 203-992-6001

Email: info@blueskystudios.com
Home Page: blueskystudios.com
IMDb: imdb.com/company/co0047265

Does not accept any unsolicited material. Project types include Feature Films. Established in 1997.

Chris Wedge
Vice-President
IMDb: imdb.com/name/nm0917188

Lisa Fragner
IMDb: imdb.com/name/nm0289591

BLUMHOUSE PRODUCTIONS

5555 Melrose Ave
Lucy Bungalow 103
Los Angeles, CA 90038
Phone: 323-956-4480

IMDb: imdb.com/company/co0098315
Home Page: blumhouse.com/index.php
Facebook: facebook.com/Blumhouse

Accepts query letter from unproduced, unrepresented writers. Preferred genres include Action, Horror, and Thriller. Established in 2000.

Jason Blum
Producer
IMDb: imdb.com/name/nm0089658

Jessica Hall
IMDb: imdb.com/name/nm4148859

BOBKER/KRUGAR FILMS

1416 N La Brea Ave
Hollywood, CA 90028
Phone: 323-469-1440
Fax: 323-802-1597

IMDb: imdb.com/company/co0163148

Accepts query letter from unproduced, unrepresented writers.

Daniel Bobker
Producer
IMDb: imdb.com/name/nm0090394

Ehren Kruger
IMDb: imdb.com/name/nm0472567

BOGNER ENTERTAINMENT INC.

269 S Beverly Dr, Suite 8
Beverly Hills, CA 90212
Phone: 310-553-0300

Email: info.beitv@gmail.com
Home Page: bognerentertainment.com
IMDb: imdb.com/company/co0068550

Accepts scripts from unproduced, unrepresented writers. Preferred genres include Horror and Thriller. Established in 2000.

Oliver Bogner
Email: oliverbogner@gmail.com
IMDb: imdb.com/name/nm3331124

Jonathan Bogner
President
Email: jsbogner@aol.com
IMDb: imdb.com/name/nm0091845

BOKU FILMS

1438 N Gower St
Box 87
Hollywood, CA 90028
Phone: 323-860-7710
Fax: 323-860-7706

IMDb: imdb.com/company/co0047458

Does not accept any unsolicited material. Project types include TV. Preferred genres include Drama and Thriller.

Alan Poul
IMDb: imdb.com/name/nm0693561

BOLD FILMS

6464 Sunset Blvd, Suite 800
Los Angeles, CA 90028
Phone: 323-769-8900
Fax: 323-769-8954

Email: info@boldfilms.com
Home Page: boldfilms.com
IMDb: imdb.com/company/co0135575

Does not accept any unsolicited material. Project types include Feature Films and TV. Preferred genres include Action, Fantasy, Horror, and Thriller.

Stephanie Wilcox
Creative Executive
IMDb: imdb.com/name/nm3432545

Jon Oakes
IMDb: imdb.com/name/nm1198333

Garrick Dion
IMDb: imdb.com/name/nm1887182

BONA FIDE PRODUCTIONS

8899 Beverly Blvd, Suite 804
Los Angeles, CA 90048
Phone: 310-273-6782
Fax: 310-273-7821

IMDb: imdb.com/company/co0063938

Accepts query letter from unproduced, unrepresented writers. Project types include Feature Films. Established in 1993.

Albert Berger
Producer
IMDb: imdb.com/name/nm0074100

Ken Furer
Director of Development
IMDb: imdb.com/name/nm1738727

BORDERLINE FILMS

545 8th Ave
11th Floor
New York, NY 10018

Email: contact@blfilm.com
Home Page: blfilm.com

Does not accept any unsolicited material. Project types include Feature Films. Preferred genres include Crime, Detective, Drama, and Thriller.

Josh Mond
IMDb: imdb.com/name/nm1317614

Sean Durkin
IMDb: imdb.com/name/nm1699934

Antonio Campos
IMDb: imdb.com/name/nm1290515

BOSS MEDIA

9440 Santa Monica Blvd.
Suite 200
Beverly Hills, CA 90210
Phone: 310-205-9900
Fax: 310-205-9909

IMDb: imdb.com/company/co0157610

Does not accept any unsolicited material. Preferred genres include Comedy, Science Fiction, and Thriller.

Frank Mancuso
President
Phone: 310-205-9900
IMDb: imdb.com/name/nm0541548

Jennifer Nieves Gordon
Vice President (Development)
Phone: 310-205-9900
IMDb: imdb.com/name/nm2707034

BOXING CAT PRODUCTIONS

11500 Hart St
North Hollywood, CA 91605
Phone: 818-765-4870
Fax: 818-765-4975

IMDb: imdb.com/company/co0080834

Does not accept any unsolicited material. Project types include Feature Films and TV. Preferred genres include Comedy and Family.

Tim Allen
IMDb: imdb.com/name/nm0000741

BOY WONDER PRODUCTIONS

68 Jay St, Suite 423
Brooklyn, NY 11201
Phone: 347-632-2961
Fax: 347-332-6953

Email: info@boywonderproductions.net
Home Page: boywonderproductions.net
IMDb: imdb.com/company/co0255525
Facebook: facebook.com/pages/Boy-Wonder-Productions/239113204508

Accepts query letter from unproduced, unrepresented writers via email. Project types include TV. Preferred genres include Comedy, Drama, and Non-Fiction. Established in 2006.

Michael Morrisesy
IMDb: imdb.com/name/nm3155184

BOZ PRODUCTIONS

429 Santa Monica Blvd, Suite 710
Santa Monica, CA 90401
Phone: 323-876-3232

Email: bozenga@sbcglobal.net
Home Page: bozproductions.com
IMDb: imdb.com/company/co0068487

Accepts query letter from unproduced, unrepresented writers.

Bo Zenga
Email: bozenga@sbcglobal.net
IMDb: imdb.com/name/nm0954848

BRANDED FILMS

4000 Warner Blvd
Building 139, Suite 107
Burbank, CA 91522
Phone: 818-954-7969

Email: info@branded-films.com
Home Page: branded-films.com
IMDb: imdb.com/company/co0347637

Does not accept any unsolicited material. Project types include Feature Films and TV. Preferred genres include Comedy. Established in 2011.

Beau Bauman
President
Email: beau@branded-films.com
IMDb: imdb.com/name/nm0062149

Russell Brand
IMDb: imdb.com/name/nm1258970
Assistant: Lee Sacks

Nik Linnen
IMDb: imdb.com/name/nm3800556

BRANDMAN PRODUCTIONS

2062 N Vine St, Suite 5
Los Angeles, CA 90068
Phone: 323-463-3224
Fax: 323-463-0852

IMDb: imdb.com/company/co0082006

Accepts query letter from unproduced, unrepresented writers.

Michael Bradman
IMDb: imdb.com/name/nm0104701

BRIGHTLIGHT PICTURES

The Bridge Studios
2400 Boundary Rd
Burnaby, BC V5M 3Z3

Canada
Phone: 604-628-3000
Fax: 604-628-3001

Email: info@brightlightpictures.com
Home Page: brightlightpictures.com
IMDb: imdb.com/company/co0065717

Does not accept any unsolicited material. Project types include Feature Films and TV. Preferred genres include Comedy and Drama. Established in 2001.

Stephen Hegyes
IMDb: imdb.com/name/nm0373812

Shawn Williamson
IMDb: imdb.com/name/nm0932144

Rebecca Nield
Creative Executive
IMDb: imdb.com/name/nm2422059

Kyle McCachen
Creative Executive
IMDb: imdb.com/name/nm5131630

BROKEN CAMERA PRODUCTIONS

San Antonio, TX
Phone: 210-454-8103

Email: info@brokencameraproductions.com
Home Page: brokencameraproductions.com

Accepts query letter from unproduced, unrepresented writers via email. Project types include Feature Films. Preferred genres include Comedy, Drama, and Thriller.

Matthew Garth
Producer
Phone: 210-454-8103
Email: matthew@brokencameraproductions.com
IMDb: imdb.com/name/nm2123288

David Y. Duncan
Producer
Phone: 210-884-5234
Email: dave@brokencameraproductions.com
IMDb: imdb.com/name/nm2839229

Lynette C. Aleman
Producer
Phone: 210-317-4647
Email: lynette@brokencameraproductions.com
IMDb: imdb.com/name/nm4074593

BROOKLYN FILMS

3815 Hughes Ave.
Culver City, CA 90232
Phone: 310-841-4300
Fax: 310-204-3464

IMDb: imdb.com/company/co0088618

Accepts query letter from unproduced, unrepresented writers. Project types include Feature Films and TV. Preferred genres include Crime and Drama.

Marsha Oglesby
Producer
IMDb: mdb.com/name/nm0644749

Jon Avnet
IMDb: imdb.com/name/nm0000816

BRUCE COHEN PRODUCTIONS

8292 Hollywood Blvd
Los Angeles, CA 90069
Phone: 323-650-4567
Fax: 323-843-9534

Does not accept any unsolicited material. Project types include TV. Preferred genres include Drama.

Jessica Leventhal
Creative Executive
IMDb: imdb.com/name/nm4202199

Bruce Cohen
IMDb: imdb.com/name/nm0169260

BUCKAROO ENTERTAINMENT

10202 W Washington Blvd
David Lean Bldg, Suite 100
Culver City, CA 90232
Phone: 310-244-4646

Does not accept any unsolicited material. Project types include Feature Films. Preferred genres include Crime, Detective, Fantasy, Horror, and Thriller.

Sam Raimi
Partner
IMDb: imdb.com/name/nm0000600

Joshua Donen
Partner
IMDb: imdb.com/name/nm0232433

Ryan Carroll
Executive
IMDb: imdb.com/name/nm1498070

BUENA VISTA HOME ENTERTAINMENT

500 S. Buena Vista St.
Burbank, CA 91521-6369
USA
Phone: 818-560-1000

Home Page: bvhe.com
IMDb: imdb.com/company/co0049546

Does not accept any unsolicited material. Project types include Feature Films, Short Films, and TV. Preferred genres include Action, Animation, Comedy, Crime, Documentary, Drama, Family, Fantasy, Horror, Non-Fiction, Romance, Science Fiction, and Thriller. Established in 1952.

BUENA VISTA TELEVISION

500 S Buena Vista St
Burbank, CA 91521
Phone: 818-560-1000

Home Page: disney.com
IMDb: imdb.com/company/co0044279

Does not accept any unsolicited material. Project types include Feature Films, Short Films, and TV. Preferred genres include Action, Animation, Comedy, Crime, Documentary, Drama, Family, Fantasy, Horror, Non-Fiction, Romance, Science Fiction, and Thriller. Established in 1932.

Louanne Brickhouse
IMDb: imdb.com/name/nm1749168

Nadia Aleyd
IMDb: imdb.com/name/nm0019022

Kristin Burr
IMDb: imdb.com/name/nm0123013

Jeanne Hobson
IMDb: imdb.com/name/nm2653496

Todd Murata
Executive
IMDb: imdb.com/name/nm0613611

John Lasseter
IMDb: imdb.com/name/nm0005124

Cherise McVicar
IMDb: imdb.com/name/nm2660270

BUNIM-MURRAY PRODUCTIONS

6007 Sepulveda Blvd
Van Nuys, CA 91411
Phone: 818-756-5100
Fax: 818-756-5140

Email: bmp@bunim-murray.com
Home Page: bunim-murray.com

Does not accept any unsolicited material. Project types include TV. Preferred genres include Documentary and Reality.

Jonathan Murray
Chairman
IMDb: imdb.com/name/nm0615086

Gil Goldschein
President
IMDb: imdb.com/name/nm2251455

Scott Freeman
IMDb: imdb.com/name/nm1321720

Jeff Jenkins
IMDb: imdb.com/name/nm0420870

Erin Cristall
IMDb: imdb.com/name/nm0188058

John Greco

Cara Goldberg

BURLEIGH FILMWORKS

22287 Mulholland Highway, Suite 129
Calabasas, CA 91302
Phone: 818-224-4686
Fax: 818-223-9089

IMDb: imdb.com/company/co0176271

Accepts query letter from unproduced, unrepresented writers.

Steve Burleigh
Producer
Email: steve.burleigh@burleighfilmworks.com
IMDb: imdb.com/name/nm0122114

BURNSIDE ENTERTAINMENT, INC.

2424 N Ontario St
Burbank, CA 91504
Phone: 818-565-5986

265 W 19th St
New York, NY 10011
Phone: 323-902-7384

Email: mail@burnsideentertainment.com
Home Page: burnsideentertainment.com
IMDb: imdb.com/company/co0180518

Accepts query letter from unproduced, unrepresented writers.

Seth William Meier
Partner
Phone: 323-902-7384
Email: sethwilliammeier@burnsideentertainment.com
IMDb: imdb.com/name/nm0576720

Glen Trotiner
Owner
Phone: 212-727-7665
Email: gtrotiner@burnsideentertainment.com
IMDb: imdb.com/name/nm0873641

CALIBER MEDIA COMPANY

5670 Wilshire Blvd.
Ste 1600
Los Angeles, CA 90036
Phone: 310-786-9210

Home Page: calibermediaco.com
IMDb: imdb.com/company/co0228420

Accepts query letter from unproduced, unrepresented writers. Project types include Feature Films. Preferred genres include Action, Crime, Drama, Family, Horror, Sociocultural, and Thriller. Established in 2008.

Jack Heller
IMDb: imdb.com/name/nm2597331

Dallas Sonnier
IMDb: imdb.com/name/nm2447772

Morgan White
IMDb: imdb.com/name/nm4765803

CALLAHAN FILMWORKS

3800 Barham Blvd
Suite 500
Los Angeles, CA 90068
Phone: 323-878-0645
Fax: 323-878-0649

Does not accept any unsolicited material. Project types include Feature Films and TV. Preferred genres include Action, Comedy, Crime, Drama, Family, Fantasy, and Romance.

Peter Segal
Partner
IMDb: imdb.com/name/nm0781842

Michael Ewing
Partner
IMDb: imdb.com/name/nm0263989

Chris Osbrink
Creative Executive
IMDb: imdb.com/name/nm1644713

Omar El-Hajoui
IMDb: imdb.com/name/nm5389420

CAMELOT ENTERTAINMENT GROUP

10 Universal City Plaza NBC/Universal Building Floor 20
Universal City, CA 91608
Phone: 949-754-3030

Email: submissions@camelotfilms.com
Email: info@camelotfilms.com
Home Page: camelotent.com/index.php
IMDb: imdb.com/company/co0006731

Accepts scripts from unproduced, unrepresented writers. Project types include Feature Films and TV. Preferred genres include Action, Animation, Comedy,

Drama, Family, Horror, Non-Fiction, Romance, Science Fiction, and Thriller.

Robert Atwell
Chairman
IMDb: imdb.com/name/nm0041164

Steven Istock
Partner
IMDb: imdb.com/name/nm1916408

Jessica Kelly
President of Distribution

CANADIAN BROADCASTING COMPANY (CBC)

181 Queen St
Ottawa, ON, Canada, K1P 1K9
Phone: 613-288-6000

Email: liaison@cbc.ca
Home Page: cbc.ca
IMDb: imdb.com/company/co0045850

Does not accept any unsolicited material. Project types include Feature Films and TV. Preferred genres include Action, Animation, Comedy, Crime, Documentary, Drama, Family, Non-Fiction, and Period. Established in 2007.

Hubert Lacroix
President
IMDb: imdb.com/name/nm4522750

Suzanne Colvin-Goulding
IMDb: imdb.com/name/nm0003681

Scott McEwen
IMDb: imdb.com/name/nm1469582

Kim Wilson

Anton Leo
IMDb: imdb.com/name/nm2502480

Jennifer Stewart
IMDb: imdb.com/name/nm4219237

Jenny Hacker
IMDb: imdb.com/name/nm4236429

Trevor Walton
IMDb: imdb.com/name/nm4280633

CAPACITY PICTURES

PO Box 96143
Las Vegas, NV 89193
Phone: 310-247-8534

Email: capacitypictures@gmail.com
IMDb: imdb.com/company/co0192878

Does not accept any unsolicited material. Project types include Feature Films. Preferred genres include Comedy, Crime, Drama, Horror, and Thriller. Established in 2008.

Rich Heller
Executive
IMDb: imdb.com/name/nm0375378

Wayne Allen Rice
Executive
IMDb: imdb.com/name/nm0723573

CAPITAL ARTS ENTERTAINMENT

23315 Clift on Plaza
Valencia, CA 91354
Phone: 818-343-8950
Fax: 818-343-8962

Email: info@capitalarts.com
Home Page: capitalarts.com
IMDb: imdb.com/company/co0009722

Accepts query letter from unproduced, unrepresented writers via email. Preferred genres include Action, Comedy, Horror, and Thriller. Established in 1995.

Mike Elliot
IMDb: imdb.com/name/nm0254291

Rob Kerchner
Partner
IMDb: imdb.com/name/nm0449246

Joe Genier
Partner
IMDb: imdb.com/name/nm0312856

CAPTIVATE ENTERTAINMENT

100 Universal City Plaza
Bungalow 4111
Universal City, CA 91608
Universal City, CA 91608

Phone: 818-777-6711
Fax: 818-733-4303

IMDb: imdb.com/company/co0263292

Does not accept any unsolicited material. Project types include Feature Films and TV. Preferred genres include Action, Comedy, Drama, Fantasy, Myth, Romance, Science Fiction, and Thriller.

Ben Smith
Producer
IMDb: imdb.com/name/nm3328356

Tony Shaw
Creative Executive
Email: tony.shaw@univfilms.com
IMDb: imdb.com/name/nm4130192

Jeffrey Weiner
IMDb: imdb.com/name/nm1788648

CARNIVAL FILMS

3rd Fl
55 New Oxford St
London WC1A 1BS
Phone: +44 0203-618-6600
Fax: +44023-618-8900

Email: info@carnivalfilms.co.uk
Home Page: carnivalfilms.co.uk

Does not accept any unsolicited material. Project types include TV. Preferred genres include Documentary, Drama, and Thriller.

Henrietta Colvin
Head of Development
IMDb: imdb.com/name/nm2188710

Sam Symons
Development Executive
IMDb: imdb.com/name/nm1599585

Steven Williams
Development Executive
IMDb: imdb.com/name/nm1034831

Kimberly Hikaka
IMDb: imdb.com/name/nm2529465

CASEY SILVER PRODUCTIONS

506 Santa Monica Blvd, Suite 322
Santa Monica, CA 90401
Phone: 310-566-3750
Fax: 310-566-3751

IMDb: imdb.com/company/co0058884

Does not accept any unsolicited material. Project types include Feature Films. Preferred genres include Action, Comedy, Drama, Family, and Thriller.

Casey Silver
Chairman
Email: casey@caseysilver.com
IMDb: imdb.com/name/nm0798661

Matthew Reynolds
Creative Executive
Email: matthew@caseysilver.com
IMDb: imdb.com/name/nm2303863

CASTLE ROCK ENTERTAINMENT

9169 W. Sunset Blvd.
Los Angeles, CA 90069
Phone: 310-285-2300
Fax: 310-285-2345

IMDb: imdb.com/company/co0040620

Accepts scripts from produced or represented writers.

Andrew Scheinman
Email: andres.scheinman@castle-rock.com
IMDb: imdb.com/name/nm0770650

Rob Reiner
Email: rob.reiner@castle-rock.com
IMDb: imdb.com/name/nm0001661

CATAPULT FILMS INC.

832 Third St, Suite 303
Santa Monica, CA 90403-1155
Phone: 310-395-1470
Fax: 310-401-0122

IMDb: imdb.com/company/co0100754

Accepts scripts from produced or represented writers.

Lisa Josefsberg
Producer
IMDb: imdb.com/name/nm2248853

Lawrence Levy
Executive
IMDb: imdb.com/name/nm0506504

CBS FILMS

11800 Wilshire Blvd
Los Angeles, CA 90025
Phone: 310-575-7700

Home Page: cbsfilms.com

Does not accept any unsolicited material. Project types include Feature Films. Preferred genres include Action, Drama, Fantasy, Romance, and Science Fiction.

Mark Ross
IMDb: imdb.com/name/nm0743653

Wolfgang Hammer
IMDb: imdb.com/name/nm1424985

Terry Press
IMDb: imdb.com/name/nm1437110

Maria Faillace
IMDb: imdb.com/name/nm1299267

CECCHI GORI PRODUCTIONS

5555 Melrose Ave
Bob Hope 203
Los Angeles, CA 90038
Phone: 323-956-5954
Fax: 323-862-2254

Email: info@cgglobalmedia.com
Home Page: cecchigoripictures.com

Project types include Feature Films. Preferred genres include Drama, Family, Horror, Romance, and Thriller.

Niels Juul
CEO
IMDb: imdb.com/name/nm3887220

Alex Shub

Jennifer Parker
IMDb: imdb.com/name/nm4487725

Andy Scott
IMDb: imdb.com/name/nm4866101

Dana Galinsky
IMDb: imdb.com/name/nm1919300

CELADOR ENTERTAINMENT

39 Long Acre
London, WC2E 9LG
United Kingdom
Phone: +44 20-7845-6800
Fax: +44 20-7845-6801

Home Page: celador.co.uk
IMDb: imdb.com/company/co0152921

Accepts scripts from produced or represented writers. Established in 1989.

Paul Smith
Email: psmith@celador.co.uk
IMDb: imdb.com/name/nm0809531

CENTROPOLIS ENTERTAINMENT

1445 N Stanley
3rd Floor
Los Angeles, CA 90046
Los Angeles, CA 90046
Phone: 323-850-1212
Fax: 323-850-1201

Email: info@centropolis.com
Home Page: centropolis.com
IMDb: imdb.com/company/co0050111

Accepts scripts from produced or represented writers. Preferred genres include Action, Fantasy, Myth, Non-Fiction, and Romance. Established in 1985.

Roland Emmerich
IMDb: imdb.com/name/nm0000386

Ute Emmerich
IMDb: imdb.com/name/nm0256498

CHAIKEN FILMS

802 Potrero Ave
San Francisco, CA 94110
Phone: 415-826-7880
Fax: 415-826-7882

Email: info@chaikenfilms.com
Home Page: chaikenfilms.com
IMDb: imdb.com/company/co0064208

Accepts query letter from unproduced, unrepresented writers. Preferred genres include Non-Fiction. Established in 1998.

Jennifer Chaiken
Producer
Email: jen@chaikenfilms.com
IMDb: imdb.com/name/nm0149671

CHARTOFF PRODUCTIONS

1250 Sixth St, Suite 101
Santa Monica, CA 90401
Phone: 310-319-1960
Fax: 310-319-3469

Email: hendeechartoff@cs.com
IMDb: imdb.com/company/co0094865

Accepts scripts from produced or represented writers. Established in 1986.

Robert Chartoff
IMDb: imdb.com/name/nm0153590

CHERNIN ENTERTAINMENT

1733 Ocean Ave, Suite 300
Santa Monica, CA 90401
Phone: 310-899-1205

Home Page: cherninent.com
IMDb: imdb.com/company/co0286257

Accepts scripts from produced or represented writers. Project types include Feature Films and TV. Preferred genres include Action, Comedy, and Drama. Established in 2009.

Peter Chernin
Principle
IMDb: imdb.com/name/nm1858656

Dylan Dark
Email: dc@cherninent.com
IMDb: imdb.com/name/nm1249995

Jenno Topping
Email: jt@cherninent.com
IMDb: imdb.com/name/nm0867768

Ivana Schechter-Garcia
Creative Executive

Katherine Pope
Email: kp@cherninent.com
IMDb: imdb.com/name/nm0691142

Pavun Shetty
Email: ps@cherninent.com

CHERRY SKY FILMS

2100 Sawtelle Blvd.,
Suite 101
Los Angeles, CA 90025
Phone: 310-479-8001
Fax: 310-479-8815

Email: contact@cherryskyfilms.com
Home Page: cherryskyfilms.com

Does not accept any unsolicited material. Project types include Feature Films. Preferred genres include Comedy, Drama, Family, and Romance. Established in 2001.

Joan Huang
Producer
IMDb: imdb.com/name/nm0399009

Jeffrey Gou
Producer
IMDb: imdb.com/name/nm2370188

CHESTNUT RIDGE PRODUCTIONS

8899 Beverly Blvd, Suite 800
Los Angeles, CA
Phone: 310-285-7011

IMDb: imdb.com/company/co0273538

Does not accept any unsolicited material. Established in 2009.

Paula Wagner
IMDb: imdb.com/name/nm0906048

CHEYENNE ENTERPRISES LLC

406 Wilshire Blvd
Santa Monica, CA 90401

Phone: 310-455-5000
Fax: 310-688-8000

IMDb: imdb.com/company/co0041195

Accepts scripts from produced or represented writers. Established in 2000.

Arnold Rifkin
IMDb: imdb.com/name/nm0726476

Joshua Rowley
Director of Development
IMDb: imdb.com/name/nm2282373

CHICAGOFILMS

253 W 72nd St
Suite 1108
New York, NY 10023
USA
Phone: 212-721-7700
Fax: 212-721-7701

IMDb: imdb.com/company/co0012485

Accepts scripts from produced or represented writers.

Bob Balaban
IMDb: imdb.com/name/nm0000837

CHICKFLICKS

8861 St Ives Dr
Los Angeles, CA 90069
Phone: 310-854-7210

Email: info@chickflicksinc.com
Home Page: chickflicksinc.com
IMDb: imdb.com/company/co0156986

Accepts scripts from produced or represented writers. Preferred genres include Comedy, Fantasy, Myth, Non-Fiction, and Romance.

Sara Risher
Phone: 310-854-7210
Email: sara@chickflicksinc.com
IMDb: imdb.com/name/nm0728260

Stephanie Austin
Phone: 310-854-7210
Email: stephanie@chickflicksinc.com
IMDb: imdb.com/name/nm0042520

CHOCKSTONE PICTURES

22355 Carbon Mesa Rd
Malibu, CA 90265
Phone: 310-456-2945

Email: steves@chockstonepictures.com
Home Page: chockstonepictures.com
IMDb: imdb.com/company/co0192912
Facebook: facebook.com/chockstonepictures?fref=ts

Accepts query letter from unproduced, unrepresented writers via email. Project types include Feature Films. Established in 2004.

Steve Schwartz
President
Email: steves@chockstonepictures.com
IMDb: imdb.com/name/nm0777455

Paula Mae Schwartz
CEO
Email: paulamae@chockstonepictures.com
IMDb: imdb.com/name/nm2445382

Roger Schwartz
Development Executive
Phone: 310-600-6840
Email: rogers@chockstonepictures.com
IMDb: imdb.com/name/nm0970118

CHOTZEN/JENNER PRODUCTIONS

4178 Dixie Canyon Ave.
Sherman Oaks, CA 91423
Phone: 323-465-9877
Fax: 323-460-6451

IMDb: imdb.com/company/co0176334

Accepts scripts from produced or represented writers. Project types include TV. Preferred genres include Comedy and Drama. Established in 1990.

Yvonne Chotzen
IMDb: imdb.com/name/nm0159278

William Jenner
IMDb: imdb.com/name/nm0421076

CHRIS/ROSE PRODUCTIONS

3131 Torreyson Place
Los Angeles, CA 90046

Phone: 323-851-8772
Fax: 323-851-0662

IMDb: imdb.com/company/co0040069

Accepts scripts from produced or represented writers. Project types include TV. Preferred genres include Comedy, Drama, and Non-Fiction.

Robert Christiansen
Executive Producer
Phone: 310-781-0833
IMDb: imdb.com/name/nm0160222

CHUBBCO FILM CO.

751 N. Fairfax Ave.
#10
Los Angeles, CA 90046
Phone: 310-729-5858
Fax: 310-933-1704

1550 E. Valley Rd.
Santa Barbara, CA 93108

Email: chubbco@gmail.com
IMDb: imdb.com/company/co0026094

Does not accept any unsolicited material. Preferred genres include Action, Crime, and Non-Fiction.

Caldecot Chubb
Producer
Email: chubbco@gmail.com
IMDb: imdb.com/name/nm0160941

CHUCK FRIES PRODUCTIONS, INC.

1880 Century Park East
Suite 213
Los Angeles, CA 90067
Phone: 310-203-9520
Fax: 310-203-9519

IMDb: imdb.com/company/co0040068

Accepts scripts from produced or represented writers. Preferred genres include Crime and Detective.

Charles Fries
IMDb: imdb.com/name/nm0295594

CINDY COWAN ENTERTAINMENT

8265 W Sunset Blvd
Suite 205
Los Angeles, CA 90046
Phone: 323-822-1082
Fax: 323-822-1086

Email: info@cowanent.com
Home Page: cowanent.com
IMDb: imdb.com/company/co0094925

Accepts scripts from produced or represented writers. Established in 1999.

Cindy Cowan
President
IMDb: imdb.com/name/nm0184546

CINEMA EPHOCH

10 Universal City Plaza, 20th Floor
Universal City, CA 91608
Phone: 818-753-2345

Email: acquisitions@cinemaepoch.com
Home Page: cinemaepoch.com
IMDb: imdb.com/company/co0028810

Accepts query letter from unproduced, unrepresented writers. Preferred genres include Action, Comedy, Crime, Detective, Horror, Myth, Non-Fiction, and Thriller. Established in 2001.

Gregory Hatanaka
IMDb: imdb.com/name/nm0368693

CINEMAGIC ENTERTAINMENT

9229 Sunset Blvd, Suite 610
West Hollywood, CA 90069
Phone: 310-385-9322
Fax: 310-385-9347

Home Page: cinemagicent.com
IMDb: imdb.com/company/co0183883

Accepts query letter from unproduced, unrepresented writers. Preferred genres include Action, Crime, Detective, Fantasy, Horror, Myth, Science Fiction, and Thriller.

Lee Cohn
IMDb: imdb.com/name/nm2325144

CINEMA LIBRE STUDIO

8328 De Soto Ave
Canoga Park, CA 91304
Phone: 818-349-8822
Fax: 818-349-9922

Email: project@CinemaLibreStudio.com
Home Page: CinemaLibreStudio.com
IMDb: imdb.com/company/co0132224

Accepts query letter from unproduced, unrepresented writers. Established in 2003.

Philippe Diaz
IMDb: imdb.com/name/nm0225034

CINE MOSAIC

130 W 25th St, 12th Floor
New York, NY 10001
Phone: 212-625-3797
Fax: 212-625-3571

Email: info@cinemosaic.net
Home Page: cinemosaic.net
IMDb: imdb.com/company/co0124029

Accepts scripts from produced or represented writers. Project types include TV. Preferred genres include Action, Drama, and Non-Fiction. Established in 2002.

Lydia Pilcher
IMDb: imdb.com/name/nm0212990

CINESON ENTERTAINMENT

4519 Varna Ave.
Sherman Oaks, CA 91423
Phone: 818-501-8246
Fax: 818-501-3647

Email: cineson@cineson.com
Home Page: cineson.com
IMDb: imdb.com/company/co0127539

Does not accept any unsolicited material. Project types include Feature Films and TV. Preferred genres include Comedy, Crime, Drama, Non-Fiction, Period, Romance, and Thriller. Established in 1999.

Andy Garcia
IMDb: imdb.com/name/nm0000412

CINETELFILMS

8255 Sunset Blvd
Los Angeles, CA 90046
Phone: 323-654-4000
Fax: 323-650-6400

Email: info@cinetelfilms.com
Home Page: cinetelfilms.com
IMDb: imdb.com/company/co0017447

Does not accept any unsolicited material. Project types include TV. Preferred genres include Crime, Drama, Horror, and Thriller. Established in 1985.

Paul Hertzberg
IMDb: imdb.com/name/nm0078473

CINEVILLE

3400 Airport Ave
Santa Monica, CA 90405
Phone: 310-397-7150
Fax: 310-397-7155

Email: info@cineville.com
Home Page: cineville.com
IMDb: imdb.com/company/co0063993

Accepts query letter from unproduced, unrepresented writers. Preferred genres include Comedy, Non-Fiction, and Romance. Established in 1990.

Carl Colpaert
President
IMDb: imdb.com/name/nm0173207

CIRCLE OF CONFUSION

8931 Ellis Ave
Los Angeles, CA 90034
Phone: 310-691-7000
Fax: 310-691-7099

Email: queries@circleofconfusion.com
Home Page: circleofconfusion.com
IMDb: imdb.com/company/co0090153

Accepts query letter from unproduced, unrepresented writers. Project types include TV. Preferred genres include Action, Comedy, Crime, Detective, Drama, Fantasy, Horror, Myth, Non-Fiction, Romance, Science Fiction, and Thriller.

Stephen Emery
Executive Vice-President Production and
Development
Email: stephen@circleofconfusion.com
IMDb: imdb.com/name/nm1765323

CITY ENTERTAINMENT

266 1/2 S Rexford Dr
Beverly Hills, CA 90212
Phone: 310-273-3101
Fax: 310-273-3676

IMDb: imdb.com/company/co0093881

Does not accept any unsolicited material.

Joshua Maurer
IMDb: imdb.com/name/nm0561027

CLARITY PICTURES, LLC

1107 Fair Oaks Ave
Ste 155
South Pasadena, CA 91030
USA
Phone: 310-226-7046
Fax: 310-388-5846

Email: info@claritypictures.net
Home Page: claritypictures.net
IMDb: imdb.com/company/co0151012

Does not accept any unsolicited material. Project types
include Feature Films and TV. Preferred genres
include Comedy, Documentary, and Horror.
Established in 2004.

David Basulto
IMDb: imdb.com/name/nm0060617

Loren Basulto
IMDb: imdb.com/name/nm1457923

CLASS 5 FILMS

200 Park Ave South, 8th Floor
New York, NY 10003
Phone: 917-414-9404

IMDb: imdb.com/company/co0113781

Accepts query letter from unproduced, unrepresented
writers.

Edward Norton
IMDb: imdb.com/name/nm0001570

CLEAR PICTURES ENTERTAINMENT

12400 Ventura Blvd, Suite 306
Studio City, CA 91604
Phone: 818-980-5460
Fax: 818-980-4716

Email: clearpicturesinc@aol.com
IMDb: imdb.com/company/co0171732

Accepts query letter from unproduced, unrepresented
writers via email. Project types include Feature Films
and TV. Preferred genres include Drama and Non-
Fiction. Established in 2009.

Elizabeth Fowler
Principle
IMDb: imdb.com/name/nm2085583

CLEARVIEW PRODUCTIONS

1180 S Beverly Dr, Suite 700
Los Angeles, CA 90035
Phone: 310-271-7698
Fax: 310-278-9978

Does not accept any unsolicited material.

Albert Ruddy
Producer
IMDb: imdb.com/name/nm0748665

CLIFFORD WERBER PRODUCTIONS

232 S Beverly Dr, Suite 224
Beverly Hills, CA 90212
Phone: 310-288-0900
Fax: 310-288-0600

IMDb: imdb.com/company/co0097249

Accepts query letter from produced or represented
writers.

Clifford Werber
Producer
IMDb: imdb.com/name/nm0921222

CLOSED ON MONDAYS ENTERTAINMENT

3800 Barham Blvd Suite 100
Los Angeles, CA 90068
Phone: 818-526-6707

IMDb: imdb.com/company/co0186526

Does not accept any unsolicited material. Established in 2003.

Joe Nozemack
IMDb: imdb.com/name/nm1060496

CLOUD EIGHT FILMS

39 Long Acre
London WC2E 9LG
United Kingdom
Phone: +44 20-7845-6877

IMDb: imdb.com/company/co0265704

Accepts scripts from produced or represented writers. Established in 2009.

Christian Colson
Phone: +44 20 7845 6988
IMDb: imdb.com/name/nm1384503

CODEBLACK ENTERTAINMENT

111 Universal Hollywood Dr, Suite 2260
Universal City, CA 91608
Phone: 818-286-8600
Fax: 818-286-8649

Email: info@codeblackentertainment.com
Home Page: codeblackentertainment.com
IMDb: imdb.com/company/co0172361

Does not accept any unsolicited material. Established in 2005.

Jeff Clanagan
CEO
IMDb: imdb.com/name/nm0163335

CODE ENTERTAINMENT

9229 Sunset Blvd, Suite 615
Los Angeles, CA 90069
Phone: 310-772-0008
Fax: 310-772-0006

Email: contact@codeentertainment.com
Home Page: codeentertainment.com
IMDb: imdb.com/company/co0143069

Accepts scripts from produced or represented writers. Established in 2005.

Bart Rosenblatt
Producer
Phone: 310-772-0008 ext. 3
IMDb: imdb.com/name/nm0742386

COLLEEN CAMP PRODUCTIONS

6464 Sunset Blvd, Suite 800
Los Angeles, CA 90028
Phone: 323-463-1434
Fax: 323-463-4379

Email: asst@ccprods.com
IMDb: imdb.com/company/co0092983

Accepts query letter from unproduced, unrepresented writers.

Colleen Camp
Producer
IMDb: imdb.com/name/nm0131974

COLLETON COMPANY

20 Fifth Ave, Suite 13F
New York, NY 10011
Phone: 212-673-0916
Fax: 212-673-1172

Accepts scripts from produced or represented writers. Project types include Feature Films and TV. Preferred genres include Crime, Detective, Drama, Non-Fiction, and Thriller.

Sara Colleton
IMDb: imdb.com/name/nm0171780

COLOR FORCE

1524 Cloverfield Blvd, Suite C
Santa Monica, CA 90404
Phone: 310-828-0641
Fax: 310-828-0672

IMDb: imdb.com/company/co0212151

Accepts query letter from unproduced, unrepresented writers. Preferred genres include Action and Comedy. Established in 2007.

Nina Jacobson
Producer
Email: nina.jacobson@colorforce.com
IMDb: imdb.com/name/nm1749221

COLOSSAL ENTERTAINMENT

PO Box 461010
Los Angeles, CA 90046
Phone: 323-656-6647

Email: clsslent@aol.com
IMDb: imdb.com/company/co0176684

Accepts query letter from unproduced, unrepresented writers.

Kelly Rowan
Producer
IMDb: imdb.com/name/nm0746414

Graham Ludlow
IMDb: imdb.com/name/nm0524905

COLUMBIA PICTURES

10202 W Washington Blvd Thalberg Building
Culver City, CA 90232
Phone: 310-244-4000
Fax: 310-244-2626

Home Page: spe.sony.com
IMDb: imdb.com/company/co0071509

Does not accept any unsolicited material. Project types include Feature Films. Preferred genres include Action, Animation, Comedy, Crime, Drama, Family, Fantasy, Horror, Non-Fiction, Period, Romance, Science Fiction, and Thriller. Established in 1939.

Amy Pascal
Chairman
IMDb: imdb.com/name/nm1166871

Doug Belgrad
President
IMDb: imdb.com/name/nm1000411

Elizabeth Cantillon
Executive Vice President of Production
IMDb: imdb.com/name/nm0134578
Assistant: Katherine Spada
katherine_spada@spe.sony.com

Samuel C. Dickerman
Executive Vice President of Production
IMDb: imdb.com/name/nm0225385

Andrea Giannetti
Executive Vice President of Production
IMDb: imdb.com/name/nm1602150

Foster Driver
Creative Executive
IMDb: imdb.com/name/nm5372839

Eric Fineman
Creative Executive
IMDb: imdb.com/name/nm2349857

Hannah Minghella
IMDb: imdb.com/name/nm1098742
Assistant: Mahsa Moayeri
mahsa_moayeri@spe.sony.com

Pete Corral
IMDb: imdb.com/name/nm0180707

DeVon Franklin
IMDb: imdb.com/name/nm2035952

Andy Given
IMDb: imdb.com/name/nm0321429

Jonathan Kadin
IMDb: imdb.com/name/nm2142367
Assistant: Ashley Johnson
ashley_johnson@spe.sony.com

Rachel O'Connor
IMDb: imdb.com/name/nm1471418

Lauren Abrahams
IMDb: imdb.com/name/nm1036268

Debra Bergman
IMDb: imdb.com/name/nm2984630

Adam Moos
IMDb: imdb.com/name/nm0602149

COMEDY ARTS STUDIOS

2500 Broadway
Santa Monica, CA 90404
Phone: 310-382-3677
Fax: 310-382-3170

IMDb: imdb.com/company/co0220109

Accepts query letter from unproduced, unrepresented writers. Project types include TV. Preferred genres include Comedy and Drama.

Stu Smiley
IMDb: imdb.com/name/nm0806979

COMPLETION FILMS

60 E 42nd St, Suite 4600
New York, NY 10165
Phone: 718-693-2057
Fax: 888-693-4133

Email: info@completionfilms.com
Home Page: completionfilms.com
IMDb: imdb.com/company/co0175660

Accepts query letter from unproduced, unrepresented writers. Preferred genres include Non-Fiction.

Kisha Imani Cameron
President
IMDb: imdb.com/name/nm0131650

CONCEPT ENTERTAINMENT

334 1/2 N Sierra Bonita Ave
Los Angeles, CA 90036
Phone: 323-937-5700
Fax: 323-937-5720

Email: enquiries@conceptentertainment.biz
Home Page: conceptentertainment.biz
IMDb: .imdb.com/company/co0096670

Accepts query letter from unproduced, unrepresented writers. Project types include TV. Preferred genres include Action, Comedy, Crime, Detective, Drama, Fantasy, Horror, Myth, Non-Fiction, Romance, Science Fiction, and Thriller.

David Faigenblum
IMDb: imdb.com/name/nm1584960

CONSTANTIN FILM

9200 W Sunset Blvd, Suite 800
West Hollywood, CA 90069
Phone: 310-247-0300
Fax: 310-247-0305

Feilitzschstr. 6
Munich, Bavaria D-80802
Germany
Phone: +49-89-44-44-60-0
Fax: +49-89-44-44-60-666

Email: zentrale@constantin-film.de
IMDb: imdb.com/company/co0002257
Home Page: constantin-film.de
Facebook: facebook.com/constantinfilm

Accepts query letter from produced or represented writers. Project types include Feature Films and TV. Preferred genres include Action, Crime, and Thriller. Established in 1950.

Robert Kultzer
Executive
Phone: 310-247-0300 ext. 3
Email: robert.kultzer@constantin-film.de
IMDb: imdb.com/name/nm0474709

CONTENT MEDIA CORPORATION PLC

225 Arizona Ave, Suite #250
Santa Monica, CA 90401
Phone: 310-576-1059
Fax: 310-576-1859

Email: jcassistant@contentmediacorp.com
Home Page: contentmediacorp.com
IMDb: imdb.com/company/co0366223

Accepts query letter from unproduced, unrepresented writers.

Jamie Carmichael
Email: jamie.carmichael@contentmediacorp.com
IMDb: imdb.com/name/nm0138430

CONTRAFILM

1531 N Cahuenga Blvd
Los Angeles, CA 90028
Phone: 323-467-8787
Fax: 323-467-7730

Accepts query letter from unproduced, unrepresented writers. Project types include Feature Films. Preferred genres include Drama, Horror, and Thriller.

Tripp Vinson
Producer
IMDb: imdb.com/name/nm1246087
Assistant: Tara Farney

Alexandra Church
Creative Executive
IMDb: imdb.com/name/nm0161344

Tucker Williams
Creative Executive
IMDb: imdb.com/name/nm2606099

CONUNDRUM ENTERTAINMENT

325 Wilshire Blvd, Suite 201
Santa Monica, CA 90401
Phone: 310-319-2800
Fax: 310-319-2808

IMDb: imdb.com/company/co0030016

Accepts scripts from produced or represented writers. Preferred genres include Comedy.

Peter Farrelly
Executive
IMDb: imdb.com/name/nm0268380

Bobby Farrelly
Executive
IMDb: imdb.com/name/nm0268370

COOPER'S TOWN PRODUCTIONS

302A West 12th St, Suite 214
New York, NY 10014
Phone: 212-255-7566
Fax: 212-255-0211

Email: info@copperstownproductions.com
Home Page: copperstownproductions.com
IMDb: imdb.com/company/co0132168

Accepts query letter from unproduced, unrepresented writers. Project types include Feature Films. Preferred genres include Non-Fiction.

Phillip Hoffman
Partner
IMDb: imdb.com/name/nm0000450

Sara Murphy
IMDb: imdb.com/name/nm2072976

COQUETTE PRODUCTIONS

8105 W Third St
Los Angeles, CA 90048
Phone: 323-801-1000
Fax: 323-801-1001

Does not accept any unsolicited material. Project types include TV. Preferred genres include Comedy, Crime, Drama, and Romance.

Thea Mann
Head of Development
IMDb: imdb.com/name/nm0542996

Jeff Bowland
Executive
IMDb: imdb.com/name/nm0101188

David Arquette
IMDb: imdb.com/name/nm0000274

Courtney Cox
IMDb: imdb.com/name/nm0001073

CORNER STORE ENTERTAINMENT

9615 Brighton Way
Ste 201
Beverly Hills, CA 90210
Phone: 310-276-6400
Fax: 310-276-6410

Home Page: cornerstore-ent.com

Does not accept any unsolicited material. Project types include Feature Films. Preferred genres include Comedy, Drama, and Romance.

Matthew Weaver
IMDb: imdb.com/name/nm2822461

Scott Prisand
IMDb: imdb.com/name/nm1964055

CRAVE FILMS

3312 Sunset Blvd
Los Angeles, CA 90026
Phone: 323-669-9000
Fax: 323-669-9002

Home Page: cravefilms.com
IMDb: imdb.com/company/co0146364

Does not accept any unsolicited material. Project types include Feature Films. Preferred genres include Drama.

David Ayer
Email: david@cravefilms.com
IMDb: imdb.com/name/nm0043742

Alex Ott
Email: alex@cravefilms.com
IMDb: imdb.com/name/nm1944773

CREANSPEAK PRODUCTIONS, LLC

120 S El Camino Dr
Beverly Hills, CA 90212
Phone: 310-273-8217

Email: info@creanspeak.com
IMDb: imdb.com/company/co0097231

Accepts query letter from unproduced, unrepresented writers via email. Project types include Feature Films, TV, and Commercials. Preferred genres include Action, Comedy, Drama, Family, Non-Fiction, and Reality.

Kelly Crean
Phone: 310-273-8217
Email: info@creanspeak.com
IMDb: imdb.com/name/nm1047631

Jon Freis
Phone: 310-273-8217
Email: info@creanspeak.com
IMDb: imdb.com/name/nm2045371

CRESCENDO PRODUCTIONS

252 N Larchmont Blvd, Suite 200
Los Angeles, CA 90004
Phone: 323-465-2222
Fax: 323-464-3750

IMDb: ww.imdb.com/company/co0025116

Accepts query letter from unproduced, unrepresented writers. Project types include Feature Films and TV. Preferred genres include Non-Fiction and Reality.

Don Cheadle
Phone: 323-465-2222
IMDb: imdb.com/name/nm0000332

CREST ANIMATION PRODUCTIONS, INC.

333 N Glenoaks Blvd, Suite 300
Burbank, CA 91502
Phone: 818-846-0166
Fax: 818-846-6074

Email: info@crestcgi.com
Home Page: crestcgi.com
IMDb: imdb.com/company/co0218880

Accepts query letter from unproduced, unrepresented writers via email. Project types include Feature Films. Preferred genres include Animation.

Richard Rich
Phone: 818-846-0166
Email: info@crestcgi.com
IMDb: imdb.com/name/nm0723704

Gregory Kasunich
Phone: 818-846-0166
Email: gkasunich@crestcgi.com
IMDb: imdb.com/name/nm3215310

CRIME SCENE PICTURES

3450 Cahuenga Blvd W, Suite 701
Los Angeles, CA 90068
Phone: 323-963-5136
Fax: 323-963-5137

Email: info@crimescenepictures.net
Home Page: crimescenepictures.net
IMDb: imdb.com/company/co0326645

Does not accept any unsolicited material. Project types include Feature Films. Established in 2010.

Brett Hedblom
Director of Development
IMDb: imdb.com/name/nm3916261

Jennifer Marmor
Creative Executive
IMDb: imdb.com/name/nm4420063

Adam Ripp
IMDb: imdb.com/name/nm0728063

CROSS CREEK PICTURES

9220 W Sunset Blvd, Suite 100
West Hollywood, CA 90069
Phone: 310-248-4061
Fax: 310-248-4068

Email: info@crosscreekpictures.com
Home Page: crosscreekpictures.com
IMDb: imdb.com/company/co0285648

Accepts query letter from unproduced, unrepresented writers via email. Project types include Feature Films and TV. Preferred genres include Drama.

Brian Oliver
President
Email: brian@crosscreekpicture.com
IMDb: imdb.com/name/nm1003922

John Shepherd
Creative Executive
Phone: 310-248-4061
Email: info@crosscreekpicture.com
IMDb: imdb.com/name/nm3005173

Stephanie Hall
Email: stephanie@crosscreekpicture.com
IMDb: imdb.com/name/nm24206

CROSSROADS FILMS

1722 Whitley Ave
Los Angeles, CA 90028
Phone: 310-659-6220
Fax: 310-659-3105

Home Page: crossroadsfilms.com
IMDb: imdb.com/company/co0061179

Accepts query letter from unproduced, unrepresented writers. Project types include Feature Films, TV, and Commercials. Preferred genres include Comedy, Crime, Drama, Romance, and Thriller.

Camille Taylor
Phone: 310-659-6220
IMDb: imdb.com/name/nm0852088

CRUCIAL FILMS

2220 Colorado Ave, 5th Floor
Santa Monica, CA 90404
Phone: 310-865-8249
Fax: 310-865-7068

Email: crucialfilms.asst@gmail.com
IMDb: imdb.com/company/co0049027

Does not accept any unsolicited material. Project types include Feature Films and TV. Preferred genres include Action, Comedy, Crime, Drama, Fantasy, Horror, Romance, and Thriller.

Daniel Schnider
Phone: 310-865-8249
Email: crucialfilms.asst@gmail.com
IMDb: imdb.com/name/nm3045845

CRYSTAL LAKE ENTERTAINMENT, INC.

4420 Hayvenhurst Ave
Encino, CA 91436
Phone: 818-995-1585
Fax: 818-995-1677

Email: sscfilms@earthlink.net
IMDb: imdb.com/company/co0067362

Accepts query letter from unproduced, unrepresented writers via email. Project types include Feature Films and TV. Preferred genres include Horror, Science Fiction, and Thriller.

Sean Cunningham
Phone: 818-995-1585
Email: sscfilms@earthlink.net
IMDb: imdb.com/name/nm0192446

Geoff Garrett
Phone: 818-995-1585
Email: sscfilms@earthlink.net
IMDb: imdb.com/name/nm0308117

CRYSTAL SKY PICTURES, LLC

10203 Santa Monica Blvd, 5th Floor
Los Angeles, CA 90067

Phone: 310-843-0223
Fax: 310-553-9895

Email: info@crystalsky.com
Home Page: crystalsky.com
IMDb: imdb.com/company/co0004724

Accepts query letter from unproduced, unrepresented writers via email. Project types include Feature Films. Preferred genres include Action, Comedy, Crime, Drama, Family, Fantasy, Horror, Science Fiction, and Thriller.

Florent Gaglio
Executive
Phone: 310-843-0223
Email: info@crystalsky.com
IMDb: imdb.com/name/nm2904382

Steven Paul
Phone: 310-843-0223
Email: info@crystalsky.com
IMDb: imdb.com/name/nm0666999

Eric Breiman
Phone: 310-843-0223
Email: info@crystalsky.com

CUBEVISION

9000 W Sunset Blvd
West Hollywood, CA 90069
Phone: 310-461-3490
Fax: 310-461-3491

Home Page: icecube.com
IMDb: imdb.com/company/co0044714

Accepts query letter from unproduced, unrepresented writers. Project types include Feature Films and TV. Preferred genres include Action, Animation, Comedy, Crime, Drama, Family, Non-Fiction, Reality, Romance, and Thriller.

Matt Alvarez
Partner
Phone: 310-461-3490
IMDb: imdb.com/name/nm0023297
Assistant: Lawtisha Fletcher

Ice Cube
Phone: 310-461-3495
IMDb: imdb.com/name/nm0001084
Assistant: Nancy Leiviska

CURB ENTERTAINMENT

3907 W Alameda Ave
Burbank, CA 91505
Phone: 818-843-8580
Fax: 818-566-1719

Email: info@curbentertainment.com
Home Page: curbentertainment.com
IMDb: mdb.com/company/co0089886

Accepts query letter from unproduced, unrepresented writers via email. Project types include Feature Films and TV. Preferred genres include Animation, Comedy, Crime, Drama, Family, Horror, Romance, Science Fiction, and Thriller. Established in 1984.

Carole Nemoy
Phone: 818-843-8580
Email: ccurb@curb.com
IMDb: imdb.com/name/nm0626002

Mona Kirton
Phone: 818-843-8580
Email: mkirton@curb.com
IMDb: imdb.com/name/nm1310398

Christy Peterson
Phone: 818-843-8580
Email: cpeterson@curb.com

CYAN PICTURES

410 Park Ave, 15th Floor
New York, NY 10022
Phone: 212-274-1085

Email: info@cyanpictures.com
IMDb: imdb.com/company/co0080910

Accepts query letter from unproduced, unrepresented writers via email. Project types include Feature Films and TV. Preferred genres include Comedy, Crime, Drama, Horror, Non-Fiction, Reality, Romance, Science Fiction, and Thriller.

Joshua Newman
CEO
Phone: 212-274-1085
Email: newman@cyanpictures.com
IMDb: imdb.com/name/nm1243333

Alexander Burns
CFO
Phone: 212-274-1085
Email: info@cyanpictures.com

Wes Schrader
Phone: 212-274-1085
Email: schrader@cyanpictures.com

CYPRESS FILMS, INC.

630 Ninth Ave, Suite 415
New York, NY 10036
Phone: 212-262-3900
Fax: 212-262-3925

Email: kmoarefi@cypressfilms.com
Home Page: cypressfilms.com
IMDb: imdb.com/company/co0044830

Accepts query letter from unproduced, unrepresented writers via email. Project types include Feature Films. Preferred genres include Comedy, Drama, Family, Romance, and Science Fiction.

Jon Glascoe
Phone: 212-262-3900
IMDb: imdb.com/name/nm0321797

Joseph Pierson
Phone: 212-262-3900
IMDb: imdb.com/name/nm0682777

Jessica Forsythe

CYPRESS POINT PRODUCTIONS

3000 Olympic Blvd
Santa Monica, CA 90404
Phone: 310-315-4787
Fax: 310-315-4785

Email: cppfilms@earthlink.net
IMDb: imdb.com/company/co0038030

Accepts query letter from unproduced, unrepresented writers via email. Project types include TV. Preferred genres include Action, Comedy, Crime, Drama, Family, Non-Fiction, Romance, Science Fiction, and Thriller.

Gerald Abrams
Chairman
Phone: 310-315-4787
Email: cppfilms@earthlink.net
IMDb: imdb.com/name/nm0009181

Michael Waldron
Phone: 310-315-4787
Email: cppfilms@earthlink.net
IMDb: imdb.com/name/nm1707236

DAKOTA PICTURES

4633 Lankershim Blvd
North Hollywood, CA 91602
Phone: 818-760-0099
Fax: 818-760-1070

Email: info@dakotafilms.com
Home Page: dakotafilms.com

Does not accept any unsolicited material. Project types include Feature Films and TV. Preferred genres include Action, Animation, Comedy, Crime, Drama, Family, Fantasy, Non-Fiction, Reality, and Thriller.

Troy Miller
Phone: 818-760-0099
Email: info@dakotafilms.com
IMDb: imdb.com/name/nm0003474

A.J. DiAntonio
Phone: 818-760-0099
Email: info@dakotafilms.com
IMDb: imdb.com/name/nm1472504

Matt Magielnicki
Phone: 818-760-0099
Email: info@dakotafilms.com
IMDb: imdb.com/name/nm2616148

DANIEL L. PAULSON PRODUCTIONS

9056 Santa Monica Blvd, Suite 203A
West Hollywood, CA 90069
Phone: 310-278-9747
Fax: 310-278-3751

Email: dlpprods@sbcglobal.net

Does not accept any unsolicited material. Project types include Feature Films and TV. Preferred genres include Action, Comedy, Crime, Detective, Drama, Family, Non-Fiction, Reality, Romance, and Thriller.

Daniel Paulson

Phone: 310-278-9747
Email: dlpprods@sbcglobal.net
IMDb: imdb.com/name/nm0667340

Steve Kennedy

Phone: 310-278-9747
Email: dlpprods@sbcglobal.net
IMDb: imdb.com/name/nm0448346

DANIEL OSTROFF PRODUCTIONS

2046 N Hillhurst Ave. #120
Los Angeles, CA 90027
Phone: 323-284-8824

Email: oteamthe@gmail.com
IMDb: imdb.com/company/co0138101

Accepts query letter from unproduced, unrepresented writers. Project types include Feature Films and TV. Preferred genres include Comedy, Detective, Non-Fiction, and Reality.

Daniel Ostroff

Producer
Phone: 323-284-8824
Email: oteamthe@gmail.com
IMDb: imdb.com/name/nm0652491

DANIEL PETRIE JR. & COMPANY

18034 Ventura Blvd, Suite 445
Encino, CA 91316
Phone: 818-708-1602
Fax: 818-774-0345

IMDb: imdb.com/company/co0120842

Accepts query letter from unproduced, unrepresented writers. Project types include Feature Films and TV. Preferred genres include Action, Comedy, Crime, Detective, Drama, Horror, Romance, Science Fiction, and Thriller.

Daniel Petrie,

Phone: 818-708-1602
IMDb: imdb.com/name/nm0677943

Rick Dugdale

Phone: 818-708-1602
IMDb: imdb.com/name/nm1067987

DANIEL SLADEK ENTERTAINMENT CORPORATION

8306 Wilshire Blvd, Suite 510
Beverly Hills, CA 90211
Phone: 323-934-9268
Fax: 323-934-7362

Email: danielsladek@mac.com
Home Page: danielsladek.com

Does not accept any unsolicited material. Project types include Feature Films and TV. Preferred genres include Action, Comedy, Crime, Drama, Fantasy, Horror, Non-Fiction, Reality, Romance, Science Fiction, and Thriller. Established in 1998.

Daniel Sladek

Phone: 323-934-9268
Email: danielsladek@mac.com
IMDb: imdb.com/name/nm0805202

DANJAQ PRODUCTIONS

2400 Broadway
Ste 310
Santa Monica, CA 90404
Phone: 310-449-3185

Does not accept any unsolicited material. Project types include Feature Films. Preferred genres include Action.

David Pope

CEO
Phone: 310-449-3185
IMDb: imdb.com/name/nm0691102

Michael Wilson

President
Phone: 310-449-3185
IMDb: imdb.com/name/nm0933865

Barbara Broccoli

IMDb: imdb.com/name/nm0110483

DAN LUPOVITZ PRODUCTIONS

936 Alandele Ave
Los Angeles, CA 90036

Phone: 323-930-0769
Fax: 310-385-0196

Email: dlupovitz@aol.com

Accepts query letter from unproduced, unrepresented writers via email. Project types include Feature Films and TV. Preferred genres include Comedy, Drama, and Romance.

Dan Lupovitz

Phone: 323-930-0769
Email: dlupovitz@aol.com
IMDb: imdb.com/name/nm0526991

Randy Albelda

Phone: 323-930-0769

DAN WINGUTOW PRODUCTIONS

534 Laguardia Pl., Suite 3
New York, NY 10012
Phone: 212-477-1328
Fax: 212-254-6902

Accepts query letter from unproduced, unrepresented writers. Project types include Feature Films and TV. Preferred genres include Comedy, Crime, Drama, Fantasy, Horror, Romance, Science Fiction, and Thriller.

Dan Wigutow

Executive Producer
Phone: 212-477-1328
IMDb: imdb.com/name/nm0927887

Caroline Moore

Phone: 212-477-1328
IMDb: imdb.com/name/nm0601006

DARIUS FILMS INCORPORATED

1020 Cole Ave, Suite 4363
Los Angeles, CA 90038
Phone: 310-728-1342
Fax: 310-494-0575

Email: info@dariusfilms.com
Home Page: dariusfilms.com
IMDb: imdb.com/company/co0133523

Accepts query letter from produced or represented writers. Project types include Feature Films and TV. Preferred genres include Comedy, Crime, Detective, Drama, Fantasy, Non-Fiction, Romance, Science Fiction, and Thriller.

Nicholas Tabarrok

Phone: 310-728-1342
Email: info@dariusfilms.com
IMDb: imdb.com/name/nm0002431

Daniel Baruela

Phone: 310-728-1342
Email: info@dariusfilms.com
IMDb: imdb.com/name/nm3758990

DARK CASTLE ENTERTAINMENT

1601 Main St
Venice, CA 90291
Phone: 310-566-6100
Fax: 310-566-6188

Accepts query letter from produced or represented writers. Project types include Feature Films. Preferred genres include Action, Crime, Drama, Horror, and Thriller. Established in 1999.

Joel Silver

Partner
IMDb: imdb.com/name/nm0005428

Steve Richards

IMDb: imdb.com/name/nm0724345

Andrew Rona

IMDb: imdb.com/name/nm0739868
Assistant: Dash Boam

DARK HORSE ENTERTAINMENT

12711 Ventura Blvd.
Suite 270
Studio City, CA 91604
Phone: 323-655-3600
Fax: 323-655-2430

Home Page: dhentertainment.com
IMDb: imdb.com/company/co0020061

Does not accept any unsolicited material. Project types include Feature Films. Preferred genres include Action, Animation, Comedy, Crime, Drama, Family, Fantasy, Horror, Non-Fiction, Romance, Science Fiction, and Thriller.

Mike Richardson
Phone: 323-655-3600
Email: miker@darkhorse.com
IMDb: imdb.com/name/nm0724700
Assistant: Pete Cacioppo

Keith Goldberg
Phone: 323-655-3600
Email: keithg@darkhorse.com
IMDb: imdb.com/name/nm1378991

DARKO ENTERTAINMENT

7164 Melrose Ave.
2nd Floor
Los Angeles, CA 90046
Phone: 323-592-3460
Fax: 323-850-2481

Email: info@darko.com
Home Page: darko.com
IMDb: imdb.com/company/co0118694

Does not accept any unsolicited material. Project types include Feature Films and TV. Preferred genres include Fantasy, Horror, and Thriller.

Jeff Cullota
IMDb: imdb.com/name/nm2261214

DARK SKY FILMS

16101 S 108th Ave
Orland Park, IL 60467
Phone: 800-323-0442

Email: info@darkskyfilms.com
Home Page: darkskyfilms.com

Does not accept any unsolicited material. Project types include Feature Films. Preferred genres include Horror and Thriller.

Malik Ali
Executive
IMDb: imdb.com/name/nm0019446

Greg Newman
Executive
IMDb: imdb.com/name/nm0628103

Todd Wieneke
Producer
IMDb: imdb.com/name/nm2663562

DARKWOODS PRODUCTIONS

301 E Colorado Blvd, Suite 705
Pasadena, CA 91101
Phone: 323-454-4580
Fax: 323-454-4581

IMDb: imdb.com/company/co0029398

Does not accept any unsolicited material. Project types include Feature Films. Preferred genres include Comedy, Crime, Drama, Fantasy, Horror, Non-Fiction, Romance, Science Fiction, and Thriller.

Frank Darobont
Phone: 323-454-4582
IMDb: imdb.com/name/nm0001104
Assistant: Alex Whit

DARREN STAR PRODUCTIONS

9200 Sunset Blvd, Suite 430
Los Angeles, CA 90069
Phone: 310-274-2145
Fax: 310-274-1455

Email: d.star.prodco@gmail.com
IMDb: imdb.com/company/co0020963

Accepts query letter from unproduced, unrepresented writers. Project types include Feature Films and TV. Preferred genres include Comedy, Crime, Drama, Non-Fiction, and Romance.

Darren Star
Phone: 310-274-2145
IMDb: imdb.com/name/nm0823015

Charles Pugliese
Phone: 310-274-2145
IMDb: imdb.com/name/nm1551399

DAVE BELL ASSOCIATES

3211 Cahuenga Blvd West
Los Angeles, CA 90068
Phone: 323-851-7801
Fax: 323-851-9349

Email: dbamovies@aol.com
IMDb: imdb.com/company/co0033679

Accepts query letter from unproduced, unrepresented writers via email. Project types include Feature Films and TV. Preferred genres include Drama, Family, Horror, Non-Fiction, Reality, Romance, and Science Fiction.

Ted Weiant
Phone: 323-851-7801
Email: dbamovies@aol.com
IMDb: imdb.com/name/nm1059707

Dave Bell
President
Phone: 323-851-7801
Email: dbamovies@aol.com
IMDb: imdb.com/name/nm1037012

Fred Putman
Phone: 323-851-7801
IMDb: imdb.com/name/nm1729656

DAVID EICK PRODUCTIONS

100 Universal City Plaza
Universal City, CA 91608
Phone: 818-501-0146
Fax: 818-733-2522

IMDb: imdb.com/company/co0176813

Accepts query letter from unproduced, unrepresented writers. Project types include TV. Preferred genres include Action, Drama, Science Fiction, and Thriller.

David Eick
President
Phone: 818-501-0146
IMDb: imdb.com/name/nm0251594

DAVIS ENTERTAINMENT

10201 W Pico Blvd
31-301
Los Angeles, CA 90064
Phone: 310-556-3550
Fax: 310-556-3688

150 S. Barrington Place
Los Angeles, CA 90049

IMDb: imdb.com/company/co0022730

Accepts scripts from produced or represented writers.

John Davis
IMDb: imdb.com/name/nm0204862

John Fox
IMDb: imdb.com/name/nm2470810

DEED FILMS

Phone: 419-685-4842

Email: sdonely@deedfilms.com
Home Page: deedfilms.com
IMDb: imdb.com/company/co0323092

Accepts query letter from unproduced, unrepresented writers via email. Project types include Feature Films. Preferred genres include Comedy and Crime. Established in 2008.

Scott Donley
President
IMDb: imdb.com/name/nm4238094

DEERJEN FILMS

222 W 23rd St
New York, NY 10011

Home Page: deerjen.com

Accepts query letter from produced or represented writers. Project types include Feature Films. Preferred genres include Comedy, Drama, Period, Romance, and Thriller.

Jen Gatien
Producer
Email: jen@deerjen.com
IMDb: imdb.com/name/nm0309684

DEFIANCE ENTERTAINMENT

6605 Hollywood Blvd, Suite 100
Los Angeles, CA 91401
Phone: 323-393-0132

Email: info@defiance-ent.com
Home Page: defiance-ent.com
IMDb: imdb.com/company/co0236811

Accepts query letter from unproduced, unrepresented writers via email. Project types include Feature Films,

TV, and Commercials. Preferred genres include Action, Comedy, Crime, Drama, Fantasy, Horror, Myth, Science Fiction, and Thriller. Established in 2006.

Clare Kramer
COO
Email: clare@defiance-ent.com
IMDb: imdb.com/name/nm0004456

Brian Keathley
Email: brian@defiance-ent.com
IMDb: imdb.com/name/nm0444080

DE LINE PICTURES

4000 Warner Blvd Building 66, Room 147
Burbank, CA 91522
Phone: 818-954-5200
Fax: 818-954-5430

IMDb: imdb.com/company/co0033149

Does not accept any unsolicited material. Project types include Feature Films. Preferred genres include Action, Animation, Comedy, Crime, Drama, Family, Fantasy, Period, Romance, Science Fiction, and Thriller. Established in 2001.

Donald De Line
President
IMDb: imdb.com/name/nm0209773
Assistant: Matt Gamboa matt@delinepictures.com

Jacob Robinson
IMDb: imdb.com/name/nm1563784

DELVE FILMS

20727 High Desert Ct
Suite 4+5
Bend, OR 97701
Phone: 424-703-3583

Email: info@delvefilms.com
Home Page: delvefilms.com

Accepts query letter from produced or represented writers. Project types include Feature Films. Preferred genres include Comedy, Documentary, Drama, Fantasy, Romance, and Thriller.

Isaac Testerman
President
Email: isaac@delvefilms.com
IMDb: imdb.com/name/nm4107099

Nate Salciccioli
Phone: 541-788-6139
Email: nate@delvefilms.com
IMDb: imdb.com/name/nm4244606

DEMAREST FILMS

100 N Crescent Dr
Suite 350
Beverly Hills, CA 90210
Phone: 310-385-4310

Does not accept any unsolicited material. Project types include Feature Films and TV. Preferred genres include Comedy, Crime, Drama, Fantasy, and Thriller.

Sam Englebardt
IMDb: mdb.com/name/nm1583132
Assistant: Linda Goetz

William D. Johnso
IMDb: imdb.com/name/nm4207924

Michael Lambert
IMDb: imdb.com/name/nm2236003

Brian Flanagan

DEPTH OF FIELD

1724 Whitley Ave
Los Angeles, CA 90028
Phone: 323-466-6500
Fax: 323-466-6501

IMDb: imdb.com/company/co0113177

Accepts scripts from produced or represented writers. Project types include Feature Films.

Andrew Miano
Executive Producer
IMDb: imdb.com/name/nm0583948

Chris Weitz
IMDb: imdb.com/name/nm0919363

DESERT WIND FILMS

13603 Marina Pointe Dr
Ste D529
Marina Del Rey, CA 90292
Phone: 661-200-3509
Fax: 310-499-5254

Email: media@desertwindfilms.com
Home Page: desertwindfilms.com

Accepts query letter from unproduced, unrepresented writers. Project types include Feature Films.

T.J. Amato
President
IMDb: imdb.com/name/nm2125600

Steven Camp
CFO
IMDb: imdb.com/name/nm3823972

Josh Mills
IMDb: imdb.com/name/nm1836231

Danny Amato
IMDb: imdb.com/name/nm3824734

Jeffrey James Ward
IMDb: imdb.com/name/nm3823932

DESTINY PICTURES

Email: destiny@destinypictures.biz
Home Page: destinypictures.biz
IMDb: imdb.com/company/co0176808
Facebook: facebook.com/pages/Destiny-Pictures/185479521464859

Does not accept any unsolicited material. Preferred genres include Drama, Non-Fiction, and Thriller.

Mark Castaldo
Founder
IMDb: imdb.com/name/nm0144431

Christine Redlin
Executive Producer

DI BONAVENTURA PICTURES

5555 Melrose Ave
DeMille Building, 2nd Floor
Los Angeles, CA 90038

Phone: 323-956-5454
Fax: 323-862-2288

Does not accept any unsolicited material. Project types include Feature Films. Preferred genres include Action, Fantasy, Science Fiction, and Thriller.

Lorenzo di Bonaventura
President
IMDb: imdb.com/name/nm0225146

David Ready
VP (Executive)
IMDb: imdb.com/name/nm2819401

Mark Vahradian
President of Production
(Executive)http://www.imdb.com/name/nm1680607/
IMDb: imdb.com/name/nm1680607

Edward Fee
Director of Development
IMDb: pro.imdb.com/name/nm1825537

Erik Howsam
Senior Vice-President Production
IMDb: imdb.com/name/nm1857184

DI BONAVENTURA PICTURES TELEVISION

500 S Buena Vista St Animation Building, Suite 3F-3
Burbank, CA 91521

IMDb: imdb.com/company/co0341152

Does not accept any unsolicited material. Project types include TV. Preferred genres include Drama, Science Fiction, and Thriller. Established in 2011.

Lorenzo di Bonaventura
Partner
IMDb: imdb.com/name/nm0225146
Assistant: Elizabeth Kiernan

Dan McDermott
Partner
IMDb: imdb.com/name/nm1908145

DIFFERENT DUCK FILMS

18 Wardell Ave.,
Rumson, NJ 07760

Email: DifferentDuckFilms@hotmail.com

Does not accept any unsolicited material. Project types include Feature Films. Preferred genres include Comedy, Drama, Family, Fantasy, and Thriller.

Rob Margolies
IMDb: imdb.com/name/nm1827689

DIMENSION FILMS

99 Hudson St
4th Floor
New York, NY 10013
Phone: 212-845-8600

9100 Wilshire Blvd.
Suite 700W
Beverly Hills, CA 90212
Phone: 424-204-4800

Home Page: weinsteinco.com

Does not accept any unsolicited material. Project types include Feature Films. Preferred genres include Action, Comedy, Horror, Science Fiction, and Thriller.

Bob Weinstein
IMDb: imdb.com/name/nm0918424

Jeff Maynard
IMDb: imdb.com/name/nm0963230

Matthew Signer
IMDb: imdb.com/name/nm1529449

DINO DE LAURENTIIS COMPANY

100 Universal City Plaza Bungalow 5195
Universal City, CA 91608
Phone: 818-777-2111
Fax: 818-886-5566

Email: ddlcoffice@ddlc.net
Home Page: ddlc.net

Does not accept any unsolicited material. Project types include Feature Films and TV. Preferred genres include Action, Crime, Detective, Drama, Horror, Romance, Science Fiction, and Thriller.

Martha De Laurentiis
President
IMDb: imdb.com/name/nm0776646

Lorenzo De Maio
IMDb: imdb.com/name/nm1298951

Stuart Boros
IMDb: imdb.com/name/nm0097214

Bobby Gonzales
IMDb: imdb.com/name/nm5260285

Meryl Pestano
IMDb: imdb.com/name/nm2535378

DINOVI PICTURES

720 Wilshire Blvd, Suite 300
Santa Monica, CA 90401
Phone: 310-458-7200
Fax: 310-458-7211

IMDb: imdb.com/company/co0062957

Accepts scripts from produced or represented writers. Project types include Feature Films. Preferred genres include Drama and Romance. Established in 1993.

Alison Greenspan
President
IMDb: imdb.com/name/nm1327019
Assistant: Rebecca Rajkowski

Denise Di Novi
Producer
IMDb: imdb.com/name/nm0224145
Assistant: Maureen Poon Fear

DMG ENTERTAINMENT

3431 Wesley St.
Suite E
Culver City, CA 90232
Phone: 310-275-3750
Fax: 310-275-3770

Email: info@dmg-entertainment.com
Home Page: h2f-entertainment.com

Accepts query letter from unproduced, unrepresented writers. Project types include Feature Films and TV. Preferred genres include Action, Comedy, Drama, Horror, Romance, Science Fiction, and Thriller.

Chris Cowles
Producer
IMDb: imdb.com/name/nm1038319

DNA FILMS

10 Amwell St
London EC1R 1UQ
Phone: +44 020-7843-4410
Fax: +44 020-7843-4411

Email: info@dnafilms.com
Home Page: dnafilms.com

Does not accept any unsolicited material. Project types include Feature Films. Preferred genres include Comedy, Crime, Drama, Horror, Romance, and Thriller. Established in 1999.

Andrew Macdonald
Partner
Phone: +44 020 7843 4410
IMDb: imdb.com/name/nm0531602

Allon Reich
Partner
Phone: +44 020 7843 4410
IMDb: imdb.com/name/nm0716924

DOBRE FILMS

Phone: 310-926-6439

Email: dobrefilms@dobrefilms.com
Home Page: dobrefilms.com

Accepts scripts from unproduced, unrepresented writers. Project types include Feature Films and TV. Preferred genres include Action, Comedy, Crime, Detective, Drama, Fantasy, Horror, Myth, Romance, and Science Fiction.

Christopher D'Elia
Producer
Phone: 310-926-6439
Email: cdelia@dobrefilms.com
IMDb: imdb.com/name/nm3179988

Michael Klein
Producer
Phone: 323-510-0818
Email: mklein@dobrefilms.com
IMDb: imdb.com/name/nm3180840

DONNERS' COMPANY

9465 Wilshire Blvd
Ste 430
Beverly Hills, CA 90212
Phone: 310-777-4600
Fax: 310-777-4610

Home Page: donnerscompany.com

Does not accept any unsolicited material. Project types include Feature Films. Preferred genres include Action, Fantasy, and Science Fiction.

Richard Donner
Principle
IMDb: imdb.com/name/nm0001149

Drew Cooke
Director of Development

DOUBLE FEATURE FILMS

8425 W 3rd St.
Suite 201
Los Angeles, CA 90048
Phone: 310-887-1100

Email: dffproducerdesk@gmail.com

Does not accept any unsolicited material. Project types include Feature Films. Preferred genres include Action, Comedy, Drama, Fantasy, Myth, and Thriller. Established in 2005.

Ameet Shukla
Creative Executive
IMDb: imdb.com/name/nm2627415

Michael Shamberg
IMDb: imdb.com/name/nm0787834

Stacey Sher
IMDb: imdb.com/name/nm0792049

Taylor Latham
IMDb: imdb.com/name/nm2281897

DOUBLE NICKEL ENTERTAINMENT

234 W 138th St
New York, NY 10030
Phone: 646-435-4390
Fax: 212-694-6205

311 N. Robertson Blvd.
Suite 385
Beverly Hills, CA 90211

Email: admin@doublenickelentertainment.com
Home Page: doublenickelentertainment.com

Accepts query letter from unproduced, unrepresented writers via email. Project types include Feature Films. Preferred genres include Drama.

Jenette Kahn
IMDb: imdb.com/name/nm1986495

Adam Richman
IMDb: imdb.com/name/nm0725013

Adam Callan
Creative Executive
IMDb: imdb.com/name/nm2565555

D. PETRIE PRODUCTIONS, INC.

13201 Haney Place
Los Angeles, CA 90049
Phone: 310-394-2608
Fax: 310-395-8530

Email: dgpetrie@aol.com

Accepts query letter from unproduced, unrepresented writers via email. Project types include TV. Preferred genres include Drama.

Dorothea Petrie
Phone: 310-394-2608
Email: dgpetrie@aol.com
IMDb: imdb.com/name/nm0677955
Assistant: John Cockrell

June Petrie
Phone: 310-394-2608
IMDb: imdb.com/name/nm0677968

DREAMBRIDGE FILMS

207 W 25th St
6th Floor
New York, NY 10001
Phone: 323-927-1907

Home Page: dreambridgefilms.com
IMDb: imdb.com/company/co0248660

Accepts query letter from unproduced, unrepresented writers. Project types include Feature Films. Preferred genres include Comedy, Drama, and Family.

Todd J. Labarowski
President
Email: todd27@mac.com
IMDb: imdb.com/name/nm1132640

DREAMWORKS ANIMATION

1000 Flower St
Glendale, CA 91201
Phone: 818-695-5000
Fax: 818-695-3510

Home Page: dreamworksanimation.com
IMDb: imdb.com/company/co0129164

Does not accept any unsolicited material. Project types include Feature Films, Short Films, TV, and Video Games. Preferred genres include Action, Animation, Comedy, Documentary, Family, Fantasy, Horror, and Science Fiction. Established in 2004.

Suzanne Buirgy
Production Executive
IMDb: imdb.com/name/nm1330174

Bill Damaschke
Chief Creative Officer
IMDb: imdb.com/name/nm0198632

Gregg Taylor
Head of Development
Assistant: Diana Theobald
Diana.Theobald@dreamworks.com

Kyle Arthur Jefferson
Director
IMDb: imdb.com/name/nm2200868

Ben Cawood
Creative Executive
IMDb: imdb.com/name/nm1374730

Karen Foster
Development Executive
IMDb: imdb.com/name/nm2259946

Jeffrey Katzenberg
IMDb: imdb.com/name/nm0005076

Chris Kuser
Senior Executive (Development)
IMDb: imdb.com/name/nm1936914
Assistant: Beth Cannon

Damon Ross
Senior Executive (Development)
IMDb: imdb.com/name/nm1842613

Nancy Bernsein
IMDb: imdb.com/name/nm0077110

Tom McGrath
IMDb: imdb.com/name/nm0569891

Jeffrey Wike
IMDb: imdb.com/name/nm5204969

Amie Karp
Creative Executive (Development)
IMDb: imdb.com/name/nm2047897

DREAMWORKS STUDIOS

100 Universal City Plaza
Building 5121
Universal City, CA 91608
Phone: 818-733-7000

Email: info@dreamworksstudios.com
Home Page: dreamworksstudios.com
IMDb: imdb.com/company/co0252576

Does not accept any unsolicited material. Project types include Feature Films and TV. Preferred genres include Action, Comedy, Crime, Drama, Fantasy, Period, Romance, Science Fiction, and Thriller.

Steven Spielberg
Chairman
IMDb: imdb.com/name/nm0000229

Mia Maniscalco
Creative Executive
Email: mia_maniscalco@dreamworksstudios.com
IMDb: imdb.com/name/nm4103271

Holly Bario
President
Email: info@wif.org
IMDb: imdb.com/name/nm2302370

DUNE ENTERTAINMENT

2121 Ave of the Stars
Suite 2570
Los Angeles, CA 90067
Phone: 310-432-2288

623 Fifth Ave.
New York, NY 10022
Phone: 212-301-8400

Does not accept any unsolicited material. Project types include Feature Films. Preferred genres include Action, Comedy, Drama, Fantasy, Horror, Romance, Science Fiction, and Thriller.

Greg Coote

Wendy Weller
IMDb: imdb.com/name/nm2956152

Larry Bernstein
IMDb: imdb.com/name/nm2955628

DUPLASS BROTHERS PRODUCTIONS

902 E Fifth St
Austin, TX 78702

Email: info@duplassbrothers.com
Home Page: duplassbrothers.com

Accepts query letter from unproduced, unrepresented writers via email. Project types include Feature Films. Preferred genres include Comedy, Drama, Horror, and Thriller.

Jay Duplass
Producer
IMDb: imdb.com/name/nm0243231

Mark Duplass
Producer
IMDb: imdb.com/name/nm0243233

Stephanie Langhoff
Producer
IMDb: imdb.com/name/nm1293297

EALING STUDIOS

Ealing Studios
Ealing Green
London, England W5 5EP
Phone: +44-0-20-8567-6655
Fax: +44-0-20-8758-8658

Email: info@ealingstudios.com
Home Page: ealingstudios.com

Does not accept any unsolicited material. Project types include Feature Films and TV. Preferred genres include Comedy, Documentary, Drama, Family, Romance, and Thriller.

Sophie Meyer
Head of Development
IMDb: mdb.com/name/nm1623306

Nic Martin
Development Executive

Barnaby Thompson
IMDb: imdb.com/name/nm0859877

James Spring
IMDb: imdb.com/name/nm2020191

ECHO BRIDGE ENTERTAINMENT

8383 Wilshire Blvd, Suite 530
Beverly Hills, CA 90211
Phone: 323-658-7900
Fax: 323-658-7922

Email: info@ebellc.com
Home Page: echobridgeentertainment.com

Does not accept any unsolicited material. Project types include Feature Films. Preferred genres include Action, Detective, Drama, Fantasy, Horror, Romance, Science Fiction, and Thriller.

Leonard Shapiro
Email: lshapiro@ebellc.com
IMDb: imdb.com/name/nm0788558

Bobby Rock
Email: brock@echobridgehe.com
IMDb: imdb.com/name/nm0734148

ECHO FILMS

c/o Allen Keshishian/Brillstein Entertainment Partners
9150 Wilshire Blvd, Suite 350
Beverly Hills, CA 90212
Phone: 323-935-2909

Does not accept any unsolicited material. Project types include Feature Films. Preferred genres include Comedy, Drama, and Romance.

Jennifer Aniston
Producer

Kristin Hahn
Producer

ECHO LAKE ENTERTAINMENT

421 S Beverly Dr,
6th Floor
Beverly Hills, CA 90212
Phone: 310-789-4790
Fax: 310-789-4791

Email: contact@echolakeproductions.com
Home Page: echolakeproductions.com

Does not accept any unsolicited material. Project types include Feature Films and TV. Preferred genres include Drama, Non-Fiction, Reality, and Thriller.

Douglas Mankoff
President
IMDb: imdb.com/name/nm0542551

Ida Diffley
Director of Development
IMDb: imdb.com/name/nm3000066

Andrew Spaulding
IMDb: imdb.com/name/nm1051748

Jessica Staman
IMDb: imdb.com/name/nm1698445

James Smith

ECLECTIC PICTURES

7119 Sunset Blvd, Suite 375
Los Angeles, CA 90046
Phone: 323-656-7555
Fax: 323-848-7761

Email: info@eclecticpictures.com
Home Page: eclecticpictures.com

Accepts query letter from unproduced, unrepresented writers via email. Project types include Feature Films.

John Yarincik
Email: john@eclecticpictures.com
IMDb: imdb.com/name/nm2432490

EDEN ROCK MEDIA, INC.

1416 N LaBrea Ave
Hollywood, CA 90028
Phone: 323-802-1718
Fax: 323-802-1832

Email: taugsberger@edenrockmedia.com
Home Page: edenrockmedia.com

Does not accept any unsolicited material. Project types include Feature Films, TV, and Commercials. Preferred genres include Crime, Drama, Family, Non-Fiction, Science Fiction, and Thriller.

Thomas Ausberger
Producer
IMDb: imdb.com/name/nm0041835

EDMONDS ENTERTAINMENT

1635 N Cahuenga Blvd, 6th Floor
Los Angeles, CA 90028
Phone: 323-860-1550
Fax: 323-860-1537

Home Page: edmondsent.com/site/main.html

Accepts scripts from produced or represented writers. Project types include Feature Films and TV. Preferred genres include Drama, Family, Non-Fiction, Reality, and Romance.

Sheila Ducksworth

Tracey Edmonds
IMDb: imdb.com/name/nm0249525
Assistant: Amy Ficken

Kenneth Edmonds
IMDb: imdb.com/name/nm0004892

EDWARD R. PRESSMAN FILM CORPORATION

1639 11th St, Suite 251
Santa Monica, CA 90404
Phone: 310-450-9692
Fax: 310-450-9705

Home Page: pressman.com/default.asp.html

Does not accept any unsolicited material. Project types include Feature Films. Preferred genres include Action, Comedy, Drama, Fantasy, Myth, and Thriller. Established in 1969.

Edward Pressman
IMDb: imdb.com/name/nm0696299
Assistant: Danielle Halagarda

Jon Katz
IMDb: imdb.com/name/nm1853997

Sarah Ramey
Phone: 212-489-3333
IMDb: imdb.com/name/nm2269975

EDWARD SAXON PRODUCTIONS

1526 14th St #105
Santa Monica, CA 90404
Phone: 310-893-0903

Email: esaxon@saxonproductions.net
Home Page: saxonproductions.net

Accepts query letter from unproduced, unrepresented writers via email. Project types include Feature Films and TV. Preferred genres include Action, Drama, Family, Non-Fiction, and Romance.

Ed Saxon
Producer
IMDb: imdb.com/name/nm0768324

EFISH ENTERTAINMENT, INC.

4236 Arch St, Suite 407
Studio City, CA 91604
Phone: 818-509-9377

Email: info@efishentertainment.com
Home Page: efishentertainment.com

Accepts query letter from unproduced, unrepresented writers via email. Project types include Feature Films. Preferred genres include Action, Crime, Horror, and Science Fiction. Established in 2009.

Brianna Johnson
Email: briannaasst@efishentertainment.com
IMDb: imdb.com/name/nm3776636

Eric Fischer
Email: ericasst@efishentertainment.com
IMDb: imdb.com/name/nm2737789
Assistant: Tatjana Bluchel

Mike Williams
Email: mikeasst@efishentertainment.com
IMDb: imdb.com/name/nm3552724

EGO FILM ARTS

80 Niagara St
Toronto, ON M5V 1C5
Phone: 416-703-2137

Email: questions@egofilmarts.com
Home Page: egofilmarts.com

Does not accept any unsolicited material. Project types include Feature Films and TV. Preferred genres include Action, Comedy, Crime, Documentary, Drama, Horror, Romance, and Thriller.

Atom Egoyan
Founder
IMDb: imdb.com/name/nm0000382

EIGHTH SQUARE ENTERTAINMENT

606 N Larchmont Blvd, Suite 307
Los Angeles, CA 90004
Phone: 323-469-1003
Fax: 323-469-1516

Does not accept any unsolicited material. Project types include Feature Films, TV, and Theater. Preferred genres include Comedy, Crime, Drama, and Thriller.

Jeff Melnick
Producer
IMDb: imdb.com/name/nm0578179

ELECTRIC CITY ENTERTAINMENT

8409 Santa Monica Blvd
West Hollywood, CA 90069
Phone: 323-654-7800
Fax: 323-654-7808

Home Page: electriccityent.com

Accepts query letter from unproduced, unrepresented writers via email. Project types include Feature Films. Preferred genres include Comedy, Drama, and Romance. Established in 2012.

Lynette Howell
IMDb: imdb.com/name/nm1987578
Assistant: Jess Engel

Jamie Patricof
IMDb: imdb.com/name/nm1364232
Assistant: Jack Hart

Katie McNeill
IMDb: imdb.com/name/nm3336352

Crystal Powell
IMDb: imdb.com/name/nm2476235

ELECTRIC DYNAMITE

1741 Ivar Ave
Los Angeles, CA 90028
Phone: 323-790-8040
Fax: 818-733-2651

Home Page: electricdynamite.com
IMDb: imdb.com/company/co0190357

Accepts query letter from unproduced, unrepresented writers. Project types include Feature Films, TV, and Commercials. Preferred genres include Comedy, Fantasy, and Science Fiction.

Jack Black
Phone: 323-790-8000
IMDb: imdb.com/name/nm0085312

Priyanka Mattoo
IMDb: imdb.com/name/nm3339192

ELECTRIC ENTERTAINMENT

940 N Highland Ave, Suite A
Los Angeles, CA 90038
Phone: 323-817-1300
Fax: 323-467-7155

Home Page: electric-entertainment.com

Does not accept any unsolicited material. Project types include Feature Films, TV, and Commercials. Preferred genres include Action, Animation, Comedy, Drama, Non-Fiction, Reality, Science Fiction, and Thriller.

Dean Devlin
President
IMDb: imdb.com/name/nm0002041
Assistant: Chase Friedman

Rachel Olschan
IMDb: imdb.com/name/nm1272673

Marc Roskin
IMDb: imdb.com/name/nm0743059

ELECTRIC FARM ENTERTAINMENT

3000 Olympic Blvd
Building 3, Suite 1366
Santa Monica, CA 90404
Phone: 310-264-4199
Fax: 310-264-4196

Email: contact@electricfarment.com
Home Page: ef-ent.com

Accepts query letter from unproduced, unrepresented writers via email. Project types include Feature Films, TV, and Commercials. Preferred genres include Action, Drama, Fantasy, and Science Fiction.

Stan Rogow
Assistant: Allison Lurie

Brent Friedman

ELECTRIC SHEPHERD PRODUCTIONS, LLC

c/o Anonymous Content
3532 Hayden Ave
Culver City, CA 90232
Phone: 310-558-6538

Email: admin@electricshepherdproductions.com
Home Page: electricshepherdproductions.com

Accepts query letter from unproduced, unrepresented writers via email. Project types include Feature Films, TV, and Commercials. Preferred genres include Action, Drama, Fantasy, Myth, Science Fiction, and Thriller.

Kalen Egan

Isa Dick Hackett
IMDb: imdb.com/name/nm2357313

Laura Leslie

ELEMENT PICTURES

21 Mespil Rd
Dublin 4
Ireland
Phone: 353-1-618-5032
Fax: 353-1-664-3737

Email: info@elementpictures.ie
Home Page: elementpictures.ie

Does not accept any unsolicited material. Project types include Feature Films and TV. Preferred genres include Action, Comedy, Documentary, Drama, Horror, and Science Fiction.

Lee Magiday
Producer
IMDb: imdb.com/name/nm3717662

Emma Norton
Head of Development
IMDb: imdb.com/name/nm4499999

Ed Guiney
IMDb: imdb.com/name/nm0347384

Andrew Lowe
IMDb: imdb.com/name/nm1103466

ELEPHANT EYE FILMS

89 Fifth Ave
Ste 306
New York, NY 10003
Phone: 212-488-8877
Fax: 212-488-8878

Email: info@elephanteyefilms.com
Home Page: elephanteyefilms.com

Does not accept any unsolicited material. Project types include Feature Films. Preferred genres include Action, Comedy, Drama, Fantasy, and Non-Fiction.

Kim Jose
Email: Kim@elephanteyefilms.com

Dave Robinson
Email: Dave@elephanteyefilms.com

Toni Branson
Email: Toni@elephanteyefilms.com

ELEVATE ENTERTAINMENT

6255 W Sunset Blvd Suite 800
Los Angeles, CA 90028
Phone: 310-788-3490
Fax: 323-848-9867

Email: info@elevate-ent.com
Home Page: elevate-ent.com

Accepts query letter from unproduced, unrepresented writers via email. Project types include Feature Films and TV. Preferred genres include Action, Animation, Comedy, Crime, Drama, Family, Fantasy, Non-Fiction, Romance, and Science Fiction.

Alex Cole
Phone: 310-557-0100
Email: acole@elevate-ent.com
IMDb: imdb.com/name/nm2251162
Assistant: Stephen Hale

Jenny M. Wood
Phone: 323-951-9310
Email: jwood@elevate-ent.com

ELIXIR FILMS

8033 W Sunset Blvd, Suite 867
West Hollywood, CA 90046
Phone: 323-848-9867
Fax: 323-848-5945

Email: info@elixirfilms.com
Home Page: elixirfilms.com

Does not accept any unsolicited material. Project types include Feature Films. Preferred genres include Drama and Family.

David Alexanian
Producer

Alexis Alexanian
Producer
Assistant: Joe Brinkman

ELKINS ENTERTAINMENT

8306 Wilshire Blvd
PMB 3643
Beverly Hills, CA 90211
Phone: 323-932-0400
Fax: 323-932-6400

Email: info@elkinsent.com
Home Page: elkinsent.com

Accepts query letter from unproduced, unrepresented writers via email. Project types include Feature Films and TV. Preferred genres include Comedy, Drama, Non-Fiction, Reality, and Romance.

Sandi Love

EMBASSY ROW, LLC

325 Hudson St
Ste 601
New York, NY 10013
Phone: 212-507-9700
Fax: 212-507-9701

6565 Sunset Blvd Suite 200
Los Angeles, CA 90028
Phone: 323-417-6560
Fax: 323-469-0015

Email: info@embassyrow.com
Home Page: embassyrow.com

Does not accept any unsolicited material. Project types include Feature Films, TV, and Commercials. Preferred genres include Action, Comedy, Drama, Fantasy, Non-Fiction, Reality, and Science Fiction.

Michael Davies

Tammy Johnston

EMBER ENTERTAINMENT GROUP

11718 Barrington Court, Suite 116
Los Angeles, CA 90049
Phone: 310-230-9759
Fax: 310-589-4850

Email: eeg.bronson@verizon.net

Accepts query letter from unproduced, unrepresented writers via email. Project types include Feature Films and TV. Preferred genres include Action, Comedy, Drama, Fantasy, and Science Fiction.

T.S. Goldberg

J.A. Keller

Lindsay Dunlap
Producer
IMDb: imdb.com/name/nm0242397

Randall Frakes
President
IMDb: imdb.com/name/nm0289696

EMERALD CITY PRODUCTIONS, INC.

c/o Stankevich-Gochman
9777 Wilshire Blvd, Suite 550
Beverly Hills, CA 90212
Phone: 310-859-8825
Fax: 310-859-8830

Does not accept any unsolicited material. Project types include Feature Films. Preferred genres include Drama, Fantasy, and Science Fiction.

Barrie M. Osborne
Producer
IMDb: imdb.com/name/nm0651614

EM MEDIA

Antenna Media Centre
Beck St
Nottingham
NG1 1EQ
Phone: +44-115-993-23-33

Email: info@em-media.org.uk
Home Page: em-media.org.uk

Accepts query letter from unproduced, unrepresented writers. Project types include Feature Films. Preferred genres include Comedy, Drama, and Romance. Established in 2002.

Debbie Williams
CEO
Phone: 0115-993-2333
Email: Debbie.Williams@em-media.org.uk
IMDb: imdb.com/name/nm3527737

Anna Seifert-Speck
Development Executive
IMDb: imdb.com/name/nm3527106

Suzanne Alizart
Email: Suzanne.Alizart@em-media.org
IMDb: imdb.com/name/nm2355251

John Tobin
IMDb: imdb.com/name/nm3527690

ENDEMOL ENTERTAINMENT

9255 W Sunset Blvd
Suite 1100
Los Angeles, CA 90069
Phone: 310-860-9914
Fax: 310-860-0073

Home Page: endemolusa.tv

Accepts query letter from produced or represented writers. Project types include TV. Preferred genres include Comedy, Drama, and Reality.

Michael Weinberg

David Goldberg
Chairman
IMDb: imdb.com/name/nm2499880

Aaron Bilgrad

Caroline Baumgard
IMDb: imdb.com/name/nm0062313

Rob Day
IMDb: imdb.com/name/nm1691117

Jeremy Gold
IMDb: imdb.com/name/nm0325005

Noah Beery

Dave Hamilton

Sean Loughlin

Chris Dickie

ENDGAME ENTERTAINMENT

9100 Wilshire Blvd, Suite 100W
Beverly Hills, CA 90212
Phone: 310-432-7300
Fax: 310-432-7301

Email: reception@endgameent.com
Home Page: endgameent.com

Does not accept any unsolicited material. Project types include Feature Films, TV, and Theater. Preferred genres include Action, Animation, Comedy, Crime,

Detective, Drama, Non-Fiction, Reality, Romance, Science Fiction, and Thriller.

Adam Del Deo
IMDb: imdb.com/name/nm0215534

Lucas Smith
IMDb: imdb.com/name/nm0809156

James Stern
IMDb: imdb.com/name/nm0827726

Julie Goldstein
IMDb: imdb.com/name/nm0326252

ENERGY ENTERTAINMENT

9107 Wilshire Blvd Suite #600
Beverly Hills, CA 90212
Phone: 310-746-4872

Email: info@energyentertainment.net
Home Page: energyentertainment.net

Does not accept any unsolicited material. Project types include Feature Films. Preferred genres include Comedy, Drama, Fantasy, Horror, Non-Fiction, Science Fiction, and Thriller. Established in 2001.

Angelina Chen
Manager

Brooklyn Weaver
IMDb: imdb.com/name/nm0915819
Assistant: David Binns

Michelle Arenal

ENTERTAINMENT ONE GROUP

9465 Wilshire Blvd, Suite 500
Los Angeles, CA 90212
Phone: 310-407-0960

Email: eonetv@entonegroup.com
Home Page: entonegroup.com

Does not accept any unsolicited material. Project types include Feature Films, TV, and Commercials. Preferred genres include Animation, Comedy, Drama, Family, Horror, Non-Fiction, Reality, Romance, and Thriller.

Michael Rosenberg

Jeff Hevert

ENTITLED ENTERTAINMENT

2038 Redcliff St
Los Angeles, CA 90039
Phone: 323-469-9000
Fax: 323-660-5292

Home Page: entitledentertainment.com/index.html

Does not accept any unsolicited material. Project types include Feature Films, TV, and Theater. Preferred genres include Comedy, Crime, Drama, Family, and Non-Fiction.

James Burke
Partner
IMDb: imdb.com/name/nm0121711

Scott Disharoon
Partner
IMDb: imdb.com/name/nm0228318

ENVISION MEDIA ARTS

5555 Melrose Ave
Building 221, Suite 110
Los Angeles, CA 90038
Phone: 323-956-9687
Fax: 323-862-2205

Email: info@envisionma.com
Home Page: envisionma.com

Accepts query letter from unproduced, unrepresented writers via email. Project types include Feature Films and TV. Preferred genres include Action, Comedy, Drama, Family, Fantasy, Myth, and Romance. Established in 2002.

Lee Nelson
CEO
Email: lnelson@envisionma.com
IMDb: imdb.com/name/nm0625540

David Buelow
Email: dbuelow@envisionma.com
IMDb: imdb.com/name/nm2149164

David Tish
Director of Development
Email: dtish@envisionma.com
IMDb: imdb.com/name/nm2953843

EPIC LEVEL ENTERTAINMENT, LTD.

7095 Hollywood Blvd #688
Hollywood, CA 91604
Phone: 818-752-6800
Fax: 818-752-6814

Email: info@epiclevel.com
Home Page: epiclevel.com

Accepts query letter from unproduced, unrepresented writers via email. Project types include Feature Films, TV, and Commercials. Preferred genres include Action, Animation, Fantasy, Horror, Myth, Non-Fiction, Reality, Science Fiction, and Thriller.

Cindi Rice
Producer

Paige Barnett

John Rosenblum
Producer
Email: jfr@jfr.com
IMDb: jfr.com

EPIGRAM ENTERTAINMENT

3745 Longview Valley Rd
Sherman Oaks, CA 91423
Phone: 818-461-8937
Fax: 818-461-8919

Email: epigrament@sbcglobal.net

Accepts query letter from unproduced, unrepresented writers via email. Project types include Feature Films, TV, and Commercials. Preferred genres include Comedy, Drama, and Romance.

Val McLeroy
Partner

Ellen Baskin

EPIPHANY PICTURES, INC.

10625 Esther Ave
Los Angeles, CA 90064
Phone: 310-815-1266
Fax: 310-815-1269

Email: submissions@epiphanypictures.com
Home Page: epiphanypictures.com

Accepts query letter from unproduced, unrepresented writers via email. Project types include Feature Films, TV, and Commercials. Preferred genres include Action, Animation, Comedy, Drama, Family, Fantasy, Myth, Non-Fiction, Reality, Romance, Science Fiction, Sociocultural, and Thriller.

Scott Frank
Email: scott@epiphanypictures.com

Dan Halperin
Phone: 310-452-0242
Email: dan@epiphanypictures.com

Joey DePaolo
Director of Development

EQUILIBRIUM MEDIA COMPANY

1259 S. Orange Grove Ave.
Los Angeles, CA 90019
Phone: 323-939-3555
Fax: 323-939-7523

Email: info@eq-ent.com
Home Page: eq-ent.com
IMDb: imdb.com/company/co0232623

Accepts query letter from unproduced, unrepresented writers. Project types include Feature Films. Preferred genres include Action and Comedy.

Demian Lichtenstein
IMDb: imdb.com/company/co0232623

ESCAPE ARTISTS

10202 W Washington Blvd
Astaire Building, 3rd Floor
Culver City, CA 90232
Phone: 310-244-8833
Fax: 310-204-2151

Email: info@escapeartistsent.com
Home Page: escapeartistsent.com

Does not accept any unsolicited material. Project types include Feature Films and TV. Preferred genres include Action, Comedy, Drama, Fantasy, Myth, Reality, Romance, and Science Fiction.

Todd Black

Email: todd_black@spe.sony.com
IMDb: imdb.com/name/nm0085542

Steve Tisch

Email: steve_tisch@spe.sony.com

Jason Blumenthal

Email: jason_blumenthal@spe.sony.com
IMDb: imdb.com/name/nm0089820

E-SQUARED

531A North Hollywood Way
Suite 237
Burbank, CA 91505
Phone: 818-760-1901

Email: info@e2-esquared.com
Home Page: e2-esquared.com
IMDb: imdb.com/company/co0109424

Accepts query letter from unproduced, unrepresented writers.

Chris Emerson

Email: esquaredasst@sbcglobal.net
IMDb: imdb.com/name/nm0256193

EVENSTART FILMS

Phone: 212-219-2020
Fax: 212-219-2323

Email: info@evenstarfilms.com
Home Page: evenstarfilms.com

Does not accept any unsolicited material. Project types include Feature Films. Preferred genres include Drama.

Elizabeth Cuthrell

Producer
IMDb: imdb.com/name/nm0193876

David Urrutia

Producer
IMDb: imdb.com/name/nm0882102

Jeremy Bloom

Steven Rinehart

EVERYMAN PICTURES

Santa Monica
1512 16th St Suite 3
Santa Monica, CA 90404
Phone: 310-460-7080
Fax: 310-460-7081

Does not accept any unsolicited material. Project types include Feature Films and TV. Preferred genres include Comedy and Drama.

Jay Roach

Email: jay.roach@fox.com
IMDb: imdb.com/name/nm0005366

Jennifer Perini

Assistant: Kristopher Fogel and Lauren Downey

EXCLUSIVE MEDIA

9100 Wilshire Blvd,
Suite 401 East,
Beverly Hills,
Phone: 310-300-9000
Fax: 310-300-9001

Email: info@exclusivemedia.com
Home Page: exclusivemedia.com

Accepts query letter from produced or represented writers. Project types include Feature Films. Preferred genres include Action, Comedy, Crime, Documentary, Drama, Fantasy, Horror, Romance, and Thriller.

Nigel Sinclair

Email: nigelsinclair@spitfirepix.com
IMDb: imdb.com/name/nm0801691
Assistant: Patricia Scott

Guy East

Email: geast@exclusivemedia.com
IMDb: imdb.com/name/nm0247524

EXILE ENTERTAINMENT

732 El Medio Ave.
Pacific Palisades, CA 90272
Phone: 310-573-1523
Fax: 310-573-0109

Email: exile_ent@yahoo.com
IMDb: imdb.com/company/co0063047

Accepts query letter from unproduced, unrepresented writers. Project types include Feature Films. Preferred genres include Comedy, Drama, and Horror.

Gary Ungar

IMDb: imdb.com/name/nm1316083

EXODUS FILM GROUP

1211 Electric Ave
Venice, CA 90291
Phone: 310-684-3155

Email: info@exodusfilmgroup.com
Home Page: exodusfilmgroup.com
IMDb: imdb.com/company/co0080906

Does not accept any unsolicited material. Project types include Feature Films. Preferred genres include Animation, Comedy, and Family.

Max Howard

Producer
Email: max@exodusfilmgroup.com
IMDb: imdb.com/name/nm0397492

EYE ON THE BALL

PO Box 46877
Los Angeles, CA 90046
Phone: 323-935-0634
Fax: 323-935-4188

IMDb: imdb.com/company/co0102936

Accepts query letter from unproduced, unrepresented writers. Project types include Feature Films. Preferred genres include Comedy.

Yareli Arizmendi

Producer
Email: arauarizmendi@aol.com
IMDb: imdb.com/name/nm0034976

Sergio Arau

Producer
Email: keepyoureye@aol.com
IMDb: imdb.com/name/nm0033190

FACE PRODUCTIONS

335 N Maple Dr, Suite 135
Beverly Hills, CA 90210
Phone: 310-205-2746
Fax: 310-285-2386

Does not accept any unsolicited material. Project types include Feature Films. Preferred genres include Action, Comedy, and Drama.

Billy Crystal

IMDb: imdb.com/name/nm0000345
Assistant: Kia Hellman

Samantha Sprecher

IMDb: imdb.com/name/nm0819616
Assistant: Kia Hellman

FAKE EMPIRE FEATURES

5555 Melrose Ave
Marx Brothers Building #207
Hollywood, CA 90038
Phone: 323-956-8766

Accepts scripts from produced or represented writers. Project types include Feature Films. Preferred genres include Comedy, Drama, and Family.

Jay Marcus

Creative Executive
IMDb: imdb.com/name/nm1682408

Lisbeth Rowinski

President
IMDb: imdb.com/name/nm2925164
Assistant: Ritu Moondra

FAKE EMPIRE TELEVISION

400 Warner Blvd
Building 138, Room 1101
Burbank, CA 91522
Phone: 818-954-2420

Home Page: fakeempire.com/about

Accepts scripts from produced or represented writers. Project types include TV. Preferred genres include Comedy, Drama, and Family.

Josh Schwatz
IMDb: imdb.com/name/nm0777300

Leonard Goldstein
IMDb: imdb.com/name/nm2325264
Assistant: Brittany Sever

Stephanie Savage
IMDb: imdb.com/name/nm1335634

Stephanie Savage
IMDb: imdb.com/name/nm1335634
Assistant: Kendall Sand

FALCONER PICTURES

100 Wilshire Blvd. Suite 400
Santa Monica, CA 90401
Phone: 310-452-3350
Fax: 310-388-5910

Home Page: http://www.falconerpictures.com
IMDb: imdb.com/company/co0395531

Does not accept any unsolicited material. Project types include Feature Films. Preferred genres include Action, Comedy, Crime, Drama, and Thriller.

Douglas Falconer
CEO
Email: doug@falconerpictures.com
IMDb: imdb.com/name/nm0266000

Sam Saab
Partner
IMDb: imdb.com/name/nm5668114

FARRELL PAURA PRODUCTIONS

11150 Santa Monica Blvd, Suite 450
Los Angeles, CA 90025
Phone: 310-477-7776
Fax: 310-477-7710

Accepts query letter from unproduced, unrepresented writers via email. Project types include Feature Films. Preferred genres include Comedy, Crime, Drama, and Thriller.

Catherine Paura
Executive

Wayne Kline
Executive

Joseph Farrell
Executive

FASTBACK PICTURES

Phone: 323-469-5719

Email: info@fastbackpictures.com
Home Page: fastbackpictures.com
IMDb: imdb.com/company/co0151624

Accepts query letter from unproduced, unrepresented writers. Project types include Feature Films. Preferred genres include Drama and Thriller.

Pascal Franchot
Producer
Phone: 323-717-5569
Email: pascal@fastbackpictures.com
IMDb: imdb.com/name/nm0289994

FASTNET FILMS

1st Fl
75-76 Camden St Lower
Dublin 2
Ireland
Phone: +353 1 478 9566
Fax: +353 1 478 9567

Email: enquiries@fastnetfilms.com
Home Page: fastnetfilms.com

Does not accept any unsolicited material. Project types include Feature Films. Preferred genres include Documentary, Drama, and Reality.

Megan Everett
Head of Development
IMDb: imdb.com/name/nm3210746

Ian Jackson
Head of Development
IMDb: imdb.com/name/nm4127212

Aoife McGonigal
IMDb: imdb.com/name/nm3502464

FEDORA ENTERTAINMENT

11846 Ventura Blvd
Suite 140
Studio City, CA 91604
Phone: 818-508-5310

Does not accept any unsolicited material. Project types include TV. Preferred genres include Comedy and Drama.

Peter Tolan
Producer
IMDb: imdb.com/name/nm0865847

Michael Wimer
Producer
IMDb: imdb.com/name/nm1057590

Marla A. White
IMDb: imdb.com/name/nm0925187

FILM 360

9111 Wilshire Blvd
Beverly Hills, CA 90210
Phone: 310-272-7000

IMDb: imdb.com/company/co0192833

Does not accept any unsolicited material. Project types include Feature Films. Preferred genres include Action, Comedy, Crime, Drama, Family, Fantasy, Period, Science Fiction, and Thriller. Established in 2009.

Eric Kranzler
Producer
IMDb: imdb.com/name/nm1023394

Daniel Rappaport
Producer
IMDb: imdb.com/name/nm0710883

Scott Lambert
Producer
IMDb: imdb.com/name/nm0483300

FILM 44

1526 Cloverfield Blvd
Santa Monica, CA 90404
Phone: 310-586-4949
Fax: 310-586-4959

Email: info@film44.com
IMDb: imdb.com/company/co0152188

Does not accept any unsolicited material. Project types include Feature Films and TV. Preferred genres include Action, Drama, Fantasy, Myth, Science Fiction, and Thriller.

Peter Berg
Partner
IMDb: imdb.com/name/nm0000916

Rebecca Hobbs
IMDb: imdb.com/name/nm1778008

Braden Aftergood
IMDb: imdb.com/name/nm2302240

FILMCOLONY

4751 Wilshire Blvd Third Floor Los Angeles, CA 90010
Phone: 323-549-4343
Fax: 323-549-9824

Email: info@filmcolony.com
Home Page: filmcolony.com
IMDb: imdb.com/company/co0159642

Does not accept any unsolicited material. Project types include Feature Films and TV. Preferred genres include Comedy, Crime, Drama, Family, Fantasy, Romance, and Thriller. Established in 1998.

Richard Gladstein
President
IMDb: imdb.com/name/nm0321621

Melanie Donkers
Director of Development
IMDb: imdb.com/name/nm1410650

Anand Shah
IMDb: imdb.com/name/nm4337795

FILMDISTRICT

1540 2nd St Suite 200
Santa Monica, CA 90401
Phone: 310-315-1722
Fax: 310-315-1723

Email: info@filmdistrict.com
Home Page: filmdistrict.com
IMDb: imdb.com/company/co0314851

Does not accept any unsolicited material. Project types include Feature Films. Preferred genres include Action, Crime, Drama, Fantasy, Horror, Romance, and Thriller. Established in 2010.

Tim Headington

Partner
IMDb: imdb.com/name/nm2593874

Graham King

Partner
IMDb: imdb.com/name/nm0454752

Josie Liang

IMDb: imdb.com/name/nm4169347

Josh Peters

IMDb: imdb.com/name/nm5444016

Peter Schlessel

IMDb: imdb.com/name/nm0772283
Assistant: Jessica Freenborn

Lia Buman

IMDb: imdb.com/name/nm2513975
Assistant: Patrick Reese

FILM GARDEN ENTERTAINMENT

6727 Odessa Ave
Van Nuys, CA 91406
Phone: 818-783-3456
Fax: 818-752-8186

Home Page: filmgarden.tv
IMDb: imdb.com/company/co0011492

Project types include TV. Preferred genres include Non-Fiction, Period, and Reality.

Eric J. Christensen

Executive

FILM HARVEST

750 Lillian Way, Suite 6
LA, CA 90038
Phone: 310-926-4131
Fax: 323-481-8499

Email: info@filmharvest.com
Home Page: filmharvest.com

Does not accept any unsolicited material. Project types include Feature Films. Preferred genres include Action, Documentary, Drama, Horror, Non-Fiction, Science Fiction, and Thriller. Established in 2009.

Joseph McKelheer

Executive Producer
Email: joe@filmharvest.com
IMDb: imdb.com/name/nm1559624

Eben Kostbar

Producer
Email: eben@filmharvest.com
IMDb: imdb.com/name/nm1670295

Elana Kostbar

Email: info@filmharvest.com
IMDb: imdb.com/name/nm3657939

FILMNATION ENTERTAINMENT

345 N Maple Dr, Suite 202
Beverly Hills, CA 90210
Phone: 310-859-0088
Fax: 310-859-0089

150 W 22nd St.
9th Floor
New York, NY 10011
Phone: 917-484-8900
Fax: 917-484-8901

Home Page: wearefilmnation.com

Accepts query letter from unproduced, unrepresented writers. Project types include Feature Films. Preferred genres include Action, Crime, Drama, Fantasy, Horror, and Thriller. Established in 2008.

Patrick Chu

Director of Development
Email: pchu@wearefilmnation.com
IMDb: imdb.com/name/nm1776958

Glen Basner

Email: gbasner@wearefilmnation.com
IMDb: imdb.com/name/nm0059984

FILM SCIENCE

201 Lavaca St Suite 502
Austin, TX 78701
Phone: 917-501-5197

Email: info@filmscience.com
Home Page: filmscience.com

Accepts query letter from unproduced, unrepresented writers. Project types include Feature Films. Preferred genres include Comedy, Drama, and Family.

Anish Savjani
Executive
Email: anish@filmscience.com
IMDb: imdb.com/name/nm1507013

FILMSMITH PRODUCTIONS

3400 Airport Dr
Bldg D
Santa Monica, CA 90405
Phone: 310-260-8866
Fax: 310-397-7155

Email: filmsmith@mac.com
IMDb: imdb.com/company/co0017423

Accepts query letter from unproduced, unrepresented writers. Project types include Feature Films and TV. Preferred genres include Comedy, Crime, Drama, and Thriller.

Zachary Matz
Producer
IMDb: imdb.com/name/nm0560693

FIRST RUN FEATURES

The Film Center Building, 630 Ninth Ave, Suite 1213
New York City, NY 10036
Phone: 212-243-0600
Fax: 212-989-7649

Email: info@firstrunfeatures.com
Home Page: firstrunfeatures.com
IMDb: imdb.com/company/co0002318

Does not accept any unsolicited material. Project types include Feature Films and Short Films. Preferred genres include Comedy, Drama, Fantasy, Romance, and Thriller. Established in 1979.

Seymour Wishman
President
IMDb: imdb.com/name/nm0936544

Marc Mauceri
IMDb: imdb.com/name/nm1439609

FIVE BY EIGHT PRODUCTIONS

4312 Clarissa Ave
Los Angeles, CA 90027
Phone: 917-658-7545

Home Page: fivebyeight.com

Accepts query letter from unproduced, unrepresented writers via email. Project types include Feature Films and TV. Preferred genres include Drama. Established in 2006.

Michael Connors
Email: mike@fivebyeight.com
IMDb: imdb.com/name/nm2155421

Sean Mullen
Email: sean@fivebyeight.com
IMDb: imdb.com/name/nm2013693

FIVE SMOOTH STONE PRODUCTIONS

106 Oakland Hills Court
Duluth, GA 30097
Phone: 770-476-7171

Home Page: 5ivesmoothstones.com

Does not accept any unsolicited material. Project types include Feature Films. Preferred genres include Action, Drama, and Non-Fiction.

Rick Middlemas
Partner

Morgan Middlemas
Partner

FLASHPOINT ENTERTAINMENT

9150 Wilshire Blvd, Suite 247
Beverly Hills, CA 90212
Phone: 310-205-6300

Email: info@flashpointentertainment.com
Home Page: flashpointent.com

Does not accept any unsolicited material. Project types include Feature Films. Preferred genres include Drama and Romance.

Andrew Tennenbaum
IMDb: imdb.com/name/nm0990025

Tom Johnson
Phone: 310-205-6300
IMDb: imdb.com/name/nm1927361

Laura Roman-Rockhold
Phone: 310-205-6300
Email: info@flashpointent.com
IMDb: imdb.com/name/nm4099178

FLAVOR UNIT ENTERTAINMENT

119 Washington Ave, Suite 400
Miami Beach, FL 33139
Phone: 201-333-4883
Fax: 973-556-1770

155 Morgan St.
Jersey City, NJ 07302

Email: info@flavorunitentertainment.com
Home Page: flavorentertainment.com

Accepts query letter from unproduced, unrepresented writers via email. Project types include Feature Films and TV. Preferred genres include Comedy, Drama, Family, and Romance.

Queen Latifah
CEO
Phone: 201-333-4883
IMDb: imdb.com/name/nm0001451

Otis Best
Phone: 201-333-4883
IMDb: imdb.com/name/nm1454006

Shakim Compere
CEO
Phone: 201-333-4883
IMDb: imdb.com/name/nm1406277
Assistant: Mark Jean

FLOREN SHIEH PRODUCTIONS

20 W 22nd St
Ste 415

New York, NY 10010
Phone: 212-898-0890

Email: katherine@florenshieh.com
IMDb: imdb.com/company/co0287709

Accepts query letter from unproduced, unrepresented writers. Project types include Feature Films. Preferred genres include Drama.

Clay Floren
Producer
IMDb: imdb.com/name/nm2850202

Aimee Shieh
Producer
IMDb: imdb.com/name/nm1848263

FLOWER FILMS INC.

7360 Santa Monica Blvd
West Hollywood, CA 90046
Phone: 323-876-7400
Fax: 323-876-7401

Accepts scripts from produced or represented writers. Project types include Feature Films and TV. Preferred genres include Comedy, Drama, Family, Fantasy, Romance, and Thriller. Established in 1995.

Drew Barrymore
Partner
IMDb: imdb.com/name/nm0000106

Chris Miller
IMDb: imdb.com/name/nm0588091
Assistant: Steven Acosta

Ember Truesdell
Email: ember@flowerfilms.com
IMDb: imdb.com/name/nm1456092

FOCUS FEATURES

100 Universal City Plaza Building 9128
Universal City, CA 91608
Phone: 818-777-7373

Email: press@filminfocus.com
Home Page: focusfeatures.com
IMDb: imdb.com/company/co0042399

Does not accept any unsolicited material. Project types include Feature Films and TV. Preferred genres include Action, Animation, Comedy, Crime, Documentary, Drama, Fantasy, Horror, Non-Fiction, Romance, and Thriller. Established in 1975.

James Schamus
IMDb: imdb.com/name/nm0770005

Jeb Brody
IMDb: imdb.com/name/nm1330162
Assistant: Rebecca Arzoian

Andrew Karpen
IMDb: imdb.com/name/nm2537917

Peter Kujawski
IMDb: imdb.com/name/nm1081654

Josh McLaughlin
IMDb: imdb.com/name/nm2249958

Christopher Koop
IMDb: imdb.com/name/nm3096137

FORENSIC FILMS

1 Worth St, 2nd Floor
New York, NY 10013
Phone: 212-966-1110
Fax: 212-966-1125

Email: forensicfilms@gmail.com

Accepts query letter from unproduced, unrepresented writers via email. Project types include Feature Films. Preferred genres include Comedy, Crime, Drama, Romance, and Thriller.

Scott Macauley
Producer
IMDb: imdb.com/name/nm0531337

Robin O'Hara
Producer
IMDb: imdb.com/name/nm0641327

FORESIGHT UNLIMITED

2934 1/2 Beverly Glen Circle
Suite 900
Bel Air, CA 90077
Phone: 310-275-5222
Fax: 310-275-5202

Email: info@foresight-unltd.com
Home Page: foresight-unltd.com

Accepts query letter from unproduced, unrepresented writers via email. Project types include Feature Films. Preferred genres include Action, Comedy, Crime, Drama, Romance, Science Fiction, and Thriller.

Mark Damon
CEO
IMDb: imdb.com/name/nm0198941

Tamara Birkemoe
IMDb: imdb.com/name/nm1736077

Scott Collette

FOREST PARK PICTURES

11210 Briarcliff Ln
Studio City, CA 91604-4277
Phone: 323-654-2735
Fax: 323-654-2735

Accepts query letter from unproduced, unrepresented writers. Project types include Feature Films. Preferred genres include Drama, Horror, and Thriller. Established in 2002.

Hayden Christensen
Partner
Phone: 323-848-2942 ext. 265
IMDb: imdb.com/name/nm0159789

Tove Christensen
Partner
Phone: 323-848-2942 ext. 265
IMDb: imdb.com/name/nm0159922

FORGET ME NOT PRODUCTIONS

New York

Email: info@4getmenotproductions.com
Home Page: 4getmenotproductions.com

Accepts query letter from unproduced, unrepresented writers via email. Project types include Feature Films. Preferred genres include Drama.

Jennifer Gargano
Email: jennifergargano@4getmenotproductions.com
IMDb: imdb.com/name/nm2470854

Harry Azano
Producer
Email: harryazano@gmail.com

FORTIS FILMS

8581 Santa Monica Blvd, Suite 1
West Hollywood, CA 90069
Phone: 310-659-4533
Fax: 310-659-4373

Accepts query letter from unproduced, unrepresented writers. Project types include Feature Films and TV. Preferred genres include Comedy, Drama, and Romance.

Sandra Bullock
Partner
Phone: 310-659-4533
IMDb: imdb.com/name/nm0000113

Maggie Biggar
Partner
Phone: 310-659-4533
IMDb: imdb.com/name/nm0081772

Bryan Moore

FORTRESS FEATURES

2727 Main St Suite E
Santa Monica, CA 90405
Phone: 323-467-4700
Fax: 310-275-2214

Home Page: fortressfeatures.com

Does not accept any unsolicited material. Project types include Feature Films. Preferred genres include Action, Comedy, Crime, Drama, Horror, and Thriller. Established in 2004.

Brett Forbes
Partner
IMDb: imdb.com/name/nm1771405

Patrick Rizzotti
Partner
IMDb: imdb.com/name/nm0729948

Bonnie Forbes
IMDb: imdb.com/name/nm1424832

FORWARD ENTERTAINMENT

9255 Sunset Blvd, Suite 805
West Hollywood, CA 90069
Phone: 310-278-6700
Fax: 310-278-6770

Accepts query letter from unproduced, unrepresented writers via email. Project types include Feature Films and TV. Preferred genres include Non-Fiction.

Connie Tavel
Partner
Email: ctavel@forward-ent.com
IMDb: imdb.com/name/nm0851679

Vera Mihailovich
Partner
Email: vmihailovich@forward-ent.com
IMDb: imdb.com/name/nm2250568

FORWARD PASS

12233 W Olympic Blvd
Ste 340
Los Angeles, CA 90064
Phone: 310-207-7378
Fax: 310-207-3426

IMDb: imdb.com/company/co0035930

Does not accept any unsolicited material. Project types include Feature Films. Preferred genres include Crime, Detective, Drama, Non-Fiction, Period, Sociocultural, and Thriller.

Michael Mann
IMDb: imdb.com/name/nm0000520

FOURBOYS FILMS

4000 Warner Blvd
Burbank, CA 91522
Phone: 818-954-4378
Fax: 818-954-5359

Email: info@fourboysfilms.com
Home Page: fourboysfilms.com

Does not accept any unsolicited material. Project types include Feature Films and TV. Preferred genres include Animation, Comedy, and Drama.

David Hunt
Partner
IMDb: imdb.com/name/nm0402408

A.J. Morewitz
President
Phone: 818-954-4378
IMDb: imdb.com/name/nm1031450

Patricia Heaton
Partner
IMDb: imdb.com/name/nm0005004

FOX 2000 PICTURES

10201 W Pico Blvd
Building 7B
Los Angeles, CA 90035
Phone: 310-369-2000
Fax: 310-369-4258

Home Page: fox.com

Does not accept any unsolicited material. Preferred genres include Action, Animation, Comedy, Crime, Drama, Family, Fantasy, Horror, Myth, Romance, Science Fiction, and Thriller. Established in 1996.

Elizabeth Gabler
Email: elizabeth.gabler@fox.com
IMDb: imdb.com/name/nm1992894

Riley Kathryn Ellis
Executive
Email: riley.ellis@fox.com

FOX DIGITAL STUDIOS

10201 W Pico Blvd
Los Angeles, CA 90035
Phone: 310-369-1000

Email: david.brooks@fox.com

Accepts query letter from produced or represented writers. Project types include Feature Films and TV. Preferred genres include Comedy, Crime, Drama, Horror, and Thriller.

David Worthen Brooks
Creative Director
IMDb: imdb.com/name/nm3652161

FOX INTERNATIONAL PRODUCTIONS (FIP)

10201 W Pico Blvd
Los Angeles, CA 90035
Phone: 310-369-1000

Home Page: foxinternational.com

Does not accept any unsolicited material. Preferred genres include Action, Crime, Drama, Family, Romance, and Thriller. Established in 2008.

Sanford Panitch
President
Phone: 310-369-1000
Email: sanford.panitch@fox.com
IMDb: imdb.com/name/nm0659529

Anna Kokourina
IMDb: imdb.com/name/nm3916463

Marco Mehlitz
IMDb: imdb.com/name/nm0576438

FOX SEARCHLIGHT PICTURES

10201 W Pico Blvd
Building 38
Los Angeles, CA 90035
Phone: 310-369-1000
Fax: 310-369-2359

Home Page: foxsearchlight.com

Does not accept any unsolicited material. Preferred genres include Action, Comedy, Crime, Drama, Family, Fantasy, Horror, Romance, and Thriller. Established in 1994.

Stephen Gilula
Phone: 310-369-1000
Email: stephen.gilula@fox.com
IMDb: imdb.com/name/nm2322989

FREDERATOR STUDIOS

231 W Olive Ave.
Burbank CA 91504
Phone: 818-736-3606
Fax: 818-736-3449

419 Park Ave South Suite 807
New York City, NY 10016
Phone: 212-779-4113

Email: hey@frederator.com
Home Page: frederator.com

Accepts query letter from unproduced, unrepresented writers via email. Project types include Short Films and TV. Preferred genres include Animation, Comedy, and Family. Established in 1998.

Fred Selbert
Phone: 646-274-4601
Email: fred@frederator.com
IMDb: imdb.com/name/nm0782288
Assistant: Zoe Barton - zoe@frederator.com

Eric Homan
Email: eric@frederator.com
IMDb: imdb.com/name/nm2302704

FREDERIC GOLCHAN PRODUCTIONS

c/o Radar Pictures
10900 Wilshire Blvd, 14th Floor
Los Angeles, CA 90024
Phone: 310-208-8525
Fax: 310-208-1764

Email: fgfilm@aol.com

Does not accept any unsolicited material. Preferred genres include Action, Comedy, Crime, Drama, and Thriller.

Frederic Golchan
Email: asstgolchan@gmail.com
IMDb: imdb.com/name/nm0324907
Assistant: Gaillaume Chiasoda

FRED KUENERT PRODUCTIONS

1601 Hilts Ave. #2
Los Angeles, CA 90024
Phone: 310-470-3363
Fax: 310-470-0060

Accepts query letter from unproduced, unrepresented writers via email. Project types include Feature Films. Preferred genres include Action, Fantasy, Horror, Science Fiction, and Thriller.

Fred Kuenert
Email: fkuehnert@earthlink.net
IMDb: imdb.com/name/nm0473896

Sandra Chouinard
Partner

FREEDOM FILMS

15300 Ventura Blvd. #508
Sherman Oaks, CA 91403
Phone: 818-906-2339
Fax: 818-906-2342

Email: info@freedomfilmsllc.com
Home Page: freedomfilms.com

Does not accept any unsolicited material. Project types include Feature Films. Preferred genres include Action, Crime, Drama, Family, Horror, and Thriller.

Brain Presley
CEO
IMDb: imdb.com/name/nm0696169

Warren Davis
Head of Development

Alexandria Klipstein
Creative Executive
IMDb: imdb.com/name/nm2317077

Carissa Buffel-Matusow

Kevin J Matusow

Scott Robinson
IMDb: imdb.com/name/nm1558904

FRELAINE

8383 Wilshire Blvd
5th Fl
Beverly Hills, CA 90211
Phone: 323-848-9729
Fax: 323-848-7219

IMDb: imdb.com/company/co0176000

Accepts query letter from unproduced, unrepresented writers. Project types include Feature Films. Preferred genres include Action, Fantasy, Period, and Thriller.

James Jacks
Executive
IMDb: imdb.com/name/nm0413208

FRESH & SMOKED

Studio City
10700 Ventura Blvd. Ste. 2D
Studio City, CA 91604
Phone: 818-505-1311
Fax: 818-301-2135

Email: bdtd@freshandsmoked.com
Home Page: freshandsmoked.com

Accepts scripts from unproduced, unrepresented writers. Project types include Feature Films, TV, and Commercials. Preferred genres include Action, Animation, Comedy, Crime, Detective, Drama, Family, Fantasy, Horror, Myth, Non-Fiction, Reality, Romance, Science Fiction, and Thriller.

Monika Gosch
Producer
Email: monika@freshandsmoked.com
IMDb: imdb.com/name/nm2815838

Jeremy Gosch
Director
Email: jeremy@freshandsmoked.com
IMDb: imdb.com/name/nm0331443

Angela McIntyre
Email: angela@freshandsmoked.com

FRIED FILMS

100 N Crescent Dr, Suite 350
Beverly Hills, CA 90210
Phone: 310-694-8150
Fax: 310-861-5454

Accepts query letter from unproduced, unrepresented writers. Project types include Feature Films and TV. Preferred genres include Action, Comedy, Crime, Detective, Drama, Family, Romance, and Thriller. Established in 1990.

Robert Fried
Producer
IMDb: imdb.com/name/nm0294975

Tyrrell Shaffner
Development Executive
Phone: 424-210-3607
IMDb: imdb.com/name/nm1656222

FRIENDLY FILMS

100 N Crescent Dr, Suite 350
Beverly Hills, CA 90210
Phone: 310-432-1818
Fax: 310-432-1801

Email: info@friendly-films.com
Home Page: friendly-films.com

Accepts query letter from unproduced, unrepresented writers. Project types include Feature Films. Preferred genres include Comedy, Crime, Drama, Family, and Science Fiction. Established in 2006.

David Friendly
Phone: 310-432-1800
IMDb: imdb.com/name/nm0295560

FRONT STREET PICTURES

1950 Franklin St
Vancouver, BC V5L 1R2
Canada
Phone: 604-257-4720
Fax: 604-257-4739

Email: info@frontstreetpictures.com
Home Page: frontstreetpictures.com
IMDb: imdb.com/company/co0149567

Accepts query letter from unproduced, unrepresented writers. Project types include Feature Films and TV. Preferred genres include Action, Comedy, Crime, Drama, Fantasy, and Thriller.

Harvey Kahn
Producer
Email: harvey@frontstreetpictures.com
IMDb: imdb.com/name/nm0434838

FR PRODUCTIONS

1531 Colorado Ave.
Santa Monica, CA 90404
Phone: 310-470-9212
Fax: 310-470-4905

Accepts query letter from unproduced, unrepresented writers via email. Project types include Feature Films. Preferred genres include Comedy, Crime, Drama, Family, Romance, and Thriller.

Fred Roos

Email: frprod@earthlink.net
IMDb: imdb.com/name/nm0740407

FULLER FILMS

P.O. BOX 976
Venice, CA 90294
Phone: 310-717-8842

Does not accept any unsolicited material. Project types include Feature Films. Preferred genres include Comedy, Crime, and Drama.

Paul De Souza

Producer
Email: gopics@verizon.net
IMDb: imdb.com/name/nm0996278

Henry Bean

IMDb: imdb.com/name/nm0063785

FUN LITTLE FILMS

2227 W Olive Ave
Burbank, CA 91506
Phone: 323-467-6868

Email: Contact@funlittlemovies.com
Home Page: funlittlemovies.com
IMDb: imdb.com/company/co0161105

Accepts query letter from unproduced, unrepresented writers. Project types include TV. Preferred genres include Animation and Comedy.

Frank Chindamo

President
Email: frank@funlittlemovies.com
IMDb: imdb.com/name/nm0157828

FURST FILMS

8954 W Pico Blvd
2nd Floor
Los Angeles, CA 90035
Phone: 310-278-6468
Fax: 310-278-7401

Email: info@furstfilms.com
Home Page: furstfilms.com

Accepts query letter from unproduced, unrepresented writers via email. Project types include Feature Films and TV. Preferred genres include Action, Crime, Detective, Drama, Horror, Non-Fiction, Reality, and Thriller.

Bryan Furst

Principal/Producer
IMDb: imdb.com/name/nm1227576

Sean Furst

Partner
IMDb: imdb.com/name/nm0299120

FURTHUR FILMS

100 Universal City Plaza
Building 5174
Universal City, CA 91608
Phone: 818-777-6700
Fax: 818-866-1278

Accepts query letter from unproduced, unrepresented writers. Project types include Feature Films. Preferred genres include Comedy, Crime, Drama, Romance, and Thriller.

Michael Douglas

Producer
IMDb: imdb.com/name/nm0000140

Andy Ziskin

FUSEFRAME

2332 Cotner Ave, Suite 200
Los Angeles, CA 90064
Phone: 424-208-1765

Does not accept any unsolicited material. Project types include Feature Films. Preferred genres include Horror and Thriller. Established in 2011.

Marcus Chait

Director of Film and New Media
IMDb: imdb.com/name/nm1483939

Eva Konstantopoulos

IMDb: imdb.com/name/nm2192285

FUSION FILMS

2355 Westwood Blvd, Suite 117
Los Angeles, CA 90064
Phone: 310-441-1496

Email: info@fusionfilms.net
Home Page: fusionfilms.net

Accepts query letter from unproduced, unrepresented writers. Project types include Feature Films and TV. Preferred genres include Action, Animation, Comedy, Crime, Drama, Fantasy, Horror, and Thriller.

John Baldecchi
IMDb: imdb.com/name/nm0049689

Jay Judah
Creative Executive

FUZZY DOOR PRODUCTIONS

5700 Wilshire Blvd
Suite 325
Los Angeles, CA 90036
Phone: 323-857-8826
Fax: 323-857-8945

Does not accept any unsolicited material. Project types include Feature Films and TV. Preferred genres include Animation, Comedy, and Family.

Seth MacFarlane
President
IMDb: imdb.com/name/nm0532235

GAETA ROSENZWEIG FILMS

Santa Monica, CA
Phone: 310-399-7101

Accepts query letter from unproduced, unrepresented writers. Project types include Feature Films and TV. Preferred genres include Comedy, Crime, Drama, Horror, and Thriller.

Alison R. Rosenzweig
Partner
IMDb: imdb.com/name/nm0742851

Michael J. Gaeta
Partner
IMDb: imdb.com/name/nm1357812

GALATEE FILMS

19 Ave de Messine
Paris, France 75008
Phone: +33 1 44 29 21 40
Fax: +33 1 44 29 25 90

Accepts query letter from unproduced, unrepresented writers via email. Project types include Feature Films. Preferred genres include Drama, Non-Fiction, and Romance.

Jacques Perrin
IMDb: imdb.com/name/nm0674742

Nicolas Mauvernay
Producer
IMDb: imdb.com/name/nm1241814

Christophe Barratier
Producer
IMDb: imdb.com/name/nm0056725

GALLANT ENTERTAINMENT

16161 Ventura Blvd, Suite 664
Encino, CA 91436
Phone: 818-905-9848
Fax: 818-906-9965

Email: mog@gallantentertainment.com
Home Page: gallantentertainment.com

Accepts query letter from unproduced, unrepresented writers via email. Project types include Feature Films, TV, and Commercials. Preferred genres include Drama, Family, Non-Fiction, Reality, Romance, and Thriller. Established in 1992.

Michael Gallant
IMDb: imdb.com/name/nm0302572

K.R. Gallant
Email: krg@gallantentertainment.com

GARY HOFFMAN PRODUCTIONS

3931 Puerco Canyon Rd
Malibu, CA 90265
Phone: 310-456-1830
Fax: 310-456-8866

Email: garyhofprods@charter.net

Accepts query letter from unproduced, unrepresented writers via email. Project types include Feature Films and TV. Preferred genres include Action, Comedy, Crime, Drama, Romance, and Thriller.

Gary Hoffman
IMDb: imdb.com/name/nm0388888

Ann Ryan

GARY SANCHEZ PRODUCTIONS

729 Seward St
2nd Fl
Los Angeles, CA 90038
USA
Phone: 323-465-4600
Fax: 323-465-0782

Email: gary@garysanchezprods.com
Home Page: garysanchezprods.com

Does not accept any unsolicited material. Project types include Feature Films and TV. Preferred genres include Comedy.

Will Ferrell
IMDb: imdb.com/name/nm0002071

GENEXT FILMS

5610 Soto St
Huntington Park, CA 90255

Email: contact@genextfilms.com
Home Page: genextfilms.com

Accepts query letter from unproduced, unrepresented writers via email. Project types include Feature Films and TV. Preferred genres include Comedy.

Carlos Salas
IMDb: imdb.com/name/nm2972624
Assistant: Kathy Snyder

Rossana Salas
IMDb: imdb.com/name/nm2970664

GENREBEND PRODUCTIONS

233 Wilshire Blvd, Suite 400
Santa Monica, CA 90401
Phone: 310-860-0878
Fax: 310-917-1065

Email: genrebend@elvis.com

Accepts query letter from unproduced, unrepresented writers via email. Project types include Feature Films and TV. Preferred genres include Comedy and Drama.

David Nutter
IMDb: imdb.com/name/nm0638354

Tom Lavagnino
IMDb: imdb.com/name/nm0491706

GEORGE LITTO PRODUCTIONS

339 N Orange Dr
Los Angeles, CA 90036
Phone: 323-936-6350
Fax: 323-936-6762

Accepts query letter from unproduced, unrepresented writers. Project types include Feature Films. Preferred genres include Action, Comedy, Crime, Drama, Non-Fiction, and Romance. Established in 1997.

George Litto
IMDb: imdb.com/name/nm0514788

Linda Lee

GERARD BUTLER ALAN SIEGEL ENTERTAINMENT / EVIL TWINS

345 N Maple Dr
Beverly Hills, CA 90210
Phone: 310-278-8400

Does not accept any unsolicited material. Project types include Feature Films. Preferred genres include Comedy, Drama, and Thriller.

Danielle Robinson
Director of Development

Gerard Butler
IMDb: imdb.com/name/nm0124930

Alan Siegel
Executive

GERBER PICTURES

4000 Warner Blvd
Building 138, Suite 1202
Burbank, CA 91522

Phone: 818-954-3046
Fax: 818-954-3706

Does not accept any unsolicited material. Project types include Feature Films and TV. Preferred genres include Action, Animation, Comedy, Drama, Family, and Romance.

Bill Gerber
President
IMDb: imdb.com/name/nm0314088
Assistant: James Leffler

GHOST HOUSE PICTURES

315 S Beverly Dr, Suite 216
Beverly Hills, CA 90212
Phone: 310-785-3900
Fax: 310-785-9176

Email: info@ghosthousepictures.com
Home Page: ghosthousepictures.com

Does not accept any unsolicited material. Project types include Feature Films and TV. Preferred genres include Comedy, Drama, Horror, and Thriller.

Sam Raimi
IMDb: imdb.com/name/nm0000600

GIGANTIC PICTURES

New York
207 W 25th St Suite 504
New York, NY 10001
Phone: 212-925-5075
Fax: 212-925-5061

Email: info@giganticpictures.com
Home Page: giganticpictures.com

Accepts query letter from produced or represented writers. Project types include Feature Films and TV. Preferred genres include Comedy, Drama, Non-Fiction, and Romance.

Brian Devine
Founder
IMDb: imdb.com/name/nm0222601

GIL ADLER PRODUCTIONS

c/o Peter Franciosa's office/United Talent Agency
9560 Wilshire Blvd, Suite 500
Beverly Hills, CA 90212

Does not accept any unsolicited material. Project types include Feature Films, TV, and Commercials. Preferred genres include Action, Horror, Non-Fiction, Reality, and Thriller.

Gil Adler
Producer
IMDb: imdb.com/name/nm0012155
Assistant: Ryan Lough

GILBERT FILMS

8409 Santa Monica Blvd.
West Hollywood, CA 90069
Phone: 310-650-6800

IMDb: imdb.com/company/co0084122

Accepts query letter from unproduced, unrepresented writers via email. Project types include Feature Films. Preferred genres include Comedy, Drama, and Family.

Gary Gilbert
President
IMDb: imdb.com/name/nm1344784

Jordan Horowitz
Vice-President, Production and Development
IMDb: imdb.com/name/nm0395302

GIL NETTER PRODUCTIONS

1645 Abbot Kinney Blvd, Suite 320
Venice, CA 90291
Phone: 310-394-1644
Fax: 310-899-6722

Does not accept any unsolicited material. Project types include Feature Films. Preferred genres include Action, Comedy, Drama, Family, and Romance.

Gil Netter
Producer
IMDb: imdb.com/name/nm0626696

Jennifer Ho
Executive

GIRLS CLUB ENTERTAINMENT

30 Sir Francis Drake Blvd
PO Box 437
Ross, CA 94957
Phone: 415-233-4060
Fax: 415-233-4082

Email: info@girlsclubentertainment.com
Home Page: girlsclubentertainment.com

Does not accept any unsolicited material. Project types include Feature Films and TV. Preferred genres include Comedy, Crime, Drama, Non-Fiction, Reality, and Romance.

Jennifer Siebel
Founder
IMDb: imdb.com/name/nm1308076

GITLIN PRODUCTIONS

1310 Montana Ave Second Floor
Santa Monica, CA 90403
Phone: 310-209-8443
Fax: 310-728-1749

Email: gitlinproduction@aol.com

Accepts query letter from unproduced, unrepresented writers via email. Project types include Feature Films and TV. Preferred genres include Action, Comedy, Drama, Non-Fiction, and Reality.

Mimi Gitlin
IMDb: imdb.com/name/nm0689316

Richard Gitlin

GITTES, INC.

Los Angeles
16615 Park Ln Place
Los Angeles, CA 90049
Phone: 310-472-2689

Accepts query letter from unproduced, unrepresented writers. Project types include Feature Films. Preferred genres include Comedy and Drama.

Harry Gittes
Producer
Email: harry_gittes@spe.sony.com
IMDb: imdb.com/name/nm0321228

Edward Wang
Director of Development
Phone: 310-244-4334
Email: edward_wang@spe.sony.com
IMDb: imdb.com/name/nm0910882

GK FILMS

1540 2nd St, Suite 200
Santa Monica, CA 90401
Phone: 310-315-1722
Fax: 310-315-1723

Email: contact@gk-films.com
Home Page: gk-films.com

Does not accept any unsolicited material. Project types include Feature Films and TV. Preferred genres include Action, Animation, Comedy, Crime, Drama, Family, Fantasy, Non-Fiction, Romance, Science Fiction, and Thriller. Established in 2007.

Graham King
CEO
IMDb: imdb.com/name/nm0454752
Assistant: Leah Williams, Michelle Reed

David Crocket
Creative Executive

GLASS EYE PIX

296 Elizabeth St.
Suite BF
New York City, NY 10012
Phone: 718-643-6911

Email: feedback@glasseyepix.com
Home Page: glasseyepix.com

Accepts query letter from unproduced, unrepresented writers via email. Preferred genres include Crime, Drama, Horror, Science Fiction, and Thriller.

Larry Fessenden
Executive
Email: larry@glasseyepix.com
IMDb: imdb.com/name/nm0275244

Brent Kunkle
Executive
Email: brentkunkle@gmail.com
IMDb: imdb.com/name/nm2390962

Peter Phok
Executive
Email: peter@peterphok.com
IMDb: imdb.com/name/nm1490961

GLORY ROAD PRODUCTIONS

23638 Lyons Ave.
Suite #470
Newhall, CA 91321
Phone: 661-367-7545

Email: info@gloryroadproductions.com
Facebook: facebook.com/pages/Glory-Road-Productions/152847784771624?ref=br_tf

Does not accept any unsolicited material. Project types include Feature Films. Preferred genres include Action, Comedy, Drama, Family, Fantasy, and Horror.

Michael Reymann
President
IMDb: imdb.com/name/nm1478831

Erik Elseman
Executive Vice President
IMDb: imdb.com/name/nm4831920

Tara Bonacci
Producer
IMDb: imdb.com/name/nm1742721

Val Mancini
Director of Development
IMDb: imdb.com/name/nm4441689

GOFF-KELLAM PRODUCTIONS

8491 Sunset Blvd, Suite 1000
West Hollywood, CA 90069
Phone: 310-666-9082
Fax: 323-656-1002

Email: info@goffproductions.com
Home Page: goffproductions.com

Accepts query letter from unproduced, unrepresented writers via email. Project types include Feature Films. Preferred genres include Comedy, Drama, Myth, Non-Fiction, Romance, and Thriller. Established in 1998.

Gina Goff
Producer
IMDb: imdb.com/name/nm0324574

Laura Kellam
Producer
IMDb: imdb.com/name/nm0445496

GO GIRL MEDIA

3450 Cahuenga Blvd West #802
Los Angeles, CA 90068
Phone: 310-472-8910
Fax: 818-924-9369

Email: info@gogirlmedia.com
Home Page: gogirlmedia.com

Accepts query letter from unproduced, unrepresented writers via email. Project types include Feature Films and TV. Preferred genres include Animation, Comedy, Drama, Family, Non-Fiction, and Reality. Established in 2004.

Don Priess
IMDb: imdb.com/name/nm1043744

Susie Carter
Email: Susie@gogirlmedia.com
IMDb: imdb.com/name/nm0802053

GOLD CIRCLE ENTERTAINMENT

233 Wilshire Blvd, Suite 650
Santa Monica, CA 90401
Phone: 310-278-4800
Fax: 310-278-0885

Email: info@goldcirclefilms.com
Home Page: goldcirclefilms.com

Does not accept any unsolicited material. Project types include Feature Films. Preferred genres include Action, Comedy, Drama, Family, Horror, Romance, Science Fiction, and Thriller. Established in 2000.

Paul Brooks
President
IMDb: imdb.com/name/nm0112189

Brad Kessell
IMDb: imdb.com/name/nm1733186

GOLDCREST FILMS

65/66 Dean St
London W1D 4PL
United Kingdom
Phone: +44207-437-8696
Fax: +44207-437-4448

799 Washington St.
New York City, NY 10014
Phone: 212-243-4700
Fax: 212-624-1701

Email: info@goldcrestfilms.com
Home Page: goldcrestfilms.com

Does not accept any unsolicited material. Project types include Feature Films and TV. Preferred genres include Animation, Comedy, Drama, Non-Fiction, Reality, and Romance. Established in 1977.

Stephen Johnston
President
IMDb: imdb.com/name/nm1158125

GOLDENRING PRODUCTIONS

4804 Laurel Canyon Blvd
Room 570
Valley Village, CA 91607
Phone: 818-508-7425

Email: info@goldenringproductions.net
Home Page: goldenringproductions.net

Accepts query letter from unproduced, unrepresented writers via email. Project types include Feature Films and TV. Preferred genres include Animation, Comedy, Drama, Family, and Non-Fiction.

Jane Goldenring
IMDb: imdb.com/name/nm0325553

Jon King
Email: jonnyfking@gmail.com

GOLDSMITH-THOMAS PRODUCTIONS

239 Central Park West, Suite 6A
New York, NY 10024
Phone: 212-243-4147
Fax: 212-799-2545

Accepts query letter from unproduced, unrepresented writers. Project types include Feature Films and TV. Preferred genres include Comedy, Drama, Family, Non-Fiction, and Romance.

Elaine Goldsmith-Thomas
IMDb: imdb.com/name/nm0326063
Assistant: Anabel Graff

GOOD HUMOR TELEVISION

9255 W Sunset Blvd #1040
West Hollywood, CA 90069
Phone: 310-205-7361
Fax: 310-550-7962

Accepts query letter from unproduced, unrepresented writers. Project types include TV. Preferred genres include Animation and Comedy.

Tom Werner
IMDb: imdb.com/name/nm0921492

GORILLA PICTURES

2000 W Olive Ave
Burbank, CA 91506
Phone: 818-848-2198
Fax: 818-848-2232

Email: info@gorillapictures.net
Home Page: gorillapictures.net

Does not accept any unsolicited material. Project types include Feature Films. Preferred genres include Action, Animation, Crime, Drama, Family, Fantasy, Science Fiction, and Thriller. Established in 1999.

Bill Gottlieb
CEO
Email: bill.gottlieb@gorillapictures.net
IMDb: imdb.com/name/nm1539281

Don Wilson
Email: don.wilson@gorillapictures.net
IMDb: imdb.com/name/nm0933310

GOTHAM ENTERTAINMENT GROUP

Los Angeles, CA

85 John St Penthouse 1
New York City, NY 10038

Phone: 814-253-5151
Fax: 801-439-6998

Email: newyork@gothamcity.com
Email: losangeles@gothamcity.com
Home Page: gothamentertainmentgroup.com

Accepts query letter from unproduced, unrepresented writers via email. Project types include Feature Films and TV. Preferred genres include Action, Comedy, Crime, Drama, Non-Fiction, Reality, Romance, Science Fiction, and Thriller.

Joel Roodman
Partner
Email: joel@gothamentertainmentgroup.com
IMDb: imdb.com/name/nm0740211

Eric Kopeloff
Partner
IMDb: imdb.com/name/nm0465740

GRACIE FILMS

10201 W. Pico Blvd., Bldg. 41/42 Los Angeles, CA 90064
Phone: 310-369-7222

Email: graciefilms@aol.com
Home Page: graciefilms.com

Does not accept any unsolicited material. Project types include Feature Films and TV. Preferred genres include Animation, Comedy, Drama, Family, Non-Fiction, and Romance.

James Brooks
IMDb: imdb.com/name/nm0000985

Richard Sakai
President
IMDb: imdb.com/name/nm0757017

Julie Ansell
IMDb: imdb.com/name/nm0030572

GRADE A ENTERTAINMENT

149 S Barrington Ave, Suite 719
Los Angeles, CA 90049
Phone: 310-358-8600
Fax: 310-919-2998

Email: development@gradeaent.com
Home Page: gradeaent.com

Accepts query letter from unproduced, unrepresented writers via email. Project types include Feature Films and TV. Preferred genres include Fantasy.

Andy Cohen
Email: andy@gradeaent.com
IMDb: imdb.com/name/nm2221597

GRAMMNET PRODUCTIONS

2461 Santa Monica Blvd #521
Santa Monica, CA 90404
Phone: 310-317-4231
Fax: 310-317-4260

Does not accept any unsolicited material. Project types include Feature Films, TV, and Theater. Preferred genres include Comedy, Drama, Family, Non-Fiction, and Reality.

Stella Bulochnikov
Executive
Phone: 310-255-5089
Assistant: Melissa Panzer, mpanzer@lionsgate.com

Kelsey Grammar
IMDb: imdb.com/name/nm0001288
Assistant: Xochitl L. Olivas

GRAND CANAL FILM WORKS

1187 Coast Village Rd
Montecito, CA 93108
Phone: 818-259-8237

11135 Magnolia, SU 160
North Hollywood, CA 91601

Does not accept any unsolicited material. Project types include Feature Films, TV, and Theater. Preferred genres include Non-Fiction and Reality.

Rick Brookwell
Partner
Email: RBrookwell@GrandCanalFW.com
IMDb: imdb.com/name/nm2162558

Craig Haffner
Partner
Email: CHaffner@GrandCanalFW.com
IMDb: imdb.com/name/nm0353121

GRAND PRODUCTIONS

16255 Venture Blvd, Suite 400
Encino, CA 91436
Phone: 818-981-1497
Fax: 818-380-3006

Email: grandproductions@mac.com

Does not accept any unsolicited material. Project types include Feature Films and TV. Preferred genres include Comedy and Drama.

Gary Randall
IMDb: imdb.com/name/nm0709592

GRAN VIA PRODUCTIONS

1888 Century Park East
14th Floor
Los Angeles, CA 90067
Phone: 310-859-3060
Fax: 310-859-3066

Does not accept any unsolicited material. Project types include Feature Films and TV. Preferred genres include Comedy, Drama, Fantasy, and Science Fiction.

Mark Ceryak
Creative Executive
IMDb: imdb.com/name/nm1641437

Mark Johnson
IMDb: imdb.com/name/nm0425741
Assistant: Emily Eckert (Story Editor)

GRAY ANGEL PRODUCTIONS

69 Windward Ave
Venice, CA 90291
Phone: 310-581-0010
Fax: 310-396-0551

Accepts query letter from unproduced, unrepresented writers. Project types include Feature Films.

Anjelica Huston
IMDb: imdb.com/name/nm0001378

Jaclyn Bashoff
IMDb: imdb.com/name/nm1902472

GRAZKA TAYLOR PRODUCTIONS

409 N Camden Dr, Suite 202
Beverly Hills, CA 90210
Phone: 310-246-1107

Home Page: grazkat.com

Does not accept any unsolicited material. Project types include Feature Films and TV. Preferred genres include Drama, Non-Fiction, Reality, and Romance.

Grazka Taylor
Producer
Email: grazka@grazkat.com
IMDb: imdb.com/name/nm0852429

GREASY ENTERTAINMENT

6345 Balboa Blvd
Building 4, Suite 375
Encino, CA 91316
Phone: 310-586-2300

Email: info@greasy.biz
Home Page: greasy.biz

Accepts query letter from unproduced, unrepresented writers via email. Project types include Feature Films and TV. Preferred genres include Action and Comedy.

Dan Heder
Executive

Jon Heder
IMDb: imdb.com/name/nm1417647

Doug Heder

GREEN HAT FILMS

4000 Warner Blvd
Building 66
Burbank, CA 91522
Phone: 818-954-3210
Fax: 818-954-3214

Does not accept any unsolicited material. Project types include Feature Films. Preferred genres include Comedy, Drama, Non-Fiction, and Thriller.

Mark O'Connor
Director of Development

Todd Phillips
IMDb: imdb.com/name/nm0680846
Assistant: Joseph Garner

Diana Davis-Dyer

GREENSTREET FILMS

430 W Broadway 2nd Floor
New York City, NY 10012
Phone: 212-609-9000
Fax: 212-609-9099

Email: general@gstreet.com
Home Page: greenestreetfilms.com

Accepts query letter from unproduced, unrepresented writers via email. Project types include Feature Films. Preferred genres include Comedy, Drama, Horror, Romance, and Thriller.

John M Penotti
President
IMDb: imdb.com/name/nm0006597

Matthew Honovic
Creative Executive
Email: http://www.imdb.com/name/
nm2416270/?ref_=fn_al_nm_1

GREENTREES FILMS

854-A 5th St
Santa Monica, CA 90403
Phone: 310-899-1522
Fax: 310-496-2082

Email: info@greentreesfilms.com
Home Page: greentreesfilms.com

Accepts query letter from unproduced, unrepresented writers via email. Project types include Feature Films, TV, and Commercials. Preferred genres include Comedy, Drama, Non-Fiction, and Reality.

Jack Binder
IMDb: imdb.com/name/nm0082784

GRINDSTONE ENTERTAINMENT GROUP

2700 Colorado Ave
Suite 200
Santa Monica, CA 90404

Phone: 310-255-5761
Fax: 310-255-3766

Home Page: thegrindstone.net

Accepts query letter from produced or represented writers. Project types include Feature Films. Preferred genres include Action, Drama, Period, and Thriller.

Barry Brooker
President
Email: barry@thegrindstone.net
IMDb: imdb.com/name/nm1633269

Ryan Black
Director of Development
Email: ryan@thegrindstone.net
IMDb: imdb.com/name/nm3337383

Stan Wertlieb
Email: stanwertlieb@gmail.com
IMDb: imdb.com/name/nm0921627

Teresa Sabatine
Email: teresa@thegrindstone.net
IMDb: imdb.com/name/nm3466608

GRIZZLY ADAMS PRODUCTIONS

201 Five Cities Dr SPC 172, Pismo Beach
CA 93449
Phone: 877-556-8536
Fax: 805-556-0393

Home Page: grizzlyadams.com

Does not accept any unsolicited material. Project types include Feature Films and TV. Preferred genres include Documentary, Drama, Family, Non-Fiction, and Reality.

David W. Balsiger
IMDb: imdb.com/name/nm1901322

GROSSO JACOBSON COMMUNICATIONS CORP.

767 Third Ave
New York, NY 10017

373 Front St East
Toronto, Ontario MSA 1G4
Canada

1801 Ave of the Stars, Suite 911
Los Angeles, CA 90067
Phone: 310-788-8900

Email: grossojacobson@grossojacobson.com

Accepts query letter from unproduced, unrepresented writers via email. Project types include Feature Films, TV, and Theater. Preferred genres include Comedy, Crime, Drama, Horror, Non-Fiction, Reality, and Thriller. Established in 1999.

Sonny Grosso
Executive Producer
Phone: 212-644-6909
IMDb: imdb.com/name/nm0343780

Keith Johnson
Sr. VP Development
Phone: 310-788-8900
IMDb: imdb.com/name/nm1702242

GROSS-WESTON PRODUCTIONS

10560 Wilshire Blvd, Suite 801
Los Angeles, CA 90024
Phone: 310-777-0010
Fax: 310-777-0016

Email: gross-weston@sbcglobal.net

Accepts scripts from produced or represented writers. Project types include Feature Films, TV, and Theater. Preferred genres include Action, Comedy, Drama, Family, Non-Fiction, Reality, Romance, Science Fiction, and Thriller.

Mary Gross
Executive Producer
IMDb: imdb.com/name/nm0343437

Ann Weston
Executive Producer
IMDb: imdb.com/name/nm0922912

GROUNDSWELL PRODUCTIONS

12424 Wilshire Blvd.
Suite 1120
Los Angeles, CA 90025
Phone: 310-385-7540
Fax: 310-385-7541

Email: info@groundswellfilms.com
Home Page: groundswellfilms.com

Does not accept any unsolicited material. Project types include Feature Films, TV, and Theater. Preferred genres include Action, Comedy, Crime, Drama, Horror, Non-Fiction, Romance, and Thriller. Established in 2006.

Kelly Mullen
Vice-President
IMDb: imdb.com/name/nm4133402

Janice Williams
IMDb: imdb.com/name/nm1003921

GUARDIAN ENTERTAINMENT, LTD

71 5th Ave
New York, NY 10003
Phone: 212-727-4729
Fax: 212-727-4713

Email: guardian@guardianltd.com
Home Page: guardianltd.com

Accepts query letter from unproduced, unrepresented writers via email. Project types include Feature Films, TV, and Commercials. Preferred genres include Drama, Horror, Non-Fiction, Reality, Science Fiction, and Thriller.

Richard Miller
Email: rmiller@guardianltd.com

Anita Agair
Email: agair@guardianltd.com

GUNN FILMS

500 S Buena Vista St
Old Animation Building, Suite 3-A7
Burbank, CA 91521
Phone: 818-560-6156
Fax: 818-842-8394

Does not accept any unsolicited material. Project types include Feature Films and TV. Preferred genres include Action, Comedy, Drama, Family, Fantasy, Romance, Science Fiction, and Thriller. Established in 2001.

Andrew Gunn
Producer
Email: andrew.gunn@disney.com
IMDb: imdb.com/name/nm0348151

GUY WALKS INTO A BAR

236 W 27th St #1000
New York, NY 10001
Phone: 212-941-1509

Email: info@guywalks.com
Home Page: guywalks.com

Does not accept any unsolicited material. Project types include Feature Films, TV, and Commercials. Preferred genres include Animation, Comedy, Family, Fantasy, Romance, and Science Fiction.

Jonathan Coleman
Director of Development

Todd Komarnicki
IMDb: imdb.com/name/nm0464548

H2O MOTION PITURES

111 E 10th St Suite 8
New York, NY 10003
Phone: 212-533-3923

23 Denmark St
Third Floor
London WC2H 8NH
United Kingdom

317 Warren Rd
Toronto, Ontario, M5P 2M7
Canada
Phone: 416-484-6754
Fax: 416-484-9229

PO Box 990
1000 AZ Amsterdam
The Netherlands
Phone: +44207-240-5656
Fax: +44207-240-5647

Email: h2o@h2omotionpictures.com
Home Page: h2omotionpictures.com

Accepts query letter from unproduced, unrepresented writers via email. Project types include Feature Films.

Andras Hamori
Producer
IMDb: imdb.com/name/nm0358877

HAMMER FILMS

52 Haymarket
London, United Kingdom,
SW1Y 4RP
Phone: +44 20 3002 9510

Email: info@hammerfilms.com
Home Page: hammerfilms.com

Does not accept any unsolicited material. Project types include Feature Films and TV. Preferred genres include Action, Comedy, Documentary, Drama, Horror, and Thriller. Established in 1934.

Simon Oakes
IMDb: imdb.com/name/nm2649227

HANDPICKED FILMS

2893 Sea Ridge Dr
Malibu, CA 90265
Phone: 310-361-6832
Fax: 310 456 1166

Email: info@handpickedfilms.net
Home Page: handpickedfilms.net

Does not accept any unsolicited material. Project types include Feature Films, TV, and Commercials. Preferred genres include Animation, Comedy, Detective, Drama, Horror, Non-Fiction, and Reality. Established in 2005.

Anthony Romano
Producer
IMDb: imdb.com/name/nm0738853

Michel Shane
IMDb: imdb.com/name/nm0788062

Darren VanCleave
Executive
IMDb: imdb.com/name/nm2168166

HANDSOMECHARLIE FILMS

1720-1/2 Whitley Ave
Los Angeles, CA 90028
Phone: 323-462-6013

Does not accept any unsolicited material. Project types include Feature Films. Preferred genres include Action, Comedy, Drama, Non-Fiction, and Romance.

Natalie Portman
President
IMDb: imdb.com/name/nm0000204

Kimberly Barton
Creative Executive

Annette Savitch

HANNIBAL PICTURES

8265 Sunset Blvd, Suite 107
West Hollywood, CA 90046
Phone: 323-848-2945
Fax: 323-848-2946

Email: contactus@hannibalpictures.com
Home Page: hannibalpictures.com
Facebook: facebook.com/pages/Hannibal-Pictures/158994507487285

Accepts query letter from unproduced, unrepresented writers via email. Project types include Feature Films. Preferred genres include Action, Comedy, Crime, Drama, Non-Fiction, Romance, Science Fiction, and Thriller. Established in 1999.

Richard Rionda Del Castro
IMDb: imdb.com/name/nm0215502

Cam Cannon
Director of Development
IMDb: imdb.com/name/nm1359191

Patricia Rionda Del Castro
President

Kristy Eberle-Adams
IMDb: imdb.com/name/nm5554723

HAPPY MADISON PRODUCTIONS

10202 W Washington Blvd Judy Garland Building
Culver City, CA 90232

Phone: 310-244-3100
Fax: 310-244-3353

Home Page: adamsandler.com/happy-madison
IMDb: imdb.com/company/co0059609

Does not accept any unsolicited material. Project types include Feature Films, Short Films, and TV. Preferred genres include Action, Animation, Comedy, Drama, Fantasy, Romance, and Thriller. Established in 1999.

Adam Sandler
Partner
IMDb: imdb.com/name/nm0001191

Jack Giarraputo
Partner
IMDb: imdb.com/name/nm0316406
Assistant: Rachel Simmer

Judit Maull
Executive
IMDb: imdb.com/name/nm1263796

Heather Parry
IMDb: imdb.com/name/nm1009782

Doug Robinson
IMDb: imdb.com/name/nm2120562
Assistant: Brianna Riofrio

Billy Wee

HARPO FILMS, INC.

345 N Maple Dr, Suite 315
Beverly Hills, CA 90210
Phone: 310-278-5559

Does not accept any unsolicited material. Project types include Feature Films and TV. Preferred genres include Comedy, Drama, Fantasy, Horror, Non-Fiction, and Romance.

Oprah Winfrey
IMDb: imdb.com/name/nm0001856

HARTSWOOD FILMS

3A Paradise Rd
Richmond
Surrey
TW9 1RX

Phone: +44 (0) 20-3668-3060
Fax: +44 (0) 20-3668-3050

Nations and Regions Office
17 Cathedral Rd
Cardiff
CF11 9HA
Phone: +44 (0)29-2023-3333
Fax: +44 (0)29-2022-5878

Email: films.tv@hartswoodfilms.co.uk
Home Page: hartswoodfilms.co.uk
IMDb: imdb.com/company/co0023675

Does not accept any unsolicited material. Project types include TV. Preferred genres include Comedy, Crime, Detective, Drama, Horror, and Thriller. Established in 1980.

Elaine Cameron
Head of Development
IMDb: imdb.com/name/nm0131569

Beryl Vertue
Chairman
IMDb: imdb.com/name/nm0895054

Debbie Vertue
General Manager
IMDb: imdb.com/name/nm0895055

Sue Vertue
Producer
IMDb: imdb.com/name/nm0895056

HASBRO, INC./HASBRO FILMS

Burbank
2950 N Hollywood Way Suite 100
Burbank, CA 91504
Phone: 818-478-4320

Home Page: hasbro.com/?US

Accepts query letter from unproduced, unrepresented writers. Project types include Feature Films. Preferred genres include Action, Animation, Comedy, Family, Fantasy, Non-Fiction, and Science Fiction.

Daniel Persitz
Creative Executive
IMDb: imdb.com/name/nm1974626

HAXAN FILMS

PO Box 261370
Encino, CA 91426
USA
Fax: 310-888-4242

Home Page: haxan.com
IMDb: imdb.com/company/co0112898

Accepts query letter from unproduced, unrepresented writers. Project types include Feature Films and TV. Preferred genres include Comedy, Documentary, Drama, Horror, Science Fiction, and Thriller. Established in 2004.

Robin Cowie
Producer
Email: rob@haxan.com
IMDb: imdb.com/name/nm0184770

Eduardo Sánchez
IMDb: imdb.com/name/nm0844896

Gregg Hale
Executive
IMDb: imdb.com/name/nm0354918

Andy Jenkins
IMDb: imdb.com/name/nm1075637

David Saunder
Phone: 310-888-4200

HAZY MILLS PRODUCTIONS

4024 Radford Ave
Building 7 - 2nd Floor
Studio City, CA 91604
Phone: 818-840-7568

Home Page: hazymills.com

Does not accept any unsolicited material. Project types include Feature Films and TV. Preferred genres include Comedy, Drama, Family, Horror, Non-Fiction, and Reality. Established in 2004.

Sean Hayes
IMDb: imdb.com/name/nm0005003
Assistant: Jessie Kalick

Kiel Elliott
Development Executive

HBO FILMS & MINISERIES

2500 Broadway, Suite 400
Santa Monica, CA 90404
Phone: 310-382-3000
Fax: 310-382-3552

Does not accept any unsolicited material. Project types include TV. Preferred genres include Comedy, Drama, Family, Non-Fiction, Romance, and Thriller.

Len Amato
IMDb: imdb.com/name/nm0024163

Kary Antholis
IMDb: imdb.com/name/nm0030794

HDNET FILMS

c/o Magnolia Pictures
49 W 27th St, 7th Fl
New York, NY 10001
USA
Phone: 212-924-6701
Fax: 212-924-6742

IMDb: imdb.com/company/co0094788

Accepts query letter from unproduced, unrepresented writers. Project types include Feature Films and TV. Preferred genres include Comedy, Crime, Documentary, Drama, Reality, Romance, Science Fiction, and Thriller.

HEAVY DUTY ENTERTAINMENT

6605 Hollywood Blvd.
Suite 100
Los Angeles, CA 90028
Phone: 323-209-3545
Fax: 323-653-1720

Email: info@heavydutyentertainment.com
Home Page: heavydutyentertainment.com

Does not accept any unsolicited material. Project types include Feature Films and TV. Preferred genres include Action, Comedy, Drama, Horror, and Science Fiction.

Jeff Balis
Producer
IMDb: imdb.com/name/nm0050276

Rhoades Rader
Producer
IMDb: imdb.com/name/nm0705476

HEEL & TOE PRODUCTIONS

1702 Olympic Blvd.
Studio C
Santa Monica, CA 90404

Does not accept any unsolicited material. Project types include Feature Films and TV. Preferred genres include Action, Drama, and Romance.

Paul Attanasio
Email: paul.attanasio@fox.com
IMDb: imdb.com/name/nm0001921

Katie Jacobs
Email: katie.jacobs@fox.com
IMDb: imdb.com/name/nm0414498

HEMISPHERE ENTERTAINMENT

20058 Ventura Blvd
#316
Woodland Hills, CA 91364
Phone: 818-888-2263
Fax: 818-888-3651

Home Page: hemisphereentertainment.com

Accepts query letter from unproduced, unrepresented writers. Project types include Feature Films. Preferred genres include Action, Crime, Drama, Family, Horror, Romance, and Thriller.

Ralph E. Portillo
IMDb: imdb.com/name/nm1589685

Jamie Elliot
IMDb: imdb.com/name/nm0254242

Brad Wilson
IMDb: imdb.com/name/nm0933085

HENCEFORTH PICTURES

1411 Fifth St, Suite 200
Santa Monica, CA 90401
Phone: 424-832-5517
Fax: 424-832-5564

Does not accept any unsolicited material. Project types include Feature Films and TV. Preferred genres include Action, Crime, Drama, and Thriller.

William Monahan
IMDb: imdb.com/name/nm1184258

Justine Jones
IMDb: imdb.com/name/nm3540960

HENDERSON PRODUCTIONS

4252 Riverside Dr
Burbank, CA 91505
Phone: 818-955-5702
Fax: 818-955-7703

Does not accept any unsolicited material. Project types include Feature Films and Theater. Preferred genres include Comedy, Drama, Family, and Romance.

Garry Marshall
IMDb: imdb.com/name/nm0005190

HEYDAY FILMS

4000 Warner Blvd
Building 81, Room 207
Burbank, CA 91522
Phone: 818-954-3004
Fax: 818-954-3017

Email: office@heydayfilms.com

Does not accept any unsolicited material. Project types include Feature Films and TV. Preferred genres include Action, Comedy, Crime, Drama, and Fantasy.

Jeffrey Clifford
President
IMDb: imdb.com/name/nm0166641
Assistant: Kate Phillips

David Heyman
Partner
IMDb: imdb.com/name/nm0382268
Assistant: Ollie Wiseman (011) 442078366333

HGTV

9721 Sherrill Blvd
Knoxville, TN 37932

Phone: 865-694-2700
Fax: 865-690-6595

Home Page: hgtv.com
IMDb: imdb.com/company/co0004908

Does not accept any unsolicited material. Project types include Feature Films and TV. Preferred genres include Documentary and Reality.

Burton Jablin

Freddy James

Chris Moore

Steven Lerner

Courtney White

HIGH HORSE FILMS

100 Universal City Plaza
Building 2128, Suite E
Universal City, CA 91608
Phone: 323-939-8802
Fax: 323-939-8832

Accepts query letter from unproduced, unrepresented writers. Project types include Feature Films and TV. Preferred genres include Comedy, Drama, and Romance. Established in 1990.

Cynthia Chvatal
Producer
IMDb: imdb.com/name/nm0161558

William Petersen
IMDb: imdb.com/name/nm0676973

HIGH INTEGRITY PRODUCTIONS

11054 Ventura Blvd
Suite 324
Studio City, CA 91604 USA
Phone: 714-313-9606

Home Page: highintegrityproductions.com

Accepts query letter from unproduced, unrepresented writers. Project types include Feature Films. Preferred genres include Animation, Horror, Romance, and Thriller.

Dale Noble

Phone: 909-883-0417
Email: dale@highintegrityproductions.com
IMDb: imdb.com/name/nm2303672

HOLLYWOOD GANG PRODUCTIONS

4000 Warner Blvd
Building 139, Room 201
Burbank, CA 91522
Phone: 818-954-4999
Fax: 818-954-4448

Does not accept any unsolicited material. Project types include Feature Films. Preferred genres include Action, Drama, Fantasy, Science Fiction, and Thriller.

Gianni Nunnari

IMDb: imdb.com/name/nm0638089

HOME BOX OFFICE (HBO)

1100 Ave of the Americas
New York City, New York 10036
Phone: 212-512-1000
Fax: 212-512-5698

2500 Broadway Suite 400
Santa Monica, CA 90404
Phone: 310-382-3000
Fax: 310-201-9293

Home Page: hbo.com
IMDb: imdb.com/company/co0008693

Does not accept any unsolicited material. Project types include Feature Films and TV. Preferred genres include Action, Comedy, Crime, Documentary, Drama, Family, Fantasy, Non-Fiction, Period, Romance, Science Fiction, and Sociocultural. Established in 1972.

HORIZON ENTERTAINMENT

1025 S Jefferson Parkway
New Orleans, LA 70125
Phone: 504-483-1177
Fax: 504-483-1173

Email: jsasst@horizonent.tv
Home Page: horizonent.tv
IMDb: imdb.com/company/co0225725

Accepts query letter from unproduced, unrepresented writers. Project types include Feature Films and TV. Preferred genres include Action, Comedy, Crime, Drama, Family, Reality, Romance, and Thriller. Established in 2000.

Jason Sciavicco
Executive Producer
IMDb: imdb.com/name/nm2217296

Melissa Dembrun Sciavicco
IMDb: imdb.com/name/nm2847926

HUGHES CAPITAL ENTERTAINMENT

22817 Ventura Blvd, Suite 471
Woodland Hills, CA 91364
Phone: 818-484-3205

Email: info@trihughes.com
Home Page: trihughes.com

Accepts scripts from produced or represented writers. Project types include Feature Films. Preferred genres include Action, Comedy, Drama, Family, and Romance.

Jacob Clymore
Email: jc@trihughes.com

Patrick Hughes
IMDb: imdb.com/name/nm1449018

HUTCH PARKER ENTERTAINMENT

204 Santa Monica Blvd Suite A
Santa Monica, CA 90401

Email: hutchparkerentertainment@gmail.com

Accepts scripts from produced or represented writers. Project types include Feature Films. Preferred genres include Romance and Thriller. Established in 2012.

Aaron Ensweiler
Vice-President
IMDb: imdb.com/name/nm3943221

Hutch Parker
Founder
IMDb: imdb.com/name/nm0404446

HYDE PARK ENTERTAINMENT

14958 Ventura Blvd Suite 100
Sherman Oaks, CA 91423
Phone: 818-783-6060
Fax: 818-783-6319

Home Page: hydeparkentertainment.com

Does not accept any unsolicited material. Project types include Feature Films and Commercials. Preferred genres include Action, Comedy, Crime, Drama, Fantasy, Romance, Science Fiction, and Thriller. Established in 1999.

Marc Fiorentino

Ashtok Amritraj
IMDb: imdb.com/name/nm0002170

HYPNOTIC

12233 W Olympic Blvd, Suite 255
Los Angeles, CA 90064
Phone: 310-806-6930
Fax: 310-806-6931

Does not accept any unsolicited material. Project types include Feature Films and TV. Preferred genres include Action, Comedy, Crime, Drama, Horror, and Thriller.

Lindsay Sloane
Development Executive

Doug Liman
IMDb: imdb.com/name/nm0510731

ICON PRODUCTIONS

808 Wilshire Blvd, Suite 400
Santa Monica, CA 90401
Phone: 310-434-7300
Fax: 310-434-7377

Home Page: iconmovies.com

Does not accept any unsolicited material. Project types include Feature Films and TV. Preferred genres include Action, Comedy, Crime, Drama, Horror, Non-Fiction, Science Fiction, and Thriller.

Mel Gibson
IMDb: imdb.com/name/nm0000154

ILLUMINATION ENTERTAINMENT

2230 Broadway Ave
Santa Monica, CA 90404
Phone: 310-593-8800
Fax: 310-593-8850

100 Universal City Plaza Bungalow 4132
Universal City, CA 91608
Phone: 818-777-6183
Fax: 818-733-0222

Email: info@illuminationent.com
Home Page: illuminationentertainment.com
IMDb: imdb.com/company/co0221986

Does not accept any unsolicited material. Project types include Feature Films and Short Films. Preferred genres include Animation, Comedy, Drama, and Family. Established in 2010.

Dana Krupinski
Director of Development
IMDb: imdb.com/name/nm2145735

Christopher Meledandri
IMDb: imdb.com/name/nm0577560
Assistant: Rachel Feinberg and Katie Kirnan

Brooke Breton
IMDb: imdb.com/name/nm0107868
Assistant: Jenna Anderson

IMAGEMOVERS

100 Universal City
Bungalow 5170
Los Angeles, CA 91608
Phone: 818-733-4000

Does not accept any unsolicited material. Project types include Feature Films and TV. Preferred genres include Action, Animation, Comedy, Drama, Family, Fantasy, Period, Romance, and Thriller.

Robert Zemeckis
Partner
IMDb: imdb.com/name/nm0000709

Steve Starkey
Partner
IMDb: imdb.com/name/nm0823330

Jack Rapke
Partner
IMDb: imdb.com/name/nm0710759

Jimmy Skodras
Development Executive

Jackie Levine

IMAGINE ENTERTAINMENT

9465 Wilshire Blvd
7th Floor
Beverly Hills, CA 90212
Phone: 310-858-2000
Fax: 310-858-2020

Home Page: imagine-entertainment.com

Does not accept any unsolicited material. Project types include Feature Films and TV. Preferred genres include Action, Animation, Comedy, Crime, Drama, Family, Fantasy, Horror, Non-Fiction, Romance, Science Fiction, and Thriller.

Ron Howard
IMDb: imdb.com/name/nm0000165

IM GLOBAL

8201 Beverly Blvd.
5th Floor
Los Angeles, CA 90048
Phone: 323-677-2486
Fax: 323-657-5354

Email: info@imglobalfilm.com
Home Page: imglobalfilm.com
IMDb: imdb.com/company/co0323227

Does not accept any unsolicited material. Project types include Feature Films and TV. Preferred genres include Action, Comedy, Fantasy, and Thriller.

Brian Kavanaugh-Jones
Head (Automatik Film Division)
Phone: 323-677-2486
Email: office@automatikent.com
IMDb: imdb.com/name/nm2271939
Assistant: Alex Saks

IMPACT PICTURES

9200 W Sunset Blvd, Suite 800
West Hollywood, CA 90069
Phone: 310-247-1803

Accepts query letter from unproduced, unrepresented writers via email. Project types include Feature Films. Preferred genres include Action, Comedy, Crime, Drama, Fantasy, Horror, Romance, Science Fiction, and Thriller.

Jeremy Bolt
Producer
IMDb: imdb.com/name/nm0093337

Paul Anderson
IMDb: imdb.com/name/nm0027271
Assistant: Sarah Crompton

IMPRINT ENTERTAINMENT

100 Universal City Plaza
Bungalow 7125
Universal City, CA 91608
Phone: 818-733-5410
Fax: 818-733-4307

Email: info@imprint-ent.com
Home Page: imprint-ent.com

Does not accept any unsolicited material. Project types include Feature Films, TV, and Commercials. Preferred genres include Action, Comedy, Crime, Drama, Fantasy, Horror, Non-Fiction, Reality, Romance, and Thriller. Established in 2008.

Lee Arter
Creative Executive
Email: larter@imprint-ent.com

Michael Becker
Executive

IN CAHOOTS

4024 Radford Ave
Editorial Building 2, Suite 7
Studio City, CA 91604
Phone: 818-655-6482
Fax: 818-655-8472

Does not accept any unsolicited material. Project types include Feature Films and TV. Preferred genres include Comedy, Drama, and Thriller.

Ken Kwapis
IMDb: imdb.com/name/nm0477129

Reynolds Anderson
Creative Executive
IMDb: imdb.com/name/nm1568030

INCOGNITO PICTURES

16027 Ventura Blvd
Suite 650
Encino, CA 91436
Phone: 818-724-4727

Email: info@incognitopictures.com
Home Page: incognitopictures.com
Facebook: facebook.com/pages/Incognito-Pictures/
167198753371256

Does not accept any unsolicited material. Project types include Feature Films. Preferred genres include Crime, Drama, and Thriller.

Jack Selby
Chairman
IMDb: imdb.com/name/nm3095212

Scott G. Stone
CEO
IMDb: imdb.com/name/nm1680597

INDIAN PAINTBRUSH

1660 Euclid St
Santa Monica, CA 90404
Phone: 310-566-0160
Fax: 310-566-0161

Email: info@indianpaintbrush.com
Home Page: indianpaintbrush.com

Does not accept any unsolicited material. Project types include Feature Films. Preferred genres include Action, Animation, Comedy, Drama, Family, Horror, Romance, Science Fiction, and Thriller.

Sam Roston
Creative Executive

INDICAN PRODUCTIONS

2565 Broadway, Suite 138
New York, NY 10025
Phone: 212-666-1500

Does not accept any unsolicited material. Project types include Feature Films. Preferred genres include Crime, Drama, and Non-Fiction.

Julia Ormond
Email: julia.ormond@fox.com
IMDb: imdb.com/name/nm0000566

INDIE GENIUS PRODUCTIONS

361 Stryker Ave
St. Paul, MN 55107
Phone: 646-596-0937

IMDb: imdb.com/company/co0097647

Accepts query letter from unproduced, unrepresented writers. Project types include Feature Films. Preferred genres include Documentary. Established in 2007.

Curt Johnson
Email: curt_johnson@indiegeniusprod.com

INDOMITABLE ENTERTAINMENT

225 Varick St
Ste 304
New York, NY 10014
Phone: 212-352-1071
Fax: 212-727-3860

1920 Main St, Suite A
Santa Monica, CA 90405
Phone: 310-664-8700
Fax: 310-664-8711

Email: info@indomitable.com
Home Page: indomitableentertainment.com
Facebook: facebook.com/pages/Indomitable-Entertainment/20750471594844

Accepts query letter from unproduced, unrepresented writers via email. Project types include Feature Films and TV. Preferred genres include Action, Comedy, Drama, and Thriller.

Dominic Ianno
Founder, CEO
IMDb: imdb.com/name/nm1746156

Robert Deege
Vice President of Business & Creative Affairs
IMDb: imdb.com/name/nm1830098

Chris Mirosevic
Director of Film Services
IMDb: imdb.com/name/nm1746156

Stuart Pollok
Executive Producer
IMDb: imdb.com/name/nm0689415

INDUSTRY ENTERTAINMENT

955 S Carrillo Dr, Suite 300
Los Angeles, CA 90048
Phone: 323-954-9000
Fax: 323-954-9009

Accepts scripts from produced or represented writers.
Project types include Feature Films and TV. Preferred
genres include Comedy, Drama, Family, Fantasy,
Horror, Romance, and Thriller.

Keith Addis
Chairman
IMDb: imdb.com/name/nm0011688

INEFFABLE PICTURES

9247 Alden Dr
Beverly Hills, CA 90210
Phone: 424-653-1122

Email: info@ineffablepictures.com
Home Page: ineffablepictures.com
IMDb: imdb.com/company/co0343339

Does not accept any unsolicited material. Project types
include Feature Films. Preferred genres include Action,
Comedy, Drama, Fantasy, and Science Fiction.
Established in 2010.

Raphael Kryszek
President
IMDb: o.imdb.com/name/nm1398360

Ross Putman
Creative Executive
IMDb: imdb.com/name/nm3819444

Jesse Israel
Executive
IMDb: imdb.com/name/nm2368220

INFERNO ENTERTAINMENT

1888 Century Park East, Suite 1540
Los Angeles, CA 90067
Phone: 310-598-2550
Fax: 310-598-2551

Home Page: inferno-entertainment.com

Does not accept any unsolicited material. Project types
include Feature Films. Preferred genres include Action,
Comedy, Crime, Drama, Family, Fantasy, Horror,
Romance, Science Fiction, and Thriller.

Campbell McInnes
IMDb: imdb.com/name/nm0570577
Assistant: Roger Porter

D.J. Gugenheim
IMDb: imdb.com/name/nm1486759
Assistant: Aaron Himmel

INFINITUM NIHIL

Phone: 323-651-2034

Home Page: infinitumnihil.com

Does not accept any unsolicited material. Project types
include Feature Films. Preferred genres include Action,
Comedy, Family, Fantasy, Myth, and Romance.

Christi Dembrowski
President
IMDb: imdb.com/name/nm0218259
Assistant: Dawn Sierra & Erik Schmudde

Norman Todd
Director of Development
IMDb: imdb.com/name/nm0865249

Johnny Depp
IMDb: imdb.com/name/nm0000136

Margaret French Isaac
IMDb: imdb.com/name/nm0410504
Assistant: Brandon Zamel

Sam Sarkar
IMDb: imdb.com/name/nm0765274

Bobby DeLeon
IMDb: imdb.com/name/nm3765677

INFORMANT MEDIA

10866 Wilshire Blvd
4th Floor, Suite 422
Los Angeles, CA 90024
Phone: 310-470-9309
Fax: 310-347-4497

Email: development@informantmedia.com
Home Page: informantmedia.com

Accepts query letter from unproduced, unrepresented writers via email. Project types include Feature Films and TV. Preferred genres include Action, Comedy, Drama, Fantasy, Romance, and Thriller.

Rick Bitzelberger
Email: development@informantmedia.com

INFRONT PRODUCTIONS

2000 Ave Of The Stars
Century City, CA 90067
Phone: 424-288-2000

Email: aelkin@caa.com
IMDb: imdb.com/company/co0077065

Project types include TV. Established in 1992.

Danny Jacobson
Manager
IMDb: imdb.com/name/nm0414816

INK FACTORY

73 Wells St
London W1T 3QG
UK
Phone: +44-20-7096-1698

13400 Ventura Blvd.
Los Angeles, CA 91423
Phone: 310-721-5409

Email: info@inkfactoryfilms.com
Home Page: inkfactoryfilms.com

Does not accept any unsolicited material. Project types include Feature Films. Preferred genres include Action, Drama, and Thriller. Established in 2010.

Rhodri Thomas
Executive
Email: rhodri@inkonscreen.co.uk
IMDb: imdb.com/name/nm2905579

Stephen Cornwell
Principle
Phone: 310-721-5409
Email: steven@inkonscreen.co.uk
IMDb: imdb.com/name/nm4051169

INPHENATE

9701 Wilshire Blvd
10th Floor
Beverly Hills, CA 90212
Phone: 310-601-7117
Fax: 310-601-7110

Does not accept any unsolicited material. Project types include Feature Films and TV. Preferred genres include Comedy, Drama, Non-Fiction, and Reality.

Glenn Rigberg
Producer
IMDb: imdb.com/name/nm0726572

INTREPID PICTURES

1880 CENTURY PARK EAST, SUITE 900
LOS ANGELES, CA 90067
Phone: 310-566-5000

Email: info@intrepidpictures.com
Home Page: intrepidpictures.com

Does not accept any unsolicited material. Project types include Feature Films. Preferred genres include Action, Comedy, Horror, and Thriller. Established in 2004.

Marc D. Evans
IMDb: imdb.com/name/nm2162955

Trevor Macy
IMDb: imdb.com/name/nm1006167

Melinda Nishioka

Email: melinda@intrepidpictures.com
IMDb: imdb.com/name/nm2325559

IRISH DREAMTIME

3000 W Olympic Blvd
Building 3, Suite 2332
Santa Monica, CA 90404
Phone: 310-449-4081

Email: info@irishdreamtime.com
Home Page: irishdreamtime.com

Does not accept any unsolicited material. Project types include Feature Films and TV. Preferred genres include Action, Comedy, Crime, Drama, Non-Fiction, Romance, and Thriller. Established in 1996.

Pierce Brosnan

IMDb: imdb.com/name/nm0000112

Keith Arnold

Head of Development
IMDb: imdb.com/name/nm2993265

Beau St. Clair

IMDb: imdb.com/name/nm0820429

IRON OCEAN FILMS

1317 Luanne Ave
Fullerton, CA 92831
Phone: 323-957-9706

Does not accept any unsolicited material. Project types include Feature Films. Preferred genres include Crime, Drama, and Thriller.

Jessica Biel

IMDb: imdb.com/name/nm0004754

Michelle Purple

IMDb: imdb.com/name/nm0321977

IRONWORKS PRODUCTIONS

517 W 35th St 2nd Floor
New York City, NY 10001
Phone: 212-216-9780
Fax: 212-239-9180

Email: ironworksproductions@pobox.com

Accepts query letter from unproduced, unrepresented writers via email. Project types include Feature Films and TV. Preferred genres include Comedy, Drama, Non-Fiction, Reality, Romance, and Thriller.

Bruce Weiss

IMDb: imdb.com/name/nm0918933

Isa Freeling

IMDb: imdb.com/name/nm2303742

IRWIN ENTERTAINMENT

710 Seward St
Los Angeles, CA 90038
Phone: 323-468-0700
Fax: 323-464-1001

IMDb: imdb.com/company/co0193199

Does not accept any unsolicited material. Project types include Feature Films and TV. Preferred genres include Comedy and Reality.

John Irwin

President
Email: john@irwinentertainment.com
IMDb: imdb.com/name/nm1685815

ISH ENTERTAINMENT

104 W 27th St Second Floor
New York, NY 10001
Phone: 212-654-6445

Email: info@ish.tv
Home Page: ish.tv
IMDb: imdb.com/name/nm4851905

Does not accept any unsolicited material. Project types include Feature Films, Short Films, and TV. Preferred genres include Documentary and Reality. Established in 2008.

Michael Hirschorn

President
IMDb: imdb.com/name/nm1337695

Wendy Roth

Executive Vice President of Production
IMDb: imdb.com/name/nm0745046

Melissa Cooper
Director of Development
IMDb: imdb.com/name/nm2435108

Michael Saffran
Executive
IMDb: imdb.com/name/nm5249575

Madison Merritt
IMDb: imdb.com/name/nm3117402

Chris Choun
IMDb: imdb.com/name/nm1780111

Larissa Neal

ITHACA PICTURES

8711 Bonner Dr
West Hollywood, CA 90048
Phone: 310-967-0112
Fax: 310-967-3053

Does not accept any unsolicited material. Project types include Feature Films. Preferred genres include Drama and Non-Fiction.

Michael Fitzgerald
Executive
IMDb: imdb.com/name/nm028033

Richard Romero
Producer
IMDb: imdb.com/name/nm2484143

JACKHOLE PRODUCTIONS

6834 Hollywood Blvd
Los Angeles, CA 90028
Phone: 323-860-5900

Accepts query letter from produced or represented writers. Project types include TV. Preferred genres include Comedy and Reality.

Jimmy Kimmel
Partner
IMDb: imdb.com/name/nm0453994

Adam Carolla
Partner
IMDb: imdb.com/name/nm0004805

Daniel Kellison
Partner
IMDb: imdb.com/name/nm0446058

Doug DeLuca
Producer
IMDb: imdb.com/name/nm0217891

JAFFE/BRAUNSTEIN FILMS

12301 Wilshire Blvd Suite 110 Los Angeles, CA 90025
Phone: 310-207-6600
Fax: 310-207-6069

Accepts scripts from produced or represented writers. Project types include Feature Films and TV. Preferred genres include Comedy, Drama, Horror, Romance, Science Fiction, and Thriller.

Howard Braunstein
IMDb: imdb.com/name/nm0105946

Michael Jaffe
Partner
IMDb: imdb.com/name/nm0415468
Assistant: Lynn Delaney

JANE STARTZ PRODUCTIONS

244 Fift h Ave, 11th Floor
New York, NY 10001
Phone: 212-545-8910
Fax: 212-545-8909

Accepts query letter from unproduced, unrepresented writers. Project types include Feature Films and TV. Preferred genres include Animation, Comedy, Drama, Family, Fantasy, Romance, and Thriller.

Jane Startz
President
IMDb: imdb.com/name/nm0823661

Kane Lee
Vice-President
IMDb: imdb.com/name/nm1634508

JEAN DOUMANIAN PRODUCTIONS

595 Madison Ave Suite 2200
New York City, NY 10022

Phone: 212-486-2626
Fax: 212-688-6236

Accepts query letter from unproduced, unrepresented writers. Project types include Feature Films and TV. Preferred genres include Comedy, Drama, Horror, Non-Fiction, Period, Romance, and Thriller.

Jean Doumanian
Founder
IMDb: imdb.com/name/nm0235389

Patrick Daily
IMDb: imdb.com/name/nm4794210

Saul Nathan-Kazis
IMDb: imdb.com/name/nm2651163

Kathryn Willingham
IMDb: imdb.com/name/nm5187379

JEFF MORTON PRODUCTIONS

10201 W Pico Blvd Building 226
Los Angeles, CA 90035
Phone: 310-467-1123
Fax: 818-981-4152

Does not accept any unsolicited material. Project types include Feature Films and TV.

Jeff Morton
Producer
Email: scoutspence@mindspring.com
IMDb: imdb.com/name/nm0608005

JERRY BRUCKHEIMER FILMS

1631 10th St
Santa Monica, CA 90404
Phone: 310-664-6260
Fax: 310-664-6261

Home Page: jbfilms.com
IMDb: imdb.com/company/co0217391

Accepts query letter from unproduced, unrepresented writers. Project types include Feature Films and TV. Preferred genres include Action, Comedy, Crime, Detective, Drama, Family, Fantasy, Horror, Myth, Non-Fiction, Reality, Science Fiction, and Thriller.

Jerry Bruckheimer
IMDb: imdb.com/name/nm0000988

Mike Stenson
President
IMDb: google.com/
url?sa=t&rct=j&q=&esrc=s&source=web&cd=1&cad=rja&ved=0CCsQ
oPsqEUJxpZlR-vg&sig2=bp-
k29QvNQCORVidApCQHw&bvm=bv.54934254,d.cGE

Charlie Vignola
Director of Development

JERRY WEINTRAUB PRODUCTIONS

190 N Canon Dr, Suite 204
Beverly Hills, CA 90210
Phone: 310-273-8800
Fax: 310-273-8502

Does not accept any unsolicited material. Project types include Feature Films. Preferred genres include Action, Comedy, Crime, Drama, Family, Non-Fiction, Science Fiction, and Thriller.

Jerry Weintraub
Producer
Assistant: Kimberly Pinkstaff

Susan Ekins
Vice-President
Assistant: Betsy Dennis

JERSEY FILMS

PO Box 491246
Los Angeles, CA 90049
Phone: 310-550-3200
Fax: 310-550-3210

IMDb: imdb.com/company/co0010434

Accepts query letter from unproduced, unrepresented writers. Project types include Feature Films. Preferred genres include Action, Comedy, Drama, Non-Fiction, Romance, and Thriller.

Danny DeVito
Executive
IMDb: imdb.com/name/nm0000362

Nikki Grosso
Phone: 310-477-7704
IMDb: imdb.com/name/nm0343777

JET TONE PRODUCTIONS

21/F Park Commercial Centre
No. 180 Tung Lo Wan Rd
Hong Kong
China
Phone: 852-2336-1102
Fax: 852-2337-9849

Email: jettone@netvigator.com
Home Page: jettone.net

Accepts query letter from unproduced, unrepresented writers via email. Project types include Feature Films. Preferred genres include Action, Animation, Comedy, Crime, Drama, Romance, Science Fiction, and Thriller.

Wong Kar-wai
IMDb: imdb.com/name/nm0939182

JOEL SCHUMACHER PRODUCTIONS

10960 Wilshire Bvld. Suite 1900
Los Angeles, CA 90024
Phone: 310-472-7602
Fax: 310-270-4618

IMDb: imdb.com/company/co0094915

Does not accept any unsolicited material. Project types include Feature Films, TV, and Commercials. Preferred genres include Action, Comedy, Crime, Drama, Fantasy, Romance, Science Fiction, and Thriller.

Aaron Cooley
Producer
Phone: 818-260-6065
IMDb: imdb.com/name/nm0177583

Joel Schumacher
Phone: 310-472-7602
IMDb: imdb.com/name/nm0001708
Assistant: Jeff Feuerstein

JOHN CALLEY PRODUCTIONS

10202 W Washington Blvd
Crawford Building
Culver City, CA 90232
Phone: 310-244-7777
Fax: 310-244-4070

IMDb: imdb.com/company/co0125552

Does not accept any unsolicited material. Project types include Feature Films and TV. Preferred genres include Action, Comedy, Detective, Drama, Romance, and Thriller.

John Calley
Producer
Phone: 310-244-7777
IMDb: imdb.com/name/nm1886942

Lisa Medwid
Phone: 310-244-7777
IMDb: imdb.com/name/nm1886942

JOHN GOLDWYN PRODUCTIONS

5555 Melrose Ave, Dressing Room. 112
Los Angeles, CA 90038
Phone: 323-956-5054
Fax: 323-862-0055

IMDb: imdb.com/company/co0177677

Does not accept any unsolicited material. Project types include Feature Films and TV. Preferred genres include Action, Comedy, Crime, Detective, Drama, Non-Fiction, and Thriller. Established in 1991.

John Goldwyn
President
IMDb: imdb.com/name/nm0326415
Assistant: Jasen Laks

Hilary Marx
Creative Executive
IMDb: imdb.com/name/nm1020576
Assistant: Rebecca Crow

Erin David
Creative Executive
IMDb: imdb.com/name/nm1716252
Assistant: Rebecca Crow

JOHN WELLS PRODUCTIONS

4000 Warner Blvd
Building 1
Burbank, CA 91522-0001
Phone: 818-954-1687
Fax: 818-954-3657

Email: jwppa@warnerbros.com
IMDb: imdb.com/company/co0037310

Accepts query letter from unproduced, unrepresented writers. Project types include Feature Films and TV. Preferred genres include Action, Comedy, Drama, Family, Horror, Romance, Science Fiction, and Thriller.

Claire Polstein
President
IMDb: imdb.com/name/nm0689856
Assistant: Tessie Groff

Andrew Stearn
President
IMDb: imdb.com/name/nm1048942
Assistant: Quinn Tivey quinn.tivey@jwprods.com

John Wells
Principle
IMDb: imdb.com/name/nm2187561
Assistant: Kristin Martini

Jinny Joung
Vice-President
Assistant: Irene Lee irene.lee@jwprods.com

JON SHESTACK PRODUCTIONS

409 N Larchmont Blvd
Los Angeles, CA 90004
Phone: 323-468-1113
Fax: 323-468-1114

IMDb: imdb.com/company/co0168855

Does not accept any unsolicited material. Project types include Feature Films. Preferred genres include Animation, Comedy, Crime, Drama, Family, Fantasy, Romance, Science Fiction, and Thriller. Established in 2006.

Jonathan Shestack
IMDb: imdb.com/name/nm0792871

Ginny Brewer Pennekamp
IMDb: imdb.com/name/nm2555285

JOSEPHSON ENTERTAINMENT

1201 W 5th St Suite M-170 Los Angeles, CA 90017
Phone: 213-534-3995

IMDb: imdb.com/company/co0046572

Does not accept any unsolicited material. Project types include Feature Films and TV. Preferred genres include Action, Animation, Comedy, Crime, Drama, Family, Fantasy, Horror, Romance, Science Fiction, Sociocultural, and Thriller.

Barry Josephson
Principle
IMDb: imdb.com/name/nm0430742
Assistant: Sean Bennett

Tia Maggini
Assistant: Mekita Faiye
mekita.faiye@josephsonent.com

JUNCTION FILMS

9615 Brighton Way, Suite M110
Beverly Hills, CA 90210
Phone: 310-246-9799
Fax: 310-246-3824

IMDb: imdb.com/company/co0099841

Accepts query letter from unproduced, unrepresented writers. Preferred genres include Action, Comedy, Crime, Drama, Horror, Reality, Science Fiction, and Thriller. Established in 2001.

Brad Wyman
Producer
Phone: 310-246-9799
IMDb: imdb.com/name/nm0943829

Donald Kushner
Producer
IMDb: imdb.com/name/nm0476291

Alwyn Kushner
Producer
IMDb: imdb.com/name/nm1672379

JUNIPER PLACE PRODUCTIONS

4024 Radford Ave, Bungalow 1
Studio City, CA 91604
Phone: 818-655-5043
Fax: 818-655-8402

Accepts query letter from unproduced, unrepresented writers. Project types include TV. Preferred genres include Drama.

Jeffrey Kramer
Principle
IMDb: imdb.com/name/nm0469552

Jennifer Stempel
Director of Development
IMDb: google.com/

KAPITAL ENTERTAINMENT

8687 Melrose Ave
9th Floor
West Hollywood, CA 90069
Phone: 310-854-3221

Does not accept any unsolicited material. Project types include TV. Preferred genres include Comedy and Drama.

Cailey Buck
Director of Development

Aaron Kaplan
Email: akaplan@kapital-ent.com
IMDb: imdb.com/name/nm3483168

KAPLAN/PERRONE ENTERTAINMENT

280 S Beverly Dr, #513
Beverly Hills, CA 90212
Phone: 310-285-0116

Home Page: kaplanperrone.com
IMDb: imdb.com/company/co0094257

Accepts scripts from produced or represented writers. Project types include Feature Films and TV. Preferred genres include Action, Comedy, Drama, Romance, and Thriller.

Josh Goldenberg
Manager

Alex Lerner
Manager

Aaron Kaplan
Partner

Sean Perrone
Partner

Tobin Babst

KARZ ENTERTAINMENT

4000 Warner Blvd Building 138, Suite 1205
Burbank, CA 91522
Phone: 818-954-1698
Fax: 818-954-1700

Email: karzent@aol.com
IMDb: imdb.com/company/co0033868

Does not accept any unsolicited material. Project types include Feature Films and TV. Preferred genres include Action, Comedy, Crime, Documentary, Drama, Family, Fantasy, Horror, Romance, and Thriller. Established in 1998.

Mike Karz
President
IMDb: imdb.com/name/nm0440344

KASSEN BROTHERS PRODUCTIONS

141 W 28th St, Suite 301
New York, NY 10001
Phone: 212-244-2865
Fax: 212-244-2874

IMDb: imdb.com/company/co0183529

Accepts query letter from unproduced, unrepresented writers. Project types include TV. Preferred genres include Action, Comedy, Drama, and Non-Fiction.

Adam Kassen
Phone: 212-244-2865
IMDb: imdb.com/name/nm0440859

Mark Kassen
President
IMDb: imdb.com/name/nm0440860

Patrick Petrocelli
IMDb: imdb.com/name/nm2332569

Mark Olsen
Director of Development
IMDb: imdb.com/name/nm1565746

KATALYST FILMS

6806 Lexington Ave
Los Angeles, CA 90038
Phone: 323-785-2700
Fax: 323-785-2715

Email: info@katalystfilms.com
Home Page: katalystfilms.com
IMDb: imdb.com/company/co0102320

Accepts scripts from unproduced, unrepresented writers. Project types include Feature Films and TV. Preferred genres include Action, Animation, Comedy, Crime, Drama, Reality, Romance, Science Fiction, and Thriller.

Ashton Kutcher
Partner
IMDb: imdb.com/name/nm0005110

Jason Goldberg
Partner
IMDb: imdb.com/name/nm0325229

KENNEDY/MARSHALL COMPANY

619 Arizona Ave
Second Floor
Santa Monica, CA 90401
Phone: 310-656-8400
Fax: 310-656-8430

Home Page: kennedymarshall.com

Does not accept any unsolicited material. Project types include Feature Films and TV. Preferred genres include Action, Comedy, Detective, Drama, Family, Non-Fiction, Romance, Science Fiction, and Thriller.

Frank Marshall
IMDb: imdb.com/name/nm0550881

Grey Rembert
IMDb: imdb.com/name/nm0718880

Robert D. Zotnowski

KERNER ENTERTAINMENT COMPANY

1888 Century Park East
Suite 1005
Los Angeles, CA 90067

Phone: 310-815-5100
Fax: 310-815-5110

Does not accept any unsolicited material. Project types include Feature Films. Preferred genres include Action, Animation, Comedy, Drama, Family, and Fantasy.

Jordan Kerner
President
IMDb: imdb.com/name/nm0449549

Ben Haber
IMDb: imdb.com/name/nm1852209

KGB FILMS

5555 Melrose Ave, Lucy Bungalow 101
Los Angeles, CA 90038
Phone: 323-956-5000
Fax: 323-224-1876

Email: turbo@kgbfilms.com
Home Page: kgbfilms.com

Accepts query letter from unproduced, unrepresented writers via email. Project types include Feature Films, Short Films, and TV. Preferred genres include Comedy, Crime, Drama, Non-Fiction, and Romance. Established in 1994.

Justin Hogan
Producer
IMDb: imdb.com/name/nm0389556

Rosser Goodman
President
IMDb: imdb.com/name/nm0329223

KICKSTART PRODUCTIONS

3212 Nebraska Ave
Santa Monica, CA 90404
Phone: 310-264-1757

Home Page: kickstartent.com
IMDb: imdb.com/company/co0163548

Does not accept any unsolicited material. Project types include Feature Films. Preferred genres include Action, Animation, Comedy, Family, and Science Fiction.

Loris Lunsford
Executive Producer
IMDb: imdb.com/name/nm0469603

Jason Netter
President
IMDb: imdb.com/name/nm0626697

Susan Norkin
IMDb: imdb.com/name/nm0635379

Samantha Olsson Shear
IMDb: imdb.com/name/nm2427387

KILLER FILMS

18th East 16th St, 4th Floor
New York, NY 10003
Phone: 212-473-3950
Fax: 212-807-1456

Home Page: killerfilms.com
IMDb: imdb.com/company/co0030755

Accepts query letter from unproduced, unrepresented writers. Project types include Feature Films, Short Films, and TV. Preferred genres include Comedy, Crime, Drama, Family, Horror, Romance, and Thriller. Established in 1995.

Christine Vachon
Partner
IMDb: imdb.com/name/nm0882927
Assistant: Gabrielle Nadig

Pamela Koffler
Partner
IMDb: imdb.com/name/nm0463025
Assistant: Gabrielle Nadig

David Hinojosa
Director of Development
IMDb: imdb.com/name/nm3065267
Assistant: Gabrielle Nadig

KIM AND JIM PRODUCTIONS

787 N. Palm Canyon Dr
Palm Springs, CA 92262
Phone: 760-289-5464

Email: info@kimandjimproductions.com
Home Page: kimandjimproductions.com

Accepts query letter from unproduced, unrepresented writers. Project types include Feature Films. Preferred genres include Action, Comedy, Drama, Fantasy, Horror, Romance, and Thriller.

Kim Waltrip
Vice Chairman
Email: assist@kimandjimproductions.com
IMDb: imdb.com/name/nm0910601

Jim Casey
Vice Chairman
Email: jim@kimandjimproductions
IMDb: imdb.com/name/nm2816633

KINETIC FILMWORKS

11018 Moorpark St Suite 114
Toluca Lake, CA 91602
Phone: 818-505-3347

Email: kineticfilmworks@aol.com
Home Page: kineticfilmworks.com
IMDb: imdb.com/company/co0224342

Accepts query letter from unproduced, unrepresented writers via email. Project types include Feature Films. Preferred genres include Horror. Established in 2013.

Gary Jones
Partner
IMDb: imdb.com/name/nm0428109

Jeffrey Miller
Partner
IMDb: imdb.com/name/nm0588577

KINTOP PICTURES

7955 W Third St
Los Angeles, CA 90048
Phone: 323-634-1570
Fax: 323-634-1575

Email: kintopfilm@aol.com

Accepts query letter from unproduced, unrepresented writers. Project types include Feature Films and TV. Preferred genres include Comedy, Documentary, Drama, Family, Horror, Romance, and Thriller.

Deepak Nayar
Founder
IMDb: imdb.com/name/nm0623235

KIPPSTER ENTERTAINMENT

420 W End Ave, Suite 1G
New York, NY 10024
Phone: 212-496-1200

IMDb: imdb.com/company/co0310346

Does not accept any unsolicited material. Project types include Feature Films and TV. Preferred genres include Drama and Non-Fiction.

Perri Kipperman
Founder
IMDb: imdb.com/name/nm1069530

David Sterns
Founder
IMDb: imdb.com/name/nm3992907

KOMUT ENTERTAINMENT

4000 Warner Blvd Building 140, Suite 201
Burbank, CA 91522
Phone: 818-954-7631

IMDb: imdb.com/company/co0028360

Does not accept any unsolicited material. Project types include TV. Preferred genres include Comedy, Drama, and Thriller.

David Kohan
Partner
IMDb: imdb.com/name/nm0463172
Assistant: Melissa Strauss
Melissa.Strauss@wbconsultant.com

Max Mutchnick
Partner
IMDb: imdb.com/name/nm0616083

Heather Hicks
IMDb: imdb.com/name/nm1337402

K/O PAPER PRODUCTS

100 Universal City Plaza
Building 5125
Universal City, CA 91608
Phone: 818-733-9645
Fax: 818-733-6988

IMDb: imdb.com/company/co0315120

Does not accept any unsolicited material. Project types include Feature Films and TV. Preferred genres include Action, Animation, Drama, Fantasy, and Science Fiction. Established in 1997.

Alex Kurtzman
Principle
IMDb: imdb.com/name/nm0476064

Roberto Orci
Principle
IMDb: imdb.com/name/nm0649460

KRANE MEDIA, LLC.

7932 Woodrow Wilson Dr
Los Angeles, CA 90046
Phone: 323-650-0942
Fax: 323-650-9132

Email: info@thekranecompany.com
Home Page: TheKraneCompany.com
IMDb: imdb.com/company/co0323526

Does not accept any unsolicited material. Project types include Feature Films and TV. Preferred genres include Action, Comedy, Crime, Drama, Romance, Science Fiction, and Thriller. Established in 1993.

Konni Corriere
Email: konni@thekranecompany.com
IMDb: pro.imdb.com/name/nm0180955

Jonathan Krane
IMDb: imdb.com/name/nm0006790

KRASNOFF FOSTER ENTERTAINMENT

5555 Melrose Ave Marx Brothers Building, Suite 110
Los Angeles, CA 90038
Phone: 323-956-4668

IMDb: imdb.com/company/co0174525

Accepts query letter from unproduced, unrepresented writers. Project types include Feature Films and TV. Preferred genres include Action, Comedy, Drama, Non-Fiction, and Romance.

Russ Krasnoff
Partner
Phone: 310-244-3282
IMDb: imdb.com/name/nm0469929
Assistant: Beth Maurer

Gary Foster
Partner
IMDb: imdb.com/name/nm0287811
Assistant: Haley Totten

KROFFT PICTURES

4024 Radford Ave
Building 5, Suite 102
Studio City, CA 91604
Phone: 818-655-5314
Fax: 818-655-8235

Email: smkroft@aol.com

Accepts query letter from unproduced, unrepresented writers via email. Project types include Feature Films and TV. Preferred genres include Animation, Comedy, and Family.

Marty Krofft
President
Email: marty@krofft pictures.com

Sid Krofft

LAGO FILM GMBH

6399 Wilshire Blvd, Suite 1002
Los Angeles, CA 90048
Phone: 310-653-7826

Email: lago@lagofilm.com
Home Page: lagofilm.com

Does not accept any unsolicited material. Project types include Feature Films. Preferred genres include Comedy, Drama, and Horror.

Marco Mehlitz
Producer

Luane Gauer

LAKESHORE ENTERTAINMENT

9268 W Third St
Beverly Hills, CA 90210
Phone: 310-867-8000
Fax: 310-300-3015

Email: info@lakeshoreentertainment.com
Home Page: lakeshoreentertainment.com
IMDb: imdb.com/company/co0005323

Accepts query letter from produced or represented writers. Project types include Feature Films. Preferred genres include Action, Comedy, Crime, Drama, Fantasy, Horror, Romance, Science Fiction, and Thriller. Established in 1994.

Tom Rosenberg
CEO
Phone: 310-867-8000
IMDb: imdb.com/name/nm0742347
Assistant: Tiffany Shinn

Robert McMinn
Sr. Vice-President
Phone: 310-867-8000
IMDb: imdb.com/name/nm0573372

Richard Wright
Executive Vice President of Production
IMDb: imdb.com/name/nm0002999

LANDSCAPE ENTERTAINMENT

9465 Wilshire Blvd Suite 500 Beverly Hills, CA 90212
Phone: 310-248-6200
Fax: 310-248-6300

IMDb: imdb.com/company/co0070807

Accepts query letter from unproduced, unrepresented writers. Project types include Feature Films and TV. Preferred genres include Action, Animation, Comedy, Crime, Drama, Family, Non-Fiction, Science Fiction, and Thriller. Established in 2007.

Bob Cooper
Chairman
IMDb: imdb.com/name/nm0178341
Assistant: Sandy Shenkman

Tyler Mitchell
Head of Development
IMDb: imdb.com/name/nm1624685

LANGLEY PARK PRODUCTIONS

4000 Warner Blvd
Building 144
Burbank, CA 91522
Phone: 818-954-2930

Home Page: langleyparkpix.com
IMDb: imdb.com/company/co0297907

Does not accept any unsolicited material. Project types include Feature Films. Preferred genres include Action, Comedy, Crime, Drama, Romance, and Thriller.

Kevin McCormick
Producer
Phone: 818-954-2930
IMDb: imdb.com/name/nm0566557
Assistant: Shamika Pryce

Aaron Schmidt
Creative Executive
Phone: 818-954-2930
Email: aaron.schmidt@langleyparkpix.com
IMDb: imdb.com/name/nm2087164

Rory Koslow
Phone: 818-954-2930
IMDb: imdb.com/name/nm1739372
Assistant: Kari Cooper

LARRIKIN ENTERTAINMENT

1801 Ave Of The Stars, Suite 921
Los Angeles, CA 90067
Phone: 310-461-3030

Home Page: larrikin-ent.com
IMDb: imdb.com/company/co0369620

Accepts scripts from produced or represented writers. Project types include Feature Films.

David Jones
IMDb: imdb.com/name/nm1965869

Greg Coote
Email: linw@larrikin-ent.com
IMDb: imdb.com/name/nm0178505
Assistant: Wayne Lin

Robert Lundberg
Email: rll@larrikin-ent.com
IMDb: imdb.com/name/nm2302909

LAUNCHPAD PRODUCTIONS

4335 Van Nuys Blvd Suite 339
Sherman Oaks, CA 91403
Phone: 818-788-4896

IMDb: imdb.com/company/co0164701

Accepts query letter from unproduced, unrepresented writers via email. Project types include Feature Films. Preferred genres include Comedy, Crime, Drama, Horror, Period, Science Fiction, and Thriller. Established in 2005.

David Higgins
Partner
IMDb: imdb.com/name/nm0383370

Angelique Higgins
President
Email: ahiggins@launchpadprods.com
IMDb: imdb.com/name/nm1583157

LAURA ZISKIN PRODUCTIONS

10202 W Washington Blvd
Astaire Building, Suite 1310
Culver City, CA 90232
Phone: 310-244-7373
Fax: 310-244-0073

IMDb: imdb.com/company/co0095403

Accepts query letter from unproduced, unrepresented writers. Project types include Feature Films and TV. Preferred genres include Action, Drama, Fantasy, Romance, Science Fiction, and Thriller. Established in 1995.

Pamela Williams
President
IMDb: imdb.com/name/nm0931423

David Jacobson
Director of Development
IMDb: imdb.com/name/nm5138376

LAURENCE MARK PRODUCTIONS

10202 W Washington Blvd
Poitier Building
Culver City, CA 90232
Phone: 310-244-5239
Fax: 310-244-0055

IMDb: imdb.com/company/co0027956

Accepts query letter from unproduced, unrepresented writers. Project types include Feature Films and TV. Preferred genres include Action, Comedy, Drama,

Family, Fantasy, Horror, Romance, Science Fiction, and Thriller.

Tamara Chestna
Director of Development
Phone: 310-244-5239
IMDb: imdb.com/name/nm2309894

Laurence Mark
Principle
Phone: 310-244-5239
IMDb: imdb.com/name/nm0548257

David Blackman
Phone: 310-244-5239
IMDb: imdb.com/name/nm1844320
Assistant: Peter Richman

LAVA BEAR FILMS

3201-B South La Cienega Blvd
Los Angeles, CA 90016
Phone: 310-815-9600

Home Page: lavabear.com
IMDb: imdb.com/company/co0296971

Does not accept any unsolicited material. Project types include Feature Films. Preferred genres include Action, Comedy, Crime, Drama, Family, Fantasy, Romance, Science Fiction, and Thriller. Established in 2011.

David Linde
Principle
Phone: 310-815-9603
Email: Dlinde@lavabear.com
IMDb: imdb.com/name/nm0511482
Assistant: Allison Warren

Tory Metzger
President
Email: Tmetzger@lavabear.com
IMDb: imdb.com/name/nm0582762
Assistant: Jon Frye

Zachary Studin
Vice-President
Email: Zstudin@lavabear.com
IMDb: imdb.com/name/nm1713122
Assistant: Jake Thomas

LAWRENCE BENDER PRODUCTIONS

1015 Gayley Ave Suite 1017
Los Angeles, CA 90024
Phone: 323-951-4600
Fax: 323-951-4601

IMDb: imdb.com/company/co0093776

Accepts query letter from unproduced, unrepresented writers. Project types include Feature Films. Preferred genres include Action, Comedy, Crime, Drama, and Thriller.

Lawrence Bender
Partner
IMDb: imdb.com/name/nm0004744
Assistant: Vincent Gatewood

Janet Jeffries
IMDb: imdb.com/name/nm0420377

Kevin Brown
IMDb: imdb.com/name/nm0114019

LD ENTERTAINMENT

9000 Sunset Blvd
Suite 600
West Hollywood, CA 90069
Phone: 310-275-9600

Email: info@identertainment.com
Home Page: identertainment.com

Does not accept any unsolicited material. Project types include Feature Films. Preferred genres include Action, Comedy, Crime, Drama, Horror, and Thriller. Established in 2007.

Mickey Liddell
President
IMDb: imdb.com/name/nm0509176

Patrick Raymond
Director of Development
IMDb: imdb.com/name/nm4811895

David Dinerstein
IMDb: imdb.com/name/nm2517209

Liz Berger
IMDb: imdb.com/name/nm0074266

Jennifer Hilton Monroe
IMDb: imdb.com/name/nm0385268

LEE DANIELS ENTERTAINMENT

315 W 36th St Suite 1002
New York City, NY 10018
Phone: 212-334-8110
Fax: 212-334-8290

Email: info@leedanielsentertainment.com
Home Page: leedanielsentertainment.com
IMDb: imdb.com/company/co0048235

Accepts query letter from unproduced, unrepresented writers via email. Project types include Feature Films and TV. Preferred genres include Comedy, Crime, Drama, Period, Romance, and Thriller. Established in 2001.

Lee Daniels
IMDb: imdb.com/name/nm0200005
Assistant: Tito Crafts

Lisa Cortes
IMDb: imdb.com/name/nm0181263

LEGENDARY PICTURES

4000 Warner Blvd
Building 76
Burbank, CA 91522
Phone: 818-954-3888
Fax: 818-954-3884

Home Page: legendarypictures.com
IMDb: imdb.com/company/co0159111

Does not accept any unsolicited material. Project types include Feature Films and TV. Preferred genres include Action, Comedy, Crime, Drama, Family, Fantasy, Non-Fiction, Romance, Science Fiction, and Thriller. Established in 2005.

Alex Hedlund
Creative Executive
Phone: 818-954-3888
IMDb: imdb.com/name/nm2906163

Thomas Tull
Phone: 818-954-3888
IMDb: imdb.com/name/nm2100078

Jennifer Preston Bosari
Creative Executive
Email: jpreston@legendary.com

Alex Garcia
IMDb: imdb.com/name/nm1247503

Jillan Share
Email: jillian.zaks@legendarypictures.com
IMDb: imdb.com/name/nm2949271

LESLIE IWERKS PRODUCTIONS

1322 2nd St Suite 35
Santa Monica, 90401 CA
Phone: 310-458-0490
Fax: 310-458-7212

Email: info@leslieiwerks.com
Home Page: leslieiwerks.com/new
IMDb: imdb.com/company/co0188417

Does not accept any unsolicited material. Project types include Feature Films, Short Films, and TV. Preferred genres include Documentary. Established in 2006.

Leslie Iwerks
President
Email: leslie@leslieiwerks.com
IMDb: imdb.com/name/nm0412649

Jane Kelly Kosek
Producer
IMDb: imdb.com/name/nm1165704

Michael Tang
IMDb: imdb.com/name/nm4046664

LIAISON FILMS

44 Rue Des Acacias
Paris 75017
France
Phone: +33-1-55-37-28-28
Fax: +33-1-55-37-98-44

Email: contact@liasonfilms.com
Home Page: liasonfilms.com
IMDb: imdb.com/company/co0120310

Does not accept any unsolicited material. Project types include Feature Films. Preferred genres include Action, Crime, Drama, and Thriller.

Stephane Sperry
President
Email: stephane.sperry@liasonfilms.com
IMDb: imdb.com/name/nm0818373

LIGHTSTORM ENTERTAINMENT

919 Santa Monica Blvd
Santa Monica, CA 90401
Phone: 310-656-6100
Fax: 310-656-6102

Does not accept any unsolicited material. Project types
include Feature Films. Preferred genres include Action,
Crime, Drama, Family, Fantasy, Horror, Romance,
Science Fiction, and Thriller.

James Cameron
CEO
IMDb: imdb.com/name/nm0000116

Jon Landau
COO
IMDb: imdb.com/name/nm0484457

Rae Sanchini
Partner
IMDb: imdb.com/name/nm0761093

Geoff Burdick

LIKELY STORY

150 W 22nd St, 9th Floor
New York, NY 10011
Phone: 917-484-8931

345 N. Maple Dr.
Suite 202
Beverly Hills, CA 90210

Email: info@likely-story.com
Home Page: likely-story.com
IMDb: imdb.com/company/co0190175

Does not accept any unsolicited material. Project types
include Feature Films.

Anthony Bregman
Phone: 917-484-8931
Email: info@likely-story.com
IMDb: imdb.com/name/nm0106835

Stefanie Azpiazu
Vice President (Development & Production)
Phone: 917-484-8931
Email: info@likely-story.com
IMDb: imdb.com/name/nm1282412

LIN PICTURES

4000 Warner Blvd. Bldg 143
Burbank, CA 91522
Phone: 818-954-6759
Fax: 818-954-2329

Home Page: linpictures.com

Does not accept any unsolicited material. Project types
include Feature Films and TV. Preferred genres
include Action, Comedy, Crime, Drama, Family,
Fantasy, Romance, Science Fiction, and Thriller.

Dan Lin
CEO
IMDb: imdb.com/name/nm1469853
Assistant: Ryan Halprin

Seanne Winslow Wehrenfennig
Head of Development
IMDb: imdb.com/name/nm2253990

Mark Bauch
Creative Executive
IMDb: imdb.com/name/nm3113076

Jennifer Gwartz
IMDb: imdb.com/name/nm0350311
Assistant: Jeremy Katz

LIONSGATE

2700 Colorado Ave, Suite 200
Santa Monica, CA 90404
Phone: 310-449-9200
Fax: 310-255-3870

Email: general-inquiries@lgf.com
Home Page: lionsgate.com

Does not accept any unsolicited material. Project types
include Feature Films and TV. Preferred genres
include Action, Comedy, Crime, Drama, Family,
Fantasy, Horror, Non-Fiction, Romance, Science
Fiction, and Thriller. Established in 1997.

Matthew Janzen
Director of Development
Phone: 310-449-9200
IMDb: imdb.com/name/nm0418432

Jina Jones
Director of Development
IMDb: imdb.com/name/nm1061205

Jon Feltheimer
Chairman
Phone: 310-449-9200
Email: jfeltheimer@lionsgate.com
IMDb: imdb.com/name/nm1410838

LIQUID THEORY

6725 Sunset Blvd Ste 240
Los Angeles, CA 90028
Phone: 323-460-5658
Fax: 323-460-4814

Home Page: liquid-theory.com
IMDb: imdb.com/company/co0113186

Accepts query letter from produced or represented writers. Project types include Feature Films and TV. Preferred genres include Animation, Comedy, Documentary, Drama, Horror, Reality, Romance, Science Fiction, and Thriller. Established in 2001.

Austin Reading
President
IMDb: imdb.com/name/nm1474879

Julie Reading
President
IMDb: imdb.com/name/nm1474880

Matt Lambert
Email: matt@liquid-theory.com
IMDb: imdb.com/name/nm1479457

LITTLE ENGINE

500 S Buena Vista St
Animation Building 3F-6
Burbank, CA 91521
Phone: 818-560-4670
Fax: 818-560-4014

Home Page: littleenginefilms.com
IMDb: imdb.com/company/co0014340

Accepts query letter from unproduced, unrepresented writers. Project types include Feature Films and TV. Preferred genres include Comedy, Crime, Drama, Non-Fiction, Reality, and Romance.

Mitchell Gutman
Director of Development
IMDb: imdb.com/name/nm1393767

Gina Matthews
Partner
IMDb: imdb.com/name/nm0560033

Grant Scharbo
Partner
IMDb: imdb.com/name/nm0770090

LLEJU PRODUCTIONS

3050 Post Oak Blvd.,
Suite 460
Houston, Texas 77056
Phone: 866-579-6444
Fax: 713-583-2214

Email: info@lleju.com
Home Page: lleju.com/index.html
IMDb: imdb.com/company/co0250136

Accepts query letter from unproduced, unrepresented writers. Project types include Feature Films. Preferred genres include Action, Comedy, Crime, Drama, Horror, and Thriller. Established in 2008.

Bill Perkins
Executive
IMDb: imdb.com/name/nm2645116

Keith Perkins
IMDb: imdb.com/name/nm1344801

Cooper Richey
IMDb: imdb.com/name/nm3295785

LONDINE PRODUCTIONS

1626 N. Wilcox Ave.
Ste. 480
Hollywood, CA 90028
Fax: 310-822-9025

IMDb: imdb.com/company/co0183894

Accepts query letter from unproduced, unrepresented writers via email. Project types include Feature Films and TV. Preferred genres include Comedy, Drama, and Thriller. Established in 1988.

Cassius Weathersby

President
Email: cassiusii@aol.com
IMDb: imdb.com/name/nm0915780

Joshua Weathersby

IMDb: imdb.com/name/nm1500833

Nadine Weathersby

IMDb: imdb.com/name/nm2325321

LUCASFILM LTD.

One Letterman Dr.
San Francisco, CA 94129
Phone: 415-662-1800

Home Page: lucasfilm.com
IMDb: imdb.com/company/co0071326

Does not accept any unsolicited material. Project types include Feature Films. Preferred genres include Action, Fantasy, and Science Fiction.

George Lucas

IMDb: imdb.com/name/nm0000184

Kathleen Kennedy

IMDb: imdb.com/name/nm0005086

LUCKY CROW FILMS

4335 Van Nuys Blvd.
Suite 355
Sherman Oaks, CA 91403
Phone: 818-783-7529
Fax: 818-783-7594

Email: info@indieproducer.net
Home Page: indieproducer.net
IMDb: imdb.com/company/co0102838

Accepts query letter from unproduced, unrepresented writers via email. Project types include Feature Films and TV. Preferred genres include Documentary and Drama. Established in 2004.

Kerry David

President
IMDb: imdb.com/name/nm0202968

Jon Gunn

President
IMDb: imdb.com/name/nm0348197

LYNDA OBST PRODUCTIONS

10202 W Washington Blvd
Astaire Building, Suite 1000
Culver City, CA 90232
Phone: 310-244-6122
Fax: 310-244-0092

Home Page: lyndaobst.com
IMDb: imdb.com/company/co0071668

Does not accept any unsolicited material. Project types include Feature Films and TV. Preferred genres include Action, Comedy, Crime, Drama, Family, Fantasy, Romance, and Thriller.

Lynda Obst

Principle
IMDb: imdb.com/name/nm0643553

Rachel Abarbanell

President
IMDb: imdb.com/name/nm1561964

M8 ENTERTAINMENT, INC.

15260 Ventura Blvd, Suite 710
Sherman Oaks, CA 91403
Phone: 818-325-8000
Fax: 818-325-8020

Email: info@media8ent.com
Home Page: media8ent.com

Does not accept any unsolicited material. Project types include Feature Films and TV. Preferred genres include Action, Comedy, Drama, and Romance. Established in 1993.

Stewart Hall

President
Phone: 818-826-8000
Email: info@media8ent.com
IMDb: imdb.com/name/nm1279593

MAD CHANCE PRODUCTIONS

4000 Warner Blvd
Building 81, Room 208
Burbank, CA 91522
Phone: 818-954-3500
Fax: 818-954-3586

IMDb: imdb.com/company/co0034487

Does not accept any unsolicited material. Project types include Feature Films. Preferred genres include Action, Comedy, Drama, Family, Fantasy, Romance, Science Fiction, and Thriller.

Andrew Lazar

Producer
IMDb: imdb.com/name/nm0493662
Assistant: Wynn Wygal

MAD HATTER ENTERTAINMENT

9229 Sunset Blvd, Suite 225
West Hollywood, CA 90069
Phone: 310-860-0441

Home Page: madhatterentertainment.com
IMDb: imdb.com/company/co0266260

Accepts scripts from unproduced, unrepresented writers. Project types include Feature Films and TV. Preferred genres include Action, Animation, Comedy, Crime, Drama, Family, Fantasy, Horror, Myth, Science Fiction, and Thriller.

Michael Connolly

Email: mike@madhatterentertainment.com
IMDb: imdb.com/name/nm0175326
Assistant: Kyle Smeehuyzen (Development Assistant)

MAD HORSE FILMS

16000 Ventura Blvd, Suite 900
Encino, CA 91436
Phone: 310-571-8048

Email: queries@madhorsefilms.com
Home Page: madhorsefilms.com
Facebook: facebook.com/mad.horse.films
IMDb: imdb.com/company/co0382776

Accepts query letter from unproduced, unrepresented writers via email. Project types include Feature Films.

Preferred genres include Action, Horror, Science Fiction, and Thriller.

John Swetnam

Principal
IMDb: imdb.com/name/nm4291727

Alexandru Celea

Vice President of Production
IMDb: imdb.com/name/nm5088556

MADHOUSE ENTERTAINMENT

10390 Santa Monica Blvd
Suite 110
Los Angeles, CA 90025
Phone: 310-587-2200
Fax: 323-782-0491

Email: query@madhouseent.net
Home Page: madhouseent.net
IMDb: imdb.com/company/co0202761

Does not accept any unsolicited material. Project types include Feature Films and TV. Preferred genres include Action, Comedy, Crime, Drama, Romance, Science Fiction, and Thriller. Established in 2010.

Robyn Meisinger

IMDb: imdb.com/name/nm1159733

Ryan Cunningham

Manager
IMDb: imdb.com/name/nm1400515

Chris Cook

Manager
IMDb: imdb.com/name/nm2303601

Adam Kolbrenner

IMDb: imdb.com/name/nm2221807

MADRIK MULTIMEDIA

Los Angeles Center Studios
1201 W Fifth St, Suite F222
Los Angeles, CA 90017
Phone: 213-596-5180

Email: info@madrik.com
Home Page: madrik.com

Accepts query letter from unproduced, unrepresented writers. Project types include Feature Films, TV, and

Commercials. Preferred genres include Comedy and Romance.

Chris Adams
Founder
Email: chris@madrik.com
IMDb: imdb.com/name/nm1886228

MAGNET RELEASING

115 W 27th St
Seventh Floor
New York City, NY 10001
Phone: 212-924-6701
Fax: 212-924-6742

Home Page: magnetreleasing.com
Facebook: facebook.com/magnetreleasing

Does not accept any unsolicited material. Project types include Feature Films. Preferred genres include Action, Comedy, Crime, Family, Fantasy, Horror, Myth, Romance, Science Fiction, and Thriller.

Eamonn Bowles
President
IMDb: imdb.com/name/nm2113054

Peter Van Steemberg
Director (Acquisitions)

MALPASO PRODUCTIONS

4000 Warner Blvd
Building 81
Suite 101
Burbank, CA 91522-0811
Phone: 818-954-3367
Fax: 818-954-4803

IMDb: imdb.com/company/co0010258

Does not accept any unsolicited material. Project types include Feature Films. Preferred genres include Crime, Drama, Fantasy, Non-Fiction, Romance, and Thriller. Established in 1967.

Clint Eastwood
IMDb: imdb.com/name/nm0000142

Robert Lorenz
IMDb: imdb.com/name/nm0520749

MANDALAY PICTURES

4751 Wilshire Blvd, 3rd Floor
Los Angeles, CA 90010
Phone: 323-549-4300
Fax: 323-549-9832

380 Lafayette St Suite 202
New York City, NY 10003
Phone: 212-725-3550

Email: info@mandalay.com
Home Page: mandalay.com
IMDb: imdb.com/company/co0013922

Accepts query letter from produced or represented writers. Project types include Feature Films. Preferred genres include Action, Comedy, Drama, Family, Horror, Romance, and Thriller. Established in 1995.

Peter Guber
IMDb: imdb.com/name/nm0345542

MANDALAY TELEVISION

4751 Wilshire Blvd, 3rd Floor
Los Angeles, CA 90010
Phone: 323-549-4300
Fax: 323-549-9832

Email: info@mandalay.com
Home Page: mandalay.com
IMDb: imdb.com/company/co0018094

Does not accept any unsolicited material. Project types include TV. Preferred genres include Action, Comedy, Drama, Period, Romance, and Thriller.

Paul Schaeffer
Phone: 323-549-4300
IMDb: imdb.com/name/nm2325215

MANDATE PICTURES

2700 Colorado Ave, Suite 501
Santa Monica, CA 90404
Phone: 310-360-1441
Fax: 310-360-1447

Email: info@mandatepictures.com
Home Page: mandatepictures.com
IMDb: imdb.com/company/co0142446

Accepts query letter from unproduced, unrepresented writers via email. Project types include Feature Films. Preferred genres include Comedy, Crime, Drama, Fantasy, Horror, Romance, Science Fiction, and Thriller. Established in 2003.

Nathan Kahane
President
Phone: 310-255-5700
IMDb: imdb.com/name/nm1144042

Aaron Ensweiler
Creative Executive
Phone: 310-255-5721
Email: aensweiler@mandatepictures.com
IMDb: imdb.com/name/nm3943221

Nicole Brown
Phone: 310-255-5710
Email: nbrown@mandatepictures.com
IMDb: imdb.com/name/nm0114352

MANDEVILLE FILMS

500 S Buena Vista St
Animation Building, 2G
Burbank, CA 91521-1783
Phone: 818-560-7662
Fax: 818-842-2937

Home Page: mandfilms.com
IMDb: imdb.com/company/co0064942

Does not accept any unsolicited material. Project types include Feature Films and TV. Preferred genres include Action, Drama, Family, and Romance. Established in 1994.

David Hoberman
Partner
IMDb: imdb.com/name/nm0387674
Assistant: Derek Steiner

Todd Lieberman
Partner
IMDb: imdb.com/name/nm0509414
Assistant: Jacqueline Lesko

Laura Cray
Creative Executive
IMDb: imdb.com/name/nm1733050
Assistant: Liz Bassin

MANDY FILMS

9201 Wilshire Blvd, Suite 206
Beverly Hills, CA 90210
Phone: 310-246-0500
Fax: 310-246-0350

IMDb: imdb.com/company/co0032786

Accepts query letter from unproduced, unrepresented writers. Project types include Feature Films and TV. Preferred genres include Action, Comedy, Drama, Fantasy, Science Fiction, and Thriller.

Leonard Goldberg
President
IMDb: imdb.com/name/nm0325252

Amanda Goldberg
IMDb: imdb.com/name/nm0325144

MANGUSTA PRODUCTIONS

145 6th Ave
Suite #6E
New York, NY 10013
Phone: 212-463-9503

Email: info@mangustaproductions.com
Home Page: mangustaproductions.com

Project types include Feature Films. Preferred genres include Comedy, Documentary, Drama, and Romance.

Sol Tryon
Producer
IMDb: imdb.com/name/nm0874501

Shannon McCoy Cohn
Producer
IMDb: imdb.com/name/nm3101571

Giancarlo Canavesio
IMDb: imdb.com/name/nm2184875

Blake Ashman
IMDb: imdb.com/name/nm0039137

MANIFEST FILM COMPANY

619 18th St
Santa Monica, CA 90402
Phone: 310-899-5554

Email: info@manifestfilms.com
Home Page: janetyang.com
IMDb: imdb.com/company/co0005048

Accepts query letter from unproduced, unrepresented writers. Project types include Feature Films. Preferred genres include Comedy, Crime, Drama, Period, and Thriller. Established in 1998.

Janet Yang

President
Email: janetyang2013@gmail.com
IMDb: imdb.com/name/nm0946003

MAPLE SHADE FILMS

4000 Warner Blvd
Building 138, Room 1103
Burbank, CA 91522
Phone: 818-954-3137

IMDb: imdb.com/company/co0100155

Accepts query letter from unproduced, unrepresented writers. Project types include Feature Films. Preferred genres include Action, Drama, Fantasy, and Thriller.

Ed McDonnell

President
IMDb: imdb.com/name/nm0568093

MARC PLATT PRODUCTIONS

100 Universal City Plaza, Bungalow 5163
Universal City, CA 91608
Phone: 818-777-8811
Fax: 818-866-6353

IMDb: imdb.com/company/co0093810

Accepts query letter from unproduced, unrepresented writers. Project types include Feature Films and TV. Preferred genres include Action, Comedy, Crime, Drama, Family, Fantasy, Horror, Romance, and Thriller.

Adam Siegel

President
Phone: 818-777-9544
IMDb: imdb.com/name/nm2132113

Marc Platt

Producer
Phone: 818-777-1122
Email: platt@nbcuni.com
IMDb: imdb.com/name/nm0686887
Assistant: Joey Levy

Jared LeBoff

Phone: 818-777-9961
IMDb: imdb.com/name/nm1545176

MARK VICTOR PRODUCTIONS

2932 Wilshire Blvd, Suite 201
Santa Monica, CA 90403
Phone: 310-828-3339
Fax: 310-828-9588

Email: info@markvictorproductions.com
Home Page: markvictorproductions.com

Accepts query letter from unproduced, unrepresented writers via email. Project types include Feature Films and TV. Preferred genres include Action, Animation, Horror, Non-Fiction, Reality, and Thriller.

Sarah Johnson

Director of Development
Phone: 310-828-3339
IMDb: imdb.com/name/nm1154417

Mark Victor

Phone: 310-828-3339
Email: markvictorproductions@hotmail.com
IMDb: imdb.com/name/nm0896131

MARK YELLEN PRODUCTION

183 S Orange Dr
Los Angeles, CA 90036
Phone: 323-935-5525
Fax: 323-935-5755

Accepts query letter from unproduced, unrepresented writers via email. Project types include Feature Films, TV, and Commercials. Preferred genres include Action and Family. Established in 2003.

Mark Yellen
Producer
Phone: 323-935-5525
Email: mark@myfilmconsult.com
IMDb: imdb.com/name/nm0947390

MARTIN CHASE PRODUCTIONS

500 S Buena Vista St
Burbank, CA 91521
Phone: 818-560-3952
Fax: 818-560-5113

Does not accept any unsolicited material. Project types include Feature Films and TV. Preferred genres include Family. Established in 2000.

Debra Chase
Phone: 818-526-4252
IMDb: imdb.com/name/nm0153744

MARTY KATZ PRODUCTIONS

22337 Pacific Coast Highway #327
Malibu, CA 90265
Phone: 310-589-1560
Fax: 310-589-1565

Email: martykatzproductions@earthlink.net

Accepts query letter from unproduced, unrepresented writers via email. Project types include Feature Films. Preferred genres include Action, Comedy, Drama, and Romance. Established in 1996.

Marty Katz
Producer
Phone: 310-589-1560
Email: martykatzproductions@earthlink.net
IMDb: imdb.com/name/nm0441794

Campbell Katz
Phone: 310-589-1560
Email: martykatzproductions@earthlink.net
IMDb: imdb.com/name/nm0441645

MARVISTA ENTERTAINMENT

12519 Venice Blvd.
Los Angeles, CA 90066
Phone: 310-737-0950
Fax: 310-737-9115

310 Grant St.
Suite 711
Pittsburgh, PA 15219
Phone: 412-918-1638
Fax: 412-918-1663

Email: info@marvista.net
Home Page: marvista.net

Accepts query letter from unproduced, unrepresented writers via email. Project types include Feature Films and TV.

Fernando Szew
CEO
Phone: 310-737-0950
Email: fszew@marvista.net
IMDb: imdb.com/name/nm2280496

Matt Freeman
Phone: 310-737-0950
IMDb: pro.imdb.com/name/nm0293513

Robyn Snyder
Phone: 310-737-0950
Email: rsnyder@marvista.net
IMDb: imdb.com/name/nm2237557

MASIMEDIA

11620 Oxnard St
North Hollywood, California 91606
Phone: 818-358-4803

Email: submissions@masimedia.net
Home Page: masimedia.net
IMDb: imdb.com/company/co0155931

Accepts scripts from unproduced, unrepresented writers via email. Project types include Feature Films and TV. Preferred genres include Documentary and Horror. Established in 2006.

Anthony Masi
President
IMDb: imdb.com/name/nm1502845

MASS HYSTERIA ENTERTAINMENT

8899 Beverly Blvd, Suite 710
Los Angeles, CA 90048
Phone: 310-285-7800
Fax: 310-285-7801

Email: info@masshysteriafilms.com
Home Page: masshysteriafilms.com

Accepts query letter from unproduced, unrepresented writers via email. Project types include Feature Films and TV.

Daniel Grodnik

President
Phone: 310-285-7800
Email: grodzilla@earthlink.net
IMDb: imdb.com/name/nm0342841

MATADOR PICTURES

159 Wardour St
London, United Kingdom, W1F 8WH
Phone: 011-442-077344544
Fax: 011-442-077347794

Email: admin@matadorpictures.com
Home Page: matadorpictures.com

Accepts query letter from unproduced, unrepresented writers via email. Project types include Feature Films. Preferred genres include Action, Comedy, Drama, and Romance. Established in 1999.

Nigel Thomas

Producer
Phone: +44 (0) 20-7009-9640
IMDb: imdb.com/name/nm0859302

Orlando Cubit

Development Executive
Phone: +44 (0) 20-7009-9640
IMDb: imdb.com/name/nm4919747

Lucia Lopez

Phone: +44 (0) 20-7009-9640
IMDb: imdb.com/name/nm2389416

MAVEN PICTURES

148 Spring St
Fourth Floor
New York, NY 10012
Phone: 212-725-3550
Fax: 646-442-7500

Does not accept any unsolicited material. Project types include Feature Films. Preferred genres include Action, Comedy, Drama, Romance, and Thriller.

Jenny Halper

Development Executive
IMDb: imdb.com/name/nm3794516

Celine Rattray

IMDb: imdb.com/name/nm1488027

Trudie Styler

IMDb: imdb.com/name/nm0836548

Alex Francis

IMDb: imdb.com/name/nm2123360

Hardy Justice

IMDb: imdb.com/name/nm1155511

Anita Sumner

IMDb: imdb.com/name/nm0838856

Nic Marshall

IMDb: imdb.com/name/nm2090942

MAXIMUM FILMS & MANAGEMENT

33 W 17th St, 11th Floor
New York, NY 10011
Phone: 212-414-4801
Fax: 212-414-4803

Email: lauren@maximumfilmsny.com
Home Page: maximumfilmsny.com

Does not accept any unsolicited material. Project types include Feature Films, TV, and Theater.

Marcy Drogin

Phone: 212-414-4801
IMDb: imdb.com/name/nm1216320

MAYA ENTERTAINMENT GROUP

1201 W 5th St, Suite T210
Los Angeles, CA 90017
Phone: 213-542-4420
Fax: 213-534-3846

Email: info@maya-entertainment.com
Home Page: maya-entertainment.com

Accepts query letter from unproduced, unrepresented writers via email. Project types include Feature Films and TV. Preferred genres include Comedy, Drama, Non-Fiction, and Reality. Established in 2008.

Christina Hirigoyen
Development Executive
Phone: 213-542-4420
IMDb: imdb.com/name/nm3491113

Moctesuma Esparza
Phone: 213-542-4420
IMDb: imdb.com/name/nm0260800

MAYHEM PICTURES

725 Arizona Ave, Suite 402
Santa Monica, CA 90401
Phone: 310-393-5005
Fax: 310-393-5017

Does not accept any unsolicited material. Project types include Feature Films and TV. Preferred genres include Comedy, Family, Non-Fiction, and Reality. Established in 2003.

Mark Ciardi
Producer
Phone: 310-393-5005
Email: mark@mayhempictures.com
IMDb: imdb.com/name/nm0161891

Brad Butler
Creative Executive
Phone: 310-393-5005
Email: brad@mayhempictures.com
IMDb: imdb.com/name/nm2744089

MBST ENTERTAINMENT

345 N Maple Dr, Suite 200
Beverly Hills, CA 90210
Phone: 310-385-1820
Fax: 310-385-1834

Accepts query letter from unproduced, unrepresented writers. Project types include Feature Films, TV, and Theater. Preferred genres include Action, Comedy, Drama, and Romance. Established in 2005.

Larry Brezner
Partner
Phone: 310-385-1820
IMDb: imdb.com/name/nm010836

Jonathan Brandstein
Partner
Phone: 310-385-1820
IMDb: imdb.com/name/nm0104844

MEDIA RIGHTS CAPITAL

1800 Century Park East/ 10th Floor
Los Angeles, CA 90067
Phone: 310-786-1600
Fax: 310-786-1601

Email: info@mrclp.com
Home Page: mrcstudios.com

Does not accept any unsolicited material. Project types include Feature Films and TV. Preferred genres include Animation, Comedy, Drama, Romance, and Thriller.

Alex Jackson
Creative Executive

Asif Satchu
Email: www.imdb.com/name/nm2640007
Assistant: Maggie Settli

Modi Wiczyk
IMDb: imdb.com/name/nm1582943
Assistant: Maggie Settli

Brye Adler

Charlie Goldstein
IMDb: imdb.com/name/nm0326177

Joe Hipps

Whitney Timmons

MEDIA TALENT GROUP

9200 Sunset Blvd, Suite 550
West Hollywood, CA 90069
Phone: 310-275-7900
Fax: 310-275-7910

Accepts query letter from unproduced, unrepresented writers. Project types include Feature Films and TV. Established in 2009.

Geyer Kosinski
Phone: 310-275-7900
IMDb: imdb.com/name/nm0467083

Chris Davey
Phone: 310-275-7900
IMDb: imdb.com/name/nm1312702

MEDUSA FILM

Via Aurelia Antica 422/424
Rome, Lazio 00165
Italy
Phone: +39-06-663-901
Fax: +39-06-66-39-04-50

Email: info.medusa@medusa.it
Home Page: medusa.it
IMDb: imdb.com/company/co0117688

Does not accept any unsolicited material. Project types include Feature Films. Preferred genres include Comedy, Crime, Documentary, Drama, Family, Horror, Romance, and Thriller. Established in 1916.

Faruk Alatan
IMDb: imdb.com/name/nm0016092

Luciana Migliavacca
IMDb: imdb.com/name/nm3096618

Pier Paolo Zerilli
IMDb: imdb.com/name/nm1047259

MELEE ENTERTAINMENT

144 S Beverly Dr, Suite 402
Beverly Hills, CA 90212
Phone: 310-248-3931
Fax: 310-248-3921

Email: acquisitions@melee.com
Home Page: melee.com

Does not accept any unsolicited material. Project types include Feature Films. Established in 2003.

Bryan Turner
CEO
Phone: 310-248-3931
IMDb: imdb.com/name/nm0877440

Brittany Williams
Creative Executive
Phone: 310-248-3931
IMDb: imdb.com/name/nm2950356

MERCHANT IVORY PRODUCTIONS

250 W. 57th St.
Suite 1825
New York, NY 10019
Phone: 212-582-8049
Fax: 212-706-8340

Email: contact@merchantivory.com
Home Page: merchantivory.com
Facebook: facebook.com/pages/Merchant-Ivory-Productions/105682432798518

Accepts query letter from unproduced, unrepresented writers via email. Project types include Feature Films and TV. Preferred genres include Drama, Non-Fiction, and Reality. Established in 1961.

Neil Jesuele
Director of Development
Phone: 212-582-8049
Email: njesuele@merchantivory.com
IMDb: imdb.com/name/nm3134373

Paul Bradley
Producer
Email: paul@merchantivory.co.uk
IMDb: imdb.com/name/nm0103364

Simon Oxley
Producer
Email: simon@merchantivory.co.uk
IMDb: imdb.com/name/nm1774746

James Ivory
Principle
IMDb: imdb.com/name/nm0412465

MERV GRIFFIN ENTERTAINMENT

130 S El Camino Dr
Beverly Hills, CA 90212
Phone: 310-385-2700
Fax: 310-385-2728

Email: firstname_lastname@griffgroup.com
IMDb: imdb.com/company/co0093384

Does not accept any unsolicited material. Project types include Feature Films, Short Films, and TV. Preferred genres include Action, Comedy, Crime, Documentary, Drama, Non-Fiction, Period, Reality, Romance, and Thriller. Established in 1964.

Ron Ward
Vice Chairman
IMDb: imdb.com/name/nm2302243

Robert Pritchard
President
IMDb: imdb.com/name/nm2923017

Mike Eyre

Tony Griffin

METRO-GOLDWYN MEYER (MGM)

245 N Beverly Dr
Beverly Hills, CA 90210
Phone: 310-449-3000

Home Page: mgm.com

Does not accept any unsolicited material. Project types include Feature Films. Preferred genres include Action, Comedy, Crime, Drama, Family, Horror, Myth, Romance, Science Fiction, and Thriller.

Dene Stratton
CFO
Phone: 310-449-3000
IMDb: imdb.com/name/nm4682676

Gary Barber
Phone: 310-449-3000
IMDb: imdb.com/name/nm0053388

Cassidy Lange
Phone: 310-449-3000
IMDb: imdb.com/name/nm3719738

MICHAEL DE LUCA PRODUCTIONS

10202 W Washington Blvd
Astaire Building, Suite 3028
Culver City, CA 90232
Phone: 310-244-4990
Fax: 310-244-0449

Does not accept any unsolicited material. Project types include Feature Films. Preferred genres include Action, Comedy, Drama, and Thriller.

Michael De Luca
Producer
Phone: 310-244-4990
IMDb: imdb.com/name/nm0006894
Assistant: Kristen Detwiler

Josh Bratman
Development Executive
Phone: 310-244-4916
IMDb: imdb.com/name/nm2302300
Assistant: Sandy Yep

Alissa Phillips
Phone: 310-244-4918
IMDb: imdb.com/name/nm1913014
Assistant: Bill Karesh

MICHAEL GRAIS PRODUCTIONS

321 S Beverly Dr, Suite M
Beverly Hills, CA 90210
Phone: 323-857-4510
Fax: 323-319-4002

Accepts query letter from unproduced, unrepresented writers via email. Project types include Feature Films and TV. Preferred genres include Horror and Thriller.

Michael Grais
Phone: 323-857-4510
Email: michaelgrais@yahoo.com
IMDb: imdb.com/name/nm0334457

MICHAEL TAYLOR PRODUCTIONS

2370 Bowmont Dr
Beverly Hills, CA 90210
Phone: 213-821-3113
Fax: 213-740-3395

Email: taycoprod@aol.com

Accepts query letter from unproduced, unrepresented writers via email. Project types include Feature Films and TV. Preferred genres include Non-Fiction and Reality.

Michael Taylor
Producer
Phone: 213-821-3113
IMDb: imdb.com/name/nm0852888
Assistant: Yolanda Rodriguez

MIDD KIDD PRODUCTIONS

10202 W Washington Blvd
Fred Astaire Building, Suite 2010
Culver City, CA 90232
Phone: 310-244-2688
Fax: 310-244-2603

Accepts query letter from unproduced, unrepresented writers. Project types include TV. Preferred genres include Crime, Detective, and Drama.

Shawn Ryan

Phone: 310-244-2688
IMDb: imdb.com/name/nm0752841
Assistant: Kent Rotherham

Marney Hochman Nash

Phone: 310-244-2688
IMDb: imdb.com/name/nm2701117
Assistant: Kent Rotherham

MIDNIGHT SUN PICTURES

10960 Wilshire Blvd, Suite 700
Los Angeles, CA 90024
Phone: 310-902-0431
Fax: 310-450-4988

Accepts query letter from produced or represented writers. Project types include Feature Films and TV. Preferred genres include Comedy, Drama, Horror, and Romance.

Renny Harlin

Phone: 310-902-0431
IMDb: imdb.com/name/nm0001317

MIKE LOBELL PRODUCTIONS

9477 Lloydcrest Dr
Beverly Hills, CA 90210
Phone: 323-822-2910
Fax: 310-205-2767

Accepts query letter from unproduced, unrepresented writers. Project types include Feature Films. Preferred genres include Action, Comedy, Drama, and Romance. Established in 1973.

Mike Lobell

Producer
Phone: 323-822-2910
IMDb: imdb.com/name/nm0516465
Assistant: JanetChiarabaglio

MILLAR/GOUGH INK

500 S Buena Vista St
Animation Building 1E16
Burbank, CA 91521
Phone: 818-560-4260
Fax: 818-560-4216

Accepts query letter from unproduced, unrepresented writers. Project types include Feature Films and TV. Preferred genres include Action, Drama, Family, and Science Fiction.

Miles Millar

Phone: 818-560-4260
IMDb: imdb.com/name/nm0587692
Assistant: Mal Stares

Alfred Gough

Phone: 818-560-4260
IMDb: imdb.com/name/nm0332184
Assistant: Mal Stares

MILLENNIUM FILMS

6423 Wilshire Blvd
Los Angeles, CA 90048
Phone: 310-388-6900
Fax: 310-388-6901

Email: info@millenniumfilms.com
Home Page: millenniumfilms.com

Accepts query letter from unproduced, unrepresented writers via email. Project types include Feature Films. Preferred genres include Action, Comedy, Detective, Drama, Fantasy, Non-Fiction, Science Fiction, and Thriller. Established in 1992.

Avi Lerner

IMDb: imdb.com/name/nm0503592

Trevor Short

IMDb: imdb.com/name/nm0795121

Boaz Davidson

IMDb: imdb.com/name/nm0203246

MIMRAN SCHUR PICTURES

1411 5th St
Suite 200
Santa Monica, CA 90401
Phone: 310-526-5410
Fax: 310-526-5405

Email: info@mimranschurpictures.com
Home Page: mimranschurpictures.com

Accepts query letter from produced or represented writers. Project types include Feature Films. Preferred genres include Drama. Established in 2009.

Lauren Pettit
Creative Executive
Phone: 310-526-5410
IMDb: imdb.com/name/nm2335692

Jordan Schur
Phone: 310-526-5410
IMDb: imdb.com/name/nm2028525

David Mimran
Phone: 310-526-5410
IMDb: imdb.com/name/nm3450764
Assistant: Caroline Haubold

MIRADA

4235 Redwood Ave
Los Angeles, CA 90066
Phone: 424-216-7470

Home Page: mirada.com

Does not accept any unsolicited material. Project types include Feature Films, TV, and Theater. Preferred genres include Animation, Drama, Fantasy, and Myth. Established in 2010.

Guillermo del Toro
IMDb: imdb.com/name/nm0868219

Guillermo Navarro
IMDb: imdb.com/name/nm0622897

Javier Jimenez
IMDb: imdb.com/name/nm3901643

MIRANDA ENTERTAINMENT

7337 Pacific View Dr
Los Angeles, CA 90068
Phone: 323-874-3600
Fax: 323-851-5350

Does not accept any unsolicited material. Project types include Feature Films and TV. Preferred genres include Comedy, Horror, and Thriller.

Carsten Lorenz
Producer
Phone: 323-874-3600
Email: clorenz1@aol.com
IMDb: imdb.com/name/nm0520696

MISHER FILMS

12233 Olympic Blvd, Suite 354
Los Angeles, CA 90064
Phone: 310-405-7999
Fax: 310-405-7991

Home Page: misherfilms.com

Does not accept any unsolicited material. Project types include Feature Films and TV. Preferred genres include Action, Crime, and Drama.

Kevin Misher
Phone: 310-405-7999
Email: kevin.misher@misherfilms.com
IMDb: pro.imdb.com/name/nm0592746
Assistant: Sarah Ezrin

MOCKINGBIRD PICTURES

Los Angeles, CA

Email: info@mockingbirdpictures.com
Home Page: mockinbirdpictures.com

Accepts query letter from unproduced, unrepresented writers via email. Project types include Feature Films. Preferred genres include Drama.

Bonnie Curtis
IMDb: imdb.com/name/nm0193268

Julie Lynn
IMDb: imdb.com/name/nm0528724

Kelly Thomas
Executive Producer
IMDb: imdb.com/name/nm1684437

MODERCINE

18 4th Place, Suite 2
Brooklyn, NY 11231

Email: info@moderncine.com
Home Page: http://www.moderncine.com/index.php
IMDb: imdb.com/company/co0100731

Does not accept any unsolicited material. Project types include Feature Films and Short Films. Preferred genres include Comedy, Crime, Horror, and Thriller.

Andrew van den Houten
CEO
IMDb: imdb.com/name/nm0886156

Robert Tonino
CFO
IMDb: imdb.com/name/nm1720736

MOJO FILMS

CBS Studios
4024 Radford Ave.
Bungalow 1
Studio City, CA 91604
Phone: 818-655-6292

Accepts query letter from unproduced, unrepresented writers. Project types include Feature Films and TV. Established in 2007.

Gary Fleder
President
Phone: 818-560-8370
IMDb: imdb.com/name/nm0001219

Mary-Beth Basile
Phone: 818-560-8370
IMDb: imdb.com/name/nm1039389

MOMENTUM ENTERTAINMENT GROUP

8687 Melrose Ave
8th Floor
Los Angeles, CA 90069

Accepts query letter from unproduced, unrepresented writers via email. Project types include TV and Commercials. Preferred genres include Action, Animation, Comedy, Crime, Detective, Drama, Family, Fantasy, Horror, Myth, Non-Fiction, Reality, Romance, Science Fiction, Sociocultural, and Thriller.

Nick Hamm
Head of Scripted Development
Email: nick.hamm@megww.com
IMDb: imdb.com/name/nm0358327

MONSTERFOOT PRODUCTIONS

3450 Cahuenga Blvd West
Loft 105
Los Angeles, CA 90068
Phone: 323-850-6116
Fax: 323-378-5232

Accepts query letter from unproduced, unrepresented writers. Project types include Feature Films and TV. Preferred genres include Non-Fiction and Reality.

Ahmet Zappa
CEO
Phone: 323-850-6116
IMDb: imdb.com/name/nm0953257

Devon Schiff
Executive
Phone: 323-850-6116
IMDb: imdb.com/name/nm3825595

MONTAGE ENTERTAINMENT

2118 Wilshire Blvd. #297
Santa Monica, CA 90403
USA
Phone: 818-248-0070
Fax: 818-248-0071

Email: david@montageentertainment.com
Home Page: montageentertainment.com

Accepts query letter from unproduced, unrepresented writers via email. Project types include Feature Films and TV.

David Peters
Producer
Phone: 310-966-0222
Email: david@montageentertainment.com
IMDb: imdb.com/name/nm0007070

Bill Ewart
Producer
Phone: 310-966-0222
Email: bill@montageentertainment.com
IMDb: imdb.com/name/nm0263867

MONTECITO PICTURES

9465 Wilshire Blvd, Suite 920
Beverly Hills, CA 90212
Phone: 310-247-9880
Fax: 310-247-9498

1482 E. Valley Rd
Suite 477
Montecito, CA 93108
Phone: 805-565-8590
Fax: 805-565-1893

Home Page: montecitopicturecompany.com

Accepts query letter from unproduced, unrepresented writers. Project types include Feature Films and TV. Preferred genres include Action, Comedy, Drama, Family, Non-Fiction, Period, and Thriller. Established in 2000.

Ivan Reitman
Partner
IMDb: imdb.com/name/nm0718645
Assistant: Eric Reich

Alex Plapinger
Executive Vice President of Production
Phone: 310-247-9880
IMDb: imdb.com/name/nm3292687

Tom Pollock
Partner
IMDb: imdb.com/name/nm0689696
Assistant: Krystee Morgan

Joe Medjuck
Partner
IMDb: imdb.com/name/nm0575817

MONTONE/YORN (UNNAMED YORN PRODUCTION COMPANY)

2000 Ave of the Stars
3rd Floor North Tower
Los Angeles, CA 90067

Accepts query letter from unproduced, unrepresented writers. Preferred genres include Action, Comedy, Family, and Fantasy. Established in 2008.

Rick Yorn
IMDb: imdb.com/name/nm0948833

MOONSTONE ENTERTAINMENT

PO Box 7400
Studio City, CA 91614
Phone: 818-985-3003
Fax: 818-985-3009

Email: submissions@moonstonefilms.com
Home Page: moonstonefilms.com

Accepts query letter from unproduced, unrepresented writers via email. Project types include Feature Films. Established in 1992.

Shahar Stroh
Phone: 818-985-3003
IMDb: imdb.com/name/nm2325576

MORGAN CREEK PRODUCTIONS

10351 Santa Monica Blvd
Suite 200
Los Angeles, CA 90025
Phone: 310-432-4848
Fax: 310-432-4844

Accepts query letter from unproduced, unrepresented writers. Project types include Feature Films. Established in 1988.

Andrew Moncrief
Creative Executive

MORNINGSTAR ENTERTAINMENT

350 N Glenoaks Blvd
Suite 300
Burbank, CA 91502

Phone: 818-559-7255
Fax: 818-559-7251

Accepts query letter from unproduced, unrepresented writers via email. Project types include TV. Preferred genres include Non-Fiction and Reality. Established in 1980.

Gary Tarpinian
President
Phone: 818-559-7255

MOSAIC/ MOSAIC MEDIA GROUP

9200 W Sunset Blvd
10th Floor
Los Angeles, CA 90069
Phone: 310-786-4900
Fax: 310-777-2185

Accepts query letter from unproduced, unrepresented writers. Project types include Feature Films and TV. Preferred genres include Action, Comedy, Drama, Family, and Myth.

David Householter
Phone: 310-786-4900
Email: dhouseholter@mosaicla.com
IMDb: imdb.com/name/nm0396720
Assistant: Brendan Clougherty

Mike Falbo
Phone: 310-786-4900
Email: mfalbo@mosaicla.com
IMDb: imdb.com/name/nm3824648
Assistant: Mark Acomb

Jimmy Miller
Phone: 310-786-4900
Email: jmiller@mosaicla.com
IMDb: imdb.com/name/nm0588612
Assistant: Alyx Carr

MOSHAG PRODUCTIONS

c/o Mark Mower
1531 Wellesley Ave
Los Angeles, CA 90025
Phone: 310-820-6760
Fax: 310-820-6960

Email: moshag@aol.com

Accepts query letter from unproduced, unrepresented writers via email. Project types include Feature Films and TV.

Mark Mower
Producer
Phone: 310-820-6760
IMDb: imdb.com/name/nm0610272

MOXIE PICTURES

5890 W Jefferson Blvd
Los Angeles, CA 90016
Phone: 310-857-1000
Fax: 310-857-1004

18 E. 16th St.
4th Floor
New York City, NY 10003
Phone: 212-807-6901
Fax: 212-807-1456

Home Page: moxiepictures.com
IMDb: imdb.com/company/co0119462

Does not accept any unsolicited material. Project types include Feature Films and TV. Preferred genres include Comedy, Documentary, Drama, Reality, and Romance. Established in 2005.

Dan Levinson
President
IMDb: imdb.com/name/nm1829495

Robert Fernandez
IMDb: imdb.com/name/nm0273045

Lizzie Schwartz
IMDb: imdb.com/name/nm2594272

Katie Connell
Phone: 212-807-6901

Dawn Laren

David Casey

MRB PRODUCTIONS

311 N. Robertson Blvd., #513
Beverly HIlls, CA 90211
Phone: 323-965-8881
Fax: 323-965-8882

Home Page: mrbproductions.com

Does not accept any unsolicited material. Project types include Feature Films and TV. Preferred genres include Comedy, Documentary, Drama, Romance, and Thriller.

Matthew Brady
Executive Producer
Email: matthew@mrbproductions.com
IMDb: imdb.com/name/nm0103683

Lori Huck
Director of Development

Brenda Bank
Producer
Email: brenda@mrbproductions.com
IMDb: imdb.com/name/nm1870773
Assistant: Erica Weiss

Yvette Lubinsky
Executive

Luke Watson
Email: luke@mrbproductions.com
IMDb: imdb.com/name/nm2362830

MR. MUDD

137 N Larchmont Blvd, #113
Los Angeles, CA 9004
Phone: 323-932-5656
Fax: 323-932-5666

Does not accept any unsolicited material. Project types include Feature Films. Preferred genres include Comedy, Drama, Family, and Romance. Established in 1998.

Lianne Halfon
Producer
IMDb: imdb.com/name/nm0355147

Russell Smith
Producer
IMDb: imdb.com/name/nm0809833

John Malkovich
IMDb: imdb.com/name/nm0000518

MYRIAD PICTURES

3015 Main St, Suite 400
Santa Monica, CA 90405
Phone: 310-279-4000
Fax: 310-279-4001

Email: info@myriadpictures.com
Home Page: myriadpictures.com
IMDb: imdb.com/company/co0033226

Does not accept any unsolicited material. Project types include Feature Films. Preferred genres include Comedy, Drama, Fantasy, Horror, Non-Fiction, and Romance. Established in 1998.

Kirk D'Amico
CEO
IMDb: imdb.com/name/nm0195136

NALA INVESTMENTS

233 Wilshire Blvd.
Suite 990
Santa Monica, CA 90401
Phone: 310-935-3867

Email: info@nalafilms.com
Home Page: nalafilms.com

Does not accept any unsolicited material. Project types include Feature Films and TV. Preferred genres include Drama and Thriller.

Emilio Barroso
CEO
IMDb: imdb.com/name/nm1950898

NANCY TENENBAUM FILMS

43 Lyons Plain Rd
Weston, CT 06883
Phone: 203-221-6830
Fax: 203-221-6832

Email: ntfilms2@aol.com
IMDb: imdb.com/company/co0012648

Accepts query letter from unproduced, unrepresented writers via email. Project types include Feature Films. Preferred genres include Comedy and Drama. Established in 1996.

Meredith Hall
Director of Development

Nancy Tenenbaum
President
Assistant: Lyndsy Celestino

NBC PRODUCTIONS

3000 W Alameda Ave
Burbank, CA 91523-0001
USA
Phone: 818-840-4444

Home Page: nbcuni.com
IMDb: imdb.com/company/co0065874

Does not accept any unsolicited material. Project types include Feature Films and TV. Preferred genres include Action, Comedy, Crime, Documentary, Drama, Family, Fantasy, Horror, Non-Fiction, Romance, Science Fiction, and Thriller. Established in 1947.

NBC STUDIOS

3000 W Alameda Ave
Burbank, CA 91523-0001
USA
Phone: 818-526-7000

Home Page: nbcuni.com
IMDb: imdb.com/company/co0022762

Does not accept any unsolicited material. Project types include Feature Films and TV. Preferred genres include Action, Comedy, Crime, Detective, Documentary, Drama, Non-Fiction, and Thriller. Established in 1950.

NBCUNIVERSAL

30 Rockefeller Plaza
New York, NY 10112
Phone: 212-664-4444

Home Page: nbcumv.com/mediavillage

Project types include Feature Films and TV. Preferred genres include Comedy, Crime, Documentary, Drama, Period, Reality, and Thriller. Established in 2009.

Steve Burke
President
IMDb: imdb.com/name/nm4446434

Marci Klein
Executive Producer
IMDb: imdb.com/name/nm0458885

Jessica Franks
Development Executive

Jon Dakss

Josie Ventura

Dan Berkowitz

Pearlena Igbokwe
IMDb: imdb.com/name/nm2303684

NBCUNIVERSAL TELEVISION DISTRIBUTION

3400 W. Olive Ave.
Burbank, CA 91505
Phone: 818-840-4444
Fax: 818-866-1430

30 Rockafeller Plaza
New York City, NY 10112
Phone: 212-664-4444

454 N. Columbus Dr.
5th Floor
Chicago, IL 60611
Phone: 312-836-5725

3340 Peachtree Rd. NE
Suite 711
Atlanta, GA 30326
Phone: 404-812-3712

Home Page: nbcuni.com
IMDb: imdb.com/company/co0129175

Does not accept any unsolicited material. Project types include Feature Films and TV. Preferred genres include Action, Animation, Comedy, Crime, Detective, Documentary, Drama, Family, Fantasy, Horror, Reality, Science Fiction, and Thriller. Established in 1971.

Jennifer Nicholson-Salke
President
IMDb: imdb.com/name/nm2323622

Jerry DiCanio
IMDb: imdb.com/name/nm3034292

NECROPIA ENTERTAINMENT

9171 Wilshire Blvd, Suite 300
Beverly Hills, CA 9021
Phone: 323-865-0547

Does not accept any unsolicited material. Project types include Feature Films. Preferred genres include Action, Fantasy, Horror, Myth, and Science Fiction.

Guillermo de Toro
Director
IMDb: imdb.com/name/nm0868219

NEO ART & LOGIC

5225 Wilshire Blvd Ste. 501
Los Angeles, CA 90036
Phone: 323-451-2040

Email: aaron@neoartandlogic.com
Home Page: neoartandlogic.com
IMDb: imdb.com/company/co0038165

Accepts query letter from unproduced, unrepresented writers via email. Project types include Feature Films and TV. Preferred genres include Action, Animation, Comedy, Documentary, Drama, Family, Fantasy, Horror, Science Fiction, and Thriller. Established in 2000.

Kirk Morri
Executive
IMDb: imdb.com/name/nm0606294

W. K. Border
IMDb: imdb.com/name/nm0096176

Joel Soisson
IMDb: imdb.com/name/nm0812373

Aaron Ockman
IMDb: imdb.com/name/nm1845744

NEW AMSTERDAM ENTERTAINMENT

1133 Ave. Of The Americas
Suite 1621
New York, NY 10036

Phone: 212-922-1930
Fax: 212-922-0674

Email: mail@newamsterdamnyc.com
Home Page: newamsterdamnyc.com
IMDb: imdb.com/company/co0010962

Does not accept any unsolicited material. Project types include Feature Films and TV. Preferred genres include Action, Documentary, Drama, Fantasy, Horror, Science Fiction, and Thriller. Established in 1996.

Richard Rubinstein
CEO
IMDb: imdb.com/name/nm0748283

Katherine Kolbert
IMDb: imdb.com/name/nm0463946

Michael Messina
IMDb: imdb.com/name/nm0582175

Sarah Reiner
IMDb: imdb.com/name/nm2200017

NEW ARTISTS ALLIANCE

16633 Ventura Blvd, #1440
Encino, CA 91436
Phone: 818-784-8341

Email: info@newartistsalliance.com
Home Page: newartistsalliance.com

Accepts query letter from unproduced, unrepresented writers via email. Project types include Feature Films. Preferred genres include Action, Drama, Horror, and Thriller. Established in 2003.

Gabe Cowan
Email: gabe@naafilms.com
IMDb: imdb.com/name/nm1410462

John Suits
Email: john@naafilms.com
IMDb: imdb.com/name/nm2986811

NEW CRIME PRODUCTIONS

1041 N Formosa Ave
Formosa Building, Room 219
West Hollywood, CA 90016
Phone: 323-850-2525

Email: newcrime@aol.com
Home Page: newcrime.com
IMDb: imdb.com/company/co0079035

Accepts query letter from unproduced, unrepresented writers via email. Project types include Feature Films. Preferred genres include Comedy, Drama, Romance, and Thriller.

John Cusack
Executive
IMDb: imdb.com/name/nm0000131

NEW LINE CINEMA

116 N Robertson Blvd
Los Angeles, CA 90048
Phone: 310-854-5811
Fax: 310-854-1824

Home Page: warnerbros.com
IMDb: imdb.com/company/co0046718

Does not accept any unsolicited material. Project types include Feature Films and TV. Preferred genres include Action, Comedy, Crime, Documentary, Drama, Family, Fantasy, Non-Fiction, Period, Romance, Science Fiction, and Thriller. Established in 1967.

Toby Emmerich
President
IMDb: imdb.com/name/nm0256497
Assistant: Joshua Mack

Andrea Johnston
Creative Executive

Richard Brener
IMDb: imdb.com/name/nm0107196
Assistant: Kristin Schmidt

Sam Brown
IMDb: imdb.com/name/nm1354041
Assistant: Celia Khong

Michael Disco

Walter Hamada
IMDb: imdb.com/name/nm1023578

NEW REGENCY FILMS

10201 W Pico Blvd
Bldg 12
Los Angeles, CA 90035
Phone: 310-369-8300
Fax: 310-969-0470

270 Lafayette St.
Suite 1505
New York City, NY 10012
Phone: 212-966-3166
Fax: 212-966-3443

Email: info@newregency.com
Home Page: newregency.com

Project types include Feature Films. Preferred genres include Action, Comedy, Crime, Drama, Family, Romance, and Science Fiction.

Justin Lam
Creative Executive
IMDb: imdb.com/name/nm3528759

Arnon Milchan
Chairman
IMDb: imdb.com/name/nm0586969

Mimi Tseng
CFO
IMDb: imdb.com/name/nm2303729

David Manpearl
IMDb: imdb.com/name/nm1818404

NEW SCHOOL MEDIA, LLC

9229 Sunset Blvd, Suite 301
West Hollywood, CA 90069
Phone: 310-858-2989
Fax: 310-858-1841

Accepts query letter from unproduced, unrepresented writers. Project types include Feature Films.

Brian Levy
IMDb: imdb.com/name/nm2546392

NEW WAVE ENTERTAINMENT

2660 W Olive Ave
Burbank, CA 91505

Phone: 818-295-5000
Fax: 818-295-5002

35 W. 36th St.
10th Floor
New York, NY 10018
Phone: 212-594-2414
Fax: 212-239-1034

Home Page: nwe.com

Does not accept any unsolicited material. Project types include Feature Films, TV, and Commercials. Preferred genres include Action, Animation, Comedy, Crime, Detective, Drama, Family, Fantasy, Horror, Myth, Non-Fiction, Reality, Romance, Science Fiction, Sociocultural, and Thriller.

Paul Apel
CEO
Phone: 818-295-5000
IMDb: pro.imdb.com/name/nm1318269

Gregory Woertz
Phone: +818-295-5000
Email: gwoertz@nwe.com
IMDb: pro.imdb.com/name/nm0937343

NICK WECHSLER PRODUCTIONS

Santa Monica, CA
Phone: 310-309-5759
Fax: 310-309-5716

Email: info@nwprods.com
Home Page: nwprods.com

Does not accept any unsolicited material. Project types include Feature Films and TV. Preferred genres include Action, Animation, Comedy, Crime, Drama, Family, Fantasy, Horror, Science Fiction, and Thriller. Established in 2005.

Elizabeth Bradford
Director of Development
Email: lizzy@nwprods.com
IMDb: imdb.com/name/nm4504768

Felicity Aldridge
Creative Executive
Email: felicity@nwprods.com
IMDb: imdb.com/name/nm4504820

Nick Wechsler
Email: nick@nwprods.com
IMDb: imdb.com/name/nm0917059

NIGHT AND DAY PICTURES

527 W. 7th St.
Suite 402
Los Angeles, CA 90036
Phone: 323-930-2212

Email: info@nightanddaypictures.com
Home Page: nightanddaypictures.com
IMDb: imdb.com/company/co0253348

Accepts query letter from unproduced, unrepresented writers via email. Project types include Feature Films.

Rachel Berk
Creative Executive
IMDb: imdb.com/company/co0157684

Michael Roiff
President
Email: michael@nightanddaypictures.com
IMDb: imdb.com/name/nm1988698

NINJAS RUNNIN' WILD PRODUCTIONS

7024 Melrose Ave, Suite 420
Los Angeles, CA 90038
Phone: 323-937-6100

Accepts scripts from produced or represented writers. Project types include Feature Films.

Jason Barrett
Producer
IMDb: imdb.com/name/nm2249074

Zac Effron
IMDb: imdb.com/name/nm1374980

NORTH BY NORTHWEST ENTERTAINMENT

903 W Broadway
Spokane, WA 99201
Phone: 509-324-2949
Fax: 509-324-2959

4838 Willowcrest Dr.
North Hollywood, CA 91601

Phone: 818-506-7015
Fax: 818-506-7265

Email: moviesales@nxnw.net
Home Page: nxnw.net

Does not accept any unsolicited material. Project types include Feature Films. Preferred genres include Thriller.

Rich Cowen
CEO
Phone: 509-324-2949
Email: rcowan@nxnw.net
IMDb: imdb.com/name/nm0184616

NOVA PICTURES

6496 Ivarene Ave.
Los Angeles, CA 90068
Phone: 323-462-5502
Fax: 323-463-8903

Email: pbarnett@novapictures.com
Home Page: novapictures.com

Does not accept any unsolicited material. Project types include Feature Films.

Peter Barnett
Executive Producer
IMDb: imdb.com/name/nm0055963

NUBIA FILMWORKS LLC

1516 K St S.E, Suite #303
Washington, DC 20003
Phone: 202-547-1591
Fax: 202-547-0013

Home Page: nubiafilmworks.com

Accepts query letter from unproduced, unrepresented writers. Project types include Feature Films and TV. Preferred genres include Drama.

Tara Hayman
Creative Executive

Calvin "C-Note" Jackson
Development Executive

Mary Colbert
Creative Executive

Shuaib Mitchell
President

NU IMAGE FILMS

6423 Wilshire Blvd
Los Angeles, CA 90048
Phone: 310-388-6900
Fax: 310-388-6901

Email: info@millenniumfilms.com
Home Page: millenniumfilms.com

Does not accept any unsolicited material. Preferred genres include Action, Comedy, Drama, and Science Fiction.

Christine Crow
Director of Development
Phone: 310-388-6900
IMDb: imdb.com/name/nm4579268

Mark Gill
President
Phone: 310-388-6900
IMDb: imdb.com/name/nm1247584

Boaz Davidson
Phone: 310-388-6900
IMDb: imdb.com/name/nm0203246

John Thompson
Phone: 310-388-6900
IMDb: imdb.com/name/nm0860315

NUYORICAN PRODUCTIONS

1100 Glendon Ave, Suite 920
Los Angeles, CA 90024
Phone: 310-943-6600
Fax: 310-943-6609

Does not accept any unsolicited material. Project types include Feature Films, TV, and Commercials. Preferred genres include Action, Comedy, Drama, Non-Fiction, and Reality.

Jennifer Lopez
IMDb: imdb.com/name/nm0000182

Tiana Rios
Creative Executive

O2 FILMES

Rua Baumann, 930
Vila Leopoldina
São Paulo, SP 05318-000
Brazil
Phone: +55 1138 39 94 00
Fax: +55 11 38 32 48 11

Email: faleconosco@o2filmes.com
Home Page: o2filmes.com

Does not accept any unsolicited material. Project types include Feature Films. Preferred genres include Documentary and Drama.

Paulo Morelli

ODDLOT ENTERTAINMENT

9601 Jefferson Blvd, Suite A
Culver City, CA 90232
Phone: 310-652-0999
Fax: 310-652-0718

2141 N. Southport Ave.
Chicago, IL 60614

Email: info@oddlotent.com
Home Page: oddlotent.com

Does not accept any unsolicited material. Project types include Feature Films. Preferred genres include Drama.

Gigi Pritzker
CEO
IMDb: imdb.com/name/nm0698133

Stacy Keppler
Director of Development

OFFSPRING ENTERTAINMENT

8755 Colgate Ave
Los Angeles, CA 90048
Phone: 310-247-0019
Fax: 310-550-6908

Does not accept any unsolicited material. Project types include Feature Films. Preferred genres include Comedy, Drama, and Family.

Adam Shankman
Executive
IMDb: imdb.com/name/nm0788202

Jennifer Gibgot
Executive
IMDb: imdb.com/name/nm0316774

OLIVE BRIDGE ENTERTAINMENT

10202 W Washington Blvd
Culver City, CA 90232
Phone: 310-244-1269

Home Page: olivebridge.com
IMDb: imdb.com/company/co0219609

Does not accept any unsolicited material. Project types include Feature Films and TV. Preferred genres include Action, Comedy, Drama, Period, and Romance. Established in 2003.

Will Gluck
IMDb: imdb.com/name/nm0323239

Alicia Emmrich
IMDb: imdb.com/name/nm1445355

Jodi Hildebrand
IMDb: imdb.com/name/nm1637492

Richard Schwartz
IMDb: imdb.com/name/nm1108160

OLMOS PRODUCTIONS INC.

500 S Buena Vista St
Old Animation Building, Suite 1G
Burbank, CA 91521
Phone: 818-560-8651
Fax: 818-560-8655

Email: olmosonline@yahoo.com

Does not accept any unsolicited material. Project types include Feature Films, TV, and Commercials. Preferred genres include Comedy, Drama, Family, Non-Fiction, and Reality. Established in 1980.

Edward Olmos
President
IMDb: imdb.com/name/nm0001579

OLYMPUS PICTURES

12424 Whilshire Blvd.
Suite 1120
Los Angeles, CA 90025
Phone: 310-452-3335
Fax: 310-452-0108

Email: getinfo@olympuspics.com
Home Page: olympuspics.com

Accepts query letter from unproduced, unrepresented writers via email. Project types include Feature Films. Established in 2007.

Leslie Urdang
IMDb: imdb.com/name/nm0881811

Amanda Beckner
Creative Executive
Email: rrdecter@olympuspics.com

OMBRA FILMS

12444 Ventura Blvd, Suite 103
Studio City, CA 91604
Phone: 818-509-0552

Email: info@ombrafilms.com
Home Page: ombrafilms.com

Accepts query letter from unproduced, unrepresented writers via email. Project types include Feature Films and TV. Preferred genres include Fantasy, Horror, and Thriller. Established in 2011.

Juan Sola
Producer
IMDb: imdb.com/name/nm4928159

Jaume Collet-Serra
Producer
IMDb: imdb.com/name/nm1429471

O.N.C.

11150 Santa Monica Blvd, Suite 450
Los Angeles, CA 90025
Phone: 310-477-0670
Fax: 310-477-7710

Home Page: oncentertainment.com

Does not accept any unsolicited material. Project types include Feature Films. Preferred genres include Action, Comedy, Crime, Family, Romance, and Thriller.

Michael Nathanson
Producer
Email: michaelnathanson@oncentertainment.com
IMDb: imdb.com/name/nm0622296
Assistant: Robyn Altman

ONE RACE FILMS

9100 Wilshire Blvd
East Tower, Suite 535
Beverly Hills, CA 90212
Phone: 310-401-6880
Fax: 310-401-6890

Email: info@oneracefilms.com
Home Page: oneracefilms.com

Accepts query letter from unproduced, unrepresented writers via email. Project types include Feature Films and TV. Preferred genres include Action, Crime, Drama, Science Fiction, and Thriller. Established in 1995.

Vin Diesel
IMDb: imdb.com/name/nm0004874

Samantha Vincent
Email: samantha@oneracefilms.com
IMDb: imdb.com/name/nm2176972

Thyrale Thai
Email: thyrale@oneracefilms.com
IMDb: imdb.com/name/nm1394166

OOPS DOUGHNUTS PRODUCTIONS

6030 Wilshire Blvd.
Suite 101
Los Angeles, CA 90036
Phone: 323-936-9811
Fax: 818-560-6185

IMDb: imdb.com/company/co0248742

Accepts query letter from unproduced, unrepresented writers. Project types include Feature Films, TV, and Commercials.

Andy Fickman
IMDb: imdb.com/name/nm0275698
Assistant: Whitney Engstrom

Betsy Sullenger
Producer
IMDb: imdb.com/name/nm0998095

OPEN CITY FILMS

122 Hudson St.
5th Floor
New York, NY 10013
Phone: 212-255-0500
Fax: 212-255-0455

Email: oc@opencityfilms.com
Home Page: opencityfilms.com

Accepts query letter from unproduced, unrepresented writers via email. Project types include Feature Films and TV. Preferred genres include Non-Fiction and Reality.

Jason Kilot
IMDb: imdb.com/name/nm0459852

Joana Vicente

OPEN ROAD FILMS

12301 Wilshire Blvd.
Suite 600
Los Angeles, CA 90025
Phone: 310-696-7575

IMDb: imdb.com/company/co0178575
Home Page: openroadfilms.com

Does not accept any unsolicited material. Project types include Feature Films, Short Films, and TV. Preferred genres include Action, Crime, Documentary, and Drama. Established in 2002.

Keri Safran

ORIGINAL FILM

11466 San Vicente Blvd
Los Angeles, CA 90049
Phone: 310-575-6950
Fax: 310-575-6990

Accepts query letter from unproduced, unrepresented writers. Project types include Feature Films. Preferred genres include Action, Comedy, and Drama.

Toby Ascher
Producer
IMDb: imdb.com/name/nm4457111

Toby Jaffe
Producer
IMDb: imdb.com/name/nm0003993
Assistant: Hanna Ozer

Vivian Cannon
Television Executive
IMDb: imdb.com/name/nm0134279
Assistant: Ashley Deaton

Ori Marmur
Production Executive
IMDb: imdb.com/name/nm1506459

ORIGINAL MEDIA

175 Varick St
7th Floor
New York, NY 10014
Phone: 212-683-3086
Fax: 212-683-3162

933 N. La Brea Ave.
Suite 400
Los Angeles, CA 90038
Phone: 323-850-7809

Home Page: originalmedia.com

Does not accept any unsolicited material. Project types include Feature Films and TV. Preferred genres include Comedy, Drama, Family, Romance, and Thriller.

Patrick Moses

Jessica Matthews

Charlie Corwin
IMDb: imdb.com/name/nm1231965

Michael Saffran

Colleen Ocean Hall
IMDb: imdb.com/name/nm5066841

Chelsey Trowbridge
IMDb: imdb.com/name/nm2399791

OSCILLOSCOPE PICTURES

511 Canal St Suite 5E
New York City, NY 10013
Phone: 212-219-4029
Fax: 212-219-9538

Email: info@oscilloscope.net
Home Page: oscilloscope.net

Does not accept any unsolicited material. Project types include Feature Films. Preferred genres include Drama and Romance.

Aaron Katz
Executive

Dan Berger
IMDb: imdb.com/name/nm3088964

David Laub
IMDb: imdb.com/name/nm3000864

Tom Sladek

Amanda Lebow
IMDb: imdb.com/name/nm4144904

O'TAYE PRODUCTIONS

12001 Ventura Place
Suite 340
Studio City, CA 91604
USA
Phone: 818-232-8580
Fax: 818-232-8108

Accepts query letter from unproduced, unrepresented writers. Project types include TV.

Jennifer Bozell
Head of Development

Taye Diggs
IMDb: imdb.com/name/nm0004875

OUTERBANK ENTERTAINMENT

4000 Warner Blvd.
Burbank, CA 91522

Phone: 818-954-3281
Fax: 818-977-9990

Accepts query letter from unproduced, unrepresented writers via email. Project types include Feature Films and TV.

Kevin Williamson
President
Phone: 310-858-8711
Email: kevin@outerbanks-ent.com
IMDb: imdb.com/name/nm0932078

OUT OF THE BLUE ENTERTAINMENT

c/o Sony Pictures Entertainment
10202 W Washington Blvd
Astaire Building, Suite 1200
Culver City, CA 90232-3195
Phone: 310-244-7811
Fax: 310-244-1539

Email: info@outoftheblueent.com
Home Page: outoftheblueent.com

Accepts query letter from unproduced, unrepresented writers via email. Project types include Feature Films and TV.

Toby Conroy
Creative Executive
IMDb: imdb.com/name/nm1926762

Sidney Ganis
IMDb: imdb.com/name/nm0304398

OVERBROOK ENTERTAINMENT

10202 W. Washington Blvd.
Poitier Building
Culver City, CA 90232
Phone: 310-432-2400
Fax: 310-432-2401

Home Page: overbrookent.com

Accepts query letter from unproduced, unrepresented writers. Project types include Feature Films and TV. Established in 1998.

Will Smith
Phone: 310-432-2400
IMDb: imdb.com/name/nm0000226

Gary Glushon
Phone: 310-432-2400
IMDb: imdb.com/name/nm2237223

OVERNIGHT PRODUCTIONS

15 Mercer St, Suite 4
New York, NY 10013
Phone: 212-625-0530

Does not accept any unsolicited material. Project types include Feature Films. Established in 2008.

Rick Schwartz
Phone: 212-625-0530
IMDb: imdb.com/name/nm0777408

OWN: OPRAH WINFREY NETWORK

5700 Wilshire Blvd
Ste 120
Los Angeles, CA 90036
Phone: 323-602-5500

Home Page: oprah.com/own

Does not accept any unsolicited material. Preferred genres include Animation, Documentary, Family, and Reality.

Oprah Winfrey
CEO
IMDb: imdb.com/name/nm0001856

OZLA PICTURES INC.

1800 Camino Palmero St
Los Angeles, CA 90046
Phone: 323-876-0180
Fax: 323-876-0189

Email: ozla@ozla.com
Home Page: ozla.com

Does not accept any unsolicited material. Project types include Feature Films and TV. Established in 1992.

Takashige Ichise
Producer
Phone: 323-876-0180
IMDb: imdb.com/name/nm0406772
Assistant: Chiaki Yanagimoto

PACIFICA INTERNATIONAL FILM & TV CORPORATION

PO Box 8329
Northridge, CA 91237
Phone: 818-831-0360
Fax: 818-831-0352

Email: pacifica@pacifica.la
Home Page: pacifica.la

Does not accept any unsolicited material.

Christine Iso
Executive Producer
IMDb: imdb.com/name/nm1259606

PACIFIC STANDARD

9720 Wilshire Blvd
4th Floor
Beverly Hills, CA 90212
Phone: 310-777-3119
Fax: 310-777-0150

IMDb: imdb.com/company/co0373561

Does not accept any unsolicited material. Project types include Feature Films. Established in 2012.

Reese Witherspoon
IMDb: imdb.com/name/nm0000702

Bruna Papandrea
IMDb: imdb.com/name/nm0660295

PALERMO PRODUCTIONS

c/o Twentieth Century Fox
10201 W Pico Blvd
Building 52, Room 103
Los Angeles, CA 90064
Phone: 310-369-1900

Accepts query letter from unproduced, unrepresented writers. Project types include Feature Films and TV.

John Palermo
Producer
Phone: 310-369-1911
IMDb: imdb.com/name/nm0657561
Assistant: Mike Belyea

PALMSTAR ENTERTAINMENT

36 E. 20th St
Third Floor
New York City, NY 10003
Phone: 646-775-4180

14622 Ventura Blvd.
Suite 755
Sherman Oaks, CA 91403
Phone: 646-277-7356
Fax: 310-469-7855

Email: contact@palmstar.com
Home Page: palmstar.com
Facebook: facebook.com/PalmStarEntertainment

Does not accept any unsolicited material. Project types include Feature Films. Preferred genres include Action, Comedy, Drama, Family, Non-Fiction, Romance, and Thriller. Established in 2004.

Courtney Andrialis
Producer

Stephan Paternot
Chairman
IMDb: imdb.com/name/nm0665456

Kevin Scott Frakes
CEO
IMDb: imdb.com/name/nm0289694

Michael Bassick
Co-CEO

PALOMAR PICTURES

PO Box 491986
Los Angeles, CA 90049
Phone: 310-440-3494

Email: ad@palomarpics.com

Does not accept any unsolicited material. Project types include Feature Films and TV. Established in 1992.

Aditya Ezhuthachan
Head of Development
Phone: 310-440-3494
IMDb: imdb.com/name/nm2149074

Joni Sighvatsson
Phone: 310-440-3494
IMDb: imdb.com/name/nm0797451

PANAY FILMS

500 S Buena Vista
Old Animation Bldg, Rm 3c-6
Burbank, CA 91521
Phone: 818-560-4265

Does not accept any unsolicited material. Project types include Feature Films. Preferred genres include Action, Comedy, Drama, and Fantasy.

Andrew Panay
IMDb: imdb.com/name/nm0659123
Assistant: Lukas Stuart-Fry

Adam Blum
IMDb: imdb.com/name/nm3597471

PANDEMONIUM

9777 Wilshire Blvd, Suite 700
Beverly Hills, CA 90212
Phone: 310-550-9900
Fax: 310-550-9910

Accepts query letter from unproduced, unrepresented writers via email. Project types include Feature Films.

Bill Mechanic
Phone: 310-550-9900
IMDb: imdb.com/name/nm0575312
Assistant: David Freedman

Suzanne Warren
Phone: 310-550-9900
IMDb: imdb.com/name/nm0913049

PANTELION FILMS

2700 Colorado Ave.
Suite 200
Santa Monica, CA 90404
Phone: 310-449-9200
Fax: 310-255-3870

1601 Cloverfield Blvd.
Suite 200
South Tower
Santa Monica, CA 90404
Phone: 310-255-3000
Fax: 310-255-3908

2000 Avendia Vasco de Quiroga
Álvaro Obregón, Mexico 01210
Phone: 011-525-552612000

Email: info@pantelionfilms.com
IMDb: imdb.com/company/co0325194
Home Page: pantelionfilms.com
Facebook: facebook.com/PantelionFilms

Does not accept any unsolicited material. Project types include Feature Films and TV. Preferred genres include Action, Comedy, Drama, Family, Romance, and Science Fiction.

Ben Odell
Head of Production & Development
Phone: 310-255-5778
IMDb: imdb.com/name/nm0643967

James McNamara
Chairman
IMDb: imdb.com/name/nm2241044

Paul Presburger
CEO
IMDb: imdb.com/name/nm0643967

Sandra Condito
President (Acquisitions & Production)
IMDb: imdb.com/name/nm1354700

PANTHER FILMS

1888 Century Park East
14th Floor
Los Angeles, CA 90067
Phone: 424-202-6630
Fax: 310-887-1001

Does not accept any unsolicited material. Project types include Feature Films.

Lindsay Culpepper
Phone: 424-202-6630
IMDb: imdb.com/name/nm0258431

Brad Epstein
Phone: 424-202-6630
IMDb: imdb.com/name/nm0258431

PAPA JOE ENTERTAINMENT

14804 Greenleaf St
Sherman Oaks, CA 91403
Phone: 818-788-7608
Fax: 818-788-7612

Email: info@papjoefilms.com
Home Page: papjoefilms.com

Accepts query letter from unproduced, unrepresented writers via email. Project types include Feature Films and TV.

Joe Simpson
CEO
Phone: 818-788-7608
IMDb: imdb.com/name/nm1471425
Assistant: Heath Pliler

Erin Alexander
Phone: 818-788-7608
IMDb: imdb.com/name/nm0018408
Assistant: Amelia Garrison

PAPER STREET FILMS

265 Canal St., Suite 212
New York, NY 10013
Phone: 646-524-6954
Fax: 646-417-6460

Email: info@paperstreetfilms.com
Home Page: paperstreetfilms.com
IMDb: imdb.com/company/co0222800

Does not accept any unsolicited material. Project types include Feature Films. Preferred genres include Comedy, Drama, Horror, and Thriller. Established in 2007.

Benji Kohn
Partner
IMDb: imdb.com/name/nm2803928

Bingo Gubelmann
Partner
IMDb: imdb.com/name/nm1292502

Austin Stark
Partner
IMDb: imdb.com/name/nm0823133

Emily Buder
Creative Executive
IMDb: imdb.com/name/nm1692758

Chris Papavasiliou
Partner
IMDb: imdb.com/name/nm2830113

PARADIGM STUDIO

2701 2nd Ave North
Seattle, WA 98109
Phone: 206-282-2161
Fax: 206-283-6433

Email: info@paradigmstudio.com
Home Page: paradigmstudio.com

Accepts query letter from unproduced, unrepresented writers via email. Project types include Feature Films and TV.

John Comerford
President
Phone: 206-282-2161
IMDb: imdb.com/name/nm0173766

B Dahlia
Manager
Phone: 206-282-2161
IMDb: imdb.com/name/nm1148338

PARADOX ENTERTAINMENT

8484 Wilshire Blvd
Suite 870
Beverly Hills, CA 90211
Phone: 323-655-1700
Fax: 323-655-1720

Email: info@paradox entertainment.com
Home Page: paradoxentertainment.com

Does not accept any unsolicited material. Project types include Feature Films. Preferred genres include Action, Comedy, Drama, Fantasy, Romance, and Science Fiction.

Janet Sheppard
CFO
IMDb: imdb.com/name/nm5128822

Fredrik Malmberg
IMDb: imdb.com/name/nm1573406

PARALLEL MEDIA

301 N Canon Dr,
Suite 223
Beverly Hills, CA 90210
Phone: 310-858-3003
Fax: 310-858-3034

11054 Ventura Blvd.
Suite 371
Studio City, CA 91604
Phone: 323-319-3944
Fax: 323-843-9921

Email: info@parallelmediallc.com
Home Page: parallelmediafilms.com

Does not accept any unsolicited material. Project types include Feature Films. Established in 2006.

Armen Mahdessian
Executive

PARAMOUNT PICTURES

5555 Melrose Ave
Los Angeles, CA 90038
Phone: 323-956-5000

Home Page: paramount.com

Does not accept any unsolicited material. Project types include Feature Films.

Allison Small
Creative Executive
IMDb: imdb.com/name/nm1861333

Marc Evans
IMDb: imdb.com/name/nm0263010

Ashley Brucks
IMDb: imdb.com/name/nm2087318

PARIAH

9229 Sunset Blvd
Ste 208
West Hollywood, CA 90069
USA

Phone: 310-461-3460
Fax: 310-246-9622

Does not accept any unsolicited material. Project types include Feature Films and TV.

Gavin Polone

Owner
Phone: 310-461-3460
IMDb: imdb.com/name/nm0689780
Assistant: Stephen Iwanyk

PARKER ENTERTAINMENT GROUP

8581 Santa Monica Blvd #261
West Hollywood, CA 90069
Phone: 323-400-6622
Fax: 323-400-6655

Email: cparker@parkerentgroup.com
Home Page: parkerentgroup.com

Accepts scripts from produced or represented writers. Project types include Feature Films. Established in 2008.

Christopher Parker

President
Email: cparker@parkerentgroup.com
IMDb: imdb.com/name/nm2034521

Gregory Parker

CEO
Phone: 323-400-6622
Email: gparker@parkerentgroup.com
IMDb: imdb.com/name/nm2027023

PARKES/MACDONALD PRODUCTIONS

1663 Euclid St
Santa Monica, CA 90404
Phone: 310-581-5990
Fax: 310-581-5999

Accepts query letter from unproduced, unrepresented writers. Project types include Feature Films and TV. Established in 2007.

Walter Parkes

Producer
Phone: 310-581-5990
IMDb: imdb.com/name/nm0662748

Laurie MacDonald

Producer
Phone: 310-581-5990
IMDb: imdb.com/name/nm0531827

PARKWAY PRODUCTIONS

7095 Hollywood Blvd, Suite 1009
Hollywood, CA 90028
Phone: 323-874-6207

Email: parkwayprods@aol.com

Accepts query letter from unproduced, unrepresented writers via email. Project types include Feature Films and TV.

Penny Marshall

Phone: 323-874-6207
IMDb: imdb.com/name/nm0001508

PARTICIPANT MEDIA

331 Foothill Rd
3rd Floor
Beverly Hills, CA 90210
Phone: 310-550-5100
Fax: 310-550-5106

Email: info@participantproductions.com
Home Page: participantmedia.com

Does not accept any unsolicited material. Project types include Feature Films and TV. Preferred genres include Non-Fiction and Reality. Established in 2004.

Jonathan King

Executive Vice President of Production
Phone: 310-550-5100
IMDb: imdb.com/name/nm2622896

Erik Andreasen

Phone: 310-550-5100
IMDb: imdb.com/name/nm1849675

PARTIZAN ENTERTAINMENT

1545 Wilcox Ave Suite 200
Hollywood, CA 90028
Phone: 323-468-0123
Fax: 323-468-0129

285 W. Broadway
Suite 330
New York, NY 10013
Phone: 212-388-0123
Fax: 212-625-2040

Home Page: partizan.com
IMDb: Feature Films, Television

Does not accept any unsolicited material. Project types include Feature Films and TV. Preferred genres include Action, Animation, Comedy, Crime, Drama, Fantasy, Horror, Romance, Science Fiction, and Thriller. Established in 1991.

Sheila Stepanek
Executive Producer
Email: sstepanek@partizan.us

Lori Stonebraker
Email: lstonebraker@partizan.us

Matt Tucker
Email: matt.tucker@partizan.com

Li-Wei Chu
Head of Production & Development
Email: liwei.chu@partizan.us

PATHE PICTURES

6 Ramillies St
4th Floor
London W1F 7TY
United Kingdom
Phone: +44207-462-4429
Fax: +44207-631-3568

Email: reception.desk@pathe-uk.com
Home Page: pathe-uk.com

Accepts query letter from unproduced, unrepresented writers via email. Project types include Feature Films and TV. Preferred genres include Non-Fiction and Reality.

Bradley Quirk
Creative Executive

PATRIOT PICTURES

PO Box 46100
West Hollywood, CA 90046

Phone: 323-874-8850
Fax: 323-874-8851

Email: info@patriotpictures.com
Home Page: patriotpictures.com

Accepts query letter from unproduced, unrepresented writers via email. Project types include Feature Films and TV. Preferred genres include Non-Fiction and Reality.

Michael Mendelsohn
Phone: 323-874-8850
IMDb: imdb.com/name/nm0578861

PCH FILM

3380 Motor Ave
Los Angeles, CA 90034
Phone: 310-841-5817

Home Page: pchfilms.com

Does not accept any unsolicited material. Project types include Feature Films. Preferred genres include Comedy and Romance.

Kayla Thorton
Phone: 310-841-5817
Email: kayla@pchfilm.com
IMDb: imdb.com/name/nm4267414

PEACE ARCH ENTERTAINMENT

4640 Admiralty Way, Suite 710
Marina del Rey, CA 90292
Phone: 310-776-7200
Fax: 310-823-7147

Email: info@peacearch.com
Home Page: peacearch.com

Does not accept any unsolicited material. Project types include Feature Films and TV. Established in 1986.

Sudhanshu Saria
Phone: 310-776-7200
Email: ssaria@peacearch.com
IMDb: imdb.com/name/nm2738818

PEACE BY PEACE PRODUCTIONS

c/o Michael Katcher/CAA
2000 Ave of the Stars

Los Angeles, CA 90067
Phone: 323-552-1097

Email: peacebypeace1@mac.com

Accepts query letter from unproduced, unrepresented writers via email. Project types include Feature Films and TV.

Alyssa Milano
Producer
Phone: 323-552-1097
IMDb: imdb.com/name/nm0000192
Assistant: Kelly Kall

PEGGY RAJSKI PRODUCTIONS

2 Washington Square Village
Suite 14I
New York, NY 10012
Phone: 323-634-7020
Fax: 323-634-7021

Does not accept any unsolicited material. Project types include Feature Films and TV. Preferred genres include Non-Fiction and Reality.

Peggy Rajski
Producer
Phone: 323-634-7020
Email: rajskip@aol.com
IMDb: imdb.com/name/nm0707475

PERFECT STORM ENTERTAINMENT

1850 Industrial St, Penthouse
Los Angeles, CA 90021
Phone: 323-546-8886

Email: info@theperfectstorment.com

Does not accept any unsolicited material. Project types include Feature Films.

Justin Lin
Director
IMDb: imdb.com/name/nm0510912

PERMUT PRESENTATIONS

3535 Hayden Ave
4th Floor
Culver City, CA 90232

USA
Phone: 310-838-0100
Fax: 310-838-0105

Email: info@permutpres.com

Accepts query letter from unproduced, unrepresented writers. Project types include Feature Films and TV.

Chris Mangano
Development Executive
Phone: 310-248-2792
IMDb: imdb.com/name/nm2032016

David Permut
Phone: 310-248-2792
IMDb: imdb.com/name/nm0674303

PHOENIX PICTURES

10203 Santa Monica Blvd
Suite 400
Los Angeles, CA 90067
Phone: 424-298-2788
Fax: 424-298-2588

Email: info@phoenixpictures.com
Home Page: phoenixpictures.com

Accepts query letter from unproduced, unrepresented writers via email. Project types include Feature Films and TV.

Ali Toukan
Creative Executive
Phone: 424-298-2788
IMDb: imdb.com/name/nm4371255

Edward McGurn
Phone: 424-298-2788
IMDb: imdb.com/name/nm0570342

Douglas McKay
Phone: 424-298-2788
IMDb: imdb.com/name/nm1305822

PIERCE WILLIAMS ENTERTAINMENT

1531 14th St
Santa Monica, CA 90404
Phone: 310-656-9440
Fax: 310-656-9441

Home Page: piercewilliams.com

Project types include Feature Films. Preferred genres include Drama, Horror, and Thriller.

Mark Williams
Executive Producer
IMDb: imdb.com/name/nm0931251

PILLER/SEGAN/SHEPHERD

7025 Santa Monica Blvd
Hollywood, CA 90038
Phone: 323-817-1100
Fax: 323-817-1131

Accepts query letter from unproduced, unrepresented writers. Project types include Feature Films and TV. Established in 2010.

Shawn Piller
Phone: 323-817-1100
IMDb: imdb.com/name/nm0683525

Lloyd Segan
Phone: 323-817-1100
IMDb: imdb.com/name/nm0781912

Scott Shepherd
Phone: 323-817-1100
IMDb: imdb.com/name/nm0791863

PINK SLIP PICTURES

1314 N. Coronado St.
Los Angeles, CA 90026
USA
Phone: 213-483-7100
Fax: 213-483-7200

Email: pinkslip@earthlink.net

Does not accept any unsolicited material. Project types include Feature Films and TV.

Max Wong
Producer
Phone: 213-483-7100
IMDb: imdb.com/name/nm0939246

Karen Firestone
Producer
Phone: 949-228-2354
Email: karenfirestone@hotmail.com
IMDb: imdb.com/name/nm0278652

PIPELINE ENTERTAINMENT INC.

Rutherford Place
305 2nd Ave.
Suite 519
New York, NY 10003
Phone: 212-372-7509

Home Page: pipeline-talent.com

Accepts query letter from unproduced, unrepresented writers. Project types include Feature Films and TV. Preferred genres include Action, Comedy, Crime, Drama, and Thriller.

Dan De Fillipo
Email: Dan@pipeline-talent.com
IMDb: imdb.com/name/nm2496568

Dave Marken
Email: Dave@pipeline-talent.com
IMDb: mdb.com/name/nm2441741

Patrick Wood
Email: Patrick@pipeline-talent.com
IMDb: imdb.com/name/nm3161377

Virginia Donovan
Email: Virginia@pipeline-talent.com
IMDb: imdb.com/name/nm3270342

PIXAR

1200 Park Ave
Emeryville, CA 94608
Phone: 510-922-3000
Fax: 510-922-3151

Email: publicity@pixar.com
Home Page: pixar.com
IMDb: imdb.com/company/co0017902

Does not accept any unsolicited material. Project types include Feature Films. Preferred genres include Animation, Comedy, Family, and Fantasy.

Ed Catmull
President
IMDb: imdb.com/name/nm0146216

Jim Morris
Producer
IMDb: imdb.com/name/nm0606640

John Lasseter
IMDb: imdb.com/name/nm0005124

PLAN B ENTERTAINMENT

9150 Wilshire Blvd, Suite 350
Beverly Hills, CA 90210
Phone: 310-275-6135
Fax: 310-275-5234

Does not accept any unsolicited material. Project types
include Feature Films and TV. Preferred genres
include Action, Animation, Drama, Fantasy, and
Myth. Established in 2004.

Sarah Esberg
Creative Executive
Phone: 310-275-6135
IMDb: imdb.com/name/nm1209665

Brad Pitt
Phone: 310-275-6135
IMDb: imdb.com/name/nm0000093

PLATFORM ENTERTAINMENT

128 Sierra St
El Segundo, CA 90425
Phone: 310-322-3737
Fax: 310-322-3729

Home Page: platformentertainment.com

Accepts query letter from unproduced, unrepresented
writers. Project types include Feature Films.
Established in 1998.

Daniel Levin
Producer
Phone: 310-322-3737
IMDb: imdb.com/name/nm0505575

Larry Gabriel
Producer
Phone: 310-322-3737
IMDb: imdb.com/name/nm0300181

Scott Sorrentino
Producer
Phone: 310-322-3737
IMDb: imdb.com/name/nm1391744

PLATINUM DUNES

631 Colorado Ave
Santa Monica, CA 90401
Phone: 310-319-6565
Fax: 310-319-6570

Does not accept any unsolicited material. Project types
include Feature Films and TV. Established in 2001.

Michael Bay
Partner
Phone: 310-319-6565
IMDb: imdb.com/name/nm0000881

PLAYTONE PRODUCTIONS

PO Box 7340
Santa Monica, CA 90406
Phone: 310-394-5700
Fax: 310-394-4466

Home Page: playtone.com

Does not accept any unsolicited material. Project types
include Feature Films and TV. Established in 1996.

Tom Hanks
Partner
Phone: 310-394-5700
IMDb: imdb.com/name/nm0000158

PLUM PICTURES

New York City, New York
Phone: 212-529-5820

IMDb: imdb.com/company/co0113146

Does not accept any unsolicited material. Project types
include Feature Films. Preferred genres include
Comedy and Drama. Established in 2003.

Joy Goodwin
Head of Development
Email: joy@pulmpic.com
IMDb: imdb.com/name/nm2205476

POLSKY FILMS

9220 Sunset Blvd., Suite 309
West Hollywood, CA 90069
Phone: 310-271-4300
Fax: 310-271-4301

Email: info@polskyfilms.com
Home Page: polskyfilms.com

Does not accept any unsolicited material. Project types include Feature Films. Preferred genres include Crime, Documentary, and Drama.

Alan Polsky
Producer
IMDb: imdb.com/name/nm2611223

Gabe Polsky
Producer
IMDb: imdb.com/name/nm2126907

Liam Satre-Meloy
Executive
IMDb: imdb.com/name/nm3176310

POLYMORPHIC PICTURES

4000 Warner Blvd
Building 81, Suite 212
Burbank, CA 91522
Phone: 818-954-3822

Does not accept any unsolicited material. Project types include Feature Films. Established in 2010.

Polly Johnsen
Phone: 818-954-3822
IMDb: imdb.com/name/nm1882593

PORCHLIGHT FILMS

94 Oxford St
Suite 31
Darlinghurst NSW 2010
Australia
Phone: 61-2-9326-9916
Fax: 61-2-9357-1479

Email: admin@porchlightfilms.com.au
Home Page: porchlightfilms.com.au

Project types include Feature Films and TV. Preferred genres include Comedy, Crime, Drama, Horror, and Thriller. Established in 1996.

Vincent Sheehan
Email: vincent@porchlightfilms.com.au
IMDb: imdb.com/name/nm0790636

Anita Sheehan
IMDb: mdb.com/name/nm1618460

Liz Watts
IMDb: imdb.com/name/nm0915192

PORTERGELLER ENTERTAINMENT

6352 De Longpre Ave
Los Angeles, CA 90028
Phone: 323-822-4400
Fax: 323-822-7270

Email: info@portergeller.com
Home Page: portergeller.com

Does not accept any unsolicited material. Project types include Feature Films and TV.

Aaron Geller
Producer
Phone: 323-822-4400
IMDb: imdb.com/name/nm1510467

Darryl Porter
Producer
Phone: 323-822-4400
IMDb: imdb.com/name/nm0692080

Michael Tyree
Producer
Phone: 323-822-4400
IMDb: imdb.com/name/nm2699784

POW! ENTERTAINMENT

9440 Santa Monica Blvd, Suite 620
Beverly Hills, CA 90210
Phone: 310-275-9933
Fax: 310-285-9955

Email: info@powentertainment.com
Home Page: powentertainment.com

Accepts query letter from unproduced, unrepresented writers via email. Project types include Feature Films and TV. Established in 2001.

Stan Lee
Phone: 310-275-9933
IMDb: imdb.com/name/nm0498278
Assistant: Mike Kelly

Ron Hawk

Phone: 310-275-9933
IMDb: imdb.com/name/nm4078012

POWER UP

419 N Larchmont Blvd #283
Los Angeles, CA 90004
Phone: 323-463-3154
Fax: 323-467-6249

Email: info@powerupfilms.org
Home Page: powerupfilms.org

Accepts query letter from unproduced, unrepresented writers via email. Project types include Feature Films and TV. Established in 2000.

Stacy Codikow

Phone: 323-463-3154
IMDb: imdb.com/name/nm0168499

Lisa Thrasher

Phone: 323-463-3154
IMDb: imdb.com/name/nm1511212

PRACTICAL PICTURES

2211 Corinth Ave, Suite 303
Los Angeles, CA 90064
Phone: 310-405-7777
Fax: 310-405-7771

Does not accept any unsolicited material.

Jason Koffeman

Creative Executive
IMDb: imdb.com/name/nm1788896

PRANA STUDIOS

1145 N McCadden Place
Los Angeles, CA 90038
Phone: 323-645-6500
Fax: 323-645-6710

Email: info@pranastudios.com
Home Page: pranastudios.com

Project types include Feature Films. Preferred genres include Action, Animation, Comedy, Drama, Family, and Fantasy.

Samir Hoon

President

Kristin Dornig

Co-Creative Director & CEO
IMDb: imdb.com/name/nm0233921

Arish Fyzee

Creative Director
IMDb: imdb.com/name/nm0299564

Danielle Sterling

VP of Development
IMDb: imdb.com/name/nm1306678

PREFERRED CONTENT

6363 Wilshire Blvd, Suite 350
Los Angeles, CA 90048
Phone: 323-782-9193

Email: info@preferredcontent.net
Home Page: preferredcontent.net

Does not accept any unsolicited material. Project types include Feature Films. Preferred genres include Action.

Trace Sheehan

Head of Development
IMDb: imdb.com/name/nm2618717

Ross Dinerstein

IMDb: imdb.com/name/nm1895871

Kevin Iwashina

IMDb: imdb.com/name/nm2250990

PRETTY MATCHES PRODUCTIONS

1100 Ave of the Americas
G26, Suite 32
New York, NY 10036
Phone: 212-512-5755
Fax: 212-512-5716

IMDb: imdb.com/company/co0173730

Accepts query letter from unproduced, unrepresented writers. Project types include Feature Films and TV. Preferred genres include Comedy, Non-Fiction, Reality, and Romance.

Sarah Parker
President
IMDb: imdb.com/name/nm0000572

Alison Benson
Producer
IMDb: imdb.com/name/nm3929030
Assistant: Matt Nathanson

PRETTY PICTURES

100 Universal City Plaza
Building 2352-A, 3rd Floor
Universal City, CA 91608
Phone: 818-733-0926
Fax: 818-866-0847

Does not accept any unsolicited material. Project types include Feature Films and TV. Preferred genres include Comedy, Drama, Non-Fiction, Romance, and Thriller.

Gail Mutrux
Producer

Tore Schmidt
Creative Executive

PRINCIPATO-YOUNG ENTERTAINMENT

9465 Wilshire Blvd, Suite 900
Beverly Hills, CA 90212
Phone: 310-274-4474
Fax: 310-274-4108

261 Madison Ave.
9th Floor
New York, NY 10016
Phone: 212-725-0010

Accepts query letter from unproduced, unrepresented writers. Project types include Feature Films and TV. Preferred genres include Comedy.

Peter Principato
President
Phone: 310-274-4130
Assistant: Max Suchov

Susan Solomon
Manager
Phone: 310-274-4408

Tucker Voorhees
Manager
Phone: 310-432-5992

PROSPECT PARK

2049 Century Park East #2550
Century City, CA 90067
Phone: 310-746-4900
Fax: 310-746-4890

IMDb: imdb.com/company/co0276484

Accepts query letter from unproduced, unrepresented writers via email. Project types include Feature Films and TV. Preferred genres include Drama, Non-Fiction, and Reality.

Jeff Kwatinetz
Executive Producer
IMDb: imdb.com/name/nm0477153

Paul Frank
IMDb: imdb.com/name/nm1899773

PROTOZOA PICTURES

104 N 7th St
Brooklyn, NY 11211
Phone: 718-388-5280
Fax: 718-388-5425

Home Page: aronofsky.net

Does not accept any unsolicited material. Project types include Feature Films. Preferred genres include Action, Fantasy, Horror, Science Fiction, and Thriller.

Darren Aronofsky
IMDb: imdb.com/name/nm0004716

PURE GRASS FILMS, LTD.

1st Floor, 16 Manette St
London, W1D 4AR

Email: info@puregrassfilms.com
Home Page: puregrassfilms.com

Accepts query letter from unproduced, unrepresented writers via email. Project types include Feature Films. Preferred genres include Action, Drama, Horror, Non-Fiction, Science Fiction, and Thriller.

Ben Grass
IMDb: imdb.com/name/nm2447240

QED INTERNATIONAL

1800 N Highland Ave, 5th Floor
Los Angeles, CA 90028
Phone: 323-785-7900
Fax: 323-785-7901

Email: info@qedintl.com
Home Page: qedintl.com

Accepts scripts from unproduced, unrepresented writers. Project types include Feature Films. Preferred genres include Action, Comedy, Crime, Drama, Fantasy, Horror, Myth, Romance, and Thriller. Established in 2005.

Bill Block
IMDb: imdb.com/name/nm1088848

QUADRANT PICTURES

9229 Sunset Blvd, Suite 225
West Hollywood, CA 90069
Phone: 424-244-1860

Email: assistant@quadrantpictures.com
Home Page: quadrantpictures.com

Accepts query letter from unproduced, unrepresented writers via email. Project types include Feature Films and TV. Preferred genres include Action, Drama, Family, Horror, Science Fiction, and Thriller. Established in 2011.

John Schwartz
Producer
IMDb: imdb.com/name/nm1862748

Doug Davison
IMDb: imdb.com/name/nm0205713

RABBIT BANDINI PRODUCTIONS

3500 W Olive Ave
Ste 1470
Burbank, CA 91505
Phone: 818-953-7510

Home Page: rabbitbandinifilms.com

Does not accept any unsolicited material. Project types include Feature Films. Preferred genres include Thriller.

James Franco
IMDb: imdb.com/name/nm0290556

Vince Jolivette
Email: vince@rabbitbandini.com
IMDb: imdb.com/name/nm0006683

RADAR PICTURES

10900 Wilshire Blvd, Suite 1400
Los Angeles, CA 90024
Phone: 310-208-8525
Fax: 310-208-1764

Email: info@radarpictures.com
Home Page: radarpictures.com
IMDb: imdb.com/company/co0023815

Does not accept any unsolicited material. Project types include Feature Films. Preferred genres include Action and Drama.

Ted Field
CEO
IMDb: imdb.com/name/nm0276059

@RADICAL MEDIA

435 Hudson St, 6th Floor
New York, NY 10014
Phone: 212-461-1500
Fax: 212-462-1600

1630 12th St
Santa Monica, CA 90404
Phone: 310-664-4500
Fax: 310-664-4600

Email: info@radicalmedia.com
Email: ckim@radicalmedia.com
Home Page: radicalmedia.com
IMDb: imdb.com/company/co0029540

Does not accept any unsolicited material.

Frank Scherma
President
Email: bina@radicalmedia.com
IMDb: imdb.com/name/nm0771075

Sidney Beaumont
Executive Producer
Email: beaumont@radicalmedia.com
IMDb: imdb.com/name/nm1359013

Jon Kamen
Chairman
Email: hammer@radicalmedia.com

Bob Stein
Head (Production, Media and Entertainment)
Email: stein@radicalmedia.com

Brent Eveleth
Creative Director (Group)
Email: eveleth@radicalmedia.com

Justin WIlkes
President (Media and Entertainment)
Phone: 310-664-4500
Email: wilkes@radicalmedia.com

Adam Neuhaus
Phone: 310-664-4500
Email: neuhaus@radicalmedia.com

RAINBOW FILM COMPANY/ RAINBOW RELEASING

1301 Montanta Ave, Suite A
Santa Monica, CA 90403
Phone: 310-271-0202
Fax: 310-271-2753

Email: therainbowfilmco@aol.com

Accepts query letter from unproduced, unrepresented writers via email. Project types include Feature Films. Preferred genres include Comedy, Drama, Non-Fiction, and Romance.

Henry Jaglom
President

Sharon Kohn

Lauren Beck

RAINMAKER ENTERTAINMENT

200-2025 W Broadway
Vancouver, BC
Canada
V6J 1Z6

Phone: 604-714-2600
Fax: 604-714-2641

Home Page: rainmaker.com
IMDb: imdb.com/company/co0298750
Facebook: facebook.com/RainmakerEnt

Does not accept any unsolicited material. Project types include Feature Films and TV. Preferred genres include Animation, Family, and Fantasy.

Craig Graham
Executive Chairman & CEO

Michael Hefferon
President

Kimberly Dennison
Director of Development

Kylie Ellis
Director of Production

RAINMAKER FILMS INC.

4212 San Felipe St 399
Houston, TX 77027
Phone: 832-287-9372

Email: rainmaker.inc@gmail.com

Accepts query letter from unproduced, unrepresented writers via email. Project types include Feature Films. Preferred genres include Science Fiction.

Grant Gurthie
President - Executive Producer
IMDb: imdb.com/name/nm0349262

RAINSTORM ENTERTAINMENT, INC.

345 N Maple Dr, Suite 105
Beverly Hills, CA 90210
Phone: 818-269-3300
Fax: 310-496-0223

Email: info@rainstormentertainment.com
Home Page: rainstormentertainment.com

Accepts query letter from unproduced, unrepresented writers via email. Project types include Feature Films and TV. Preferred genres include Non-Fiction and Reality.

Alec Rossel
Development Executive
Phone: 818-269-3300
IMDb: imdb.com/name/nm1952377

RANDOM HOUSE STUDIO

1745 Broadway
New York, NY 10019
Phone: 212-782-9000

Home Page: randomhouse.com

Accepts query letter from unproduced, unrepresented writers. Project types include Feature Films. Established in 2007.

Valerie Cates
Executive Story Editor
Phone: 212-782-9000
IMDb: imdb.com/name/nm1161200

Brady Emerson
Phone: 212-782-9000
IMDb: imdb.com/name/nm3031708

RAT ENTERTAINMENT

100 Universal City Plz
Bungalow 5196
Universal City, CA 91608
Phone: 818-733-4603
Fax: 818-733-4612

Accepts query letter from unproduced, unrepresented writers. Project types include Feature Films and TV. Preferred genres include Non-Fiction and Reality.

Brett Ratner
Phone: 818-733-4603
IMDb: imdb.com/name/nm0711840
Assistant: Anita S. Chang

John Cheng
Phone: 818-733-4603
IMDb: imdb.com/name/nm1766738

RCR MEDIA GROUP

421 S Beverly Dr.
Beverly Hills, CA 90212

1169 Loma Linda Dr,
Beverly Hills, CA 90210
Phone: 310-273-3888
Fax: 310-273-2888

Email: info@rcrmg.com
Home Page: rcrmediagroup.com
Facebook: facebook.com/rcrmediagroup

Does not accept any unsolicited material. Project types include Feature Films. Preferred genres include Action, Comedy, Crime, Drama, Horror, Romance, Science Fiction, and Thriller.

Eliad Josephson
CEO
IMDb: imdb.com/name/nm4035615

Rui Costa Reis
Chairman
IMDb: imdb.com/name/nm3926066

Ricardo Costa Reis
Producer/Creative Executive
IMDb: imdb.com/name/nm4579160

RCR PICTURES

8840 Wilshire Blvd
Beverly Hills, CA 90211
Phone: 310-358-3234
Fax: 310-358-3109

Accepts query letter from unproduced, unrepresented writers. Project types include Feature Films. Preferred genres include Crime, Drama, Romance, and Science Fiction.

Robin Schorr
Producer
IMDb: imdb.com/name/nm0774908

RECORDED PICTURE COMPANY

24 Hanway St
London W1T 1UH
United Kingdom
Phone: +44 20-7636-2251
Fax: +44 20-7636-2261

Email: rpc@recordedpicture.com
Home Page: recordedpicture.com

Accepts scripts from produced or represented writers. Project types include Feature Films.

Jeremy Thomas

Phone: +44 20 7636 2251
IMDb: imdb.com/name/nm0859016
Assistant: Karin Padgham

Alainee Kent

Phone: +44 20 7636 2251
IMDb: imdb.com/name/nm1599134

Peter Watson

Phone: +44 20 7636 2251
IMDb: imdb.com/name/nm0914838

RED CROWN PRODUCTIONS

630 5th Ave, Suite 2505
New York, NY 10111
Phone: 212-355-9200
Fax: 212-719-7029

Email: info@redcrownproductions.com
Home Page: redcrownproductions.com

Does not accept any unsolicited material. Project types include Feature Films. Preferred genres include Comedy and Drama. Established in 2010.

Riva Marker

Head of Production & Development
Email: riva@redcrownproductions.com
IMDb: imdb.com/name/nm1889450

Alish Erman

Creative Executive
Email: alish@redcrownproductions.com
IMDb: imdb.com/name/nm2289542

Daniel Crown

Phone: 212-355-9200
Email: dcrown@crownnyc.com
IMDb: imdb.com/name/nm3259054

REDFIELD PRODUCTIONS

c/o The Lot
1041 N Formosa Ave
Writer's Building, Suite 321
West Hollywood, CA 90046
Phone: 323-850-3905
Fax: 323-850-3907

Email: development@renfieldproductions.com
Home Page: renfieldproductions.com

Accepts query letter from unproduced, unrepresented writers via email. Project types include TV. Preferred genres include Action, Animation, Comedy, Drama, Family, Horror, Non-Fiction, and Reality.

Mark Alan

Development Executive
Phone: 323-850-3905
IMDb: imdb.com/name/nm1591345

Joe Dante

Phone: 323-850-3905
IMDb: imdb.com/name/nm0001102

T.L. Kittle

Phone: 323-850-3905
IMDb: imdb.com/name/nm1473622

RED GIANT MEDIA

535 5th Ave, 5th Floor
New York, NY 10017
Phone: 212-989-7200
Fax: 212-937-3505

Email: info@redgiantmedia.com
Home Page: redgiantmedia.com

Does not accept any unsolicited material. Project types include Feature Films. Preferred genres include Science Fiction. Established in 2008.

Isen Robbins

Producer

Aimee Schoof

Producer

Kevin Fox

RED GRANITE PICTURES

9255 Sunset Blvd, Suite 710
Los Angeles, CA 90069
Phone: 310-703-5800
Fax: 310-246-3849

IMDb: imdb.com/company/co0325207

Does not accept any unsolicited material. Project types include Feature Films. Preferred genres include Drama.

Riza Aziz
CEO
IMDb: imdb.com/name/nm4265383

Joe Gatta
IMDb: imdb.com/name/nm2211910

RED HEN PRODUCTIONS

3607 W Magnolia
Ste. L
Burbank, CA 91505
Phone: 818-563-3600
Fax: 818-787-6637

Home Page: redhenprods.com

Accepts query letter from unproduced, unrepresented writers. Preferred genres include Drama and Thriller.

Stuart Gordon
Phone: 818-563-3600
IMDb: imdb.com/name/nm0002340

RED HOUR FILMS

629 N La Brea Ave
Los Angeles, CA 90036
Phone: 323-602-5000
Fax: 323-602-5001

Home Page: redhourfilms.com

Does not accept any unsolicited material. Project types include Feature Films and TV. Preferred genres include Action, Comedy, Family, Fantasy, and Science Fiction.

Ben Stiller
IMDb: imdb.com/name/nm0001774

Robin Mabrito
Email: robin@redhourfilms.com
IMDb: imdb.com/name/nm3142663

RED OM FILMS, INC.

3000 Olympic Blvd
Building 3, Suite 2330

Santa Monica, CA 90404
Phone: 310-594-3467

Does not accept any unsolicited material. Project types include Feature Films and TV. Preferred genres include Action, Comedy, Drama, and Family.

Lisa Gillian
Producer
IMDb: imdb.com/name/nm0731359

Philip Rose
Producer
IMDb: imdb.com/name/nm0741615

Julia Roberts
IMDb: imdb.com/name/nm0000210

RED PLANET PICTURES

13 Doolittle Mill
Froghall Rd
Ampthill, Bedfordshire MK45 2ND
UK
Phone: +44 (0)1525 408 970
Fax: +44 (0)1525 408 971

Email: info@redplanetpictures.co.uk
Home Page: redplanetpictures.co.uk

Does not accept any unsolicited material. Project types include TV. Preferred genres include Crime and Drama.

Simon Winstone
Director of Development
Email: simonwinstone@redplanetpictures.co.uk
IMDb: imdb.com/name/nm0935654

RED WAGON ENTERTAINMENT

8931 Ellis Ave.
2nd Floor
Los Angeles, CA 90034
Phone: 310-853-4600

Does not accept any unsolicited material. Project types include Feature Films and TV. Preferred genres include Animation, Drama, Fantasy, and Horror.

Douglas Wick
Producer
Phone: 310-244-4466
IMDb: imdb.com/name/nm0926824

Lucy Fisher
Producer
Phone: 310-244-4466
IMDb: imdb.com/name/nm0279651

REGENT ENTERTAINMENT

10940 Wilshire Blvd, Suite 1600
Los Angeles, CA 90024
Phone: 310-806-4290
Fax: 310-806-6351

Email: info@regententertainment.com
Home Page: regententertainment.com
IMDb: imdb.com/company/co0045895

Accepts query letter from unproduced, unrepresented writers via email. Project types include Feature Films and TV. Preferred genres include Action, Drama, Horror, and Science Fiction.

David Millbern
Director of Development
Phone: 310-806-4290
IMDb: imdb.com/name/nm0587778

Roxana Vatan
IMDb: imdb.com/name/nm2985872

REHAB ENTERTAINMENT

1416 N La Brea Ave
Hollywood, CA 90028
Phone: 323-645-6444
Fax: 323-645-6445

Email: info@rehabent.com
Home Page: rehabent.com

Accepts query letter from unproduced, unrepresented writers via email. Project types include Feature Films.

John Hyde
President

Brett Coker

REINER/GREISMAN

9169 W. Sunset Blvd.
West Hollywood, CA 90069
Phone: 310-285-2300
Fax: 310-285-2345

Accepts query letter from unproduced, unrepresented writers. Project types include Feature Films. Preferred genres include Comedy and Drama.

Alan Greisman
Producer
Phone: 310-205-2766

Rob Reiner
Phone: 310-285-2328
IMDb: imdb.com/name/nm0001661
Assistant: Pam Jones

RELATIVITY MEDIA, LLC

9242 Beverly Blvd, Suite 300
Beverly Hills, CA 90210
Phone: 310-724-7700
Fax: 310-724-7701

Accepts query letter from produced or represented writers. Project types include Feature Films, TV, and Commercials. Preferred genres include Non-Fiction and Reality.

Jonathan Karsh

Julie Link

RELEVANT ENTERTAINMENT GROUP

10323 Santa Monica Blvd
Ste 101
Los Angeles, CA 90025
Phone: 310-277-0853

Project types include Feature Films and TV. Preferred genres include Comedy.

REMEMBER DREAMING, LLC

8252 1/2 Santa Monica Blvd, Suite B
West Hollywood, CA 90046
Phone: 323-654-3333

Accepts query letter from unproduced, unrepresented writers. Project types include Feature Films and TV. Preferred genres include Non-Fiction and Reality.

Stan Spry
President

Courtney Brin

Email: courtney@freefall-films.com

RENAISSANCE PICTURES

315 S Beverly Dr, Suite 216
Beverly Hills, CA 90210
Phone: 310-785-3900
Fax: 310-785-9176

Accepts query letter from unproduced, unrepresented writers. Project types include Feature Films and TV. Preferred genres include Action, Drama, Fantasy, and Horror.

Sam Raimi

Robert Tapert
Partner

RENART FILMS

135 Grand St.
3rd Floor
New York, NY 10013
Phone: 212-274-8224
Fax: 212-274-8229

Email: info@renartfilms.com
Home Page: renartfilms.com

Accepts query letter from produced or represented writers. Project types include Feature Films. Preferred genres include Comedy, Drama, and Romance.

Caroline Dillon
Creative Director
Email: caroline@renartfilms.com
IMDb: imdb.com/name/nm0226974

Timothy Duff
President
Email: tim@renartfilms.com
IMDb: imdb.com/name/nm2178779

TJ Federico
Email: tj@renartfilms.com

Julie Christeas
Email: julie@renartfilms.com
IMDb: imdb.com/name/nm2184127

Dan Schechter
Email: dan@renartfilms.com

RENEE MISSEL MANAGEMENT

2376 Adrian St, Suite A
Newbury Park, CA 91320
Phone: 310-463-0638
Fax: 805-669-4511

Email: fi lmtao@aol.com

Accepts query letter from unproduced, unrepresented writers via email. Project types include Feature Films. Established in 1983.

Renee Missel
Producer

Bridget Stone

RENEE VALENTE PRODUCTIONS

13547 Ventura Blvd, #195
Sherman Oaks, CA 91423
Phone: 310-472-5342

Email: valenteprod@aol.com

Accepts query letter from unproduced, unrepresented writers via email. Project types include Feature Films and TV.

Renee Valente
Executive Producer

RENEGADE ANIMATION, INC.

111 E Broadway, Suite 208
Glendale, CA 91205
Phone: 818-551-2351
Fax: 818-551-2350

Email: contactus@renegadeanimation.com
Home Page: renegadeanimation.com

Accepts query letter from unproduced, unrepresented writers via email. Project types include TV.

Ashley Postlewaite

Darrell Van Citters

REVEILLE, LLC/ SHINE INTERNATIONAL

1741 Ivar Ave
Los Angeles, CA 90028

Phone: 323-790-8000
Fax: 323-790-8399

Does not accept any unsolicited material. Project types include TV. Preferred genres include Non-Fiction and Reality.

Todd Cohen

Rob Cohen

Carolyn Bernstein
Executive Vice-President, Scripted TV
IMDb: imdb.com/name/nm3009190

REVELATIONS ENTERTAINMENT

1221 Second St
4th Floor
Santa Monica, CA 90401
Phone: 310-394-3131
Fax: 310-394-3133

Email: info@revelationsent.com
Home Page: revelationsent.com

Does not accept any unsolicited material. Project types include Feature Films and TV. Preferred genres include Action, Detective, Drama, and Family.

Morgan Freeman
Phone: 310-394-3131
IMDb: imdb.com/name/nm0000151

Lori McCreary
Phone: 310-394-3131
IMDb: imdb.com/name/nm0566975

Tracy Mercer
Phone: 310-394-3131
IMDb: imdb.com/name/nm0580312

REVOLUTION FILMS

9-A Dallington St
London EC1V 0BQ
UK
Phone: +44-20-7566-0700

Email: email@revolution-films.com
Home Page: revolution-films.com
IMDb: mdb.com/company/co0103733

Does not accept any unsolicited material. Project types include Feature Films. Preferred genres include Action, Comedy, Drama, Non-Fiction, Period, and Thriller.

Michael Winterbottom
Producer
IMDb: imdb.com/name/nm0935863

Andrew Eaton
Producer
IMDb: imdb.com/name/nm0247787

RHINO FILMS

10501 Wilshire Blvd, Suite 814
Los Angeles, CA 90024
Phone: 310-441-6557
Fax: 310-441-6584

Email: contact@rhinofilms.com
Home Page: rhinofilms.com

Accepts query letter from unproduced, unrepresented writers via email. Project types include Feature Films.

Stephen Nemeth
CEO
Email: stephennemcth@rhinofilms.com
IMDb: imdb.com/name/nm0625932

RHOMBUS MEDIA, INC.

99 Spadina Ave
Ste 600
Toronto, ON M5V 3P8
Canada
Phone: 416-971-7856
Fax: 416-971-9647

Email: info@rhombusmedia.com
Home Page: rhombusmedia.com

Does not accept any unsolicited material. Project types include Feature Films. Preferred genres include Action, Comedy, Crime, Horror, Science Fiction, and Thriller.

Niv Fichman
Principle

Larry Weistein
Principle
IMDb: imdb.com/name/nm0918452

RHYTHM & HUES STUDIOS

2100 E Grand Ave
El Segundo, CA 90245
Phone: 310-448-7500
Fax: 310-448-7600

Email: webmaster@rhythm.com
Home Page: rhythm.com

Does not accept any unsolicited material. Project types include Feature Films. Preferred genres include Action, Comedy, Crime, Drama, Family, Fantasy, Romance, and Science Fiction.

Lee Burger
President
IMDb: imdb.com/name/nm0074260

Venecia Duran
Director of Development
IMDb: imdb.com/name/nm1330358

Heather Jennings
IMDb: imdb.com/name/nm0997142

Pauline Ts'o
IMDb: imdb.com/name/nm1173396

RICE & BEANS PRODUCTIONS

30 N Raymond, Suite 605
Pasadena, CA 91103
Phone: 626-792-9171
Fax: 626-792-9171

Email: vin88@pacbell.net

Accepts query letter from unproduced, unrepresented writers via email. Project types include Feature Films and TV. Preferred genres include Comedy and Drama.

Vince Cheung
IMDb: imdb.com/name/nm0156588

Ben Montanio
IMDb: imdb.com/name/nm0598996

RICHE PRODUCTIONS

9336 W Washington Blvd
Stage 4, Room 201
Culver City, CA 90232
Phone: 310-202-4850

Accepts query letter from unproduced, unrepresented writers. Project types include Feature Films and TV. Preferred genres include Action and Family.

Alan Riche
Partner
Assistant: Adrienne Novelly

Peter Riche
Partner

RIVE GAUCHE TELEVISION

15442 Ventura Blvd.
Ste. 101
Sherman Oaks, CA 91403
Phone: 818-784-9912
Fax: 818-784-9916

Home Page: rgitv.com

Project types include Feature Films. Preferred genres include Documentary.

Jonathan Kramer
CEO
IMDb: imdb.com/name/nm2883855

RIVER ROAD ENTERTAINMENT

2000 Ave of the Stars, Suite 620-N
Los Angeles, CA 90067
Phone: 213-253-4610
Fax: 310-843-9551

Home Page: riverroadentertainment.com

Does not accept any unsolicited material. Project types include Feature Films and TV. Preferred genres include Comedy, Drama, Non-Fiction, and Reality.

Tom Skapars
Creative Executive

ROADSIDE ATTRACTIONS

7920 Sunset Blvd
Suite 402
Los Angeles, CA 90046
Phone: 323-882-8490
Fax: 323-882-8493

Email: info@roadsideattractions.com
Home Page: roadsideattractions.com

Accepts query letter from produced or represented writers. Project types include Feature Films. Preferred genres include Comedy, Drama, Horror, and Thriller.

Howard Cohen
IMDb: imdb.com/name/nm1383518

Eric d'Arbeloff
IMDb: imdb.com/name/nm0195396

Gail Blumenthal
IMDb: imdb.com/name/nm0089812

ROBERT CORT PRODUCTIONS

1041 N Formosa Ave
Administration Building, Suite 196
West Hollywood, CA 90046
Phone: 323-850-2644
Fax: 323-850-2634

Accepts query letter from unproduced, unrepresented writers. Project types include Feature Films and TV. Preferred genres include Comedy and Drama.

Robert Cort
Producer
IMDb: imdb.com/name/nm0181202

Eric Hetzel
IMDb: imdb.com/name/nm0381796

Maritza Berta
Creative Executive

ROBERT GREENWALD PRODUCTIONS

10510 Culver Blvd
Culver City, CA 90232-3400
Phone: 310-204-0404
Fax: 310-204-0174

Email: info@rgpinc.com
Home Page: rgpinc.com

Does not accept any unsolicited material. Project types include Feature Films and TV. Preferred genres include Comedy, Drama, and Non-Fiction.

Robert Greenwald
IMDb: imdb.com/name/nm0339254

Philip Kleinbart
IMDb: imdb.com/name/nm0459036

ROBERT LAWRENCE PRODUCTIONS

1810 14th St
Suite 102
Santa Monica, CA 90404
Phone: 310-399-2762

Accepts query letter from unproduced, unrepresented writers. Project types include Feature Films. Preferred genres include Action, Comedy, and Drama.

Robert Lawrence
President
IMDb: imdb.com/name/nm0492994

ROBERTS/DAVID FILMS INC.

100 Universal City Plaza
Bldg. 1320
Universal City, CA 91608
Phone: 818-733-2143
Fax: 818-733-1551

Does not accept any unsolicited material. Project types include Feature Films and TV. Preferred genres include Comedy, Non-Fiction, and Reality.

Mark Roberts
Partner
Email: mark@robertsdavid.com

Lorena David
Partner
Email: lorena@robertsdavid.com

ROBERT SIMONDS COMPANY

10202 Washington Blvd
Robert Young Building
Suite 3510
Culver City, CA 90232
Phone: 310-244-5222
Fax: 310-244-0348

Home Page: rscfilms.com

Does not accept any unsolicited material. Project types include Feature Films. Preferred genres include Action, Comedy, Family, and Thriller. Established in 2012.

Robert Simonds
CEO
Email: rasst@rscfilms.com
IMDb: imdb.com/name/nm0800465
Assistant: Jennifer Jiang

ROCKLIN/ FAUST

10390 Santa Monica Blvd, Suite 200
Los Angeles, CA 90025
Phone: 310-800-5140
Fax: 310-789-3060

Does not accept any unsolicited material. Project types include Feature Films and TV. Preferred genres include Animation, Comedy, Drama, Non-Fiction, and Reality.

Blye Pagon Faust
Producer
IMDb: imdb.com/name/nm1421308

ROOM 101, INC.

9677 Charleville Blvd.
Beverly Hills 90212
Phone: 310-271-1130

Accepts query letter from unproduced, unrepresented writers. Project types include Feature Films and TV. Preferred genres include Crime, Drama, and Horror.

Steven Schneider
Producer
IMDb: imdb.com/name/nm2124081

ROOM 9 ENTERTAINMENT, LLC

9229 Sunset Blvd, Suite 505
West Hollywood, CA 90069
Phone: 310-651-2001
Fax: 310-651-2010

Email: info@room9entertainment.com
Home Page: room9entertainment.com

Does not accept any unsolicited material. Project types include Feature Films and TV. Preferred genres include Drama and Non-Fiction.

David O. Sacks
CEO
IMDb: imdb.com/name/nm1616294

Michael R. Newman
IMDb: imdb.com/name/nm1616293

Daniel Brunt
IMDb: imdb.com/name/nm1616292

ROSA ENTERTAINMENT

7288 Sunset Blvd, Suite 208
Los Angeles, CA 90046
Phone: 310-470-3506
Fax: 310-470-3509

Email: info@rosaentertainment.com
Home Page: rosaentertainment.com

Does not accept any unsolicited material. Project types include Feature Films and TV. Preferred genres include Comedy and Drama.

Sidney Sherman
Producer
Email: sidney@rosaentertainment.com
IMDb: imdb.com/name/nm0792587

ROSEROCK FILMS

4000 Warner Blvd
Building 81
Suite 216
Burbank, CA 91522
Phone: 818-954-7528
Fax: 818-954-6658

Does not accept any unsolicited material. Project types include Feature Films.

Hunt Lowry
Producer
IMDb: imdb.com/name/nm0523324

Patricia Reed
Director of Development
Phone: 818-954-7673
IMDb: imdb.com/name/nm0715623

ROTH FILMS

2900 W Olympic Blvd
Santa Monica, CA 90404
Phone: 310-255-7000

Accepts query letter from unproduced, unrepresented writers. Project types include Feature Films.

Joe Roth
Producer
IMDb: imdb.com/name/nm0005387

Palak Patel
IMDb: imdb.com/name/nm2026983

ROUGHHOUSE

1722 Whitley Ave
Hollywood, CA 90028
Phone: 323-469-3161

Accepts scripts from produced or represented writers. Project types include Feature Films. Preferred genres include Drama and Romance.

David Green
IMDb: imdb.com/name/nm0337773

ROUTE ONE FILMS

1041 N Formosa Ave
Santa Monica East #200
West Hollywood, CA 90046
Phone: 323-850-3855
Fax: 323-850-3866

Home Page: routeonefilms.com

Does not accept any unsolicited material. Project types include Feature Films.

Jay Stern
IMDb: imdb.com/name/nm0827731

Russell Levine
IMDb: imdb.com/name/nm4149902

Chip Diggins
IMDb: imdb.com/name/nm0226505

RUBICON ENTERTAINMENT

3406 Tareco Dr.
Los Angeles, CA 90068
Phone: 323-850-9200
Fax: 323-378-5584

Email: submissions@rubiconentertainment.com
Home Page: rubiconentertainment.com

Accepts query letter from unproduced, unrepresented writers via email. Project types include Feature Films. Preferred genres include Comedy and Drama.

RUNAWAY PRODUCTIONS

7336 Santa Monica Blvd.
Ste 751
West Hollywood, CA 90046
Phone: 310-801-0885

Email: lindapalmer@runawayproductions.tv
Home Page: runawayproductions.tv

Project types include Feature Films and TV. Preferred genres include Comedy.

Linda Palmer
IMDb: imdb.com/name/nm1881313

Todd Wade
IMDb: imdb.com/name/nm0905520

RYAN MURPHY PRODUCTIONS

5555 Melrose Ave Modular Building, First Floor
Los Angeles, CA 90038
Phone: 323-956-2408
Fax: 323-862-2235

IMDb: imdb.com/company/co0156994

Does not accept any unsolicited material. Project types include Feature Films and TV. Preferred genres include Comedy, Documentary, Drama, Horror, Non-Fiction, Science Fiction, and Thriller. Established in 2008.

Dante Di Loreto
President
IMDb: imdb.com/name/nm0223994

Ryan Murphy
IMDb: imdb.com/name/nm0614682

SACRED DOGS ENTERTAINMENT LLC

311 N Robertson Blvd.
Ste. 249
Beverly Hills, CA 90211
Phone: 323-656-6900

Email: victory@sacreddogs.com
Home Page: sacreddogs.com

Project types include Feature Films. Preferred genres include Documentary.

Arden Brotman
Phone: 323-656-6900
IMDb: imdb.com/name/nm2231224

Victory Tischler-Blue
Owner
Phone: 323-656-6900
IMDb: imdb.com/name/nm0089548

SALTIRE ENTERTAINMENT

6352 De Longpre Ave
Los Angeles, CA 90028

IMDb: imdb.com/company/co0104114

Does not accept any unsolicited material. Project types include Feature Films. Preferred genres include Drama, Myth, and Science Fiction.

Stuart Pollok
Producer
IMDb: imdb.com/name/nm0689415

SALTY FEATURES

104 W. 14th St.
4th Floor
New York, NY 10011
Phone: 212-924-1601
Fax: 212-924-2306

Email: info@saltyfeatures.com
Home Page: saltyfeatures.com

Accepts query letter from unproduced, unrepresented writers via email. Project types include Feature Films and TV. Preferred genres include Non-Fiction and Reality.

Yael Melamede
Producer
IMDb: imdb.com/name/nm0577336

Eva Kolodner
IMDb: imdb.com/name/nm0464286

SALVATORE/ORNSTON PRODUCTIONS

5650 Camellia Ave
North Hollywood, CA 91601

Phone: 310-466-8980
Fax: 818-752-9321

Accepts query letter from produced or represented writers. Project types include Feature Films. Preferred genres include Action, Animation, Comedy, Crime, Drama, Romance, and Thriller.

Richard Salvatore
Executive
IMDb: imdb.com/name/nm0759363

David E. Ornston
Executive
IMDb: imdb.com/name/nm0650361

SAMUELSON PRODUCTIONS LIMITED

10401 Wyton Dr
Los Angeles, CA 90024-2527
Phone: 310-208-1000
Fax: 323-315-5188

Email: info@samuelson.la
Home Page: samuelson.la

Does not accept any unsolicited material. Project types include Feature Films and TV. Preferred genres include Action, Comedy, and Drama.

Peter Samuelson
Owner
IMDb: imdb.com/name/nm0006873
Assistant: Brian Casey

Marc Samuelson
IMDb: imdb.com/name/nm0760555

Renato Celani
IMDb: imdb.com/name/nm1954607

Josie Law
IMDb: imdb.com/name/nm1656468

Saryl Hirsch
IMDb: imdb.com/name/nm1950244

SANDBAR PICTURES

1145 N. McCadden Place
Hollywood, CA 90038
Phone: 323-337-1183
Fax: 323-337-1434

760 Market St, Suite 507
San Francisco, CA 94102
Phone: 415-398-0780
Fax: 415-398-1598

Email: info@sandbarpictures.net
Home Page: sandbarpictures.net
IMDb: imdb.com/company/co0171098

Does not accept any unsolicited material. Project types include Feature Films. Preferred genres include Drama, Horror, and Thriller.

Greg Little
Founder
IMDb: imdb.com/name/nm0514571

Elizabeth Zox Friedman
Founder
IMDb: imdb.com/name/nm0295288

SANDER/MOSES PRODUCTIONS

The Lot 1041 N. Formosa Ave
Formosa Building
Suite 7
West Hollywood, CA 90046
Phone: 818-560-4500
Fax: 818-860-6284

Email: info@sandermoses.com
Home Page: sandermoses.com

Accepts query letter from unproduced, unrepresented writers via email. Project types include Feature Films, TV, and Commercials. Preferred genres include Drama, Non-Fiction, and Reality.

Ian Sander
IMDb: imdb.com/name/nm0761401

Kim Moses
IMDb: imdb.com/name/nm0608593

SANITSKY COMPANY

9200 Sunset Blvd.
Los Angeles, CA 90069
Phone: 310-274-0120
Fax: 310-274-1455

Does not accept any unsolicited material. Project types include TV. Preferred genres include Drama.

Larry Sanitsky
President
IMDb: imdb.com/name/nm0762792

SCARLET FIRE ENTERTAINMENT

561 28th Ave
Venice, CA 90291
Phone: 310-302-1001
Fax: 310-302-1002

Does not accept any unsolicited material. Project types include Feature Films and TV. Preferred genres include Comedy.

Allen Loeb
Producer
Phone: 310-302-1001
IMDb: imdb.com/name/nm1615610

Steven Pearl
Producer
Phone: 310-302-1001
IMDb: imdb.com/name/nm0669093

SCORE PRODUCTIONS, INC.

2401 Main St.
Santa Monica, CA 90405
Phone: 604-868-7377

Email: score@scoreproductions.com
Home Page: scoreproductions.com

Accepts query letter from produced or represented writers. Project types include Feature Films and TV. Preferred genres include Detective, Drama, Fantasy, and Science Fiction.

SCOTT FREE PRODUCTIONS

614 N. La Peer Dr.
Los Angeles, CA 90069
Phone: 310-360-2250
Fax: 310-360-2251

Does not accept any unsolicited material. Project types include Feature Films and TV. Preferred genres include Action, Animation, Crime, Detective, Drama, Non-Fiction, Reality, and Thriller.

Ridley Scott
IMDb: imdb.com/name/nm0000631
Assistant: Nancy Ryan

David Zucker
IMDb: imdb.com/name/nm0001878
Assistant: Mark Pfeffer

SCOTT RUDIN PRODUCTIONS

120 W 45th St
10th Floor
New York, NY 10036
Phone: 212-704-4600

Accepts query letter from unproduced, unrepresented writers. Project types include Feature Films. Established in 1993.

Scott Rudin
Producer
Phone: 212-704-4600
IMDb: imdb.com/name/nm0748784

Eli Bush
Executive
Phone: 212-704-4600
Email: eli@scottrudinprod.com
IMDb: imdb.com/name/nm4791912

SCOTT SANDERS PRODUCTIONS

Los Angeles, CA
Phone: 818-560-6350
Fax: 818-560-3541

322 8th Ave.
14th Floor
New York, NY 10001
Phone: 212-792-6390
Fax: 212-792-6399

Home Page: scottsandersproductions.com

Accepts query letter from unproduced, unrepresented writers. Project types include Feature Films and TV.

Scott Sanders
IMDb: imdb.com/name/nm0761712
Assistant: Jaime Quiroz

Bryan Kalfus
IMDb: imdb.com/name/nm0435729

SCREEN DOOR ENTERTAINMENT

15223 Burbank Blvd.
Sherman Oaks, CA 91411
Phone: 818-781-5600
Fax: 818-781-5601

Email: info@sdetv.com
Home Page: sdetv.com

Accepts query letter from unproduced, unrepresented writers. Project types include TV. Preferred genres include Reality. Established in 2001.

Joel Rizor
President
IMDb: imdb.com/name/nm1381432

M. Alessandra Ascoli
Email: generalinfo@sdetv.com
IMDb: imdb.com/name/nm0038529

Dave Shikiar

SCREEN GEMS

10202 W Washington Blvd
Culver City, CA 90232
Phone: 310-244-4000
Fax: 310-244-2037

IMDb: imdb.com/company/co0010568

Does not accept any unsolicited material. Project types include Feature Films, Short Films, and TV. Preferred genres include Action, Comedy, Documentary, Drama, Fantasy, Horror, Reality, Romance, Science Fiction, and Thriller. Established in 1926.

Clint Culpepper
President
IMDb: imdb.com/name/nm0191695

Scott Strauss
Executive Vice President of Production
IMDb: imdb.com/name/nm0833873

Pamela Kunath
IMDb: imdb.com/name/nm2242666

Loren Schwartz
IMDb: imdb.com/name/nm2817219

James Lopez
IMDb: imdb.com/name/nm5144603

Eric Paquette
IMDb: imdb.com/name/nm1789841

Glenn Gainor
IMDb: imdb.com/name/nm0004636

Carol Smithson

SE8 GROUP

PO Box 691763
West Hollywood, CA 90069
Phone: 310-285-6090
Fax: 310-285-6097

Accepts query letter from unproduced, unrepresented writers. Project types include Feature Films. Preferred genres include Drama and Thriller.

Douglas Urbanski
Producer
IMDb: imdb.com/name/nm0881703

Gary Oldman
IMDb: imdb.com/name/nm0000198

SECOND AND 10TH INC.

51 MacDougal St, Suite 383
New York, NY 10012
Phone: 347-882-4493

Does not accept any unsolicited material. Project types include Feature Films. Preferred genres include Drama.

Anne Carey
Producer
IMDb: imdb.com/name/nm0136904

SEISMIC PICTURES

Raleigh Studios
5358 Melrose Ave.
Suite 218W
Hollywood, CA 90028
Phone: 323-960-3449

Email: info@seismicpictures.com
Home Page: seismicpictures.com

Does not accept any unsolicited material. Project types include Feature Films and TV. Preferred genres include Comedy, Drama, Non-Fiction, and Reality.

Robert Schwartz
IMDb: imdb.com/name/nm0777412

Alejandro Laguette
Director of Development

SENART FILMS

555 W 25th St, 4th Floor
New York, NY 10001
Phone: 212-406-9610
Fax: 212-406-9581

Email: info@senartfilms.com
Home Page: senartfilms.com

Does not accept any unsolicited material. Project types include Feature Films and TV. Preferred genres include Drama, Non-Fiction, and Reality.

Robert May
Producer
IMDb: imdb.com/name/nm1254338

SERAPHIM FILMS

Phone: 310-888-4200 or 310-246-0050

Email: assistant@seraphimfilms.com
Home Page: seraphimfilms.com

Does not accept any unsolicited material. Project types include Feature Films. Preferred genres include Animation, Drama, Fantasy, and Horror.

Clive Barker
President

Mark Miller
Vice-President

SERENDIPITY POINT FILMS

9 Price St
Toronto, ON M4W 1Z1
Canada
Phone: 416-960-0300
Fax: 416-960-8656

Home Page: serendipitypoint.com

Does not accept any unsolicited material. Project types include Feature Films and TV. Preferred genres include Action, Comedy, Drama, and Thriller.

Robert Lantos
Producer
Assistant: Cherri Campbell

Wendy Saffer

SERENDIPITY PRODUCTIONS, INC.

15260 Ventura Blvd, Suite 1040
Sherman Oaks, CA 91403
Phone: 818-789-3035
Fax: 818-235-0150

Does not accept any unsolicited material. Project types include Feature Films and TV. Preferred genres include Drama, Horror, and Non-Fiction.

Ketura Kestin
Email: keturak@gmail.com
IMDb: imdb.com/name/nm3109585

Daniel Heffner
Email: danheffner@earthlink.net
IMDb: imdb.com/name/nm0004527

SEVEN ARTS PICTURES

1801 Century Park East
Suite 1830
Lost Angeles, CA 90067
Phone: 323-372-3080
Fax: 323-372-3088

136-144 New Kings Rd
London, United Kingdom, SW6 4LZ
Phone: 011-442-030068222
Fax: 011-442-030068220

Email: info@7artspictures.com
Home Page: 7artspictures.com

Does not accept any unsolicited material. Project types include Feature Films. Preferred genres include Comedy, Drama, Science Fiction, and Thriller.

Peter Hoffman
CEO
IMDb: imdb.com/name/nm0389056

SHADOWCATCHER ENTERTAINMENT

4701 SW Admiral Way
Box 32
Seattle, WA 98116
Phone: 206-328-6266
Fax: 206-447-1462

Email: kate@shadowcatcherent.com
Home Page: shadowcatcherent.com

Accepts query letter from unproduced, unrepresented writers via email. Project types include Feature Films, TV, and Theater. Preferred genres include Animation, Comedy, Drama, Non-Fiction, and Reality.

David Skinner
Executive Producer
IMDb: imdb.com/name/nm1623496

Tom Gorai
Producer
IMDb: imdb.com/name/nm0329753

Norman Stephens
Producer
IMDb: imdb.com/name/nm1017457

SHAFTESBURY FILMS

163 Queen St East Suite 100
Toronto, ON, Canada, M5A 1S1
Phone: 416-363-1411
Fax: 416-363-1428

4370 Tujunga Ave Suite 300
Studio City, CA 91604
Phone: 818-505-3361

Email: mailbox@shaftesbury.org
Home Page: shaftesbury.ca

Does not accept any unsolicited material. Project types include Feature Films and TV. Preferred genres include Action, Animation, Comedy, Drama, Family, Romance, and Thriller. Established in 1987.

Christina Jennings
Chairman & CEO
Email: cjennings@shaftesbury.ca
IMDb: imdb.com/name/nm0421126

Jan Peter Meyboon
Senior Vice President, Production
Email: pmeyboom@shaftesbury.ca
IMDb: imdb.com/name/nm0582978

Adam Haight
Senior Vice President, Scripted Content
Email: ahaight@shaftesbury.ca

Julie Lacey
Vice President, Creative Affairs
Email: jlacey@shaftesbury.ca
IMDb: imdb.com/name/nm0479936

SHAUN CASSIDY PRODUCTIONS

Los Angeles, CA
Phone: 818-733-5976

Accepts query letter from unproduced, unrepresented writers. Project types include TV. Preferred genres include Comedy and Drama.

Shaun Cassidy

SHEEP NOIR FILMS

438 W 17th Ave
Vancouver, BC V5Y 2A2
Fax: 604-762-8933

Email: info@sheepnoir.com
Home Page: sheepnoir.com

Does not accept any unsolicited material. Project types include Feature Films and TV. Preferred genres include Drama.

Wendy Hyman
Producer
IMDb: imdb.com/name/nm0405207

Marc Stephenson
Producer
Phone: 604-762-8933
Email: marc@sheepnoir.com

Nathaniel Geary
IMDb: imdb.com/name/nm0311303

SHEPHARD/ROBIN COMPANY

c/o Raleigh Studios
5300 Melrose Ave, Suite 225E
Los Angeles, CA 90038
Phone: 323-871-4412
Fax: 323-871-4418

Does not accept any unsolicited material. Project types include TV. Preferred genres include Drama.

Greer Shephard
Principle
IMDb: imdb.com/name/nm0791709

Michael Robin
Principle
IMDb: imdb.com/name/nm0732218

SHOE MONEY PRODUCTIONS

10202 W Washington Blvd
Poitier Building, Suite 3100
Culver City, CA 90232
Phone: 310-244-6188

Email: shoemoneyproductions@mac.com

Accepts query letter from unproduced, unrepresented writers via email. Project types include Feature Films and TV. Preferred genres include Drama.

Thomas Schlamme
IMDb: imdb.com/name/nm0772095

Julie DeJoie
Head of Production & Development

SHONDALAND

Phone: 323-671-4650

Does not accept any unsolicited material. Project types include Feature Films and TV. Preferred genres include Comedy and Drama.

Betsy Beers
Producer

Shonda Rhimes

Alison Eakle
Executive

SHORELINE ENTERTAINMENT

1875 Century Park East, Suite 600
Los Angeles, CA 90067
Phone: 310-551-2060
Fax: 310-201-0729

Email: info@shorelineentertainment.com
Home Page: shorelineentertainment.com

Does not accept any unsolicited material. Project types include Feature Films and TV. Preferred genres include Drama, Horror, Non-Fiction, Reality, Science Fiction, and Thriller.

Morris Ruskin
CEO

Sam Eigen

SHOWTIME NETWORKS

10880 Wilshire Blvd
Ste 1600
Los Angeles, CA 90024
Phone: 310-234-5200

1633 Broadway
New York, NY 10019
Phone: 212-708-1600

Home Page: sho.com

Does not accept any unsolicited material. Project types include Feature Films and TV. Preferred genres include Action, Animation, Comedy, Crime, Detective, Drama, Family, Fantasy, Horror, Myth, Non-Fiction, Romance, Science Fiction, and Thriller.

Christina Spade
CFO
IMDb: imdb.com/name/nm5268270

Matthew Blank
CEO
IMDb: imdb.com/name/nm2303194

Joan Boorstein
IMDb: imdb.com/name/nm1140886

Tim Delaney
IMDb: imdb.com/name/nm2303906

SIDNEY KIMMEL ENTERTAINMENT

9460 Wilshire Blvd., Suite 500
Beverly Hills, CA 90212
Phone: 310-777-8818
Fax: 310-777-8892

Email: reception@skefilms.com
Home Page: skefilms.com

Does not accept any unsolicited material. Project types include Feature Films. Preferred genres include Comedy, Crime, Drama, and Romance. Established in 2004.

Matt Berenson
President
IMDb: imdb.com/name/nm0073554

Sidney Kimmel
Chairman
IMDb: imdb.com/name/nm0454004

Jim Tauber
CCO
IMDb: imdb.com/name/nm0851433

Mark Mikutowicz
Vice-President
IMDb: imdb.com/name/nm2963870

SIERRA/ AFFINITY

9378 Wilshire Blvd.
Suite 210
Beverly Hills, CA 90212
Phone: 424-253-1060
Fax: 424-653-1977

Email: info@sierra-affinity.com
Home Page: sierra-affinity.com

Does not accept any unsolicited material. Project types include Feature Films. Preferred genres include Action, Comedy, Crime, Detective, Drama, Fantasy, Horror, Romance, Science Fiction, and Thriller.

Jen Gorton
Creative Executive
IMDb: imdb.com/name/nm4224815

Nicholas Meyer
CEO
IMDb: imdb.com/name/nm0583293

Kelly McCormick
Sr. Vice-President
IMDb: imdb.com/name/nm0566555

SIGNATURE PICTURES

8285 W Sunset Blvd, Suite 7
West Hollywood, CA 90046
Phone: 323-848-9005
Fax: 323-848-9305

Email: james@signaturepictures.com
Home Page: signaturepictures.com

Does not accept any unsolicited material. Project types include Feature Films. Preferred genres include Action, Drama, Non-Fiction, Romance, and Thriller.

Moshe Diamant
Partner

Illana Diamant
Partner

SIKELIA PRODUCTIONS

110 W 57th St
5th Floor
New York, NY 10019
Phone: 212-906-8800
Fax: 212-906-8891

Does not accept any unsolicited material. Project types include Feature Films. Preferred genres include Action, Crime, Drama, Romance, and Thriller.

Martin Scorsese
Principle
IMDb: imdb.com/name/nm0000217

Emma Koskoff
President
IMDb: imdb.com/name/nm0863374

Margaret Bodde
Executive Producer

SILLY ROBIN PRODUCTIONS

30 Slope Dr
Short Hills, NJ 07078
Phone: 310-487-8234
Fax: 973-376-7639

Email: ribz99@aol.com
Home Page: alanzweibel.com

Accepts query letter from unproduced, unrepresented writers via email. Project types include Feature Films, TV, and Theater. Preferred genres include Comedy and Drama.

Alan Zweibel
Writer/Producer/Director

John Robertson
Director of Development

SILVER DREAM PRODUCTIONS

3452 E Foothill Blvd, Suite 620
Pasadena, CA 91107
Phone: 626-799-3880
Fax: 626-799-5363

Email: luoyan@silverdreamprods.com
Home Page: silverdreamprods.com

Accepts query letter from unproduced, unrepresented writers via email. Project types include Feature Films. Preferred genres include Drama and Myth.

Luo Yan
Assistant: Diana Chin

SILVER/KOSTER PRODUCTIONS

353 S Reeves Dr, Penthouse
Beverly Hills, CA 90212
Phone: 310-551-5245

Email: skfi lmco@aol.com
Home Page: silvers-koster.com

Accepts query letter from unproduced, unrepresented writers via email. Project types include Feature Films, TV, and Commercials. Preferred genres include Non-Fiction and Reality.

Iren Koster
President

Tracey Silvers
Chairman

Karen Corcoran
Vice-President

SILVER NITRATE ENTERTAINMENT

12268 Ventura Blvd
Studio City, CA 91604
Phone: 818-762-9559
Fax: 818-762-9177

Does not accept any unsolicited material. Project types include Feature Films. Preferred genres include Animation, Comedy, Drama, and Science Fiction.

Ash Shah
Principle
Email: ash@silvernitrate.net

SILVER PICTURES

2434 Main St.
Santa Monica, CA 90405
Phone: 310-566-6100
Fax: 310-566-6188

Accepts query letter from unproduced, unrepresented writers. Project types include Feature Films and TV. Preferred genres include Action, Animation, Drama, Family, Non-Fiction, Reality, Science Fiction, and Thriller.

Joel Silver
Chairman

Alex Heineman

Sarah Meyer
Director of Development

SIMONSAYS ENTERTAINMENT

12 Desbrosses St
New York, NY 10013
Phone: 917-797-9704

Email: info@simonsaysentertainment.net
Home Page: simonsaysentertainment.net

Accepts scripts from unproduced, unrepresented writers. Project types include Feature Films. Preferred genres include Crime, Drama, and Romance.

Ron Simons
Principle
IMDb: imdb.com/name/nm1839399

April Yvette Thompson
IMDb: imdb.com/name/nm1690743

SIMON WEST PRODUCTIONS

3450 Cahuenga Blvd West
Building 510
Los Angeles, CA 90068
Phone: 323-845-0821
Fax: 323-845-4582

Email: submissions@simonwestproductions.com
Home Page: simonwestproductions.com

Accepts query letter from unproduced, unrepresented writers. Project types include Feature Films and TV. Preferred genres include Action, Drama, and Science Fiction.

Simon West
Principle

Jib Polhemus
President

SIMSIE FILMS/ MEDIA SAVANT PICTURES

2934 1/2 Beverly Glen Circle
Suite 264
Los Angeles, CA 90077

Email: simsiefilms@mac.com

Accepts query letter from unproduced, unrepresented writers. Project types include Feature Films. Preferred genres include Comedy and Drama.

Gwen Field
Partner
IMDb: imdb.com/name/nm0275947

SINGE CELL PICTURES

PO Box 69691
West Hollywood, CA 90069
USA
Phone: 310-360-7600
Fax: 310-360-7011

Accepts query letter from unproduced, unrepresented writers. Project types include Feature Films and TV. Preferred genres include Comedy and Drama.

Michael Stipe
Principle

Sandy Stern
Principle

SINOVOI ENTERTAINMENT

1317 N San Fernando Blvd, Suite 395
Burbank, CA 91504
Phone: 818-562-6404
Fax: 818-567-0104

Email: maxwell@sinovoientertainment.com
Home Page: sinovoientertainment.com

Accepts query letter from unproduced, unrepresented writers via email. Project types include Feature Films. Preferred genres include Comedy, Drama, and Horror.

Maxwell Sinovoi
Principle

Kimberly Estrada

SIXTH SENSE PRODUCTIONS, INC.

269 S Beverly Dr, Suite 1297
Beverly Hills, CA 90212
Phone: 310-247-2790
Fax: 310-247-2791

Email: scripts@sixthsenseproductions.com
Home Page: sixthsenseproductions.com

Accepts scripts from unproduced, unrepresented writers via email. Project types include Feature Films. Preferred genres include Action, Drama, and Sociocultural.

Richard Harding
CEO
IMDb: imdb.com/name/nm1502749

SKETCH FILMS

2332 S. Centinela Ave.
Suite B
Los Angeles, CA 90046
Phone: 310-806-4960

Does not accept any unsolicited material. Project types include Feature Films. Preferred genres include Action, Fantasy, Horror, Myth, and Science Fiction.

David Bernardi
Principle
Email: d.bernardi@sbcglobal.net
IMDb: imdb.com/name/nm2050171

Len Wiseman
Principle
IMDb: imdb.com/name/nm0936482

Malcolm Gray
Creative Executive

SKYDANCE PRODUCTIONS

5555 Melrose Ave
Dean Martin Building
2nd Floor
Hollywood, CA 90038
Phone: 323-956-9900
Fax: 323-956-9901

Email: info@skydance.com
Home Page: skydance.com

Accepts scripts from produced or represented writers. Project types include Feature Films and TV. Preferred genres include Action, Comedy, Drama, Family, Fantasy, Myth, Science Fiction, and Thriller.

David Ellison
CEO
IMDb: imdb.com/name/nm1911103
Assistant: Bill Bost

Dana Goldberg
CCO
IMDb: imdb.com/name/nm1602154
Assistant: Matt Grimm

Matthew Milam
Vice-President
IMDb: imdb.com/name/nm1297784
Assistant: Kyle Hebenstreit

Shannon Gregory
Creative Executive
IMDb: imdb.com/name/nm4087474

SKYLARK ENTERTAINMENT, INC.

12405 Venice Blvd, Suite 237
Los Angeles, CA 90066
Phone: 310-390-2659

Home Page: skylark.net

Does not accept any unsolicited material. Project types include Feature Films and TV. Preferred genres include Comedy, Drama, and Non-Fiction.

Jacobus Rose
President

SKY ONE

9220 Sunset Blvd, Suite 230
West Hollywood, CA 90069
Phone: 310-860-2740
Fax: 310-860-2471

Home Page: sky.com

Accepts query letter from unproduced, unrepresented writers. Project types include TV. Preferred genres include Action and Science Fiction.

Rebecca Siegal
Sr. Vice-President

SMART ENTERTAINMENT

9595 Wilshire Blvd, Suite 900
Beverly Hills, CA 90212
Phone: 310-205-6090
Fax: 310-205-6093

Email: assistant@smartentertainment.com
Home Page: smartentertainment.com

Accepts query letter from unproduced, unrepresented writers via email. Project types include Feature Films and TV. Preferred genres include Comedy, Horror, Non-Fiction, Reality, and Thriller.

John Jacobs
President
Email: john@smartentertainment.com

Zac Unterman
Email: zac@smartentertainment.com

SMASH MEDIA FILMS

1208 Georgina Ave
Santa Monica, CA 90402
Phone: 310-395-0058
Fax: 310-395-8850

Email: info@smashmediafilms.com
Home Page: smashmediafilms.com

Accepts query letter from unproduced, unrepresented writers via email. Project types include Feature Films and TV. Preferred genres include Comedy, Drama, and Science Fiction.

Harry Winer
President
Email: harry.winer@smashmediafilms.com

Shelley Hack
Vice-President
Email: shelley.hack@smashmediafilms.com

SMOKEHOUSE PICTURES

12001 Ventura Pl., Suite 200
Studio City, CA 91604
Phone: 818-432-0330
Fax: 818-432-0337

IMDb: imdb.com/company/co0184096

Does not accept any unsolicited material. Project types include Feature Films. Preferred genres include Comedy, Drama, and Thriller.

George Clooney
Partner
IMDb: imdb.com/name/nm0000123

Grant Heslov
Partner
IMDb: imdb.com/name/nm0381416
Assistant: Tara Oslin

Katie Murphy
Creative Executive
IMDb: imdb.com/name/nm3682023

SNEAK PREVIEW ENTERTAINMENT

6705 Sunset Blvd
2nd Floor
Hollywood, CA 90028
Phone: 323-962-0295
Fax: 323-962-0372

Email: indiefilm@sneakpreviewentertain.com
Home Page: sneakpreviewentertain.com

Accepts query letter from unproduced, unrepresented writers via email. Project types include Feature Films. Established in 1991.

Chris Hazzard
Director of Development
Phone: 323-962-0295
Email: ch@sneakpe.com
IMDb: imdb.com/name/nm3302502

Steven Wolfe
CEO
Phone: 323-962-0295
Email: sjwolfe@sneakpreviewentertain.com
IMDb: imdb.com/name/nm0938145

SOBINI FILMS

10203 Santa Monica Blvd
Suite 300B
Los Angeles, CA 90067
Phone: 310-432-6900
Fax: 310-432-6939

Home Page: sobini.com
IMDb: imdb.com/company/co0086773

Does not accept any unsolicited material. Project types include Feature Films. Preferred genres include Comedy, Drama, Family, and Thriller.

Mark Amin
CEO
IMDb: imdb.com/name/nm0024909

David Higgin
President
IMDb: imdb.com/name/nm0383371

Cami Winikoff
COO
IMDb: imdb.com/name/nm0935121

SOCIAL CAPITAL FILMS

1010 Wilshire Blvd.
Suite 507
Los Angeles, CA 90017
Phone: 866-609-7098

1001 Bridgeway PMB 170
Sausalito, CA 94965

Phone: 415-332-8877
Fax: 415-332-8467

Email: info@socialcapitalfilms.com
Home Page: socialcapitalfilms.com

Does not accept any unsolicited material. Project types include Feature Films and TV. Preferred genres include Comedy, Drama, Family, Horror, Non-Fiction, Reality, Science Fiction, and Thriller.

Martin Shore
CEO

SOGNO PRODUCTIONS

PO Box 55476
Portland, OR 97238
Phone: 561-676-4696

Email: angaelica@gmail.com
Home Page: ANGAELICA.com

Accepts scripts from unproduced, unrepresented writers. Project types include Feature Films. Preferred genres include Action, Comedy, Documentary, Drama, Fantasy, Romance, and Thriller.

Breven Angaelica Warren
Producer
IMDb: imdb.com/name/nm1938686

SOLIPSIST FILMS

465 N Crescent Heights Blvd
Los Angeles, CA 90048
Phone: 323-272-3122
Fax: 323-375-1649

Email: info@solipsistfilms.com
Home Page: solipsistfilms.com

Accepts query letter from unproduced, unrepresented writers via email. Project types include Feature Films and TV. Preferred genres include Detective, Drama, Fantasy, Non-Fiction, Reality, and Thriller.

Stephen L'Heureux
Principle

David Purcell
Creative Executive

S PICTURES, INC.

4420 Hayvenhurst Ave
Encino, CA 91436
Phone: 818-995-1585
Fax: 818-995-1677

Email: info@spictures.tv
Home Page: spictures.tv

Does not accept any unsolicited material. Project types include Feature Films and TV. Preferred genres include Comedy, Non-Fiction, Reality, and Science Fiction.

Chuck Simon
Phone: 818-995-1585
Email: chuck@Spictures.TV
IMDb: imdb.com/name/nm1247168

SPITFIRE PICTURES

9100 Wilshire Blvd
#401e
Beverly Hills, CA 90212
Phone: 310-300-9000
Fax: 310-300-9001

Home Page: spitfirepictures.com

Does not accept any unsolicited material. Project types include Feature Films. Preferred genres include Documentary, Drama, Romance, and Thriller. Established in 2003.

Nigel Sinclair
CEO
IMDb: imdb.com/name/nm0801691

Nicholas Ferrall
Director
IMDb: imdb.com/name/nm5909330

SPYGLASS ENTERTAINMENT

245 N Beverly Dr
Second Floor
Beverly Hills, CA 90024
Phone: 310-443-5800
Fax: 310-443-5912

Home Page: spyglassentertainment.com

Does not accept any unsolicited material. Project types include Feature Films. Preferred genres include Action, Comedy, Drama, Family, Horror, Non-Fiction, and Thriller.

Gary Barber
Chairman
IMDb: imdb.com/name/nm0053388

Roger Birnbaum
Chairman
IMDb: imdb.com/name/nm0083696

STAGE 6 FILMS

10202 W Washington Blvd
Culver City, CA 90232
Phone: 310-244-4000
Fax: 310-244-2626

Home Page: sonypicturesworldwideacquisitions.com
IMDb: imdb.com/company/co0222021

Does not accept any unsolicited material. Project types include Feature Films. Preferred genres include Action, Animation, Comedy, Crime, Documentary, Drama, Family, Horror, Period, Romance, Science Fiction, and Thriller. Established in 2007.

ST. AMOS PRODUCTIONS

3480 Barham Blvd
Los Angeles, CA 90068
Phone: 323-850-9872

Email: st.amosproductions@earthlink.net

Accepts query letter from unproduced, unrepresented writers via email. Project types include Feature Films and TV. Preferred genres include Comedy, Drama, Non-Fiction, and Reality.

John Stamos
Principle
IMDb: imdb.com/name/nm0001764

STARRY NIGHT ENTERTAINMENT

975 Park AVe.
Suite 10C
New York, NY 10028
Phone: 212-717-2750
Fax: 212-794-6150

Los Angeles, CA
Phone: 818-895-4916

Email: mailbox@starrynightent.com
Email: info@starrynightentertainment.com
Home Page: starrynightentertainment.com
IMDb: imdb.com/company/co0183209

Accepts query letter from unproduced, unrepresented writers via email. Project types include Feature Films, TV, Commercials, and Theater. Preferred genres include Comedy, Drama, Non-Fiction, and Reality.

Craig Saavedra
Partner (LA)
Email: cs@starrynightentertainment.com

Michael Shulman
Partner (NY)
Email: ms@starrynightentertainment.com

STATE STREET PICTURES

9255 W. Sunset Blvd.
Suite 528
Los Angeles, CA 90069
Phone: 323-556-2240
Fax: 323-556-2242

Home Page: statestreetpictures.com
IMDb: imdb.com/company/co0068765

Does not accept any unsolicited material. Project types include Feature Films and TV. Preferred genres include Comedy and Drama.

Robert Teitel
Partner
IMDb: imdb.com/name/nm0854052

George Tillman, Jr.
Partner
IMDb: imdb.com/name/nm0863387

Michael Flavin
Creative Executive

STEAMROLLER PRODUCTIONS, INC.

100 Universal City Plaza #7151
Universal City, CA 91608
Phone: 818-733-4622
Fax: 818-733-4608

Email: steamrollerprod@aol.com

Accepts query letter from unproduced, unrepresented writers via email. Project types include Feature Films and TV. Preferred genres include Action, Crime, Detective, Non-Fiction, Reality, and Thriller.

Steven Seagal
Assistant: Tracy Irvine

Binh Dang

STEFANIE EPSTEIN PRODUCTIONS

427 N Canon Dr, Suite 214
Beverly Hills, CA 90210
Phone: 310-385-0300
Fax: 310-385-0302

Email: billseprods@aol.com
IMDb: imdb.com/company/co0171458

Accepts query letter from unproduced, unrepresented writers via email. Project types include Feature Films and TV. Preferred genres include Comedy and Drama.

Stefanie Epstein
Producer

Bill Gienapp
Creative Executive

STEVEN BOCHCO PRODUCTIONS

3000 Olympic Blvd, Suite 1310
Santa Monica, CA 90404
Phone: 310-566-6900

Email: yr@bochcomedia.com
IMDb: imdb.com/company/co0085628

Accepts query letter from unproduced, unrepresented writers. Project types include TV. Preferred genres include Crime, Detective, and Drama.

Steven Bochco
Chairman
IMDb: imdb.com/name/nm0004766

Craig Shenkler
CFO

Dayna Kalins
President
IMDb: imdb.com/name/nm0435861

STOKELY CHAFFIN PRODUCTIONS

1456 Sunset Plaza Dr
Los Angeles, CA 90069
Phone: 310-657-4559

Accepts query letter from unproduced, unrepresented writers via email. Project types include Feature Films and TV. Preferred genres include Action, Comedy, Horror, Non-Fiction, and Thriller.

Stokely Chaffin
Principle
IMDb: imdb.com/name/nm0149563

STONEBROOK ENTERTAINMENT

10061 Riverside Dr, Suite 813
Toluca Lake, CA 91602
Phone: 818-766-8797

Accepts query letter from unproduced, unrepresented writers via email. Project types include Feature Films and TV.

Kris Wheeler
Producer
IMDb: imdb.com/name/nm2699108

STONE & COMPANY ENTERTAINMENT

c/o Hollywood Center Studios
1040 N Las Palmas Ave, Building 1
Los Angeles, CA 90038
Phone: 323-960-2599
Fax: 323-960-2437

Email: info@stonetv.com
Home Page: stonetv.com/home.html
IMDb: imdb.com/company/co0173288

Accepts query letter from unproduced, unrepresented writers via email. Project types include TV. Preferred genres include Non-Fiction and Reality.

Scott Stone
Principle
IMDb: imdb.com/name/nm0832164

David Weintraub
Producer
IMDb: imdb.com/name/nm1479111

René Brar
Development Executive

STONE VILLAGE PICTURES

9200 W Sunset Blvd
Suite 520
West Hollywood, CA 90069
Phone: 310-402-5171
Fax: 310-402-5172

Home Page: stonevillagepictures.com

Does not accept any unsolicited material. Project types include Feature Films. Preferred genres include Drama, Romance, and Thriller.

Scott Steindorff
Executive Producer
IMDb: imdb.com/name/nm1127589

Dylan Russell
Partner
IMDb: imdb.com/name/nm1928375

STOREFRONT PICTURES

1112 Montana Ave
Santa Monica, CA 90403
Phone: 310-459-4235

Email: betty@storefrontpics.com
Home Page: storefrontpics.com

Does not accept any unsolicited material. Project types include Feature Films. Preferred genres include Comedy, Drama, Family, Fantasy, and Romance.

Susan Cartsonis
President

STORY AND FILM

2934 1/2 Beverly Glen Circle,
Suite 195
Los Angeles, CA 90077
Phone: 310-480-8833

IMDb: imdb.com/company/co0120778

Accepts query letter from unproduced, unrepresented writers via email.

Clark Peterson
Development Executive
IMDb: imdb.com/name/nm0677075

STORYLINE ENTERTAINMENT

8335 Sunset Blvd, Suite 207
West Hollywood, CA 90069
Phone: 323-337-9045
Fax: 323-210-7263

Email: info@storyline-entertainment.com
Home Page: storyline-entertainment.com
IMDb: imdb.com/company/co0091980

Does not accept any unsolicited material. Project types include Feature Films, TV, and Theater. Preferred genres include Comedy, Drama, Non-Fiction, Reality, and Romance.

Craig Zadan
Partner
Phone: 323-337-9045
Email: craig@storyline-entertainment.com

Neil Meron
Partner
Phone: 323-337-9046
Email: neil@storyline-entertainment.com

Mark Nicholson
Vice President (Development)
Phone: 323-337-9047
Email: mark@storyline-entertainment.com

STRAIGHT UP FILMS

1514 17th St.
Suite 201
Santa Monica, CA 90404
Phone: 424-238-8470

Email: hello@straightupfilms.com
Home Page: straightupfilms.com

Does not accept any unsolicited material. Project types include Feature Films and TV. Preferred genres include Comedy, Crime, and Drama.

Marisa Polvino
Co-CEO/Producer
IMDb: imdb.com/name/nm0689909

Kate Cohen
Co-CEO/Producer
IMDb: imdb.com/name/nm3154628

Casey A. Carroll
Director (Film & Television Development)
IMDb: imdb.com/name/nm3554230

STRIKE ENTERTAINMENT

3000 W Olympic Blvd
Building 5, Suite 1250
Santa Monica, CA 90404
Phone: 310-315-0550
Fax: 310-315-0560

Accepts query letter from unproduced, unrepresented writers via email. Project types include Feature Films. Preferred genres include Action, Comedy, Drama, Horror, Science Fiction, and Thriller. Established in 2002.

Marc Abraham
Producer
Assistant: Jamie Zakowski

Tom Bliss
Producer
Assistant: Mark Barclay

Eric Newman
Producer
Assistant: Jesse Rose Moore

Kristel Laiblin
Assistant: Nhu Tran

STUDIOCANAL

301 N. Canon Dr.
Suite 207
Beverly Hills, CA 90210
Phone: 310-247-0994
Fax: 310-247-0995

Does not accept any unsolicited material. Project types include Feature Films and TV. Preferred genres include Comedy, Crime, Drama, Fantasy, Horror, Non-Fiction, Reality, Romance, and Thriller.

Ron Halpern
Executive Vice President of Production

SUBMARINE ENTERTAINMENT

525 Broadway
Ste 601
New York, NY 10012
Phone: 212-625-1410
Fax: 212-625-9931

Email: info@submarine.com
Home Page: submarine.com

Accepts query letter from produced or represented writers. Project types include Feature Films. Preferred genres include Documentary and Drama.

Josh Braun
President
Email: josh@submarine.com
IMDb: imdb.com/name/nm2248562

David Koh
Executive

Dan Braun
President
Email: dan@submarine.com
IMDb: imdb.com/name/nm2250854

SUCH MUCH FILMS

Santa Monica, CA 90405

Email: info@suchmuchfilms.com
Home Page: suchmuchfilms.com

Accepts query letter from unproduced, unrepresented writers via email. Project types include Feature Films. Preferred genres include Documentary and Drama.

Judi Levine
Principle
IMDb: imdb.com/name/nm0505861

Ben Lewin
Principle
IMDb: imdb.com/name/nm0506802

SUMMIT ENTERTAINMENT

1630 Stewart St
Ste 120
Santa Monica, CA 90404
Phone: 310-309-8400
Fax: 310-828-4132

Home Page: summit-ent.com
IMDb: imdb.com/company/co0046206

Does not accept any unsolicited material. Project types include Feature Films. Preferred genres include Action, Comedy, Crime, Drama, Fantasy, Romance, Science Fiction, and Thriller.

Rob Friedman
CEO
Phone: 310-309-8400
IMDb: imdb.com/name/nm2263981

Patrick Wachsberger
President
Phone: 310-309-8400
IMDb: imdb.com/name/nm0905163

Gillian Bohrer
Vice-President
Phone: 310-309-8400
IMDb: imdb.com/name/nm2023551

Merideth Milton
Sr. Vice-President
Phone: 310-309-8400
IMDb: imdb.com/name/nm0590693

SUNDIAL PICTURES

511 Sixth Ave., Suite 375
New York, NY 10011

Email: info@sundialpicturesllc.com
Home Page: sundial-pictures.com

Does not accept any unsolicited material. Project types include Feature Films. Preferred genres include Comedy, Documentary, Drama, and Thriller.

Stefan Norwicki
President
IMDb: imdb.com/name/nm3378356

Joey Carey
Partner
IMDb: imdb.com/name/nm2909903

Benjamin Weber
IMDb: imdb.com/name/nm3373548

SUNLIGHT PRODUCTIONS

854-A Fifth St
Santa Monica, CA 90403
Phone: 310-899-1522
Fax: 310-899-1262

Email: info@sunlightproductions.com
Home Page: mikebinder.net
IMDb: imdb.com/company/co0028319

Does not accept any unsolicited material. Project types include Feature Films and TV. Preferred genres include Comedy, Drama, and Non-Fiction.

Mike Binder
Executive
IMDb: imdb.com/name/nm0082802

Jack Binder
Executive

SUNSWEPT ENTERTAINMENT

10201 W Pico Blvd
Building 45
Los Angeles, CA 90064
Phone: 310-369-0878
Fax: 310-969-0726

Sunswept Entertainment - TV
10201 W. Pico Blvd.
Building 3/Room 204
Los Angeles, CA 90035

IMDb: imdb.com/company/co0226011

Does not accept any unsolicited material. Project types include Feature Films. Preferred genres include Animation, Comedy, Family, Fantasy, and Romance. Established in 2004.

Karen Rosenfelt
Principle
IMDb: imdb.com/name/nm1651942

Caroline MacVicar
Creative Executive

SUNTAUR ENTERTAINMENT

1581 N Crescent Heights Blvd.
Los Angeles, CA 90046
Phone: 323-656-3800

Email: info@suntaurent.com
Home Page: suntaurent.com
IMDb: imdb.com/company/co0183461

Does not accept any unsolicited material. Project types include Feature Films and TV. Preferred genres include Comedy and Drama.

Paul Aaron
Executive
IMDb: imdb.com/name/nm0007477

SUPER CRISPY ENTERTAINMENT

2812 Santa Monica Blvd
Ste 205
Santa Monica, CA 90404
Phone: 310-453-4545

Email: crispyfilms@gmail.com

Does not accept any unsolicited material. Project types include Feature Films. Preferred genres include Comedy, Drama, and Romance.

Jonathan Schwartz
Producer
Phone: 310-453-4545
IMDb: imdb.com/name/nm2009933

Andrea Sperling
Producer
Phone: 310-453-4545
IMDb: imdb.com/name/nm0818304

SUPERFINGER ENTERTAINMENT

c/o Chris Hart/UTA
9560 Wilshire Blvd
Beverly Hills, CA 90212
Phone: 310-385-6715

IMDb: imdb.com/company/co0181284

Accepts query letter from unproduced, unrepresented writers via email. Project types include Feature Films and TV. Preferred genres include Animation, Comedy, Non-Fiction, and Reality.

Dane Cook
IMDb: imdb.com/name/nm0176981

SWEET 180

141 W 28th St #300
NYC, NY 10001
Phone: 212-541-4443
Fax: 212-563-9655

Home Page: sweet180.com

Does not accept any unsolicited material. Project types include Feature Films and TV. Preferred genres include Comedy, Drama, Non-Fiction, Reality, and Romance.

Lillian LaSalle
Principle
Email: lillian@sweet180.com

Nina Schreiber
Manager
Email: nina@sweet180.com

Catherine Clausi
Assistant: Lindsay Carlson

Rachel Maran
Email: assistant@sweet180.com

TAGGART PRODUCTIONS

9000 W Sunset Blvd
Suite 1020
West Hollywood, CA 90069
Phone: 424-249-3350
Fax: 424-249-3972

Home Page: taggart-productions.com
Facebook: facebook.com/taggartproductions

Does not accept any unsolicited material. Project types include Feature Films. Preferred genres include Action, Comedy, Crime, Drama, and Thriller.

Michael Nardelli
President & CEO
IMDb: imdb.com/name/nm1660148

TAGLINE PICTURES

9250 Wilshire Blvd
Ground Floor
Beverly Hills, CA 90212
Phone: 310-595-1515
Fax: 310-595-1505

Email: info@taglinela.com
Home Page: taglinela.com

Does not accept any unsolicited material. Project types include TV. Preferred genres include Comedy and Drama.

Chris Henze
Partner
IMDb: imdb.com/name/nm1771421

J.B. Roberts
Partner

William Mercer

Ron West

Kelly Kulchak
President
IMDb: imdb.com/name/nm2103544

TAMARA ASSEYEV PRODUCTION

1187 Coast Village Rd.
Suite 134
Santa Barbara, CA 93108
Phone: 323-656-4731
Fax: 323-656-2211

Email: tamaraprod@aol.com

Accepts query letter from unproduced, unrepresented writers. Project types include TV. Preferred genres include Drama.

Tamara Asseyev
Producer
Assistant: Constance Mead

TANNENBAUM COMPANY

c/o CBS Studios
4024 Radford Ave, Bungalow 16
Studio City, CA 91604
Phone: 818-655-7181
Fax: 818-655-7193

Does not accept any unsolicited material. Project types include Feature Films and TV. Preferred genres include Comedy, Drama, Non-Fiction, and Reality.

Kim Haswell-Tannenbaum
Producer

Eric Tannenbaum
Partner
IMDb: imdb.com/name/nm1383548

Jason Wang
Creative Affairs
IMDb: imdb.com/name/nm4867712

TAPESTRY FILMS, INC.

9328 Civic Center Dr, 2nd Floor
Beverly Hills, CA 90210
Phone: 310-275-1191
Fax: 310-275-1266

Does not accept any unsolicited material. Project types include Feature Films. Preferred genres include Action, Comedy, Family, Romance, and Thriller.

Michael Schreiber
President
IMDb: imdb.com/name/nm2325100

Peter Abrams
IMDb: imdb.com/name/nm0009222

Robert L. Levy
IMDb: imdb.com/name/nm0506597

Kat Blasband Page
IMDb: imdb.com/name/nm2321097

TAURUS ENTERTAINMENT COMPANY

5555 Melrose Ave
Marx Brothers Building, Suite 103/104
Hollywood, CA 90038
Phone: 818-935-5157
Fax: 323-686-5379

Email: taurusentco@yahoo.com
Home Page: taurusec.com

Accepts query letter from unproduced, unrepresented writers via email. Project types include Feature Films and TV. Preferred genres include Action, Animation, Drama, and Family. Established in 1991.

James Dudelson
Email: jgdudelson@yahoo.com
IMDb: imdb.com/name/nm0240054

Robert Dudelson
Email: rfdudelson@mac.com
IMDb: imdb.com/name/nm0240055

T&C PICTURES

3122 Santa Monica Blvd #200
Santa Monica, CA 90404
Phone: 310-828-1340
Fax: 310-828-1581

Email: info@tandcpictures.com

Accepts query letter from unproduced, unrepresented writers. Project types include Feature Films and TV. Preferred genres include Action, Comedy, Drama, Family, Non-Fiction, and Thriller.

Bill Borden
Producer
Email: christine@tandcpictures.com
IMDb: imdb.com/name/nm0096115

Barry Rosenbush
Executive
IMDb: imdb.com/name/nm0742492

Arata Matsushima
Phone: 310-828-7801
IMDb: imdb.com/name/nm2606503

TEAM DOWNEY

1311 Abbot Kinney
Venice, CA 90291
Phone: 310-450-5100

Does not accept any unsolicited material. Project types include Feature Films. Preferred genres include Action, Comedy, and Drama. Established in 2010.

Robert Downey
Producer
IMDb: imdb.com/name/nm0000375

Susan Downey
Producer
IMDb: imdb.com/name/nm1206265

David Gambino
President
IMDb: imdb.com/name/nm1312724

TEAM G

1839 Blake Ave #5 Los Angeles, CA 90039
Phone: 213-915-8106
Fax: 323-843-9210

Email: info@teamgproductions.com
Home Page: teamgproductions.com

Project types include Feature Films. Preferred genres include Comedy, Drama, and Science Fiction.

Trey Hock
Partner
IMDb: imdb.com/name/nm2465366

Jett Steiger
Partner
IMDb: imdb.com/name/nm2532520

TEAM TODD

2900 W Olympic Blvd
Santa Monica, CA 91404
Phone: 310-255-7265
Fax: 310-255-7222

Accepts scripts from produced or represented writers. Project types include Feature Films. Preferred genres include Animation, Drama, Family, Myth, and Romance.

Julianna Hays
Creative Executive
IMDb: imdb.com/name/nm3057670

Suzanne Todd
Principle
IMDb: imdb.com/name/nm0865297

TEMPLE HILL ENTERTAINMENT

9255 Sunset Blvd, Suite 801
Los Angeles, CA 90069
Phone: 310-270-4383
Fax: 310-270-4395

Home Page: templehillent.com

Does not accept any unsolicited material. Project types include Feature Films and TV. Preferred genres include Comedy, Drama, Family, Fantasy, and Thriller. Established in 2006.

Marty Bowen
Partner
IMDb: imdb.com/name/nm2125212

Wyck Godfrey
Partner
IMDb: imdb.com/name/nm0324041

Isaac Klausner
Director of Development

Isaac Klausner
Director of Development
IMDb: imdb.com/name/nm2327099

Tracy Nyberg
Sr. Vice-President
IMDb: imdb.com/name/nm2427937

TERRA FIRMA FILMS

468 N Camden Dr, Suite 365T
Beverly Hills, CA 90210
Phone: 310-480-5676
Fax: 310-862-4717

Email: info@terrafirmafilms.com
Home Page: terrafirmafilms.com

Accepts query letter from unproduced, unrepresented writers via email. Project types include Feature Films. Preferred genres include Action, Comedy, Drama, Family, and Romance. Established in 2003.

Adam Herz
President
Phone: 310-860-7480
Email: info@terrafi rmafi lms.com
IMDb: imdb.com/name/nm0381221

Josh Shader
IMDb: imdb.com/name/nm1003558

Gregory Lessans
IMDb: imdb.com/name/nm0504298

THE AMERICAN FILM COMPANY

c/o Business Affairs, Inc.
2415 Main St, 2nd Floor
Santa Monica, CA 90405
Phone: 310-392-0777

Email: info@americanfilmco.com
Home Page: theamericanfilmcompany.com

Accepts query letter from unproduced, unrepresented writers via email. Project types include Feature Films. Preferred genres include Drama, Non-Fiction, Period, and Thriller. Established in 2008.

Brian Falk
President
Email: bfalk@americanfi lmco.com
IMDb: imdb.com/name/nm1803137

Alfred Levitt
COO
IMDb: imdb.com/name/nm4662708

THE ASYLUM

72 E Palm Ave
Burbank, CA 91502
Phone: 323-850-1214
Fax: 818-260-9811

Email: theasylum@theasylum.cc
Home Page: theasylum.cc

Does not accept any unsolicited material. Project types include Feature Films. Preferred genres include Action, Fantasy, Horror, Science Fiction, and Thriller.

Micho Rutare
Director of Development
IMDb: imdb.com/name/nm3026436

Mark Quod
IMDb: imdb.com/name/nm0704517

Joseph Lawson
IMDb: imdb.com/name/nm1037472

THE AV CLUB

2629 Main St #211
Santa Monica, CA 90405
Phone: 310-396-1165

Does not accept any unsolicited material. Project types include Feature Films. Preferred genres include Comedy, Drama, Non-Fiction, Romance, and Science Fiction.

Amy Robertson
Producer
IMDb: imdb.com/name/nm1516144

THE BADHAM COMPANY

16830 Ventura Blvd, Suite 300
Encino, CA, 91436
Phone: 818-990-9495
Fax: 818-981-9163

Email: development@badhamcompany.com
Home Page: badhamcompany.com

Accepts scripts from produced or represented writers. Project types include Feature Films and TV. Preferred genres include Drama, Family, and Non-Fiction.

John Badham
Principle
IMDb: imdb.com/name/nm0000824

THE BUREAU

18 Phipp St
2nd Floor
London - EC2A 4NU
United-Kingdom
Phone: +44-0207-033-0555

Email: mail@thebureau.co.uk
Home Page: thebureau.co.uk

Does not accept any unsolicited material. Project types include Feature Films. Preferred genres include Comedy, Documentary, Drama, Romance, and Thriller. Established in 2000.

Bertrand Faivre
Producer
IMDb: imdb.com/name/nm0265724

Tristan Golighter
Producer

Soledad Gatti-Pascual
IMDb: imdb.com/name/nm0309806

Valentina Brazzini

Matthew de Braconier

THE GOLD COMPANY

499 N Canon Dr, Suite 306
Beverly Hills, CA 90210
Phone: 310-270-4653

Accepts query letter from unproduced, unrepresented writers. Project types include Feature Films. Preferred genres include Comedy.

Eric L. Gold
Principle
IMDb: imdb.com/name/nm0324970

Jessica Green
Executive Vice President of Production
IMDb: imdb.com/name/nm2783652

THE GOLDSTEIN COMPANY

1644 Courtney Ave
Los Angeles, CA 90046
Phone: 310-659-9511

Home Page: garywgoldstein.com

Accepts query letter from unproduced, unrepresented writers via email. Project types include Feature Films, TV, and Commercials. Preferred genres include Action, Comedy, Non-Fiction, Reality, Romance, and Thriller.

Gary Goldstein
Producer
Email: gary@garywgoldstein.com
IMDb: imdb.com/name/nm0326214

Sandra Tomita
IMDb: imdb.com/name/nm0866739

THE GOODMAN COMPANY

8491 Sunset Blvd, Suite 329
Los Angeles, CA 90069
Phone: 323-655-0719

Email: ilyssagoodman@sbcglobal.net

Accepts query letter from unproduced, unrepresented writers. Project types include Feature Films and TV. Preferred genres include Comedy, Drama, Family, Non-Fiction, and Reality.

Ilyssa Goodman
Executive
IMDb: imdb.com/name/nm1058415

THE GOTHAM GROUP

9255 Sunset Blvd, Suite 515
Los Angeles, CA 90069
Phone: 310-285-0001
Fax: 310-285-0077

Home Page: gotham-group.com

Does not accept any unsolicited material. Project types include Feature Films, TV, and Commercials. Preferred genres include Action, Animation, Comedy, Drama, Family, Fantasy, Non-Fiction, Reality, and Science Fiction.

Julie Kane-Ritsch
Email: jkr@gotham-group.com
IMDb: imdb.com/name/nm1415970

Peter McHugh
Email: peter@gotham-group.com

Ellen Goldsmith-Vein
Email: egv@gotham-group.com
IMDb: imdb.com/name/nm1650412

THE GREENBERG GROUP

2029 S Westgate Ave
Los Angeles, CA 90025

Email: info@greenberggroup.com
Home Page: greenberggroup.com

Accepts query letter from unproduced, unrepresented writers via email. Project types include Feature Films, TV, and Commercials. Preferred genres include Action, Non-Fiction, Reality, and Thriller.

Randy Greenberg
Email: randy@greenberggroup.com
IMDb: imdb.com/name/nm2985843

THE GROUP ENTERTAINMENT

115 W 29th St #1102
New York, NY 10001
Phone: 212-868-5233
Fax: 212-504-3082

Email: info@thegroupentertainment.com
Home Page: thegroupentertainment.com

Does not accept any unsolicited material. Project types include Feature Films and TV. Preferred genres include Action, Comedy, Drama, Non-Fiction, Reality, and Romance.

Rebecca Atwood
Creative Executive
Email: rebecca@thegroupentertainment.com

Gil Holland
Partner
IMDb: imdb.com/name/nm0390693

Kyle Luker
Partner
Email: kyle@thegroupentertainment.com

Jill McGrath
Partner
Email: jill@thegroupentertainment.com

THE HALCYON COMPANY

8455 Beverly Blvd
Suite 600
Los Angeles, CA 90048
Phone: 323-650-0222

Email: info@thehalcyoncompany.com
Home Page: thehalcyoncompany.com

Does not accept any unsolicited material. Project types include Feature Films. Preferred genres include Action, Science Fiction, and Thriller. Established in 2006.

Derek Anderson
CEO
IMDb: imdb.com/name/nm2203770

Victor Kubicek
CEO
IMDb: imdb.com/name/nm2127497

THE HAL LIEBERMAN COMPANY

8522 National Blvd, Suite 108
Culver City, CA 90232
Phone: 310-202-1929
Fax: 323-850-5132

Accepts query letter from unproduced, unrepresented writers via email. Project types include Feature Films. Preferred genres include Drama, Family, Fantasy, Horror, and Thriller.

Hal Lieberman
Principle
IMDb: imdb.com/name/nm0509386

Dan Scheinkman
Vice-President

THE HATCHERY

2950 N Hollywood Way
3rd Floor
Burbank, CA 91505
Phone: 818-748-4507
Fax: 818-748-4615/Attn: Dan Angel

Email: dangel@thehatcheryllc.com
Home Page: thehatcheryllc.com

Does not accept any unsolicited material. Project types include Feature Films and TV. Preferred genres include Comedy, Family, Horror, and Science Fiction.

Dan Angel
Founder
Email: dangel@thehatcheryllc.com
IMDb: imdb.com/name/nm0029445

THE HECHT COMPANY

3607 W Magnolia, Suite L
Burbank, CA 91505
Phone: 310-989-3467

Email: hechtco@aol.com

Accepts query letter from unproduced, unrepresented writers via email. Project types include Feature Films and TV. Preferred genres include Drama, Non-Fiction, Reality, and Thriller.

Duffy Hecht
Producer
IMDb: imdb.com/name/nm0372953

THE JIM HENSON COMPANY

1416 N La Brea Ave
Hollywood, CA 90028

Phone: 323-802-1500
Fax: 323-802-1825

117 E. 69th St.
New York, NY 10021
Phone: 212-794-2400

Email: info@henson.com
Home Page: henson.com

Does not accept any unsolicited material. Project types include Feature Films, TV, Commercials, and Theater. Preferred genres include Animation, Comedy, Family, Fantasy, Non-Fiction, Reality, and Science Fiction. Established in 1958.

Brian Henson
Chairman
IMDb: imdb.com/name/nm0005008

Halle Stanford
Executive Vice-President, Children's TV
IMDb: imdb.com/name/nm1277553

Blanca Lista
Director of Development (Feature Films)

THE LITTLEFIELD COMPANY

500 S Buena Vista St Animation Building, Suite 3D-2
Burbank, CA 91521
Phone: 818-560-2280
Fax: 818-560-3775

Does not accept any unsolicited material. Project types include TV. Preferred genres include Drama.

Warren Littlefield
Principle
Phone: 818-560-2280
IMDb: imdb.com/name/nm0514716
Assistant: Patricia Mann

Jill Young
Development Executive

THE MARK GORDON COMPANY

12200 W Olympic Blvd, Suite 250
Los Angeles, CA 90064
Phone: 310-943-6401
Fax: 310-943-6402

Does not accept any unsolicited material. Project types include Feature Films and TV. Preferred genres include Action and Drama.

Mark Gordon
Principle
IMDb: imdb.com/name/nm0330428

Sara Smith
Creative Executive

THE MAZUR/KAPLAN COMPANY

3204 Pearl St
Santa Monica, CA 90405
Phone: 310-450-5838

Email: info@mazurkaplan.com
Home Page: mazurkaplan.com

Does not accept any unsolicited material. Project types include Feature Films and TV. Preferred genres include Comedy, Family, Fantasy, Non-Fiction, Reality, Romance, and Thriller. Established in 2009.

Paula Mazur
Producer
Phone: 310-450-5838
IMDb: imdb.com/name/nm0563394

Kimi Armstrong Stein
Vice-President
Email: kimi@mazurkaplan.com
IMDb: imdb.com/name/nm2148964

Mitchell Kaplan
Producer
IMDb: imdb.com/name/nm3125086

Ally Israelson
Creative Executive

THE PITT GROUP

8750 Wilshire Blvd.
Suite 301
Beverly Hills, CA 90211
Phone: 310-246-4800
Fax: 310-275-9258

Accepts query letter from unproduced, unrepresented writers. Project types include Feature Films and TV.

Preferred genres include Animation, Comedy, Crime, Detective, Drama, and Romance. Established in 2000.

Jeremy Conrady
Creative Executive
Email: jconrady@pittgroup.com
IMDb: imdb.com/name/nm262042

Lou Pitt
Principle
Email: lpitt@pittgroup.com
IMDb: imdb.com/name/nm2229316

THE RADMIN COMPANY

9201 Wilshire Blvd, Suite 102
Beverly Hills, CA 90210
Phone: 310-274-9515
Fax: 310-274-0739

Email: queries@radmincompany.com
Home Page: radmincompany.com

Accepts query letter from unproduced, unrepresented writers via email. Project types include Feature Films. Preferred genres include Comedy, Drama, and Romance. Established in 1993.

Linne Radmin
IMDb: imdb.com/name/nm0705709

Brandon Klaus
Creative Executive

THE SAFRAN COMPANY

9663 Santa Monica Blvd.
Suite 840
Beverly Hills, CA 90210
Phone: 310-278-1450

Does not accept any unsolicited material. Project types include Feature Films and TV. Preferred genres include Comedy and Family. Established in 2006.

Peter Safran
IMDb: imdb.com/name/nm0755911

Joan Mao
Director of Development
IMDb: imdb.com/name/nm1619641

THE STEVE TISCH COMPANY

10202 W Washington Blvd
Astaire Building, 3rd Floor
Culver City, CA 90232
Phone: 310-244-6612
Fax: 310-204-2713

Accepts query letter from unproduced, unrepresented writers. Project types include Feature Films. Preferred genres include Action, Comedy, Drama, and Thriller.

Steve Tisch
Principle
IMDb: imdb.com/name/nm0005494

Lacy Boughn
Director of Development
Phone: 310-244-6620
Email: lacy_boughn@spe.sony.com
IMDb: imdb.com/name/nm2064419

THE WALT DISNEY COMPANY

500 S Buena Vista St
Burbank, CA 91521
Phone: 818-560-1000
Fax: 818-560-2500

Home Page: disney.com

Does not accept any unsolicited material. Project types include TV. Preferred genres include Action, Animation, Comedy, Drama, Family, Fantasy, Myth, and Non-Fiction. Established in 1923.

Robert Iger
President
Email: bob.iger@disney.com
IMDb: imdb.com/name/nm2250609

Rita Ferro

Mary Ann Hughes
Vice-President
IMDb: imdb.com/name/nm3134377

THE WEINSTEIN COMPANY

375 Greenwich St, Lobby A
New York, NY 10013-2376
Phone: 212-941-3800
Fax: 212-941-3949

9100 Wilshire Blvd, Suite 700W
Beverly Hills, CA 90212
Phone: 424-204-4800

Canaletto House
39 Beak St.
London, United Kingdom, W1F 9SA
Phone: 011-442-074946180

99 Hudson St.
New York, NY 10013
Phone: 212-845-8600

Email: info@weinsteinco.com
Home Page: weinsteinco.com

Does not accept any unsolicited material. Project types include Feature Films and TV. Preferred genres include Action, Animation, Comedy, Drama, Family, Myth, Non-Fiction, Romance, and Thriller. Established in 2005.

Harvey Weinstein
Co-Chairman
Assistant: Brendon Boyea

Barbara Schneeweiss
Vice President (Development & Production for TV & Film)

Collin Creighton
Vice President (Production & Development)

Bob Weinstein
Co-Chairman

THE WOLPER ORGANIZATION

4000 Warner Blvd.
Bldg. 28, Ste. 2300
Burbank, CA 91522
Phone: 818-954-1421
Fax: 818-954-1593

Home Page: wolperorg.com

Does not accept any unsolicited material. Project types include Feature Films and TV. Preferred genres include Crime, Detective, and Drama. Established in 1987.

Sam Alexander
Director of Development
Email: Sam.Alexander@wbtvprod.com
IMDb: imdb.com/name/nm3303012

Mark Wolper
President
IMDb: imdb.com/name/nm0938679

Kevin Nicklaus
Vice-President
IMDb: imdb.com/name/nm2102454

THE ZANUCK COMPANY

16 Beverly Park
Beverly Hills, CA 90210
Phone: 310-274-0261
Fax: 310-273-9217

Does not accept any unsolicited material. Project types include Feature Films and TV. Preferred genres include Action, Comedy, Crime, Drama, Family, Fantasy, Period, Romance, and Thriller. Established in 1988.

Harrison Zanuck
Producer
Phone: 310-274-5929

Lili Fini Zanuck
Phone: 310-274-0209
IMDb: imdb.com/name/nm0005572
Assistant: Aubrie Artiano

THOUSAND WORDS

110 S Fairfax Ave, Suite 370
Los Angeles, CA 90036
Phone: 323-936-4700
Fax: 323-936-4701

Email: info@thousand-words.com
Home Page: thousand-words.com

Accepts query letter from unproduced, unrepresented writers via email. Project types include Feature Films. Preferred genres include Animation, Drama, and Thriller. Established in 2000.

Michael Van Vliet
Creative Executive
Phone: 323-936-4700
Email: info@thousand-words.com
IMDb: imdb.com/name/nm2702900

Jonah Smith
Chairman
Phone: 323-936-4700
Email: info@thousand-words.com
IMDb: imdb.com/name/nm0808819

Palmer West
Chairman
Phone: 323-936-4700
Email: info@thousand-words.com
IMDb: imdb.com/name/nm0922279

THREE STRANGE ANGELS, INC.

9050 W Washington Blvd
Culver City, CA 90232
Phone: 310-840-8213

Does not accept any unsolicited material. Project types include Feature Films. Preferred genres include Action, Comedy, and Fantasy.

Lindsay Doran
Phone: 310-840-8213
IMDb: imdb.com/name/nm0233386
Assistant: Natasha Khrolenko

THUNDERBIRD FILMS

401 - 533 Smithe St
Vancouver, BC V6B 6H1
Canada
Phone: 604-683-3555
Fax: 604-707-0378

Email: info@hunderbirdfilms.net
Home Page: thunderbirdfilms.net/s/Home.asp
IMDb: imdb.com/company/co0163158

Does not accept any unsolicited material. Project types include TV. Preferred genres include Comedy and Drama.

Alex Raffe
Head of Production & Development
Email: alex@thunderbirdfilms.com
IMDb: imdb.com/name/nm0706244

Danielle Kreinik
Head of Development

Timothy Gamble
CEO
IMDb: imdb.com/name/nm0303817

THUNDER ROAD PICTURES

1411 5th St Suite 400
Santa Monica, CA 90401
Phone: 310-573-8885

Does not accept any unsolicited material. Project types include Feature Films and TV. Preferred genres include Action, Crime, Detective, Drama, Non-Fiction, and Thriller. Established in 2003.

Basil Iwanyk
Owner
IMDb: imdb.com/name/nm0412588

Kent Kubena
IMDb: imdb.com/name/nm0473423
Assistant: Noah Winter

Erica Lee
Vice-President
IMDb: imdb.com/name/nm3102707

Peter Lawson
President
IMDb: imdb.com/name/nm4498662

TIM BURTON PRODUCTIONS

8033 Sunset Blvd, Suite 7500
West Hollywood, CA 90046
Phone: 310-300-1670
Fax: 310-300-1671

Home Page: timburton.com

Does not accept any unsolicited material. Project types include Feature Films. Preferred genres include Action, Family, and Fantasy. Established in 1989.

Tim Burton
Principle
Phone: 310-300-1670
Email: kory.edwrds@timburton.com
IMDb: imdb.com/name/nm0000318

Derek Frey
Executive
Email: derek@lazerfilm.com
IMDb: imdb.com/name/nm0294553

TOM WELLING PRODUCTIONS

4000 Warner Blvd
Building 146, Room 201
Burbank, CA 91522
Phone: 818-954-4012

Does not accept any unsolicited material. Project types include TV. Preferred genres include Drama. Established in 2010.

Tom Welling
Principle
Phone: 818-954-4012
IMDb: imdb.com/name/nm0919991

Jessica Franks
Development Executive
Phone: 818-954-4012

Stephanie Levine
President
Phone: 818-954-4012

TONIK PRODUCTIONS

27 W 24th St. Suite 1108
New York, NY 10010
Phone: 212-532-6565
Fax: 212-532-6650

Email: info@tonikproductions.com
Home Page: http://www.tonikproductions.com/home
IMDb: imdb.com/company/co0078138

Accepts query letter from unproduced, unrepresented writers via email. Project types include Feature Films. Preferred genres include Comedy, Drama, Family, Fantasy, and Science Fiction.

Tonya Lewis Lee
Principle
IMDb: imdb.com/name/nm1416174

Nikki SIlver
Principle
IMDb: imdb.com/name/nm1012185

TOOL OF NORTH AMERICA

2210 Broadway
Santa Monica, CA 90404
Phone: 310-453-9244
Fax: 310-453-4185

50 W 17th St, 4th Floor
New York, NY 10011
Phone: 212-924-1100
Fax: 212-924-1156

Home Page: toolofna.com
Facebook: facebook.com/toolofna

Accepts query letter from unproduced, unrepresented writers via email. Project types include Feature Films, TV, and Commercials. Preferred genres include Drama, Horror, Non-Fiction, Reality, and Thriller.

Oliver Fuselier
Executive Producer
Email: oliver@toolofna.com
IMDb: imdb.com/name/nm0299336

Dustin Callif
Executive Producer
Email: dustin@toolofna.com
IMDb: imdb.com/name/nm2956668

Brian Latt
Email: brian@toolofna.com
IMDb: imdb.com/name/nm0490373

TORNELL PRODUCTIONS

80 Varick St, Suite 10C
New York, NY 10013
Phone: 212-625-2530
Fax: 212-625-2532

Accepts query letter from unproduced, unrepresented writers. Project types include Feature Films.

Lisa Tornell
Producer
Phone: 212-625-2530
IMDb: imdb.com/name/nm0868178

TOWER OF BABBLE ENTERTAINMENT

854 N Spaulding Ave
Los Angeles, CA 90046
Phone: 323-230-6128
Fax: 323-822-0312

Email: info@towerofb .com
Home Page: towerofb .com

Accepts query letter from unproduced, unrepresented writers via email. Project types include Feature Films and TV. Preferred genres include Comedy and Romance.

Jeff Wadlow
Phone: 323-230-6128
Email: info@towerofb .com
IMDb: imdb.com/name/nm0905592

Beau Bauman
Phone: 323-230-6128
Email: info@towerofb .com
IMDb: imdb.com/name/nm0062149

TRANCAS INTERNATIONAL FILMS, INC.

2021 Pontius Ave
2nd Floor
Los Angeles, CA 90025
Phone: 310-477-6569
Fax: 310-477-7126

Email: info@trancasfilms.com
Home Page: trancasfilms.com

Does not accept any unsolicited material. Project types include Feature Films and TV. Preferred genres include Action, Comedy, Drama, Horror, and Thriller.

Malek S. Akkad
President
IMDb: imdb.com/name/nm0015443

Louis Nader
IMDb: imdb.com/name/nm0618868

TREEHOUSE FILMS

4450 Lakeside Dr
Suite 225
Burbank, CA 91505
Phone: 818-260-8707
Fax: 818-260-0440

Does not accept any unsolicited material. Project types include Feature Films. Preferred genres include Drama and Romance.

Kevin Costner
Principle
IMDb: imdb.com/name/nm0000126

Jasa McCall
Creative Executive

TRIBECA FILMS

375 Greenwich St, 8th Floor
New York, NY 10013
Phone: 212-941-2400
Fax: 212-941-3939

345 N. Maple Dr.
Suite 202
Beverly Hills, CA 90210
Phone: 310-651-8342

Email: info@tribecafilm.com
Home Page: tribecafilm.com

Does not accept any unsolicited material. Project types include Feature Films and TV. Preferred genres include Action, Comedy, Crime, Drama, Fantasy, Non-Fiction, Period, Romance, and Thriller. Established in 1989.

Robert De Niro
Partner
Phone: 212-941-2400
IMDb: imdb.com/name/nm0000134

Berry Welsh
Director of Development
Phone: 212-941-2400
IMDb: imdb.com/name/nm2654730

Jane Rosenthal
Partner
IMDb: imdb.com/name/nm0742772

TRICOAST STUDIOS

11124 W Washington Blvd
Culver City, CA 90232
Phone: 310-458-7707
Fax: 310-204-2450

Email: tricoast@tricoast.com
Home Page: tricoast.com

Does not accept any unsolicited material. Project types include Feature Films and TV.

Marcy Levitas Hamilton
Founder
IMDb: imdb.com/name/nm0358036

Strathford Hamilton
Founder
Email: strath@tricoast.com
IMDb: imdb.com/name/nm0358175

TRICOR ENTERTAINMENT

1613 Chelsea Rd
San Marino, CA 91108
Phone: 626-282-5184
Fax: 626-282-5185

Email: ExecutiveOffices@TricorEntertainment.com
Home Page: TricorEntertainment.com

Does not accept any unsolicited material. Project types include Feature Films.

Craig Darian
Chairman
Phone: 626-282-5184
IMDb: imdb.com/name/nm1545768

Ron Mencer
Director of Development
IMDb: imdb.com/name/nm1348889

TRILOGY ENTERTAINMENT GROUP

627 S Plymouth Blvd
The Studio
Los Angeles, CA 90005
Phone: 310-656-9733
Fax: 310-424-5816

1207 4th St
Suite 400
Santa Monica, CA 90401

Home Page: trilogyent.com

Does not accept any unsolicited material. Project types include Feature Films and TV. Preferred genres include Action, Comedy, Fantasy, Romance, and Thriller.

Pen Densham
Partner
Phone: 310-656-9733
IMDb: imdb.com/name/nm0219720

Nevin Densham
Creative Executive
Email: bfl am@trilogyent.com
IMDb: imdb.com/name/nm0219719

John Watson
Partner
IMDb: imdb.com/name/nm2302370

Howard Han

TROIKA PICTURES

2019 S Westgate Ave
2nd Floor
Los Angeles, CA 90025
Phone: 310-696-2859

Email: troikapics@gmail.com
Home Page: troikapictures.com

Does not accept any unsolicited material. Project types include Feature Films. Preferred genres include Action, Crime, Fantasy, Romance, and Thriller.

Bradley Gallo
Head of Production & Development
Phone: 310-696-2859
IMDb: imdb.com/name/nm0303010

Robert Stein
CEO
Phone: 310-696-2859
IMDb: imdb.com/name/nm3355501

Michael Helfant
COO
Phone: 310-696-2859
IMDb: imdb.com/name/nm0375033

TROMA ENTERTAINMENT

36-40 11th St
Long Island City, NY 11106
Phone: 718-391-0110
Fax: 718-391-0255

Email: troma1@gmail.com
Home Page: troma.com

Accepts scripts from unproduced, unrepresented writers. Project types include Feature Films. Preferred genres include Action, Drama, Fantasy, Horror, Science Fiction, Sociocultural, and Thriller.

Lloyd Kaufman
President
Email: lloyd@troma.com
IMDb: imdb.com/name/nm0442207

Michael Herz
Vice-President
IMDb: imdb.com/name/nm0381230

TURTLEBACK PRODUCTIONS, INC.

11736 Gwynne Ln
Los Angeles, CA, CA 90077
Phone: 310-440-8587
Fax: 310-440-8903

Accepts query letter from unproduced, unrepresented writers. Project types include Feature Films and TV. Preferred genres include Crime, Drama, Fantasy, and Thriller. Established in 1988.

Howard Meltzer
President
Phone: 310-440-8587
IMDb: imdb.com/name/nm0578430

TV LAND

1515 Broadway 38th Floor
New York, NY 10036
Phone: 212-258-7500

2600 Colorado Ave.
4th Floor
Santa Monica, CA 90404
Phone: 310-752-8000

Email: info@tvland.com
Home Page: tvland.com

Accepts query letter from unproduced, unrepresented writers via email. Project types include TV. Preferred genres include Comedy and Drama. Established in 1996.

Larry W. Jones
President
Phone: 212-846-6000
Email: larry.jones@tvland.com
IMDb: imdb.com/name/nm1511130

Scott Gregory
Vice-President

Bradley Gardner
IMDb: imdb.com/name/nm3952119

Rose Catherine Pinkney
IMDb: imdb.com/name/nm0684384

TV ONE LLC

1010 Wayne Ave
Silver Spring, MD 20910
Phone: 301-755-0400

Home Page: tvoneonline.com

Accepts query letter from produced or represented writers. Project types include TV. Preferred genres include Comedy and Drama. Established in 2004.

Alfred Liggins
Chairman
Phone: 301-755-0400
Email: aliggins@tv-one.tv
IMDb: imdb.com/name/nm3447190

Toni Judkins

Jubba Seyyid

T.V. REPAIR

857 Castaic Place
Pacific Palisades, CA 90272

Phone: 310-459-3671
Fax: 310-459-4251

Email: davidjlatt@earthlink.net

Accepts query letter from unproduced, unrepresented writers via email. Project types include TV.

David Latt

Phone: 310-459-3671
Email: davidjlatt@earthlink.net
IMDb: imdb.com/name/nm0490374

TWENTIETH CENTURY FOX FILM CORPORATION

10201 W Pico Blvd
Los Angeles, CA 90035
Phone: 310-369-1000
Fax: 310-203-1558

Email: foxmovies@fox.com
Home Page: fox.com

Does not accept any unsolicited material. Project types include Feature Films and TV. Preferred genres include Action, Comedy, Crime, Detective, Drama, Family, Fantasy, Horror, Myth, Non-Fiction, Romance, and Thriller. Established in 1935.

Emma Watts
President

Kimberly Cooper

Ted Dodd

David A Starke

Steve Freedman

TWENTIETH CENTURY FOX TELEVISION

10201 W Pico Blvd
Building 103, Room 5286
Los Angeles, CA 90035
Phone: 310-369-1000

Email: info@fox.com
Home Page: fox.com

Does not accept any unsolicited material. Project types include TV. Preferred genres include Comedy and Drama. Established in 1949.

Gary Newman
Chairman
Email: gary.newman@fox.com
IMDb: imdb.com/name/nm3050096

Dana Walden
Chairman
IMDb: imdb.com/name/nm0992861

Jonathan Davis

Dana Honor

Lisa Katz

Mark Ambrose

Jennifer Carreras

TWENTIETH TELEVISION

2121 Ave of the Stars
17th Floor
Los Angeles, CA 90067
Phone: 310-369-1000

Email: info@fox.com
Home Page: fox.com

Does not accept any unsolicited material. Project types include TV. Preferred genres include Comedy and Drama. Established in 1992.

Greg Meidel
IMDb: imdb.com/name/nm2518163

Roger Ailes
Chairman

Stephen Brown

Deborah Norton

TWINSTAR ENTERTAINMENT

4041 MacArthur Blvd, Suite 475
Newport Beach, CA 92660
Phone: 949-474-8600

Email: info@twinstarentertainment.com
Home Page: twinstarentertainment.com

Accepts scripts from unproduced, unrepresented writers. Project types include TV. Preferred genres include Animation, Comedy, Drama, and Family. Established in 2003.

Russell Werdin

CEO
Phone: 949-474-8600
Email: info@twinstarentertainment.com
IMDb: imdb.com/name/nm2232609

TWISTED PICTURES

901 N Highland Ave
Los Angeles, CA 90038
Phone: 323-850-3232
Fax: 323-850-0521

Accepts query letter from unproduced, unrepresented writers. Project types include Feature Films and TV. Preferred genres include Crime, Horror, and Thriller.

Michael J. Menchel

President

Mark Burg

Principle
IMDb: imdb.com/name/nm0121117

TWO TON FILMS

375 Greenwich St
New York, NY 10013
Phone: 212-941-3863

Email: info@twotonfilms.com
Home Page: twotonfilms.com

Accepts query letter from unproduced, unrepresented writers via email. Project types include Feature Films and TV. Preferred genres include Action, Comedy, Drama, and Family.

Justin Zackham

Principle
Phone: 212-941-3863
Email: info@twotonfilms.com
IMDb: imdb.com/name/nm0951698

Clay Pecorin

Principle
Phone: 212-941-3863
Email: info@twotonfilms.com
IMDb: imdb.com/name/nm2668976

UFLAND PRODUCTIONS

963 Moraga Dr
Los Angeles, CA 90049
Phone: 310-476-4520
Fax: 310-476-4891

Email: ufland.productions@verizon.net

Does not accept any unsolicited material. Project types include Feature Films and TV. Preferred genres include Comedy, Drama, and Romance. Established in 1972.

Harry Ufland

Principle
Phone: 310-437-0805
IMDb: imdb.com/name/nm0880036

Mary Jane Ufland

Producer
IMDb: imdb.com/name/nm0880040

UNDERGROUND FILMS

447 S Highland Ave
Los Angeles, CA 90036
Phone: 323-930-2588
Fax: 323-930-2334

Email: submissions@undergroundfilms.net
Home Page: undergroundfilms.net

Accepts scripts from unproduced, unrepresented writers via email. Project types include TV. Preferred genres include Action, Animation, Comedy, Drama, Family, Fantasy, Horror, Myth, Non-Fiction, Romance, and Thriller. Established in 2003.

Trevor Engelson

Phone: 323-930-2569
Email: trevor@undergroundfilms.net
IMDb: imdb.com/name/nm0257333

Noah Rothman

Producer
Phone: 323-930-2588
Email: noah@undergroundfilms.net

Josh McGuire Turner

Producer
Phone: 323-930-2435
Email: josh@undergroundfilms.net

Evan Silverberg
Producer
Phone: 323-930-2588
Email: evan@undergroundfilms.net

Austin Bedell
Producer
Phone: 323-930-2588
Email: austin@undergroundfilms.net

Chris Dennis
Phone: 323-930-2588
Email: chris@undergroundfilms.net

UNIFIED PICTURES

19773 Bahama St
Northridge, CA 91324
Phone: 818-576-1006
Fax: 818-534-3347

Email: info@unifiedpictures.com
Home Page: unifiedpictures.com

Accepts query letter from unproduced, unrepresented writers. Project types include Feature Films. Preferred genres include Action, Comedy, Crime, Detective, Drama, Horror, and Thriller. Established in 2004.

Keith Kjarval
Founder
IMDb: imdb.com/name/nm1761309

Steve Goldstein
IMDb: imdb.com/name/nm2179640

Paul Michael Ruffman

UNION ENTERTAINMENT

9255 Sunset Blvd, Suite 528
West Hollywood, CA 90069
Phone: 310-274-7040
Fax: 310-274-1065

Email: info@unionent.com
Home Page: unionent.com
IMDb: imdb.com/company/co0183888

Does not accept any unsolicited material. Project types include Video Games. Preferred genres include Animation. Established in 2006.

Richard Leibowitz
President
Phone: 310-274-7040
Email: rich@unionent.com
IMDb: imdb.com/name/nm2325318
Assistant: Sarah Logie

Howard Bliss
Email: howard@unionent.com
IMDb: imdb.com/name/nm2973051

UNIQUE FEATURES

888 7th Ave, 16th Floor
New York, NY 10106
Phone: 212-649-4980
Fax: 212-649-4999

9200 W. Sunset Blvd.
Suite 404
West Hollywood, CA 90069
Phone: 310-492-8009
Fax: 310-492-8022

IMDb: imdb.com/company/co0242085

Does not accept any unsolicited material. Project types include Feature Films and TV. Established in 2008.

Michael Lynne
Principle
Phone: 310-492-8009
IMDb: imdb.com/name/nm1088153

UNISON FILMS

790 Madison Ave
Suite 306
New York, NY 10065
Phone: 212-226-1200
Fax: 646-349-1738

Email: info@unisonfilms.com
Home Page: unisonfilms.com

Project types include Feature Films. Preferred genres include Comedy, Drama, and Romance. Established in 2004.

Emanuel Michael
Partner
IMDb: imdb.com/name/nm1639578

Cassandra Kulukundis
Partner
IMDb: imdb.com/name/nm0474697

Ryan Brooks
Executive Producer

Cliff Curtis
Producer

UNITED ARTISTS

245 N Beverly Dr
Beverly Hills, CA 90210
Phone: 310-449-3000
Fax: 310-586-8358

Home Page: unitedartists.com
IMDb: imdb.com/company/co0026841

Does not accept any unsolicited material. Project types include Feature Films and TV. Preferred genres include Action, Crime, and Drama. Established in 1919.

Tom Cruise
Producer
Phone: 310-449-3000
IMDb: imdb.com/name/nm0000129

Elliot Kleinberg
COO
Phone: 310-449-3000
IMDb: imdb.com/name/nm2552087

Don Granger
Phone: 310-449-3000
IMDb: imdb.com/name/nm1447370

UNIVERSAL CABLE PRODUCTIONS

100 Universal City Plaza
Building 1440, 14th Floor
Universal City, CA 91608
Phone: 818-840-4444

30 Rockefeller Plaza
New York, NY 10112
Phone: 212-664-4444

Home Page: nbcumv.com
IMDb: imdb.com/company/co0242101

Accepts query letter from unproduced, unrepresented writers. Project types include TV. Preferred genres include Comedy and Drama. Established in 1997.

Alex Kerr
Development Executive
Phone: 818-840-4444

UNIVERSAL STUDIOS

100 Universal City Plaza
Universal City, CA 91608
Phone: 818-840-4444

Home Page: universalstudios.com
IMDb: imdb.com/company/co0000534

Accepts query letter from unproduced, unrepresented writers. Project types include Feature Films and TV. Preferred genres include Action, Animation, Comedy, Crime, Detective, Drama, Family, Fantasy, Horror, Myth, Non-Fiction, Romance, Science Fiction, and Thriller. Established in 1912.

Ron Meyer
Phone: 818-840-4444
IMDb: imdb.com/name/nm0005228

UNIVERSAL TELEVISION

100 Universal City Plaza
Building 1360, 3rd Floor
Universal City, CA 91608
Phone: 818-777-1000
Fax: 818-866-1430

Home Page: universalstudios.com
IMDb: imdb.com/company/co0096447

Accepts query letter from unproduced, unrepresented writers. Project types include TV. Preferred genres include Action, Animation, Comedy, Crime, Detective, Drama, Family, Fantasy, Myth, Non-Fiction, Romance, Science Fiction, and Thriller.

Bela Bajaria
Executive Vice-President, Universal Television
IMDb: imdb.com/name/nm0338612

UNSTOPPABLE

c/o Independent Talent Agency
76 Oxford St

London W1D 1BS
United Kingdom

Email: info@unstoppableentertainmentuk.com
Home Page: unstoppableentertainmentuk.com

Accepts scripts from unproduced, unrepresented writers. Project types include Feature Films. Preferred genres include Action, Comedy, Crime, Drama, Romance, Science Fiction, and Thriller. Established in 2007.

Noel Clarke
Principle
Email: noel@unstoppableentertainmentuk.com

UNTITLED ENTERTAINMENT

350 S Beverly Dr, Suite 200
Beverly Hills, CA 90212
Phone: 310-601-2100
Fax: 310-601-2344

435 Hudson St.
9th Floor
New York, NY 10014
Phone: 212-444-5630

IMDb: imdb.com/company/co0034249

Accepts query letter from unproduced, unrepresented writers. Project types include TV. Preferred genres include Comedy, Drama, Fantasy, Myth, Non-Fiction, and Romance.

Jason Weinberg
Phone: 310-601-2100
IMDb: imdb.com/name/nm4156256

UPLOAD FILMS

8522 National Blvd., #107
Culver City, CA 90232
Phone: 310-841-5805
Fax: 310-841-5804

Home Page: uploadfilms.com/index.php
IMDb: imdb.com/company/co0195173

Does not accept any unsolicited material. Project types include Feature Films. Preferred genres include Action, Detective, Drama, Horror, and Thriller. Established in 2006.

Andrew Mann
Partner

John Portnoy
Partner
Email: jportnoy@uploadfilms.com
IMDb: imdb.com/name/nm0692471

UPPITV

c/o CBS Studios
4024 Radford Ave, Bungalow 9
Studio City, CA 91604
Phone: 818-655-5000

Does not accept any unsolicited material. Project types include TV. Preferred genres include Comedy and Drama.

Samuel Jackson
Phone: 818-655-5000
IMDb: imdb.com/name/nm0000168

USA NETWORK

30 Rockefeller Plaza
21st Floor
New York, NY 10112
Phone: 212-664-4444
Fax: 212-703-8582

IMDb: imdb.com/company/co0014957

Does not accept any unsolicited material. Project types include TV. Preferred genres include Comedy and Drama. Established in 1971.

Sally Whitehill
Phone: 212-664-4444

VALHALLA MOTION PICTURES

3201 Cahuenga Blvd W
Los Angeles, CA 90068-1301
Phone: 323-850-3030
Fax: 323-850-3038

Email: vmp@valhallapix.com
Home Page: valhallapix.com

Does not accept any unsolicited material. Project types include Feature Films and TV. Preferred genres include Action, Drama, Fantasy, Horror, and Thriller.

Gale Hurd

Phone: 323-850-3030
Email: gah@valhallapix.com
IMDb: imdb.com/name/nm0005036

Kris Henigman

Director of Development
Email: vmp@valhallapix.com
IMDb: imdb.com/name/nm1898339

VANDERKLOOT FILM & TELEVISION

750 Ralph McGill Blvd N.E.
Atlanta, GA 30312
Phone: 404-221-0236
Fax: 404-221-1057

Email: billvdk@gmail.com
Home Page: vanderkloot.com

Does not accept any unsolicited material. Project types include Feature Films, Short Films, TV, and Commercials. Preferred genres include Action, Comedy, Drama, Family, and Non-Fiction. Established in 1976.

William VanDerKloot

Phone: 404-221-0236
Email: william@vanderkloot.com
IMDb: imdb.com/name/nm0886281

Lisa Ferrell

Executive Producer
Email: lisa@magicklantern.com

VANGUARD FILMS + ANIMATION

8703 W Olympic Blvd
Los Angeles, CA 90035
Phone: 310-888-8020
Fax: 310-362-8685

Email: contact@vanguardanimation.com
Home Page: vanguardanimation.com

Does not accept any unsolicited material. Project types include Feature Films. Preferred genres include Animation. Established in 2004.

Robert Moreland

President Production & Development
Phone: 310-888-8020
IMDb: imdb.com/name/nm0603668

John Williams

Chairman & CEO
Phone: 310-888-8020
IMDb: imdb.com/name/nm0930964

VANGUARD PRODUCTIONS

12111 Beatrice St
Culver City, CA 90230
Phone: 310-306-4910
Fax: 310-306-1978

Email: info@vanguardproductions.biz
Home Page: vanguardproductions.biz

Accepts query letter from unproduced, unrepresented writers via email. Project types include TV. Preferred genres include Action, Comedy, Drama, Family, and Non-Fiction. Established in 1986.

Terence O'Keefe

Phone: 310-306-4910
Email: terry@vanguardproductions.biz
IMDb: imdb.com/name/nm0641496

VANQUISH MOTION PICTURES

10 Universal City Plaza
NBC/Universal Building, 20th Floor
Universal City, CA 91608
Phone: 818-753-2319

Email: submissions@vanquishmotionpictures.com
Home Page: vanquishmotionpictures.com

Accepts query letter from unproduced, unrepresented writers via email. Project types include Feature Films and TV. Established in 2009.

Neetu Sharma

Creative Executive
Phone: 818-753-2319
Email: ns@vanquishmotionpictures.com
IMDb: imdb.com/name/nm3434485

Ryan Williams

Creative Executive
Phone: 818-753-2319
Email: rs@vanquishmotionpictures.com
IMDb: imdb.com/name/nm4426713

VARSITY PICTURES

11821 Mississippi Ave
Los Angeles, CA 90025
Phone: 310-601-1960
Fax: 310-601-1961

Accepts query letter from unproduced, unrepresented writers. Project types include Feature Films and TV. Established in 2007.

Carter Hansen

Creative Executive
Phone: 310-601-1960
IMDb: imdb.com/name/nm3255715

Shauna Phelan

Phone: 310-601-1960
IMDb: imdb.com/name/nm1016912

VELOCITY PICTURES

4132 Woodcliff Rd
Sherman Oaks, CA 91403
Phone: 310-804-8554
Fax: 310-496-1329

Accepts query letter from unproduced, unrepresented writers. Preferred genres include Action, Drama, Non-Fiction, Romance, and Thriller. Established in 2006.

Ryan Johnson

Phone: 310-804-8554
Email: ryanj@prettydangerousfilms.com
IMDb: imdb.com/name/nm1010198

Patrick Gallagher

Phone: 310-804-8554
Email: pfgla@aol.com
IMDb: imdb.com/name/nm1725050

VERISIMILITUDE

225 W 13th St
New York, NY 10011
Phone: 212-989-1038
Fax: 212-989-1943

Email: info@verisimilitude.com
Home Page: verisimilitude.com

Accepts query letter from produced or represented writers. Project types include Feature Films. Preferred genres include Comedy, Drama, Romance, and Thriller.

Tyler Brodie

Partner
IMDb: mdb.com/name/nm0110921

Phaedon Papadopoulos

Creative Executive
IMDb: imdb.com/name/nm3011396

Hunter Gray

Partner
IMDb: imdb.com/name/nm0336683

Alex Orlovsky

Partner
IMDb: imdb.com/name/nm0650164

VÉRITÉ FILMS

15 Beaufort Rd
Toronto, ON M4E 1M6
Canada
Phone: 416-693-8245

Email: verite@veritefilms.ca
Home Page: veritefilms.ca
IMDb: pro.imdb.com/company/co0121068
Facebook: facebook.com/pages/
V%C3%A9rit%C3%A9-Films-Inc/
174261756027334
Twitter: @veritecanada

Accepts query letter from unproduced, unrepresented writers. Project types include TV. Preferred genres include Comedy, Drama, and Family. Established in 2004.

Virginia Thompson

Phone: 306-585-1737
Email: virginia@veritefilms.ca
IMDb: imdb.com/name/nm1395111

VERTEBRA FILMS

1608 Vine St, Suite 503
Hollywood, CA 90028
Phone: 323-461-0021
Fax: 323-461-0031

Home Page: vertebrafilms.com

Does not accept any unsolicited material. Project types include Feature Films. Preferred genres include Horror and Thriller. Established in 2010.

Mac Cappucino

IMDb: imdb.com/name/nm2225247

VERTIGO FILMS

The Big Room Studios 77 Fortess Rd
London, United Kingdom,
NW5 1AG
Phone: +44-0-20-7428-7555
Fax: +44-0-20-7485-9713

Email: mail@vertigofilms.com
Home Page: vertigofilms.com

Does not accept any unsolicited material. Project types include Feature Films. Preferred genres include Action, Comedy, Crime, Drama, Fantasy, Horror, Romance, Science Fiction, and Thriller. Established in 2002.

James Richardson

Producer
IMDb: imdb.com/name/nm0724597

Allan Niblo

Producer
IMDb: imdb.com/name/nm0629242

Rupert Preston

Producer
IMDb: imdb.com/name/nm0696486

Jim Spencer

Producer
IMDb: imdb.com/name/nm2005794

NIck Love

IMDb: imdb.com/name/nm0522393

VH1

2600 Colorado Ave
Santa Monica, CA 90404
Phone: 310-752-8000

Email: info@vh1.com
Home Page: vh1.com

Accepts query letter from unproduced, unrepresented writers. Project types include TV. Preferred genres

include Comedy, Drama, Non-Fiction, and Romance. Established in 1986.

Van Toffler

Phone: 212-846-8000
Email: van.toffler@vh1.com
IMDb: imdb.com/name/nm0865508

VIACOM INC.

1515 Broadway
New York, NY 10036
Phone: 212-258-6000

Home Page: viacom.com

Does not accept any unsolicited material. Project types include TV. Preferred genres include Comedy, Drama, and Non-Fiction. Established in 1971.

Philippe Dauman

Phone: 212-258-6000
Email: philippe.dauman@viacom.com
IMDb: imdb.com/name/nm2449184

VILLAGE ROADSHOW PICTURES

100 N Crescent Dr, Suite 323
Beverly Hills, CA 90210
Phone: 310-385-4300
Fax: 310-385-4301

Home Page: vreg.com/films

Does not accept any unsolicited material. Project types include Feature Films. Established in 1998.

Matt Skiena

Phone: 310-385-4300
Email: mskiena@vrpe.com
IMDb: imdb.com/name/nm3466832

Bruce Berman

Phone: 310-385-4300
IMDb: imdb.com/name/nm0075732
Assistant: Suzy Figueroa

VINCENT NEWMAN ENTERTAINMENT

8840 Wilshire Blvd
3rd Floor
Los Angeles, CA 90211

Phone: 310-358-3050
Fax: 310-358-3289

Email: general@liveheart-vne.com

Accepts query letter from unproduced, unrepresented writers via email. Project types include TV. Preferred genres include Action, Comedy, Drama, Fantasy, Myth, and Thriller. Established in 2011.

Vincent Newman

Phone: 310-358-3050
Email: vincent@liveheart-vne.com
IMDb: imdb.com/name/nm0628304
Assistant: John Funk

VIN DI BONA PRODUCTIONS

12233 W Olympic Blvd, Suite 170
Los Angeles, CA 90064
Phone: 310-571-1875

Home Page: vdbp.com

Accepts query letter from unproduced, unrepresented writers. Project types include TV. Preferred genres include Comedy. Established in 1987.

Vin DiBona

Chairman
IMDb: imdb.com/name/nm0223688

Joanne Moore

President

Cara Di Bona

IMDb: imdb.com/name/nm0223685

VIRGIN PRODUCED

315 S Beverly Dr, Suite 506
Beverly Hills, CA 90212
Phone: 310-941-7300

Email: media@virginproduced.com
Home Page: virginproduced.com

Does not accept any unsolicited material. Project types include TV. Preferred genres include Action, Animation, Comedy, Drama, Fantasy, and Thriller. Established in 2010.

Jason Felts

CEO
Phone: 310-941-7300
Email: jfelts@virginproduced.com
IMDb: imdb.com/name/nm1479777

Rebecca Farrell

IMDb: imdb.com/name/nm2761874

VOLTAGE PRODUCTIONS

662 N Crescent Heights Blvd
Los Angeles, CA 90048
Phone: 323-606-7630
Fax: 323-315-7115

Email: sales@voltagepictures.com
Home Page: voltagepictures.com

Accepts scripts from produced or represented writers. Project types include Feature Films. Preferred genres include Action, Animation, Drama, Fantasy, Non-Fiction, Romance, and Science Fiction. Established in 2011.

Nicolas Chartier

Email: nicolas@voltagepictures.com
IMDb: imdb.com/name/nm1291566

Zev Foreman

Head of Development
IMDb: imdb.com/name/nm2303301

Craig Flores

IMDb: imdb.com/name/nm1997836
Assistant: Edmond Guidry

VON ZERNECK SERTNER FILMS

c/o HCVT
11444 W Olympic Blvd
11th Floor
Los Angeles, CA 90064
Phone: 310-652-3020

Email: vzs@vzsfilms.com
Home Page: vzsfilms.com
IMDb: imdb.com/company/co0094479

Does not accept any unsolicited material. Preferred genres include Crime, Detective, Drama, Non-Fiction, and Thriller. Established in 1987.

Frank Von Zerneck
Partner
Phone: 310-652-3020
Email: vonzerneck@gmail.com
IMDb: imdb.com/name/nm0903273

Robert M. Srtner
Partner
IMDb: imdb.com/name/nm0785750

VOX3 FILMS

315 Bleecker St #111
New York, NY 10014
Phone: 212-741-0406
Fax: 212-741-0424

Email: contact@vox3films.com
Home Page: vox3films.com
IMDb: imdb.com/company/co0146502

Does not accept any unsolicited material. Project types include TV. Preferred genres include Drama, Romance, and Thriller. Established in 2004.

Steven Shainberg
Partner
IMDb: imdb.com/name/nm078760

Christina Lurie
Partner
IMDb: imdb.com/name/nm1417371

Andrew Fierberg
Phone: 212-741-0406
Email: andrew.fi erberg@vox3fi lms.com
IMDb: imdb.com/name/nm0276404

VULCAN PRODUCTIONS

505 Fifth Ave. S., Suite 900
Seattle WA 98104
Phone: 206-342-2277

Email: production@vulcan.com
Home Page: vulcan.com
IMDb: imdb.com/company/co0042766

Accepts query letter from unproduced, unrepresented writers via email. Preferred genres include Action, Non-Fiction, and Thriller. Established in 1983.

Jody Allen
President
Phone: 206-342-2277
Email: jody@vulcan.com
IMDb: imdb.com/name/nm0666580

WALDEN MEDIA

1888 Century Park East
14th Floor
Los Angeles, CA 90067
Phone: 310-887-1000
Fax: 310-887-1001

Email: info@walden.com
Home Page: walden.com
IMDb: imdb.com/company/co0073388

Accepts query letter from unproduced, unrepresented writers via email. Project types include Feature Films. Established in 2001.

Eric Tovell
Creative Executive
Email: etovell@walden.com
Assistant: Carol Tang ctang@walden.com

Evan Turner
Phone: 310-887-1000
IMDb: imdb.com/name/nm1602263

Amanda Palmer
Phone: 310-887-1000
IMDb: imdb.com/name/nm2198853

WALKER/FITZGIBBON TV & FILM PRODUCTION

2399 Mt. Olympus
Los Angeles, CA 90046
Phone: 323-469-6800
Fax: 323-878-0600

Home Page: walkerfitzgibbon.com
IMDb: imdb.com/company/co0171571

Accepts query letter from unproduced, unrepresented writers via email. Project types include TV. Preferred genres include Animation, Comedy, Drama, and Non-Fiction. Established in 1996.

Mo Fitzgibbon

Phone: 323-469-6800
Email: mo@walkerfitzgibbon.com
IMDb: imdb.com/name/nm0280422

Robert W. Walker

IMDb: imdb.com/name/nm0908166

WALT BECKER PRODUCTIONS

8530 Wilshire Blvd.
Suite 550
Beverly Hills, CA 90212
USA
Phone: 323-871-8400
Fax: 323-871-2540

IMDb: imdb.com/company/co0236068

Does not accept any unsolicited material. Project types include TV.

Walt Becker

IMDb: imdb.com/name/nm0065608

Kelly Hayes

Director of Development
IMDb: imdb.com/name/nm0971886

WARNER BROS. TELEVISION GROUP

4000 Warner Blvd
Burbank, CA 91522-0001
Phone: 818-954-6000

Email: info@warnerbros.com
Home Page: warnerbros.com
IMDb: imdb.com/company/co0253255

Does not accept any unsolicited material. Project types include TV. Preferred genres include Action, Animation, Comedy, Drama, Family, Fantasy, Myth, Non-Fiction, Romance, and Thriller. Established in 2005.

Bruce Rosenblum

President
Email: bruce.rosenblum@warnerbros.com
IMDb: imdb.com/name/nm2686463

WARNER BROTHERS ANIMATION

411 N Hollywood Way
Burbank, CA 91505
Phone: 818-977-8700

Email: info@warnerbros.com
Home Page: warnerbros.com
IMDb: imdb.com/company/co0072876

Does not accept any unsolicited material. Project types include TV. Preferred genres include Animation. Established in 1930.

Sam Register

Executive Vice-President, Creative
Email: sam.register@warnerbros.com
IMDb: imdb.com/name/nm1882146

WARNER BROTHERS ENTERTAINMENT INC.

4000 Warner Blvd
Burbank, CA 91522-0001
Phone: 818-954-6000

Home Page: warnerbros.com

Does not accept any unsolicited material. Project types include TV. Preferred genres include Action, Animation, Comedy, Crime, Detective, Drama, Family, Fantasy, Myth, Non-Fiction, Romance, Science Fiction, and Thriller. Established in 1923.

Barry Meyer

Email: barry.meyer@warnerbros.com
IMDb: imdb.com/name/nm0583028

WARNER BROTHERS HOME ENTERTAINMENT

4000 Warner Blvd
Burbank, CA 91522-0001
Phone: 818-954-6000

Email: info@warnerbros.com
Home Page: warnerbros.com
IMDb: imdb.com/company/co0200179

Does not accept any unsolicited material. Project types include Feature Films, Short Films, and TV. Preferred genres include Action, Animation, Comedy, Crime, Drama, Family, Fantasy, Horror, Myth, Non-Fiction,

Romance, Science Fiction, and Thriller. Established in 2005.

Kevin Tsujihara

President
Email: kevin.tsujihara@warnerbros.com
IMDb: imdb.com/name/nm2493597

WARNER BROTHERS PICTURES

4000 Warner Blvd
Burbank, CA 91522-0001
Phone: 818-954-6000

Email: info@warnerbros.com
Home Page: warnerbros.com
IMDb: imdb.com/company/co0026840

Does not accept any unsolicited material. Project types include Feature Films. Preferred genres include Action, Animation, Comedy, Crime, Detective, Drama, Family, Fantasy, Myth, Non-Fiction, Romance, and Thriller. Established in 1923.

Jeff Robinov

President
Email: jeff.robinov@warnerbros.com
IMDb: imdb.com/name/nm0732268
Assistant: Carrie Frymer

Lynn Harris

Executive Vice President of Production
IMDb: imdb.com/name/nm0365036
Assistant: Alexandra Amin

Racheline Benveniste

Creative Executive
IMDb: imdb.com/name/nm3367909
Assistant: Matthew Crespy

Greg Silverman

IMDb: imdb.com/name/nm0798909
Assistant: Cate Adams

Andrew Fischel

Assistant: Stephanie Rosenthal

WARNER HORIZON TELEVISION

4000 Warner Blvd
Burbank, CA 91522-0001
Phone: 818-954-6000

Email: info@warnerbros.com
Home Page: warnerbros.com
IMDb: mdb.com/company/co0183230

Does not accept any unsolicited material. Project types include TV. Preferred genres include Action, Animation, Comedy, Drama, Family, Fantasy, Myth, Non-Fiction, and Romance. Established in 1999.

Peter Roth

President
Phone: 818-954-6000
Email: peter.roth@warnerbros.com
IMDb: imdb.com/name/nm2325137

WARNER SISTERS PRODUCTIONS

PO Box 50104
Santa Barbara, CA 93150
Phone: 818-766-6952

Email: info@warnersisters.com
Home Page: warnersisters.com
IMDb: imdb.com/company/co0121034

Does not accept any unsolicited material. Preferred genres include Documentary and Non-Fiction. Established in 2003.

Cass Warner

IMDb: imdb.com/name/nm2064300

WARP FILMS

Spectrum House 32-34 Gordon House Rd
London, United Kingdom, NW5 1LP
Phone: 011-442-072848350
Fax: 011-442-072848360

Email: info@warpfilms.co.uk
Home Page: warp.net/films
IMDb: imdb.com/company/co0251927

Accepts query letter from unproduced, unrepresented writers via email. Project types include Feature Films. Preferred genres include Action, Comedy, Documentary, Drama, Horror, Non-Fiction, and Romance. Established in 2004.

Mark Herbert

IMDb: imdb.com/name/nm0378591

Peter Carlton

IMDb: imdb.com/name/nm1275058

WARP X

Electric Works
Digital Campus
Sheffield S1 2BJ
UK
Phone: +44114-286-6280
Fax: +44114-286-6283

Email: info@warpx.co.uk
Home Page: warpx.co.uk
IMDb: imdb.com/company/co0202028

Does not accept any unsolicited material. Project types include Feature Films. Preferred genres include Comedy, Crime, Documentary, Drama, Horror, and Thriller. Established in 2008.

Mary Burke
Producer
IMDb: imdb.com/name/nm1537339

Mark Herbert
Producer
IMDb: imdb.com/name/nm0378591

Robin Gutch
IMDb: imdb.com/name/nm0349168

Barry Ryan
IMDb: imdb.com/name/nm1419213

WARREN MILLER ENTERTAINMENT

5720 Flatiron Parkway
Boulder CO 80301
Phone: 303-253-6300
Fax: 303-253-6380

Email: info@warrenmillertv.com
Home Page: warrenmillertv.com
IMDb: imdb.com/company/co0040142

Accepts query letter from unproduced, unrepresented writers. Project types include Feature Films and TV. Preferred genres include Action, Non-Fiction, and Reality. Established in 1952.

Jeffrey Moore
Email: jeffm@warrenmiller.com
IMDb: imdb.com/name/nm2545455

Warren Miller

Ginger Sheehy
IMDb: imdb.com/name/nm1200078

WARRIOR POETS

76 Mercer St Fourth Floor
New York, NY 10012
Phone: 212-219-7617
Fax: 212-219-2920

Email: em@warrior-poets.com
Home Page: warrior-poets.com
IMDb: imdb.com/company/co0169151

Does not accept any unsolicited material. Project types include Feature Films and TV. Preferred genres include Drama and Non-Fiction. Established in 2005.

Morgan Spurlock
IMDb: imdb.com/name/nm1041597
Assistant: Emmanuel Moran

Jeremy Chilnick
IMDb: imdb.com/name/nm2505733
Assistant: Marjon Javadi

Ethan Goldman
IMDb: imdb.com/name/nm1134121

WAYANS BROTHERS ENTERTAINMENT

8730 W Sunset Blvd, Suite 290
Los Angeles, CA 90069-2247
Phone: 323-930-6720
Fax: 424-202-3520

Email: thawkins@wayansbros.com
IMDb: imdb.com/company/co0001823

Does not accept any unsolicited material. Project types include TV. Preferred genres include Comedy, Crime, Family, and Horror. Established in 1980.

Keenan Wayans
IMDb: imdb.com/name/nm0005540

Mike Tiddes
Creative Executive

Rick Alvarez
IMDb: imdb.com/name/nm0023315

Marlon Wayans
IMDb: imdb.com/name/nm0005541
Assistant: Shane Miller

Shawn Wayans
IMDb: imdb.com/name/nm0915465

WAYFARE ENTERTAINMENT VENTURES LLC

435 W 19th St
4th Floor
New York, NY 10011
Phone: 212-989-2200

Email: info@wayfareentertainment.com
Home Page: wayfareentertainment.com
IMDb: imdb.com/company/co0239158

Does not accept any unsolicited material. Project types include Feature Films. Preferred genres include Action, Comedy, Drama, Family, Fantasy, Myth, Non-Fiction, Romance, Science Fiction, and Thriller. Established in 2008.

Ben Browning
Email: info@wayfareentertainment.com
IMDb: imdb.com/name/nm1878845

Michael Maher
IMDb: imdb.com/name/nm3052130

Sarah Shepard
IMDb: imdb.com/name/nm2416896

Jeremy Kipp Walker
IMDb: imdb.com/name/nm0907844

WEED ROAD PRODUCTIONS

4000 Warner Blvd
Building 81, Suite 115
Burbank, CA 91522
Phone: 818-954-3771
Fax: 818-954-3061

IMDb: imdb.com/company/co0093488

Does not accept any unsolicited material. Project types include Feature Films and TV. Preferred genres include Action, Animation, Drama, Family, Fantasy, Horror, Non-Fiction, Science Fiction, and Thriller. Established in 2004.

Akiva Goldsman
IMDb: imdb.com/name/nm0326040
Assistant: Bonnie Balmos

Nicki Cortese
IMDb: imdb.com/name/nm2492480
Assistant: Mike Pence

WEINSTOCK PRODUCTIONS

316 N Rossmore Ave
Los Angeles, CA 90004
Phone: 323-791-1500

IMDb: imdb.com/company/co0032259

Accepts query letter from unproduced, unrepresented writers. Project types include Feature Films. Preferred genres include Comedy, Crime, Drama, Family, and Thriller.

Charles Weinstock
Producer
IMDb: imdb.com/name/nm091848

WEINTRAUB/KUHN PRODUCTIONS

1351 Third St Promenade, Suite 206
Santa Monica, CA 90401
Phone: 310-458-3300
Fax: 310-458-3302

Email: fred@fredweintraub.com
Home Page: fredweintraub.com
IMDb: imdb.com/company/co0031680

Does not accept any unsolicited material. Project types include Feature Films and TV. Preferred genres include Action, Comedy, Drama, Family, Fantasy, Myth, Non-Fiction, Romance, Science Fiction, and Thriller. Established in 1976.

Fred Weintraub
President
Email: fred@fredweintraub.com
IMDb: imdb.com/name/nm0918518

Tom Kuhn
Producer
IMDb: imdb.com/name/nm0474166

Maxwell Meltzer
IMDb: imdb.com/name/nm0578443

Jackie Weintraub
IMDb: imdb.com/name/nm0918520

WELLER/GROSSMAN PRODUCTIONS

5200 Lankershim Blvd
5th Floor
North Hollywood, CA 91601
Phone: 818-755-4800

Email: contact@wellergrossman.com
Home Page: wellergrossman.com
IMDb: imdb.com/company/co0102774

Accepts scripts from produced or represented writers. Project types include TV. Preferred genres include Comedy, Drama, and Reality. Established in 1993.

Robb Weller
Email: contact@wellergrossman.com
IMDb: imdb.com/name/nm0919888

Gary Grossman
Partner
IMDb: imdb.com/name/nm0343646

Debbie Supnik
IMDb: imdb.com/name/nm0839489

WENDY FINERMAN PRODUCTIONS

144 S Beverly Dr, #304
Beverly Hills, CA 90212
Phone: 310-694-8088
Fax: 310-694-8088

Email: info@wendyfinermanproductions.com
Home Page: wendyfinermanproductions.com
IMDb: imdb.com/company/co0004317

Accepts query letter from unproduced, unrepresented writers via email. Project types include Feature Films and TV. Preferred genres include Comedy, Drama, Family, Fantasy, Period, and Romance.

Wendy Finerman
Producer
Email: wfinerman@wendyfinermanproductions.com
IMDb: imdb.com/name/nm0277704

Lisa Zupan
Vice-President
Email: lzupan@wendyfinermanproductions.com
IMDb: imdb.com/name/nm0958702

WESSLER ENTERTAINMENT

11661 San Vicente Blvd., Suite 609
Los Angeles, CA 90049

Accepts query letter from unproduced, unrepresented writers. Project types include Feature Films. Preferred genres include Comedy and Family.

Charles B. Wessler
President
IMDb: imdb.com/name/nm0921853

WE TV NETWORK

11 Penn Plaza
19th Floor
New York, NY 10001
Phone: 212-324-8500
Fax: 212-324-8595

Email: contactwe@wetv.com
Home Page: wetv.com
IMDb: imdb.com/company/co0340786

Does not accept any unsolicited material. Project types include TV. Preferred genres include Comedy, Family, and Reality. Established in 1997.

Laurence Gellert
IMDb: imdb.com/name/nm1557598

WHITEWATER FILMS

11264 La Grange Ave
Los Angeles, CA 90025
Phone: 310-575-5800
Fax: 310-575-5802

Email: info@whitewaterfilms.com
Home Page: whitewaterfilms.com
IMDb: imdb.com/company/co0109361

Does not accept any unsolicited material. Project types include Feature Films. Preferred genres include Comedy, Crime, Drama, Non-Fiction, Romance, and Thriller. Established in 2008.

Nick Morton
Producer
IMDb: imdb.com/name/nm1134288

Bert Kern
Producer
IMDb: imdb.com/name/nm2817387

Rick Rosenthal
IMDb: imdb.com/name/nm0742819

Trent Brion
Producer

WHYADUCK PRODUCTIONS INC.

4804 Laurel Canyon Blvd
PMB 502
North Hollywood, CA 91607-3765
Phone: 818-980-5355

Email: info@duckprods.com
Home Page: duckprods.com
IMDb: imdb.com/company/co0034143

Does not accept any unsolicited material. Project types include Feature Films and TV. Preferred genres include Comedy, Drama, Non-Fiction, Romance, and Science Fiction. Established in 1981.

Robert Weide
Email: rbw@duckprods.com
IMDb: imdb.com/name/nm0004332

WIDEAWAKE, INC.

Los Angeles
8752 Rangely Ave
Los Angeles, CA 90048
Phone: 310-652-9200

IMDb: imdb.com/company/co0145942

Does not accept any unsolicited material. Project types include Feature Films and TV. Preferred genres include Action, Comedy, Family, and Romance. Established in 2004.

Luke Greenfield
IMDb: imdb.com/name/nm0339004

Jake Detharidge
Creative Executive
IMDb: imdb.com/name/nm4681516

WIGRAM PRODUCTIONS

4000 Warner Blvd
Building 81, Room 215
Burbank, CA 91522
Phone: 818-954-2412
Fax: 818-954-6538

IMDb: imdb.com/company/co0204562

Accepts query letter from unproduced, unrepresented writers. Project types include Feature Films. Preferred genres include Action, Comedy, Crime, Fantasy, Science Fiction, and Thriller. Established in 2006.

Peter Eskelsen
Vice-President
Email: peter.eskelsen@wbconsultant.com
IMDb: imdb.com/name/nm2367411

Lionel Wigram
IMDb: imdb.com/name/nm0927880
Assistant: Jeff Ludwig jeff.ludwig@wbconsultant.com

WILD AT HEART FILMS

868 W Knoll Dr, Suite 9
West Hollywood, CA 90069
Phone: 310-855-1538
Fax: 310-855-0177

Email: wildheartfilms@aol.com
Home Page: wildatheartfilms.us
IMDb: imdb.com/company/co0096528

Does not accept any unsolicited material. Preferred genres include Animation, Comedy, Drama, Family, Myth, Non-Fiction, and Romance. Established in 2000.

James Egan
Email: jamesegan@wildatheartfilms.us
IMDb: imdb.com/name/nm0250680

Boris Geiger
IMDb: imdb.com/name/nm1788313

Jewell Sparks
IMDb: imdb.com/name/nm3876152

WILDWOOD ENTERPRISES, INC.

725 Arizona Ave, Suite 306
Santa Monica, CA 90401
Phone: 310-451-8050

IMDb: imdb.com/company/co0034515

Does not accept any unsolicited material. Project types include Feature Films, Short Films, and TV. Preferred genres include Comedy, Crime, Drama, Fantasy, Non-Fiction, Romance, and Thriller.

Robert Redford
Owner
IMDb: imdb.com/name/nm0000602

Bill Holderman
Development Executive
IMDb: imdb.com/name/nm2250139

WIND DANCER FILMS

315 S Beverly Dr, Suite 502
Beverly Hills, CA 90212
Phone: 310-601-2720
Fax: 310-601-2725

Home Page: winddancer.com
IMDb: imdb.com/company/co0028602

Does not accept any unsolicited material. Project types include Feature Films and TV. Preferred genres include Comedy, Crime, Drama, Fantasy, and Romance. Established in 1989.

Catherine Redfearn
Creative Executive
Email: Catherine_Redfearn@winddancer.com
IMDb: imdb.com/name/nm1976144

Matt Williams
IMDb: imdb.com/name/nm0931285
Assistant: Jake Perron

David McFadzean
IMDb: imdb.com/name/nm05687
Assistant: David Caruso

Judd Payne
IMDb: imdb.com/name/nm1450928

WINGNUT FILMS LTD.

PO Box 15 208
Miramar
Wellington 6003
New Zealand
Phone: +64-4-388-9939
Fax: +64-4-388-9449

Email: reception@wingnutfilms.co.nz
Home Page: wingnutfilms.co.nz
IMDb: imdb.com/company/co0046203

Does not accept any unsolicited material. Project types include Feature Films and TV. Preferred genres include Animation, Comedy, Crime, Family, Fantasy, Horror, Non-Fiction, Romance, Science Fiction, and Thriller.

Carolynne Cunningham
Producer
IMDb: imdb.com/name/nm0192254

Peter Jackson
IMDb: imdb.com/name/nm0001392

WINKLER FILMS

190 N Canon Dr Suite 500 Penthouse
Beverly Hills, CA 90210
Phone: 310-858-5780
Fax: 310-858-5799

Email: winklerfilms@sbcglobal.net
Home Page: winklerfilms.com
IMDb: imdb.com/company/co0049390

Accepts query letter from unproduced, unrepresented writers. Project types include Feature Films and TV. Preferred genres include Action, Crime, Drama, and Romance.

Irwin Winkler
CEO
Phone: 310-858-5780
IMDb: imdb.com/name/nm0005563
Assistant: Selina Gomeau

David Winkler
Producer
Phone: 310-858-5780
IMDb: imdb.com/name/nm0935210

Charles Winkler
Phone: 310-858-5780
IMDb: imdb.com/name/nm0935203
Assistant: Jose Ruisanchez

Jill Cutler
President
IMDb: imdb.com/name/nm1384594

WINSOME PRODUCTIONS

PO Box 2071
Santa Monica, CA 90406
Phone: 310-656-3300

Email: info@winsomeprods.com
Home Page: winsomeprods.com
IMDb: imdb.com/company/co0129854

Does not accept any unsolicited material. Project types include Feature Films and TV. Preferred genres include Action, Comedy, Drama, and Non-Fiction. Established in 1989.

A.D. Oppenheim
Email: info@winsomeprods.com
IMDb: imdb.com/name/nm0649148

Daniel Oppenheim
IMDb: imdb.com/name/nm0649151

WITT-THOMAS PRODUCTIONS

11901 Santa Monica Blvd, Suite 596
Los Angeles, CA 90025
Phone: 310-472-6004
Fax: 310-476-5015

Email: pwittproductions@aol.com
IMDb: imdb.com/company/co0083928

Does not accept any unsolicited material. Project types include Feature Films. Preferred genres include Action, Comedy, Crime, Drama, Period, and Romance. Established in 2010.

Paul Witt
Partner
Email: pwittproductions@aol.com
IMDb: imdb.com/name/nm0432625
Assistant: Ellen Benjamin

Tony Thomas
Partner
IMDb: imdb.com/name/nm0859597
Assistant: Marlene Fuentes

W!LDBRAIN ENTERTAINMENT, INC.

15000 Ventura Blvd
3rd Floor
Sherman Oaks, CA 91403
Phone: 818-290-7080

Email: info@wildbrain.com
Home Page: wildbrain.com
IMDb: imdb.com/company/co0077172

Accepts query letter from produced or represented writers. Project types include Feature Films, Short Films, and TV. Preferred genres include Animation, Comedy, Family, and Fantasy. Established in 1994.

Michael Polis
President
Email: mpolis@wildbrain.com
IMDb: imdb.com/name/nm1277040

Bob Higgins
IMDb: imdb.com/name/nm0383338

Lisa Ullmann
IMDb: imdb.com/name/nm0880520

WOLF FILMS, INC.

100 Universal City Plaza #2252
Universal City, CA 91608-1085
Phone: 818-777-6969
Fax: 818-866-1446

IMDb: imdb.com/company/co0019598

Does not accept any unsolicited material. Project types include Feature Films, Short Films, and TV. Preferred genres include Drama and Non-Fiction.

Dick Wolf
CEO
IMDb: imdb.com/name/nm0937725

Danielle Gelber
Executive Producer
IMDb: imdb.com/name/nm1891764

Tony Ganz
IMDb: imdb.com/name/nm0304673

WOLFMILL ENTERTAINMENT

9027 Larke Ellen Circle
Los Angeles, CA 90035
Phone: 310-559-1622
Fax: 310-559-1623

Email: info@wolfmill.com
Home Page: wolfmill.com
IMDb: imdb.com/company/co0184078

Accepts query letter from unproduced, unrepresented writers via email. Project types include Feature Films and TV. Preferred genres include Animation. Established in 1997.

Marv Wolfman
Partner
Email: marv@wolfmill.com
IMDb: imdb.com/name/nm0938379

Craig Miller
Partner
Email: craig@wolfmill.com
IMDb: imdb.com/name/nm0003653

WONDERLAND SOUND AND VISION

8739 Sunset Blvd
West Hollywood, CA 90069
Phone: 310-659-4451
Fax: 310-659-4451

Home Page: wonderlandsoundandvision.com
IMDb: imdb.com/company/co0080859

Does not accept any unsolicited material. Project types include Feature Films and TV. Preferred genres include Action, Comedy, Crime, Drama, Horror, Non-Fiction, Romance, and Science Fiction. Established in 2000.

Steven Bello
Creative Executive
IMDb: imdb.com/name/nm2086605

Mary Viola
IMDb: imdb.com/name/nm0899193

WONDERPHIL PRODUCTIONS

1032 Irving St., #130
San Francisco, CA. 94122
Phone: 310-482-1324

Home Page: wonderphil.biz

Accepts scripts from unproduced, unrepresented writers. Project types include Feature Films. Preferred genres include Action, Drama, Fantasy, Horror, Science Fiction, and Thriller.

Phil Gorn
CEO
Email: phil@wonderphil.biz

Sanders Robinson
President
Phone: 925-525-7583
Email: sandman@wonderphil.biz

WORKING TITLE FILMS

9720 Wilshire Blvd
4th Floor
Beverly Hills, CA 90212
Phone: 310-777-3100
Fax: 310-777-5243

Home Page: workingtitlefilms.com
IMDb: imdb.com/company/co0057311

Does not accept any unsolicited material. Project types include Feature Films, Short Films, and TV. Preferred genres include Action, Comedy, Crime, Drama, Family, Fantasy, Non-Fiction, Romance, Science Fiction, and Thriller. Established in 1983.

Amelia Granger
Phone: +44 20 7307 3000
IMDb: imdb.com/name/nm0335028

Liza Chasin
Email: liza.chasin@workingtitlefilms.com
IMDb: imdb.com/name/nm0153877
Assistant: Johanna Byer

Michelle Wright
IMDb: imdb.com/name/nm0942657

WORLD FILM SERVICES, INC.

150 E 58th St
29th Floor
New York, NY 10155
Phone: 212-632-3456
Fax: 212-632-3457

IMDb: imdb.com/company/co0184077

Accepts query letter from unproduced, unrepresented writers. Project types include Feature Films and TV. Preferred genres include Action, Comedy, Crime, Drama, Family, Fantasy, Horror, Non-Fiction, Romance, Science Fiction, and Thriller.

John Heyman
CEO
IMDb: imdb.com/name/nm0382274

Dahlia Heyman
Creative Executive
IMDb: imdb.com/name/nm3101094

Pamela Osowski
Creative Executive
IMDb: imdb.com/name/nm1948494

WORLD OF WONDER PRODUCTIONS

6650 Hollywood Blvd, Suite 400
Hollywood, CA 90028
Phone: 323-603-6300
Fax: 323-603-6301

Email: support@worldofwonder.net
Home Page: worldofwonder.net
IMDb: imdb.com/company/co0093416

Does not accept any unsolicited material. Project types include Feature Films and TV. Preferred genres include Action, Comedy, Crime, Drama, Family, Non-Fiction, Period, and Reality. Established in 1990.

Fenton Bailey
IMDb: imdb.com/name/nm0047259

Tom Campbell
IMDb: imdb.com/name/nm1737859

Chris Skura
IMDb: imdb.com/name/nm1048940

WORLDVIEW ENTERTAINMENT, INC.

1384 Broadway
25th Floor
New York, NY 10018
Phone: 212-431-3090
Fax: 212-431-0390

Email: info@worldviewent.com
Home Page: worldviewent.com

Does not accept any unsolicited material. Project types include Feature Films. Preferred genres include Action, Comedy, Documentary, Drama, and Romance. Established in 2007.

Sarah Johnson Redlich
Partner
IMDb: imdb.com/name/nm3164071

Christopher Woodrow
IMDb: imdb.com/name/nm2002108

Amanda Bowers
IMDb: imdb.com/name/nm4112873

Maria Cestone
IMDb: imdb.com/name/nm2906036

WORLDWIDE BIGGIES

545 W 45th St
5th Floor
New York, NY 10036
Phone: 646-442-1700
Fax: 646-557-0019

Email: info@wwbiggies.com
Home Page: wwbiggies.com
IMDb: imdb.com/company/co0173152

Does not accept any unsolicited material. Project types include Feature Films and TV. Preferred genres include Action, Animation, Comedy, Drama, Family, Fantasy, Non-Fiction, and Reality. Established in 2007.

Albie Hecht
CEO
IMDb: imdb.com/name/nm0372935

Kari Kim
IMDb: imdb.com/name/nm2004613

Scott Webb
IMDb: imdb.com/name/nm1274591

WORLDWIDE PANTS INC.

1697 Broadway
New York, NY 10019
Phone: 212-975-5300
Fax: 212-975-4780

IMDb: imdb.com/company/co0066959

Does not accept any unsolicited material. Project types include Feature Films and TV. Preferred genres include Action, Animation, Comedy, Drama, Non-Fiction, and Romance.

Rob Burnett
IMDb: imdb.com/name/nm0122427

Tom Keaney
Executive
IMDb: imdb.com/name/nm3174758

David Letterman
IMDb: imdb.com/name/nm0001468

WWE STUDIOS

12424 Wilshire Blvd, Suite 1400
Los Angeles, CA 90025
Phone: 310-481-9370
Fax: 310-481-9369

Email: talent.marketing@wwe.com
Home Page: wwe.com
IMDb: imdb.com/company/co0242604

Does not accept any unsolicited material. Project types include Feature Films and TV. Preferred genres include Action, Comedy, Crime, Detective, Drama, Family, Horror, Non-Fiction, Science Fiction, and Thriller. Established in 2002.

Michael Luisi
President
IMDb: imdb.com/name/nm0525405

Richard Lowell
IMDb: imdb.com/name/nm1144067
Assistant: Cherie Harris Cherie.harris@wwecorp.com

X FILME CREATIVE POOL

Kurfuerstenstrasse 57
10785 Berlin
Germany
Phone: 49-30-230-833-11
Fax: 49-30-230-833-22

Email: x-filme@x-filme.de
Home Page: x-filme.de
IMDb: imdb.com/company/co0055954

Does not accept any unsolicited material. Preferred genres include Action, Comedy, Drama, Family, and Romance. Established in 1994.

Stefan Arndt
Email: stefan.arndt@x-filme.de
IMDb: imdb.com/name/nm0036155

Wolfgang Becker
IMDb: imdb.com/name/nm0065615

Dani Levy
IMDb: imdb.com/name/nm0506374

XINGU FILMS LTD.

12 Cleveland Row
St. James
London SW1A 1DH
United Kingdom
Phone: 44-20-7451-0600
Fax: 44-20-7451-0601

Email: mail@xingufilms.com
Home Page: xingufilms.com

Does not accept any unsolicited material. Project types include TV. Preferred genres include Action, Animation, Comedy, Crime, Detective, Drama, Family, Fantasy, Horror, Myth, Non-Fiction, Romance, Science Fiction, and Thriller. Established in 1993.

Trudie Styler
Email: trudie@xingufilms.com
IMDb: imdb.com/name/nm0836548

Alex Francis
Producer
IMDb: imdb.com/name/nm2123360

Anita Sumner
IMDb: imdb.com/name/nm0838856

Kate Henderson

XIX ENTERTAINMENT

9000 W Sunset Blvd, Penthouse
West Hollywood, CA 90069
Phone: 310-746-1919
Fax: 310-746-1920

Email: info@xixentertainment.com
Home Page: xixentertainment.com

Does not accept any unsolicited material. Project types include Feature Films and TV. Preferred genres include Drama, Non-Fiction, Period, Reality, Romance, and Thriller. Established in 2010.

Robert Dodds
CEO
Email: robert.dodds@xixentertainment.com
IMDb: imdb.com/name/nm2142323

XYZ FILMS

4223 Glencoe Ave, Suite B119
Marina del Rey, CA 90292
Phone: 310-956-1550
Fax: 310-827-7690

Email: team@xyzfilms.com
Home Page: xyzfilms.com
IMDb: imdb.com/company/co0244345

Does not accept any unsolicited material. Project types include Feature Films. Preferred genres include Action, Comedy, Crime, Drama, Horror, Non-Fiction, Science Fiction, and Thriller.

Nate Bolotin
Partner
Email: nate@xyzfilms.com
IMDb: imdb.com/name/nm1924867

Todd Brown
Partner
Email: info@xyzfilms.com
IMDb: imdb.com/name/nm1458075

Kyle Franke
Head of Development
Phone: 310-359-9099
Email: kyle@xyzfilms.com
IMDb: imdb.com/name/nm3733941

YAHOO!

2400 Broadway
1st Floor
Santa Monica, CA 90404
Phone: 310-907-2700
Fax: 310-907-2701

Home Page: yahoo.com
IMDb: imdb.com/company/co0054481

Accepts query letter from unproduced, unrepresented writers. Project types include Short Films, TV, and Commercials. Preferred genres include Comedy, Family, Non-Fiction, and Reality. Established in 1995.

David Filo
Founder

Ryan Clifford

Jacqueline Reses

YARI FILM GROUP

10850 Wilshire Blvd
6th Floor
Los Angeles, CA 90024
Phone: 310-689-1450
Fax: 310-234-8975

Email: info@yarifilmgroup.com
Home Page: yarifilmgroup.com
IMDb: imdb.com/company/co0136740

Does not accept any unsolicited material. Project types include Feature Films and TV. Preferred genres include Action, Animation, Comedy, Crime, Drama, Family, Romance, and Thriller.

Bob Yari
Email: byari@yarifilmgroup.com
IMDb: imdb.com/name/nm0946441
Assistant: Julie Milstead

Ethen Adams
IMDb: imdb.com/name/nm2319337

David Clark
IMDb: imdb.com/name/nm1354046

YORK SQUARE PRODUCTIONS

17328 Ventura Blvd, Suite 370
Encino, CA 91316
Phone: 818-789-7372

Email: assistant@yorksquareproductions.com
Home Page: yorksquareproductions.com

Accepts query letter from unproduced, unrepresented writers via email. Project types include Feature Films, TV, and Commercials. Preferred genres include Comedy and Drama.

Jonathan Mostow
Executive
IMDb: imdb.com/name/nm0609236
Assistant: Emily Somers

YORKTOWN PRODUCTIONS

18 Gloucester Ln
4th Floor
Toronto ON M4Y 1L5
Canada
Phone: 416-923-2787
Fax: 416-923-8580

IMDb: imdb.com/company/co0184088

Does not accept any unsolicited material. Project types include Feature Films, Short Films, and TV. Preferred genres include Action, Comedy, Drama, Family, Fantasy, Romance, and Science Fiction. Established in 1986.

Norman Jewison
Founder
Phone: 416-923-2787
IMDb: imdb.com/name/nm0422484

Michael Jewison
Producer
IMDb: imdb.com/name/nm0422483

YOURFACE GOES HERE ENTERTAINMENT

1041 N Formosa Ave
Santa Monica Bldg W, #7

West Hollywood, CA 90046
Phone: 323-850-2433

Does not accept any unsolicited material. Project types include TV. Preferred genres include Drama, Fantasy, Horror, Romance, Science Fiction, and Thriller.

Alan Ball
Phone: 323-850-2433
IMDb: imdb.com/name/nm0050332

ZACHARY FEUER FILMS

9348 Civic Center Dr, 3rd Floor
Beverly Hills, CA 90210
Phone: 310-729-2110
Fax: 310-820-7535

Accepts query letter from unproduced, unrepresented writers. Project types include TV. Preferred genres include Action, Comedy, Drama, and Thriller.

Zachary Feuer
Producer
Phone: 310-729-2110
IMDb: imdb.com/name/nm0275400

ZAK PENN'S COMPANY

PO Box 5623
Beverly Hills, CA 90209
Phone: 323-939-1700
Fax: 323-930-2339

Email: TheSirenChoir@gmail.com
IMDb: imdb.com/company/co0185423

Does not accept any unsolicited material. Project types include Feature Films and TV. Preferred genres include Comedy, Family, Fantasy, Non-Fiction, Science Fiction, and Thriller.

Zak Penn
IMDb: imdb.com/name/nm0672015
Assistant: Hannah Rosner

ZANUCK INDEPENDENT

1951 N Beverly Dr
Beverly Hills, CA 90210
Phone: 310-274-5735
Fax: 310-273-9217

IMDb: imdb.com/company/co0279611

Accepts query letter from unproduced, unrepresented writers. Project types include Feature Films. Preferred genres include Action, Comedy, Drama, and Thriller.

Dean Zanuck
Principle
IMDb: imdb.com/name/nm0953124

ZEMECKIS/NEMEROFF FILMS

264 S La Cienega Blvd, Suite 238
Beverly Hills, CA 90211
Phone: 310-736-6586

Email: info@enfantsterriblesmovie.com
Home Page: enfantsterriblesmovie.com
IMDb: imdb.com/company/co0141237

Does not accept any unsolicited material. Project types include Feature Films. Preferred genres include Comedy and Drama.

Leslie Zemeckis
Producer
IMDb: imdb.com/name/nm0366667

Terry Nemeroff
IMDb: imdb.com/name/nm0625892

ZENTROPA ENTERTAINMENT

Filmbyen 22
Hvidovre, Denmark, 2650
Phone: +45-36-86-87-88
Fax: +45-36-86-87-89

Email: receptionen@filmbyen.dk
Home Page: zentropa.dk
IMDb: imdb.com/company/co0136662

Accepts scripts from unproduced, unrepresented writers. Project types include Feature Films. Preferred genres include Action, Comedy, Crime, Drama, Family, Fantasy, Horror, Non-Fiction, Romance, Science Fiction, and Thriller. Established in 1992.

Lars von Trier
IMDb: imdb.com/name/nm0001885

Peter Aalbaek Jensen
IMDb: imdb.com/name/nm0421639

ZEPHYR FILMS

33 Percy St
London, United Kingdom W1T 2DF
Phone: +44207-255-3555
Fax: +44207-255-3777

Email: info@zephyrfilms.co.uk
Home Page: zephyrfilms.co.uk

Accepts query letter from unproduced, unrepresented writers via email. Project types include Feature Films and TV. Preferred genres include Action, Animation, Comedy, Crime, Drama, Family, Fantasy, Horror, Romance, and Thriller.

Chris Curling
Producer
IMDb: imdb.com/name/nm0192770

Phil Robertson
Producer
IMDb: imdb.com/name/nm0731990

ZETA ENTERTAINMENT

3422 Rowena Ave
Los Angeles, CA 90027
Phone: 310-595-0494

IMDb: imdb.com/company/co0037026

Does not accept any unsolicited material. Project types include Feature Films and TV. Preferred genres include Action, Comedy, Crime, Drama, Family, Fantasy, Horror, and Thriller.

Zane Levitt
President
Email: zanewlevitt@gmail.com
IMDb: imdb.com/name/nm0506254

Lisa Jan Savy
Creative Executive
IMDb: imdb.com/name/nm2957586

ZIEGER PRODUCTIONS

Phone: 310-476-1679
Fax: 310-476-7928

IMDb: imdb.com/company/co0114742

Accepts query letter from unproduced, unrepresented writers.

Michele Colucci-Zieger
Producer
IMDb: imdb.com/name/nm1024135

ZING PRODUCTIONS, INC.

220 S Van Ness Ave
Hollywood, CA 90004
Phone: 323-466-9464

Home Page: zinghollywood.com

Does not accept any unsolicited material. Project types include Feature Films, Short Films, and TV. Preferred genres include Animation, Comedy, Drama, Family, Fantasy, Reality, and Romance.

Rob Loos
President
Email: rob@zinghollywood.com
IMDb: imdb.com/name/nm0519763

ZODIAK USA

520 Broadway Suite 500
Santa Monica, CA 90401
Phone: 310-460-4490
Fax: 310-460-4494

Email: contact@zodiakusa.com
Home Page: zodiakusa.com
IMDb: imdb.com/company/co0314564

Accepts query letter from unproduced, unrepresented writers via email. Project types include TV. Preferred

genres include Animation, Comedy, Non-Fiction, Reality, and Romance.

Natalka Znak
CEO
IMDb: imdb.com/name/nm1273500

Timothy Sullivan
Phone: 212-488-1699
IMDb: imdb.com/name/nm2432438

ZUCKER PRODUCTIONS

Los Angeles, CA
Phone: 310-656-9202
Fax: 310-656-9220

IMDb: imdb.com/company/co0110404

Accepts query letter from unproduced, unrepresented writers. Project types include TV. Preferred genres include Comedy, Drama, Fantasy, Romance, and Thriller. Established in 1972.

Farrell Ingle
Creative Executive
IMDb: imdb.com/name/nm3377346

Jerry Zucker
Partner
IMDb: imdb.com/name/nm0958387

Janet Zucker
Partner
IMDb: imdb.com/name/nm0958384

Index by Company Name

100% Entertainment, 52
100% Terrycloth, 52
1019 Entertainment, 52
10 by 10 Entertainment, 52
1821 Pictures, 53
19 Entertainment, 53
21 Laps Entertainment, 53
25/7 Productions, 53
26 Films, 54
2929 Productions, 54
2S Films, 54
2Waytraffic - A Sony Pictures Entertainment
    Company, 54
3311 Productions, 55
34th Street Films, 55
3 Arts Entertainment, 55
3 Ball Productions, 55
40 Acres & A Mule Filmworks, Inc., 56
44 Blue Productions, Inc., 56
495 Productions, 56
4th Row Films, 56
51 Minds Entertainment, 57
59th Street Films, 57
5ive Smooth Stones Productions, 57
72nd Street Productions, 57
72 Productions, 58
777 Group, 58
7ATE9 Entertainment, 58
8:38 Productions, 58
8790 Pictures, Inc., 58
8th Wonder Entertainment, 59
900 Films, 59
9.14 Pictures, 59
Aardman Animations, 59
Abandon Interactive Entertainment, 60
ABC Studios, 60
Aberration Films, 60
Acappella Pictures, 60
Accelerated Entertainment LLC, 60
A.C. Lyles Productions, Inc., 61
Act III Productions, 61
Actual Reality Pictures, 61
Adam Fields Productions, 61
Adelstein Productions, 61

Ad Hominem Enterprises, 61
Adult Swim, 62
Aegis Film Group, 62
AEI - Atchity Entertainment International, Inc., 62
A&E Network, 62
After Dark Films, 62
Agamemnon Films, 63
Aggregate Films, 63
Agility Studios, 63
Ahimsa Films, 63
Ahimsa Media, 63
Airmont Pictures, 64
Akil Productions, 64
Alamo Drafthouse Films, 64
Alan Barnette Productions, 64
Alan David Management, 64
Alan Sacks Productions, 64
Alchemy Entertainment, 65
Alcon Entertainment, LLC, 65
Aldamisa Films, 65
Alexander/Mitchell Productions, 65
Alex Rose Productions, 66
Alianza Films International, 66
A-Line Pictures, 66
Allan McKeown Presents, 66
Allentown Productions, 66
Alliance Films, 67
Alloy Entertainment, 67
Aloe Entertainment, 67
Al Roker Productions, 67
Alta Loma Entertainment, 67
Alturas Films, 67
A-Mark Entertainment, 68
Ambassador Entertainment, Inc., 68
Amber Entertainment, 68
Amblin Entertainment, 68
Ambush Entertainment, 69
American Moving Pictures, 69
American Work Inc., 69
American World Pictures, 69
American Zoetrope, 69
Anchor Bay Films, 70
Andrea Simon Entertainment, 70
Andrew Lauren Productions, 70

Angelworld Entertainment Ltd., 70

Animus Films, 71

Annapurna Pictures, 71

An Olive Branch Productions, Inc., 71

Anomaly Entertainment, 71

Anonymous Content, 71

Antidote Films, 72

Apatow Productions, 72

Aperture Entertainment, 72

Appleseed Entertainment, 72

Arclight Films, 73

Arenas Entertainment, 73

Argonaut Pictures, 73

ArieScope Pictures, 73

Ars Nova, 74

Artfire Films, 74

Article19 Films, 74

Artists Public Domain, 74

A. Smith & Company Productions, 75

Asylum Entertainment, 75

Atlas Entertainment (Production Branch of Mosaic), 75

Atlas Media Corporation, 75

Atmosphere Entertainment MM, LLC, 76

Automatic Pictures, 76

Bad Hat Harry Productions, 76

Bad Robot, 76

Baldwin Entertainment Group, LTD., 77

Ballyhoo, Inc., 77

Baltimore Pictures, 77

Bandito Brothers, 77

Barnstorm Films, 78

Barry Films, 78

Basra Entertainment, 78

Bauer Martinez Studios, 78

Bay Films, 78

Bayonne Entertainment, 79

Bazelevs Productions, 79

BBC Films, 79

BCDF Pictures, 79

Beacon Pictures, 79

Bedford Falls Company, 80

Bee Holder Productions, 80

Before The Door Pictures, 80

Belisarius Productions, 81

Belladonna Productions, 81

Bellwether Pictures, 81

Benaroya Pictures, 81

Benderspink, 82

Berk/Lane Entertainment, 82

Berlanti Television, 82

BermanBraun, 82

Bernero Productions, 82

Beth Grossbard Productions, 83

BET Networks, 83

Big Foot Entertainment, Ltd., 83

Big Talk Productions, 83

Birch Tree Entertainment, 83

Biscayne Pictures, 84

Bix Pix Entertainment, 84

Black Bear Pictures, 84

Blacklight Transmedia, 84

Black Sheep Entertainment, 84

Bleiberg Entertainment, 85

BlindWink Productions, 85

Blondie Girl Productions, 85

Bluegrass Films, 85

Blue Print Pictures, 86

Blue Sky Studios, 86

Blumhouse Productions, 86

Bobker/Krugar Films, 86

Bogner Entertainment Inc., 86

Boku Films, 87

Bold Films, 87

Bona Fide Productions, 87

Borderline Films, 87

Boss Media, 87

Boxing Cat Productions, 88

Boy Wonder Productions, 88

Boz Productions, 88

Branded Films, 88

Brandman Productions, 88

Brightlight Pictures, 88

Broken Camera Productions, 89

Brooklyn Films, 89

Bruce Cohen Productions, 89

Buckaroo Entertainment, 89

Buena Vista Home Entertainment, 90

Buena Vista Television, 90

Bunim-Murray Productions, 90

Burleigh Filmworks, 90

Burnside Entertainment, Inc., 91

Caliber Media Company, 91

Callahan Filmworks, 91

Camelot Entertainment Group, 91

Canadian Broadcasting Company (CBC), 92

Capacity Pictures, 92

Capital Arts Entertainment, 92

Captivate Entertainment, 92

Carnival Films, 93

Casey Silver Productions, 93

Castle Rock Entertainment, 93

Catapult Films Inc., 93
CBS Films, 94
Cecchi Gori Productions, 94
Celador Entertainment, 94
Centropolis Entertainment, 94
Chaiken Films, 94
Chartoff Productions, 95
Chernin Entertainment, 95
Cherry Sky Films, 95
Chestnut Ridge Productions, 95
Cheyenne Enterprises LLC, 95
Chicagofilms, 96
Chickflicks, 96
Chockstone Pictures, 96
Chotzen/Jenner Productions, 96
Chris/Rose Productions, 96
ChubbCo Film Co., 97
Chuck Fries Productions, Inc., 97
Cindy Cowan Entertainment, 97
Cinema Ephoch, 97
CineMagic Entertainment, 97
Cinema Libre Studio, 98
Cine Mosaic, 98
Cineson Entertainment, 98
CineTelFilms, 98
Cineville, 98
Circle of Confusion, 98
City Entertainment, 99
Clarity Pictures, LLC, 99
Class 5 Films, 99
Clear Pictures Entertainment, 99
Clearview Productions, 99
Clifford Werber Productions, 99
Closed On Mondays Entertainment, 100
Cloud Eight Films, 100
CodeBlack Entertainment, 100
CODE Entertainment, 100
Colleen Camp Productions, 100
Colleton Company, 100
Color Force, 100
Colossal Entertainment, 101
Columbia Pictures, 101
Comedy Arts Studios, 102
Completion Films, 102
Concept Entertainment, 102
Constantin Film, 102
Content Media Corporation PLC, 102
Contrafilm, 102
Conundrum Entertainment, 103
Cooper's Town Productions, 103
Coquette Productions, 103

Corner Store Entertainment, 103
Crave Films, 104
Creanspeak Productions, LLC, 104
Crescendo Productions, 104
Crest Animation Productions, Inc., 104
Crime Scene Pictures, 104
Cross Creek Pictures, 105
Crossroads Films, 105
Crucial Films, 105
Crystal Lake Entertainment, Inc., 105
Crystal Sky Pictures, LLC, 105
CubeVision, 106
Curb Entertainment, 106
Cyan Pictures, 106
Cypress Films, Inc., 107
Cypress Point Productions, 107
Dakota Pictures, 107
Daniel L. Paulson Productions, 107
Daniel Ostroff Productions, 108
Daniel Petrie Jr. & Company, 108
Daniel Sladek Entertainment Corporation, 108
Danjaq Productions, 108
Dan Lupovitz Productions, 108
Dan Wingutow Productions, 109
Darius Films Incorporated, 109
Dark Castle Entertainment, 109
Dark Horse Entertainment, 109
Darko Entertainment, 110
Dark Sky Films, 110
Darkwoods Productions, 110
Darren Star Productions, 110
Dave Bell Associates, 110
David Eick Productions, 111
Davis Entertainment, 111
Deed Films, 111
DeerJen Films, 111
Defiance Entertainment, 111
De Line Pictures, 112
Delve Films, 112
Demarest Films, 112
Depth of Field, 112
Desert Wind Films, 113
Destiny Pictures, 113
Di Bonaventura Pictures, 113
Di Bonaventura Pictures Television, 113
Different Duck Films, 113
Dimension Films, 114
Dino De Laurentiis Company, 114
Dinovi Pictures, 114
DMG Entertainment, 114
DNA Films, 115

Dobre Films, 115
Donners' Company, 115
Double Feature Films, 115
Double Nickel Entertainment, 115
D. Petrie Productions, Inc., 116
Dreambridge Films, 116
DreamWorks Animation, 116
DreamWorks Studios, 117
Dune Entertainment, 117
Duplass Brothers Productions, 117
Ealing Studios, 117
Echo Bridge Entertainment, 118
Echo Films, 118
Echo Lake Entertainment, 118
Eclectic Pictures, 118
Eden Rock Media, Inc., 119
Edmonds Entertainment, 119
Edward R. Pressman Film Corporation, 119
Edward Saxon Productions, 119
Efish Entertainment, Inc., 119
Ego Film Arts, 120
Eighth Square Entertainment, 120
Electric City Entertainment, 120
Electric Dynamite, 120
Electric Entertainment, 120
Electric Farm Entertainment, 121
Electric Shepherd Productions, LLC, 121
Element Pictures, 121
Elephant Eye Films, 121
Elevate Entertainment, 122
Elixir Films, 122
Elkins Entertainment, 122
Embassy Row, LLC, 122
Ember Entertainment Group, 122
Emerald City Productions, Inc., 123
EM Media, 123
Endemol Entertainment, 123
Endgame Entertainment, 123
Energy Entertainment, 124
Entertainment One Group, 124
entitled entertainment, 124
Envision Media Arts, 124
Epic Level Entertainment, LTD., 125
Epigram Entertainment, 125
Epiphany Pictures, Inc., 125
Equilibrium Media Company, 125
Escape Artists, 125
E-Squared, 126
Evenstart Films, 126
Everyman Pictures, 126
Exclusive Media, 126

Exile Entertainment, 127
Exodus Film Group, 127
Eye on the Ball, 127
Face Productions, 127
Fake Empire Features, 127
Fake Empire Television, 127
Falconer Pictures, 128
Farrell Paura Productions, 128
Fastback Pictures, 128
Fastnet Films, 128
Fedora Entertainment, 129
Film 360, 129
Film 44, 129
FilmColony, 129
FilmDistrict, 129
Film Garden Entertainment, 130
Film Harvest, 130
FilmNation Entertainment, 130
Film Science, 131
Filmsmith Productions, 131
First Run Features, 131
Five By Eight Productions, 131
Five Smooth Stone Productions, 131
Flashpoint Entertainment, 131
Flavor Unit Entertainment, 132
Floren Shieh Productions, 132
Flower Films Inc., 132
Focus Features, 132
Forensic Films, 133
Foresight Unlimited, 133
Forest Park Pictures, 133
Forget Me Not Productions, 133
Fortis Films, 134
Fortress Features, 134
Forward Entertainment, 134
Forward Pass, 134
FourBoys Films, 134
Fox 2000 Pictures, 135
Fox Digital Studios, 135
Fox International Productions (FIP), 135
Fox Searchlight Pictures, 135
Frederator Studios, 135
Frederic Golchan Productions, 136
Fred Kuenert Productions, 136
Freedom Films, 136
Frelaine, 136
Fresh & Smoked, 137
Fried Films, 137
Friendly Films, 137
Front Street Pictures, 137
FR Productions, 137

Fuller Films, 138
Fun Little Films, 138
Furst Films, 138
Furthur Films, 138
FuseFrame, 138
Fusion Films, 139
Fuzzy Door Productions, 139
Gaeta Rosenzweig Films, 139
Galatee Films, 139
Gallant Entertainment, 139
Gary Hoffman Productions, 139
Gary Sanchez Productions, 140
Genext Films, 140
Genrebend Productions, 140
George Litto Productions, 140
Gerard Butler Alan Siegel Entertainment / Evil Twins, 140
Gerber Pictures, 140
Ghost House Pictures, 141
Gigantic Pictures, 141
Gil Adler Productions, 141
Gilbert Films, 141
Gil Netter Productions, 141
Girls Club Entertainment, 142
Gitlin Productions, 142
Gittes, Inc., 142
GK Films, 142
Glass Eye Pix, 142
Glory Road Productions, 143
Goff-Kellam Productions, 143
Go Girl Media, 143
Gold Circle Entertainment, 143
Goldcrest Films, 144
Goldenring Productions, 144
Goldsmith-Thomas Productions, 144
Good Humor Television, 144
Gorilla Pictures, 144
Gotham Entertainment Group, 144
Gracie Films, 145
Grade A Entertainment, 145
Grammnet Productions, 145
Grand Canal Film Works, 145
Grand Productions, 146
Gran Via Productions, 146
Gray Angel Productions, 146
Grazka Taylor Productions, 146
Greasy Entertainment, 146
Green Hat Films, 146
Greenstreet Films, 147
Greentrees Films, 147
Grindstone Entertainment Group, 147

Grizzly Adams Productions, 147
Grosso Jacobson Communications Corp., 147
Gross-Weston Productions, 148
Groundswell Productions, 148
Guardian Entertainment, LTD, 148
Gunn Films, 148
Guy Walks Into A Bar, 149
H2O Motion Pitures, 149
Hammer Films, 149
Handpicked Films, 149
Handsomecharlie Films, 150
Hannibal Pictures, 150
Happy Madison Productions, 150
Harpo Films, Inc., 150
Hartswood Films, 150
Hasbro, Inc./Hasbro Films, 151
Haxan Films, 151
Hazy Mills Productions, 151
HBO Films & Miniseries, 152
HDNet Films, 152
Heavy Duty Entertainment, 152
Heel & Toe Productions, 152
Hemisphere Entertainment, 152
Henceforth Pictures, 152
Henderson Productions, 153
Heyday Films, 153
HGTV, 153
High Horse Films, 153
High Integrity Productions, 153
Hollywood Gang Productions, 154
Home Box Office (HBO), 154
Horizon Entertainment, 154
Hughes Capital Entertainment, 154
Hutch Parker Entertainment, 154
Hyde Park Entertainment, 155
Hypnotic, 155
Icon Productions, 155
Illumination Entertainment, 155
ImageMovers, 155
Imagine Entertainment, 156
IM Global, 156
Impact Pictures, 156
Imprint Entertainment, 156
In Cahoots, 156
Incognito Pictures, 157
Indian Paintbrush, 157
Indican Productions, 157
Indie Genius Productions, 157
Indomitable Entertainment, 157
Industry Entertainment, 158
Ineffable Pictures, 158

Inferno Entertainment, 158
Infinitum Nihil, 158
Informant Media, 159
Infront Productions, 159
Ink Factory, 159
INPHENATE, 159
Intrepid Pictures, 159
Irish Dreamtime, 160
Iron Ocean Films, 160
Ironworks Productions, 160
Irwin Entertainment, 160
Ish Entertainment, 160
Ithaca Pictures, 161
Jackhole Productions, 161
Jaffe/Braunstein Films, 161
Jane Startz Productions, 161
Jean Doumanian Productions, 161
Jeff Morton Productions, 162
Jerry Bruckheimer Films, 162
Jerry Weintraub Productions, 162
Jersey Films, 162
Jet Tone Productions, 163
Joel Schumacher Productions, 163
John Calley Productions, 163
John Goldwyn Productions, 163
John Wells Productions, 163
Jon Shestack Productions, 164
Josephson Entertainment, 164
Junction Films, 164
Juniper Place Productions, 164
Kapital Entertainment, 165
Kaplan/Perrone Entertainment, 165
Karz Entertainment, 165
Kassen Brothers Productions, 165
Katalyst Films, 166
Kennedy/Marshall Company, 166
Kerner Entertainment Company, 166
KGB Films, 166
Kickstart Productions, 166
Killer Films, 167
Kim and Jim Productions, 167
Kinetic Filmworks, 167
Kintop Pictures, 167
KippSter Entertainment, 168
Komut Entertainment, 168
K/O Paper Products, 168
Krane Media, LLC., 168
Krasnoff Foster Entertainment, 168
Krofft Pictures, 169
Lago Film GmbH, 169
Lakeshore Entertainment, 169

Landscape Entertainment, 169
Langley Park Productions, 169
Larrikin Entertainment, 170
Launchpad Productions, 170
Laura Ziskin Productions, 170
Laurence Mark Productions, 170
Lava Bear Films, 171
Lawrence Bender Productions, 171
LD Entertainment, 171
Lee Daniels Entertainment, 172
Legendary Pictures, 172
Leslie Iwerks Productions, 172
Liaison Films, 172
Lightstorm Entertainment, 173
Likely Story, 173
Lin Pictures, 173
Lionsgate, 173
Liquid Theory, 174
Little Engine, 174
Lleju Productions, 174
Londine Productions, 174
Lucasfilm Ltd., 175
Lucky Crow Films, 175
Lynda Obst Productions, 175
M8 Entertainment, Inc., 175
Mad Chance Productions, 176
Mad Hatter Entertainment, 176
Mad Horse Films, 176
Madhouse Entertainment, 176
Madrik Multimedia, 176
Magnet Releasing, 177
Malpaso Productions, 177
Mandalay Pictures, 177
Mandalay Television, 177
Mandate Pictures, 177
Mandeville Films, 178
Mandy Films, 178
Mangusta Productions, 178
Manifest Film Company, 178
Maple Shade Films, 179
Marc Platt Productions, 179
Mark Victor Productions, 179
Mark Yellen Production, 179
Martin Chase Productions, 180
Marty Katz Productions, 180
MarVista Entertainment, 180
MasiMedia, 180
Mass Hysteria Entertainment, 180
Matador Pictures, 181
Maven Pictures, 181
Maximum Films & Management, 181

Maya Entertainment Group, 181
Mayhem Pictures, 182
MBST Entertainment, 182
Media Rights Capital, 182
Media Talent Group, 182
Medusa Film, 183
Melee Entertainment, 183
Merchant Ivory Productions, 183
Merv Griffin Entertainment, 183
Metro-Goldwyn Meyer (MGM), 184
Michael De Luca Productions, 184
Michael Grais Productions, 184
Michael Taylor Productions, 184
Midd Kidd Productions, 185
Midnight Sun Pictures, 185
Mike Lobell Productions, 185
Millar/Gough Ink, 185
Millennium Films, 185
Mimran Schur Pictures, 186
Mirada, 186
Miranda Entertainment, 186
Misher Films, 186
Mockingbird Pictures, 186
Modercine, 187
Mojo Films, 187
Momentum Entertainment Group, 187
Monsterfoot Productions, 187
Montage Entertainment, 187
Montecito Pictures, 188
Montone/Yorn (Unnamed Yorn Production
    Company), 188
Moonstone Entertainment, 188
Morgan Creek Productions, 188
Morningstar Entertainment, 188
Mosaic/ Mosaic Media Group, 189
Moshag Productions, 189
Moxie Pictures, 189
MRB Productions, 189
Mr. Mudd, 190
Myriad Pictures, 190
NALA Investments, 190
Nancy Tenenbaum Films, 190
NBC Productions, 191
NBC Studios, 191
NBCUniversal, 191
NBCUniversal Television Distribution, 191
Necropia Entertainment, 192
Neo Art & Logic, 192
New Amsterdam Entertainment, 192
New Artists Alliance, 192
New Crime Productions, 192

New Line Cinema, 193
New Regency Films, 193
New School Media, LLC, 193
New Wave Entertainment, 193
Nick Wechsler Productions, 194
Night and Day Pictures, 194
Ninjas Runnin' Wild Productions, 194
North By Northwest Entertainment, 194
Nova Pictures, 195
Nubia Filmworks LLC, 195
Nu Image Films, 195
Nuyorican Productions, 195
O2 Filmes, 196
OddLot Entertainment, 196
Offspring Entertainment, 196
Olive Bridge Entertainment, 196
Olmos Productions Inc., 196
Olympus Pictures, 197
Ombra Films, 197
O.N.C., 197
One Race Films, 197
Oops Doughnuts Productions, 197
Open City Films, 198
Open Road Films, 198
Original Film, 198
Original Media, 198
Oscilloscope Pictures, 199
O'Taye Productions, 199
Outerbank Entertainment, 199
Out of the Blue Entertainment, 199
Overbrook Entertainment, 199
Overnight Productions, 200
OWN: Oprah Winfrey Network, 200
OZLA Pictures Inc., 200
Pacifica International Film & TV Corporation, 200
Pacific Standard, 200
Palermo Productions, 200
PalmStar Entertainment, 201
Palomar Pictures, 201
Panay Films, 201
Pandemonium, 201
Pantelion Films, 201
Panther Films, 202
Papa Joe Entertainment, 202
Paper Street Films, 202
Paradigm Studio, 203
Paradox Entertainment, 203
Parallel Media, 203
Paramount Pictures, 203
Pariah, 203
Parker Entertainment Group, 204

Parkes/MacDonald Productions, 204
Parkway Productions, 204
Participant Media, 204
Partizan Entertainment, 204
Pathe Pictures, 205
Patriot Pictures, 205
PCH Film, 205
Peace Arch Entertainment, 205
Peace By Peace Productions, 205
Peggy Rajski Productions, 206
Perfect Storm Entertainment, 206
Permut Presentations, 206
Phoenix Pictures, 206
Pierce Williams Entertainment, 206
Piller/Segan/Shepherd, 207
Pink Slip Pictures, 207
Pipeline Entertainment Inc., 207
Pixar, 207
Plan B Entertainment, 208
Platform Entertainment, 208
Platinum Dunes, 208
Playtone Productions, 208
Plum Pictures, 208
Polsky Films, 208
Polymorphic Pictures, 209
Porchlight Films, 209
PorterGeller Entertainment, 209
POW! Entertainment, 209
Power Up, 210
Practical Pictures, 210
Prana Studios, 210
Preferred Content, 210
Pretty Matches Productions, 210
Pretty Pictures, 211
Principato-Young Entertainment, 211
Prospect Park, 211
Protozoa Pictures, 211
Pure Grass Films, LTD., 211
QED International, 212
Quadrant Pictures, 212
Rabbit Bandini Productions, 212
Radar Pictures, 212
@Radical Media, 212
Rainbow Film Company/ Rainbow Releasing, 213
Rainmaker Entertainment, 213
Rainmaker Films Inc., 213
Rainstorm Entertainment, INC., 213
Random House Studio, 214
Rat Entertainment, 214
RCR Media Group, 214
RCR Pictures, 214

Recorded Picture Company, 214
Red Crown Productions, 215
Redfield Productions, 215
Red Giant Media, 215
Red Granite Pictures, 215
Red Hen Productions, 216
Red Hour Films, 216
Red Om Films, Inc., 216
Red Planet Pictures, 216
Red Wagon Entertainment, 216
Regent Entertainment, 217
Rehab Entertainment, 217
Reiner/Greisman, 217
Relativity Media, LLC, 217
Relevant Entertainment Group, 217
Remember Dreaming, LLC, 217
Renaissance Pictures, 218
Renart Films, 218
Renee Missel Management, 218
Renee Valente Productions, 218
Renegade Animation, Inc., 218
Reveille, LLC/ Shine International, 218
Revelations Entertainment, 219
Revolution Films, 219
Rhino Films, 219
Rhombus Media, Inc., 219
Rhythm & Hues Studios, 220
Rice & Beans Productions, 220
Riche Productions, 220
Rive Gauche Television, 220
River Road Entertainment, 220
Roadside Attractions, 220
Robert Cort Productions, 221
Robert Greenwald Productions, 221
Robert Lawrence Productions, 221
Roberts/David Films Inc., 221
Robert Simonds Company, 221
Rocklin/ Faust, 222
Room 101, Inc., 222
Room 9 Entertainment, LLC, 222
Rosa Entertainment, 222
Roserock Films, 222
Roth Films, 222
Roughhouse, 223
Route One Films, 223
Rubicon Entertainment, 223
Runaway Productions, 223
Ryan Murphy Productions, 223
Sacred Dogs Entertainment LLC, 223
Saltire Entertainment, 224
Salty Features, 224

Salvatore/Ornston Productions, 224
Samuelson Productions Limited, 224
Sandbar Pictures, 224
Sander/Moses Productions, 225
Sanitsky Company, 225
Scarlet Fire Entertainment, 225
Score Productions, Inc., 225
Scott Free Productions, 225
Scott Rudin Productions, 226
Scott Sanders Productions, 226
Screen Door Entertainment, 226
Screen Gems, 226
SE8 Group, 227
Second and 10th Inc., 227
Seismic Pictures, 227
SenArt Films, 227
Seraphim Films, 227
Serendipity Point Films, 227
Serendipity Productions, Inc., 228
Seven Arts Pictures, 228
Shadowcatcher Entertainment, 228
Shaftesbury Films, 228
Shaun Cassidy Productions, 229
Sheep Noir Films, 229
Shephard/Robin Company, 229
Shoe Money Productions, 229
Shondaland, 229
Shoreline Entertainment, 230
Showtime Networks, 230
Sidney Kimmel Entertainment, 230
Sierra/ Affinity, 230
Signature Pictures, 231
Sikelia Productions, 231
Silly Robin Productions, 231
Silver Dream Productions, 231
Silver/Koster Productions, 231
Silver Nitrate Entertainment, 232
Silver Pictures, 232
SimonSays Entertainment, 232
Simon West Productions, 232
Simsie Films/ Media Savant Pictures, 232
Singe Cell Pictures, 232
Sinovoi Entertainment, 233
Sixth Sense Productions, Inc., 233
Sketch Films, 233
Skydance Productions, 233
Skylark Entertainment, Inc., 233
Sky One, 234
Smart Entertainment, 234
Smash Media Films, 234
Smokehouse Pictures, 234

Sneak Preview Entertainment, 234
Sobini Films, 235
Social Capital Films, 235
Sogno Productions, 235
Solipsist Films, 235
S Pictures, Inc., 236
Spitfire Pictures, 236
Spyglass Entertainment, 236
Stage 6 Films, 236
St. Amos Productions, 236
Starry Night Entertainment, 236
State Street Pictures, 237
Steamroller Productions, Inc., 237
Stefanie Epstein Productions, 237
Steven Bochco Productions, 237
Stokely Chaffin Productions, 238
StoneBrook Entertainment, 238
Stone & Company Entertainment, 238
Stone Village Pictures, 238
Storefront Pictures, 238
Story and Film, 238
Storyline Entertainment, 239
Straight Up Films, 239
Srrike Entertainment, 239
StudioCanal, 239
Submarine Entertainment, 240
Such Much Films, 240
Summit Entertainment, 240
Sundial Pictures, 240
Sunlight Productions, 241
Sunswept Entertainment, 241
Suntaur Entertainment, 241
Super Crispy Entertainment, 241
SuperFinger Entertainment, 241
Sweet 180, 242
Taggart Productions, 242
Tagline Pictures, 242
Tamara Asseyev Production, 242
Tannenbaum Company, 242
Tapestry Films, Inc., 243
Taurus Entertainment Company, 243
T&C Pictures, 243
Team Downey, 243
Team G, 244
Team Todd, 244
Temple Hill Entertainment, 244
Terra Firma Films, 244
The American Film Company, 244
The Asylum, 245
The AV Club, 245
The Badham Company, 245

The Bureau, 245
The Gold Company, 246
The Goldstein Company, 246
The Goodman Company, 246
The Gotham Group, 246
The Greenberg Group, 246
The Group Entertainment, 246
The Halcyon Company, 247
The Hal Lieberman Company, 247
The Hatchery, 247
The Hecht Company, 247
The Jim Henson Company, 247
The Littlefield Company, 248
The Mark Gordon Company, 248
The Mazur/Kaplan Company, 248
The Pitt Group, 248
The Radmin Company, 249
The Safran Company, 249
The Steve Tisch Company, 249
The Walt Disney Company, 249
The Weinstein Company, 249
The Wolper Organization, 250
The Zanuck Company, 250
Thousand Words, 250
Three Strange Angels, Inc., 251
Thunderbird Films, 251
Thunder Road Pictures, 251
Tim Burton Productions, 251
Tom Welling Productions, 252
Tonik Productions, 252
Tool of North America, 252
Tornell Productions, 252
Tower of Babble Entertainment, 253
Trancas International Films, Inc., 253
Treehouse Films, 253
Tribeca Films, 253
TriCoast Studios, 254
Tricor Entertainment, 254
Trilogy Entertainment Group, 254
Troika Pictures, 254
Troma Entertainment, 255
Turtleback Productions, Inc., 255
TV Land, 255
TV One LLC, 255
T.V. Repair, 255
Twentieth Century Fox Film Corporation, 256
Twentieth Century Fox Television, 256
Twentieth Television, 256
TwinStar Entertainment, 256
Twisted Pictures, 257
Two Ton Films, 257

Ufland Productions, 257
Underground Films, 257
Unified Pictures, 258
Union Entertainment, 258
Unique Features, 258
Unison Films, 258
United Artists, 259
Universal Cable Productions, 259
Universal Studios, 259
Universal Television, 259
Unstoppable, 259
Untitled Entertainment, 260
Upload Films, 260
UppiTV, 260
USA Network, 260
Valhalla Motion Pictures, 260
Vanderkloot Film & Television, 261
Vanguard Films + Animation, 261
Vanguard Productions, 261
Vanquish Motion Pictures, 261
Varsity Pictures, 262
Velocity Pictures, 262
Verisimilitude, 262
Vérité Films, 262
Vertebra Films, 262
Vertigo Films, 263
VH1, 263
Viacom Inc., 263
Village Roadshow Pictures, 263
Vincent Newman Entertainment, 263
Vin di Bona Productions, 264
Virgin Produced, 264
Voltage Productions, 264
Von Zerneck Sertner Films, 264
Vox3 Films, 265
Vulcan Productions, 265
Walden Media, 265
Walker/Fitzgibbon TV & Film Production, 265
Walt Becker Productions, 266
Warner Bros. Television Group, 266
Warner Brothers Animation, 266
Warner Brothers Entertainment Inc., 266
Warner Brothers Home Entertainment, 266
Warner Brothers Pictures, 267
Warner Horizon Television, 267
Warner Sisters Productions, 267
Warp Films, 267
Warp X, 268
Warren Miller Entertainment, 268
Warrior Poets, 268
Wayans Brothers Entertainment, 268

Wayfare Entertainment Ventures LLC, 269
Weed Road Productions, 269
Weinstock Productions, 269
Weintraub/Kuhn Productions, 269
Weller/Grossman Productions, 270
Wendy Finerman Productions, 270
Wessler Entertainment, 270
We TV Network, 270
Whitewater Films, 270
Whyaduck Productions Inc., 271
WideAwake, Inc., 271
Wigram Productions, 271
Wild at Heart Films, 271
Wildwood Enterprises, Inc., 272
Wind Dancer Films, 272
Wingnut Films Ltd., 272
Winkler Films, 272
Winsome Productions, 273
Witt-Thomas Productions, 273
W!ldbrain Entertainment, Inc., 273
Wolf Films, Inc., 273
Wolfmill Entertainment, 274
Wonderland Sound and Vision, 274
Wonderphil Productions, 274
Working Title Films, 274
World Film Services, Inc., 275

World of Wonder Productions, 275
Worldview Entertainment, Inc., 275
Worldwide Biggies, 275
Worldwide Pants Inc., 276
WWE Studios, 276
X Filme Creative Pool, 276
Xingu Films Ltd., 276
XIX Entertainment, 277
XYZ Films, 277
Yahoo!, 277
Yari Film Group, 277
York Square Productions, 278
Yorktown Productions, 278
YourFace Goes Here Entertainment, 278
Zachary Feuer Films, 278
Zak Penn's Company, 278
Zanuck Independent, 278
Zemeckis/Nemeroff Films, 279
Zentropa Entertainment, 279
Zephyr Films, 279
Zeta Entertainment, 279
Zieger Productions, 279
Zing Productions, Inc., 280
Zodiak USA, 280
Zucker Productions, 280

Index of Company Websites

100% Entertainment, 52
100percent.com

100% Terrycloth, 52
terencemichael.com

1019 Entertainment, 52
1019ent.com

1821 Pictures, 53
1821pictures.com

19 Entertainment, 53
19.co.uk

25/7 Productions, 53
257productions.com

26 Films, 54
26films.com

2929 Productions, 54
2929entertainment.com

2Waytraffic - A Sony Pictures Entertainment
    Company, 54
2waytraffic.com

3311 Productions, 55
3311productions.com

3 Arts Entertainment, 55
3arts.com

3 Ball Productions, 55
3ballproductions.com

40 Acres & A Mule Filmworks, Inc., 56
40acres.com

44 Blue Productions, Inc., 56
44blue.com

495 Productions, 56
495productions.com

4th Row Films, 56
4throwfilms.com

51 Minds Entertainment, 57
51minds.com

5ive Smooth Stones Productions, 57
5ivesmoothstones.com

72nd Street Productions, 57
72ndstreetproductions.com

72 Productions, 58
72productions.com

777 Group, 58
the777group.com

7ATE9 Entertainment, 58
7ate9.com

900 Films, 59
900films.com

9.14 Pictures, 59
914pictures.com

Aardman Animations, 59
aardman.com

Abandon Interactive Entertainment, 60
abandoninteractive.com

Aberration Films, 60
aberrationfilms.com

Acappella Pictures, 60
acappellapictures.com

Accelerated Entertainment LLC, 60
acceleratedent.com

Act III Productions, 61
normanlear.com/act_iii.html

Actual Reality Pictures, 61
actualreality.tv

Adult Swim, 62
adultswim.com

Aegis Film Group, 62
aegisfilmgroup.com

AEI - Atchity Entertainment International, Inc., 62
aeionline.com

A&E Network, 62
aetv.com

After Dark Films, 62
afterdarkfilms.com

Agamemnon Films, 63
agamemnon.com

Agility Studios, 63
agilitystudios.com

Ahimsa Media, 63
ahimsamedia.com

Akil Productions, 64
akilproductions.com

Alamo Drafthouse Films, 64
drafthousefilms.com

Alcon Entertainment, LLC, 65
alconent.com

Aldamisa Films, 65
aldamisa.com

Alianza Films International, 66
alianzafilms.com

A-Line Pictures, 66
a-linepictures.com

Allan McKeown Presents, 66
ampresents.tv

Allentown Productions, 66
allentownproductions.com

Alliance Films, 67
alliancefilms.com

Alloy Entertainment, 67
alloyentertainment.com

Aloe Entertainment, 67
aloeentertainment.com

Al Roker Productions, 67
alrokerproductions.com

Alta Loma Entertainment, 67
alta-loma.com

Alturas Films, 67
alturasfilms.com

A-Mark Entertainment, 68
amarkentertainment.com

Ambassador Entertainment, Inc., 68
ambassadortv.com

Amber Entertainment, 68
amberentertainment.com

Ambush Entertainment, 69
ambushentertainment.com

American Moving Pictures, 69
americanmovingpictures.com

American World Pictures, 69
americanworldpictures.com

American Zoetrope, 69
zoetrope.com

Anchor Bay Films, 70
anchorbayent.com

Andrew Lauren Productions, 70
andrewlaurenproductions.com

Angelworld Entertainment Ltd., 70
angelworldentertainment.com

Animus Films, 71
animusfilms.com

Annapurna Pictures, 71
annapurnapics.com

An Olive Branch Productions, Inc., 71
anolivebranchmedia.com

Anonymous Content, 71
anonymouscontent.com

Antidote Films, 72
antidotefilms.com

Appleseed Entertainment, 72
appleseedent.com

Arclight Films, 73
arclightfilms.com

Arenas Entertainment, 73
arenasgroup.com

Argonaut Pictures, 73
argonautpictures.com

ArieScope Pictures, 73
ariescope.com

Ars Nova, 74
arsnovaent.com

Artfire Films, 74
artfirefilms.com

Article19 Films, 74
article19films.com

Artists Public Domain, 74
artistspublicdomain.com

A. Smith & Company Productions, 75
asmithco.com

Asylum Entertainment, 75
asylument.com

Atlas Media Corporation, 75
atlasmediacorp.com

Automatic Pictures, 76
automaticpictures.net

Bad Hat Harry Productions, 76
badhatharry.com

Bad Robot, 76
badrobot.com

Baldwin Entertainment Group, LTD., 77
baldwinent.com

Baltimore Pictures, 77
levinson.com/index_bsc.htm

Bandito Brothers, 77
banditiobrothers.com

Barry Films, 78
barryfilms.com

Basra Entertainment, 78
basraentertainment.com

Bauer Martinez Studios, 78
bauermartinez.com

Bazelevs Productions, 79
bazelevs.ru

BBC Films, 79
bbc.co.uk/bbcfilms

BCDF Pictures, 79
bcdfpictures.com

Beacon Pictures, 79
beaconpictures.com

Before The Door Pictures, 80
beforethedoor.com

Belladonna Productions, 81
belladonna.bz

Benaroya Pictures, 81
benaroyapics.com

Benderspink, 82
benderspink.com

BermanBraun, 82
bermanbraun.com

Bernero Productions, 82
berneroproductions.com

BET Networks, 83
bet.com

Big Foot Entertainment, Ltd., 83
bigfoot.com

Big Talk Productions, 83
bigtalkproductions.com

Birch Tree Entertainment, 83
birchtreeentertainment.com

Biscayne Pictures, 84
biscaynepictures.com

Bix Pix Entertainment, 84
bixpix.com

Black Bear Pictures, 84
blackbearpictures.com

Blacklight Transmedia, 84
blacklighttransmedia.com

Bleiberg Entertainment, 85
bleibergent.com

BlindWink Productions, 85
blindwink.com

Blondie Girl Productions, 85
blondiegirlproductions.com

Blue Sky Studios, 86
blueskystudios.com

Blumhouse Productions, 86
blumhouse.com/index.php

Bogner Entertainment Inc., 86
bognerentertainment.com

Bold Films, 87
boldfilms.com

Borderline Films, 87
blfilm.com

Boy Wonder Productions, 88
boywonderproductions.net

Boz Productions, 88
bozproductions.com

Branded Films, 88
branded-films.com

Brightlight Pictures, 88
brightlightpictures.com

Broken Camera Productions, 89
brokencameraproductions.com

Buena Vista Home Entertainment, 90
bvhe.com

Buena Vista Television, 90
disney.com

Bunim-Murray Productions, 90
bunim-murray.com

Burnside Entertainment, Inc., 91
burnsideentertainment.com

Caliber Media Company, 91
calibermediaco.com

Camelot Entertainment Group, 91
camelotent.com/index.php

Canadian Broadcasting Company (CBC), 92
cbc.ca

Capital Arts Entertainment, 92
capitalarts.com

Carnival Films, 93
carnivalfilms.co.uk

CBS Films, 94
cbsfilms.com

Cecchi Gori Productions, 94
cecchigoripictures.com

Celador Entertainment, 94
celador.co.uk

Centropolis Entertainment, 94
centropolis.com

Chaiken Films, 94
chaikenfilms.com

Chernin Entertainment, 95
cherninent.com

Cherry Sky Films, 95
cherryskyfilms.com

Chickflicks, 96
chickflicksinc.com

Chockstone Pictures, 96
chockstonepictures.com

Cindy Cowan Entertainment, 97
cowanent.com

Cinema Ephoch, 97
cinemaepoch.com

CineMagic Entertainment, 97
cinemagicent.com

Cinema Libre Studio, 98
CinemaLibreStudio.com

Cine Mosaic, 98
cinemosaic.net

Cineson Entertainment, 98
cineson.com

CineTelFilms, 98
cinetelfilms.com

Cineville, 98
cineville.com

Circle of Confusion, 98
circleofconfusion.com

Clarity Pictures, LLC, 99
claritypictures.net

CodeBlack Entertainment, 100
codeblackentertainment.com

CODE Entertainment, 100
codeentertainment.com

Columbia Pictures, 101
spe.sony.com

Completion Films, 102
completionfilms.com

Concept Entertainment, 102
conceptentertainment.biz

Constantin Film, 102
constantin-film.de

Content Media Corporation PLC, 102
contentmediacorp.com

Cooper's Town Productions, 103
copperstownproductions.com

Corner Store Entertainment, 103
cornerstore-ent.com

Crave Films, 104
cravefilms.com

Crest Animation Productions, Inc., 104
crestcgi.com

Crime Scene Pictures, 104
crimescenepictures.net

Cross Creek Pictures, 105
crosscreekpictures.com

Crossroads Films, 105
crossroadsfilms.com

Crystal Sky Pictures, LLC, 105
crystalsky.com

CubeVision, 106
icecube.com

Curb Entertainment, 106
curbentertainment.com

Cypress Films, Inc., 107
cypressfilms.com

Dakota Pictures, 107
dakotafilms.com

Daniel Sladek Entertainment Corporation, 108
danielsladek.com

Darius Films Incorporated, 109
dariusfilms.com

Dark Horse Entertainment, 109
dhentertainment.com

Darko Entertainment, 110
darko.com

Dark Sky Films, 110
darkskyfilms.com

Deed Films, 111
deedfilms.com

DeerJen Films, 111
deerjen.com

Defiance Entertainment, 111
defiance-ent.com

Delve Films, 112
delvefilms.com

Desert Wind Films, 113
desertwindfilms.com

Destiny Pictures, 113
destinypictures.biz

Dimension Films, 114
weinsteinco.com

Dino De Laurentiis Company, 114
ddlc.net

DMG Entertainment, 114
h2f-entertainment.com

DNA Films, 115
dnafilms.com

Dobre Films, 115
dobrefilms.com

Donners' Company, 115
donnerscompany.com

Double Nickel Entertainment, 115
doublenickelentertainment.com

Dreambridge Films, 116
dreambridgefilms.com

DreamWorks Animation, 116
dreamworksanimation.com

DreamWorks Studios, 117
dreamworksstudios.com

Duplass Brothers Productions, 117
duplassbrothers.com

Ealing Studios, 117
ealingstudios.com

Echo Bridge Entertainment, 118
echobridgeentertainment.com

Echo Lake Entertainment, 118
echolakeproductions.com

Eclectic Pictures, 118
eclecticpictures.com

Eden Rock Media, Inc., 119
edenrockmedia.com

Edmonds Entertainment, 119
edmondsent.com/site/main.html

Edward R. Pressman Film Corporation, 119
pressman.com/default.asp.html

Edward Saxon Productions, 119
saxonproductions.net

Efish Entertainment, Inc., 119
efishentertainment.com

Ego Film Arts, 120
egofilmarts.com

Electric City Entertainment, 120
electriccityent.com

Electric Dynamite, 120
electricdynamite.com

Electric Entertainment, 120
electric-entertainment.com

Electric Farm Entertainment, 121
ef-ent.com

Electric Shepherd Productions, LLC, 121
electricshepherdproductions.com

Element Pictures, 121
elementpictures.ie

Elephant Eye Films, 121
elephanteyefilms.com

Elevate Entertainment, 122
elevate-ent.com

Elixir Films, 122
elixirfilms.com

Elkins Entertainment, 122
elkinsent.com

Embassy Row, LLC, 122
embassyrow.com

EM Media, 123
em-media.org.uk

Endemol Entertainment, 123
endemolusa.tv

Endgame Entertainment, 123
endgameent.com

Energy Entertainment, 124
energyentertainment.net

Entertainment One Group, 124
entonegroup.com

entitled entertainment, 124
entitledentertainment.com/index.html

Envision Media Arts, 124
envisionma.com

Epic Level Entertainment, LTD., 125
epiclevel.com

Epiphany Pictures, Inc., 125
epiphanypictures.com

Equilibrium Media Company, 125
eq-ent.com

Escape Artists, 125
escapeartistsent.com

E-Squared, 126
e2-esquared.com

Evenstart Films, 126
evenstarfilms.com

Exclusive Media, 126
exclusivemedia.com

Exodus Film Group, 127
exodusfilmgroup.com

Fake Empire Television, 127
fakeempire.com/about

Falconer Pictures, 128
http://www.falconerpictures.com

Fastback Pictures, 128
fastbackpictures.com

Fastnet Films, 128
fastnetfilms.com

FilmColony, 129
filmcolony.com

FilmDistrict, 129
filmdistrict.com

Film Garden Entertainment, 130
filmgarden.tv

Film Harvest, 130
filmharvest.com

FilmNation Entertainment, 130
wearefilmnation.com

Film Science, 131
filmscience.com

First Run Features, 131
firstrunfeatures.com

Five By Eight Productions, 131
fivebyeight.com

Five Smooth Stone Productions, 131
5ivesmoothstones.com

Flashpoint Entertainment, 131
flashpointent.com

Flavor Unit Entertainment, 132
flavorentertainment.com

Focus Features, 132
focusfeatures.com

Foresight Unlimited, 133
foresight-unltd.com

Forget Me Not Productions, 133
4getmenotproductions.com

Fortress Features, 134
fortressfeatures.com

FourBoys Films, 134
fourboysfilms.com

Fox 2000 Pictures, 135
fox.com

Fox International Productions (FIP), 135
foxinternational.com

Fox Searchlight Pictures, 135
foxsearchlight.com

Frederator Studios, 135
frederator.com

Freedom Films, 136
freedomfilms.com

Fresh & Smoked, 137
freshandsmoked.com

Friendly Films, 137
friendly-films.com

Front Street Pictures, 137
frontstreetpictures.com

Fun Little Films, 138
funlittlemovies.com

Furst Films, 138
furstfilms.com

Fusion Films, 139
fusionfilms.net

Gallant Entertainment, 139
gallantentertainment.com

Gary Sanchez Productions, 140
garysanchezprods.com

Genext Films, 140
genextfilms.com

Ghost House Pictures, 141
ghosthousepictures.com

Gigantic Pictures, 141
giganticpictures.com

Girls Club Entertainment, 142
girlsclubentertainment.com

GK Films, 142
gk-films.com

Glass Eye Pix, 142
glasseyepix.com

Goff-Kellam Productions, 143
goffproductions.com

Go Girl Media, 143
gogirlmedia.com

Gold Circle Entertainment, 143
goldcirclefilms.com

Goldcrest Films, 144
goldcrestfilms.com

Goldenring Productions, 144
goldenringproductions.net

Gorilla Pictures, 144
gorillapictures.net

Gotham Entertainment Group, 144
gothamentertainmentgroup.com

Gracie Films, 145
graciefilms.com

Grade A Entertainment, 145
gradeaent.com

Grazka Taylor Productions, 146
grazkat.com

Greasy Entertainment, 146
greasy.biz

Greenstreet Films, 147
greenestreetfilms.com

Greentrees Films, 147
greentreesfilms.com

Grindstone Entertainment Group, 147
thegrindstone.net

Grizzly Adams Productions, 147
grizzlyadams.com

Groundswell Productions, 148
groundswellfilms.com

Guardian Entertainment, LTD, 148
guardianltd.com

Guy Walks Into A Bar, 149
guywalks.com

H2O Motion Pitures, 149
h2omotionpictures.com

Hammer Films, 149
hammerfilms.com

Handpicked Films, 149
handpickedfilms.net

Hannibal Pictures, 150
hannibalpictures.com

Happy Madison Productions, 150
adamsandler.com/happy-madison

Hartswood Films, 150
hartswoodfilms.co.uk

Hasbro, Inc./Hasbro Films, 151
hasbro.com/?US

Haxan Films, 151
haxan.com

Hazy Mills Productions, 151
hazymills.com

Heavy Duty Entertainment, 152
heavydutyentertainment.com

Hemisphere Entertainment, 152
hemisphereentertainment.com

HGTV, 153
hgtv.com

High Integrity Productions, 153
highintegrityproductions.com

Home Box Office (HBO), 154
hbo.com

Horizon Entertainment, 154
horizonent.tv

Hughes Capital Entertainment, 154
trihughes.com

Hyde Park Entertainment, 155
hydeparkentertainment.com

Icon Productions, 155
iconmovies.com

Illumination Entertainment, 155
illuminationentertainment.com

Imagine Entertainment, 156
imagine-entertainment.com

IM Global, 156
imglobalfilm.com

Imprint Entertainment, 156
imprint-ent.com

Incognito Pictures, 157
incognitopictures.com

Indian Paintbrush, 157
indianpaintbrush.com

Indomitable Entertainment, 157
indomitableentertainment.com

Ineffable Pictures, 158
ineffablepictures.com

Inferno Entertainment, 158
inferno-entertainment.com

Infinitum Nihil, 158
infinitumnihil.com

Informant Media, 159
informantmedia.com

Ink Factory, 159
inkfactoryfilms.com

Intrepid Pictures, 159
intrepidpictures.com

Irish Dreamtime, 160
irishdreamtime.com

Ish Entertainment, 160
ish.tv

Jerry Bruckheimer Films, 162
jbfilms.com

Jet Tone Productions, 163
jettone.net

Kaplan/Perrone Entertainment, 165
kaplanperrone.com

Katalyst Films, 166
katalystfilms.com

Kennedy/Marshall Company, 166
kennedymarshall.com

KGB Films, 166
kgbfilms.com

Kickstart Productions, 166
kickstartent.com

Killer Films, 167
killerfilms.com

Kim and Jim Productions, 167
kimandjimproductions.com

Kinetic Filmworks, 167
kineticfilmworks.com

Krane Media, LLC., 168
TheKraneCompany.com

Lago Film GmbH, 169
lagofilm.com

Lakeshore Entertainment, 169
lakeshoreentertainment.com

Langley Park Productions, 169
langleyparkpix.com

Larrikin Entertainment, 170
larrikin-ent.com

Lava Bear Films, 171
lavabear.com

LD Entertainment, 171
identertainment.com

Lee Daniels Entertainment, 172
leedanielsentertainment.com

Legendary Pictures, 172
legendarypictures.com

Leslie Iwerks Productions, 172
leslieiwerks.com/new

Liaison Films, 172
liasonfilms.com

Likely Story, 173
likely-story.com

Lin Pictures, 173
linpictures.com

Lionsgate, 173
lionsgate.com

Liquid Theory, 174
liquid-theory.com

Little Engine, 174
littleenginefilms.com

Lleju Productions, 174
lleju.com/index.html

Lucasfilm Ltd., 175
lucasfilm.com

Lucky Crow Films, 175
indieproducer.net

Lynda Obst Productions, 175
lyndaobst.com

M8 Entertainment, Inc., 175
media8ent.com

Mad Hatter Entertainment, 176
madhatterentertainment.com

Mad Horse Films, 176
madhorsefilms.com

Madhouse Entertainment, 176
madhouseent.net

Madrik Multimedia, 176
madrik.com

Magnet Releasing, 177
magnetreleasing.com

Mandalay Pictures, 177
mandalay.com

Mandalay Television, 177
mandalay.com

Mandate Pictures, 177
mandatepictures.com

Mandeville Films, 178
mandfilms.com

Mangusta Productions, 178
mangustaproductions.com

Manifest Film Company, 178
janetyang.com

Mark Victor Productions, 179
markvictorproductions.com

MarVista Entertainment, 180
marvista.net

MasiMedia, 180
masimedia.net

Mass Hysteria Entertainment, 180
masshysteriafilms.com

Matador Pictures, 181
matadorpictures.com

Maximum Films & Management, 181
maximumfilmsny.com

Maya Entertainment Group, 181
maya-entertainment.com

Media Rights Capital, 182
mrcstudios.com

Medusa Film, 183
medusa.it

Melee Entertainment, 183
melee.com

Merchant Ivory Productions, 183
merchantivory.com

Metro-Goldwyn Meyer (MGM), 184
mgm.com

Millennium Films, 185
millenniumfilms.com

Mimran Schur Pictures, 186
mimranschurpictures.com

Mirada, 186
mirada.com

Misher Films, 186
misherfilms.com

Mockingbird Pictures, 186
mockinbirdpictures.com

Modercine, 187
http://www.moderncine.com/index.php

Montage Entertainment, 187
montageentertainment.com

Montecito Pictures, 188
montecitopicturecompany.com

Moonstone Entertainment, 188
moonstonefilms.com

Moxie Pictures, 189
moxiepictures.com

MRB Productions, 189
mrbproductions.com

Myriad Pictures, 190
myriadpictures.com

NALA Investments, 190
nalafilms.com

NBC Productions, 191
nbcuni.com

NBC Studios, 191
nbcuni.com

NBCUniversal, 191
nbcumv.com/mediavillage

NBCUniversal Television Distribution, 191
nbcuni.com

Neo Art & Logic, 192
neoartandlogic.com

New Amsterdam Entertainment, 192
newamsterdamnyc.com

New Artists Alliance, 192
newartistsalliance.com

New Crime Productions, 192
newcrime.com

New Line Cinema, 193
warnerbros.com

New Regency Films, 193
newregency.com

New Wave Entertainment, 193
nwe.com

Nick Wechsler Productions, 194
nwprods.com

Night and Day Pictures, 194
nightanddaypictures.com

North By Northwest Entertainment, 194
nxnw.net

Nova Pictures, 195
novapictures.com

Nubia Filmworks LLC, 195
nubiafilmworks.com

Nu Image Films, 195
millenniumfilms.com

O2 Filmes, 196
o2filmes.com

OddLot Entertainment, 196
oddlotent.com

Olive Bridge Entertainment, 196
olivebridge.com

Olympus Pictures, 197
olympuspics.com

Ombra Films, 197
ombrafilms.com

O.N.C., 197
oncentertainment.com

One Race Films, 197
oneracefilms.com

Open City Films, 198
opencityfilms.com

Open Road Films, 198
openroadfilms.com

Original Media, 198
originalmedia.com

Oscilloscope Pictures, 199
oscilloscope.net

Out of the Blue Entertainment, 199
outoftheblueent.com

Overbrook Entertainment, 199
overbrookent.com

OWN: Oprah Winfrey Network, 200
oprah.com/own

OZLA Pictures Inc., 200
ozla.com

Pacifica International Film & TV Corporation, 200
pacifica.la

PalmStar Entertainment, 201
palmstar.com

Pantelion Films, 201
pantelionfilms.com

Papa Joe Entertainment, 202
papjoefilms.com

Paper Street Films, 202
paperstreetfilms.com

Paradigm Studio, 203
paradigmstudio.com

Paradox Entertainment, 203
paradoxentertainment.com

Parallel Media, 203
parallelmediafilms.com

Paramount Pictures, 203
paramount.com

Parker Entertainment Group, 204
parkerentgroup.com

Participant Media, 204
participantmedia.com

Partizan Entertainment, 204
partizan.com

Pathe Pictures, 205
pathe-uk.com

Patriot Pictures, 205
patriotpictures.com

PCH Film, 205
pchfilms.com

Peace Arch Entertainment, 205
peacearch.com

Phoenix Pictures, 206
phoenixpictures.com

Pierce Williams Entertainment, 206
piercewilliams.com

Pipeline Entertainment Inc., 207
pipeline-talent.com

Pixar, 207
pixar.com

Platform Entertainment, 208
platformentertainment.com

Playtone Productions, 208
playtone.com

Polsky Films, 208
polskyfilms.com

Porchlight Films, 209
porchlightfilms.com.au

PorterGeller Entertainment, 209
portergeller.com

POW! Entertainment, 209
powentertainment.com

Power Up, 210
powerupfilms.org

Prana Studios, 210
pranastudios.com

Preferred Content, 210
preferredcontent.net

Protozoa Pictures, 211
aronofsky.net

Pure Grass Films, LTD., 211
puregrassfilms.com

QED International, 212
qedintl.com

Quadrant Pictures, 212
quadrantpictures.com

Rabbit Bandini Productions, 212
rabbitbandinifilms.com

Radar Pictures, 212
radarpictures.com

@Radical Media, 212
radicalmedia.com

Rainmaker Entertainment, 213
rainmaker.com

Rainstorm Entertainment, INC., 213
rainstormentertainment.com

Random House Studio, 214
randomhouse.com

RCR Media Group, 214
rcrmediagroup.com

Recorded Picture Company, 214
recordedpicture.com

Red Crown Productions, 215
redcrownproductions.com

Redfield Productions, 215
renfieldproductions.com

Red Giant Media, 215
redgiantmedia.com

Red Hen Productions, 216
redhenprods.com

Red Hour Films, 216
redhourfilms.com

Red Planet Pictures, 216
redplanetpictures.co.uk

Regent Entertainment, 217
regententertainment.com

Rehab Entertainment, 217
rehabent.com

Renart Films, 218
renartfilms.com

Renegade Animation, Inc., 218
renegadeanimation.com

Revelations Entertainment, 219
revelationsent.com

Revolution Films, 219
revolution-films.com

Rhino Films, 219
rhinofilms.com

Rhombus Media, Inc., 219
rhombusmedia.com

Rhythm & Hues Studios, 220
rhythm.com

Rive Gauche Television, 220
rgitv.com

River Road Entertainment, 220
riverroadentertainment.com

Roadside Attractions, 220
roadsideattractions.com

Robert Greenwald Productions, 221
rgpinc.com

Robert Simonds Company, 221
rscfilms.com

Room 9 Entertainment, LLC, 222
room9entertainment.com

Rosa Entertainment, 222
rosaentertainment.com

Route One Films, 223
routeonefilms.com

Rubicon Entertainment, 223
rubiconentertainment.com

Runaway Productions, 223
runawayproductions.tv

Sacred Dogs Entertainment LLC, 223
sacreddogs.com

Salty Features, 224
saltyfeatures.com

Samuelson Productions Limited, 224
samuelson.la

Sandbar Pictures, 224
sandbarpictures.net

Sander/Moses Productions, 225
sandermoses.com

Score Productions, Inc., 225
scoreproductions.com

Scott Sanders Productions, 226
scottsandersproductions.com

Screen Door Entertainment, 226
sdetv.com

Seismic Pictures, 227
seismicpictures.com

SenArt Films, 227
senartfilms.com

Seraphim Films, 227
seraphimfilms.com

Serendipity Point Films, 227
serendipitypoint.com

Seven Arts Pictures, 228
7artspictures.com

Shadowcatcher Entertainment, 228
shadowcatcherent.com

Shaftesbury Films, 228
shaftesbury.ca

Sheep Noir Films, 229
sheepnoir.com

Shoreline Entertainment, 230
shorelineentertainment.com

Showtime Networks, 230
sho.com

Sidney Kimmel Entertainment, 230
skefilms.com

Sierra/ Affinity, 230
sierra-affinity.com

Signature Pictures, 231
signaturepictures.com

Silly Robin Productions, 231
alanzweibel.com

Silver Dream Productions, 231
silverdreamprods.com

Silver/Koster Productions, 231
silvers-koster.com

SimonSays Entertainment, 232
simonsaysentertainment.net

Simon West Productions, 232
simonwestproductions.com

Sinovoi Entertainment, 233
sinovoientertainment.com

Sixth Sense Productions, Inc., 233
sixthsenseproductions.com

Skydance Productions, 233
skydance.com

Skylark Entertainment, Inc., 233
skylark.net

Sky One, 234
sky.com

Smart Entertainment, 234
smartentertainment.com

Smash Media Films, 234
smashmediafilms.com

Sneak Preview Entertainment, 234
sneakpreviewentertain.com

Sobini Films, 235
sobini.com

Social Capital Films, 235
socialcapitalfilms.com

Sogno Productions, 235
ANGAELICA.com

Solipsist Films, 235
solipsistfilms.com

S Pictures, Inc., 236
spictures.tv

Spitfire Pictures, 236
spitfirepictures.com

Spyglass Entertainment, 236
spyglassentertainment.com

Stage 6 Films, 236
sonypicturesworldwideacquisitions.com

Starry Night Entertainment, 236
starrynightentertainment.com

State Street Pictures, 237
statestreetpictures.com

Stone & Company Entertainment, 238
stonetv.com/home.html

Stone Village Pictures, 238
stonevillagepictures.com

Storefront Pictures, 238
storefrontpics.com

Storyline Entertainment, 239
storyline-entertainment.com

Straight Up Films, 239
straightupfilms.com

Submarine Entertainment, 240
submarine.com

Such Much Films, 240
suchmuchfilms.com

Summit Entertainment, 240
summit-ent.com

Sundial Pictures, 240
sundial-pictures.com

Sunlight Productions, 241
mikebinder.net

Suntaur Entertainment, 241
suntaurent.com

Sweet 180, 242
sweet180.com

Taggart Productions, 242
taggart-productions.com

Tagline Pictures, 242
taglinela.com

Taurus Entertainment Company, 243
taurusec.com

Team G, 244
teamgproductions.com

Temple Hill Entertainment, 244
templehillent.com

Terra Firma Films, 244
terrafirmafilms.com

The American Film Company, 244
theamericanfilmcompany.com

The Asylum, 245
theasylum.cc

The Badham Company, 245
badhamcompany.com

The Bureau, 245
thebureau.co.uk

The Goldstein Company, 246
garywgoldstein.com

The Gotham Group, 246
gotham-group.com

The Greenberg Group, 246
greenberggroup.com

The Group Entertainment, 246
thegroupentertainment.com

The Halcyon Company, 247
thehalcyoncompany.com

The Hatchery, 247
thehatcheryllc.com

The Jim Henson Company, 247
henson.com

The Mazur/Kaplan Company, 248
mazurkaplan.com

The Radmin Company, 249
radmincompany.com

The Walt Disney Company, 249
disney.com

The Weinstein Company, 249
weinsteinco.com

The Wolper Organization, 250
wolperorg.com

Thousand Words, 250
thousand-words.com

Thunderbird Films, 251
thunderbirdfilms.net/s/Home.asp

Tim Burton Productions, 251
timburton.com

Tonik Productions, 252
http://www.tonikproductions.com/home

Tool of North America, 252
toolofna.com

Tower of Babble Entertainment, 253
towerofb .com

Trancas International Films, Inc., 253
trancasfilms.com

Tribeca Films, 253
tribecafilm.com

TriCoast Studios, 254
tricoast.com

Tricor Entertainment, 254
TricorEntertainment.com

Trilogy Entertainment Group, 254
trilogyent.com

Troika Pictures, 254
troikapictures.com

Troma Entertainment, 255
troma.com

TV Land, 255
tvland.com

TV One LLC, 255
tvoneonline.com

Twentieth Century Fox Film Corporation, 256
fox.com

Twentieth Century Fox Television, 256
fox.com

Twentieth Television, 256
fox.com

TwinStar Entertainment, 256
twinstarentertainment.com

Two Ton Films, 257
twotonfilms.com

Underground Films, 257
undergroundfilms.net

Unified Pictures, 258
unifiedpictures.com

Union Entertainment, 258
unionent.com

Unison Films, 258
unisonfilms.com

United Artists, 259
unitedartists.com

Universal Cable Productions, 259
nbcumv.com

Universal Studios, 259
universalstudios.com

Universal Television, 259
universalstudios.com

Unstoppable, 259
unstoppableentertainmentuk.com

Upload Films, 260
uploadfilms.com/index.php

Valhalla Motion Pictures, 260
valhallapix.com

Vanderkloot Film & Television, 261
vanderkloot.com

Vanguard Films + Animation, 261
vanguardanimation.com

Vanguard Productions, 261
vanguardproductions.biz

Vanquish Motion Pictures, 261
vanquishmotionpictures.com

Verisimilitude, 262
verisimilitude.com

Vérité Films, 262
veritefilms.ca

Vertebra Films, 262
vertebrafilms.com

Vertigo Films, 263
vertigofilms.com

VH1, 263
vh1.com

Viacom Inc., 263
viacom.com

Village Roadshow Pictures, 263
vreg.com/films

Vin di Bona Productions, 264
vdbp.com

Virgin Produced, 264
virginproduced.com

Voltage Productions, 264
voltagepictures.com

Von Zerneck Sertner Films, 264
vzsfilms.com

Vox3 Films, 265
vox3films.com

Vulcan Productions, 265
vulcan.com

Walden Media, 265
walden.com

Walker/Fitzgibbon TV & Film Production, 265
walkerfitzgibbon.com

Warner Bros. Television Group, 266
warnerbros.com

Warner Brothers Animation, 266
warnerbros.com

Warner Brothers Entertainment Inc., 266
warnerbros.com

Warner Brothers Home Entertainment, 266
warnerbros.com

Warner Brothers Pictures, 267
warnerbros.com

Warner Horizon Television, 267
warnerbros.com

Warner Sisters Productions, 267
warnersisters.com

Warp Films, 267
warp.net/films

Warp X, 268
warpx.co.uk

Warren Miller Entertainment, 268
warrenmillertv.com

Warrior Poets, 268
warrior-poets.com

Wayfare Entertainment Ventures LLC, 269
wayfareentertainment.com

Weintraub/Kuhn Productions, 269
fredweintraub.com

Weller/Grossman Productions, 270
wellergrossman.com

Wendy Finerman Productions, 270
wendyfinermanproductions.com

We TV Network, 270
wetv.com

Whitewater Films, 270
whitewaterfilms.com

Whyaduck Productions Inc., 271
duckprods.com

Wild at Heart Films, 271
wildatheartfilms.us

Wind Dancer Films, 272
winddancer.com

Wingnut Films Ltd., 272
wingnutfilms.co.nz

Winkler Films, 272
winklerfilms.com

Winsome Productions, 273
winsomeprods.com

W!ldbrain Entertainment, Inc., 273
wildbrain.com

Wolfmill Entertainment, 274
wolfmill.com

Wonderland Sound and Vision, 274
wonderlandsoundandvision.com

Wonderphil Productions, 274
wonderphil.biz

Working Title Films, 274
workingtitlefilms.com

World of Wonder Productions, 275
worldofwonder.net

Worldview Entertainment, Inc., 275
worldviewent.com

Worldwide Biggies, 275
wwbiggies.com

WWE Studios, 276
wwe.com

X Filme Creative Pool, 276
x-filme.de

Xingu Films Ltd., 276
xingufilms.com

XIX Entertainment, 277
xixentertainment.com

XYZ Films, 277
xyzfilms.com

Yahoo!, 277
yahoo.com

Yari Film Group, 277
yarifilmgroup.com

York Square Productions, 278
yorksquareproductions.com

Zemeckis/Nemeroff Films, 279
enfantsterriblesmovie.com

Zentropa Entertainment, 279
zentropa.dk

Zephyr Films, 279
zephyrfilms.co.uk

Zing Productions, Inc., 280
zinghollywood.com

Zodiak USA, 280
zodiakusa.com

Index by Contact Name

Aalbaek Jensen, Peter, 279
Aaron, Paul, 241
Abarbanell, Rachel, 175
Abraham, Marc, 239
Abrahams, Lauren, 101
Abrams, J.J., 76
Abrams, Peter, 243
Abrams, Gerald, 107
Abrego, Cris, 57
Adair, Andrew, 74
Adams, Ethen, 277
Adams, Chris, 177
Adams, Erik, 52
Addis, Keith, 158
Adelstein, Marty, 61
Adler, Gil, 141
Adler, Brye, 182
Aftergood, Braden, 129
Agair, Anita, 148
Agnelli, Giovanni, 73
Agor, Sarah, 57
Ailes, Roger, 256
Akers, Sean, 81
Akil, Mara, 64
Akil, Salim, 64
Akkad, Malek S., 253
Alan, Mark, 215
Alatan, Faruk, 183
Albelda, Randy, 109
Aldridge, Felicity, 194
Aleman, Lynette C., 89
Alexander, Erin, 202
Alexander, Sam, 250
Alexander, Les, 65
Alexanian, Alexis, 122
Alexanian, David, 122
Aleyd, Nadia, 90
Ali, Malik, 110
Alizart, Suzanne, 123
Allen, Tim, 88
Allen, Jody, 265
Allen Rice, Wayne, 92
Almond, Peter, 80
Aloe, Mary, 67

Alvarez, Matt, 106
Alvarez, Rick, 268
Amato, Len, 152
Amato, T.J., 113
Amato, Danny, 113
Ambrose, Mark, 256
Amin, Mark, 235
Amritraj, Ashtok, 155
Anderson, Reynolds, 157
Anderson, Derek, 247
Anderson, Paul, 156
Andreasen, Erik, 204
Andrialis, Courtney, 201
Angaelica Warren, Breven, 235
Angel, Darby, 70
Angel, Dan, 247
Angsten, David, 62
Aniston, Jennifer, 118
Ansell, Julie, 145
Antholis, Kary, 152
Apatow, Judd, 72
Apel, Paul, 194
Apfelbaum, Jillian, 74
Arau, Sergio, 127
Arenal, Michelle, 124
Argott, Don, 59
Arizmendi, Yareli, 127
Armstrong, Scot, 69
Armstrong Stein, Kimi, 248
Arndt, Stefan, 276
Arnold, Keith, 160
Aronofsky, Darren, 211
Arquette, David, 103
Arter, Lee, 156
Arthur Jefferson, Kyle, 116
Ascher, Toby, 198
Ascoli, M. Alessandra, 226
Ashman, Blake, 178
Asseyev, Tamara, 242
Attanasio, Paul, 152
Atwell, Robert, 92
Atwood, Rebecca, 247
Ausberger, Thomas, 119
Austin, Stephanie, 96

Austin, Brad, 52
Austyn Biggers, Rickey, 83
Avnet, Jon, 89
Ayer, David, 104
Azano, Harry, 134
Aziz, Riza, 216
Azpiazu, Stefanie, 173
Babst, Tobin, 165
Badham, John, 245
Bailey, Fenton, 275
Bailey, Miranda, 69
Bajaria, Bela, 259
Balaban, Bob, 96
Baldecchi, John, 139
Baldwin, Howard, 77
Baldwin, Karen, 77
Balis, Jeff, 152
Ball, Alan, 278
Bank, Josh, 67
Bank, Brenda, 190
Barber, Gary, 236
Barber, Gary, 184
Bario, Holly, 117
Barker, Clive, 227
Barlow, Nate, 76
Barnett, Paige, 125
Barnett, Peter, 195
Barnette, Alan, 64
Baron, Caroline, 66
Baronoff, David, 77
Barratier, Christophe, 139
Barratt, Will, 73
Barrett, Jason, 194
Barrett, Jason, 65
Barroso, Emilio, 190
Barrymore, Drew, 132
Barton, Kimberly, 150
Baruela, Daniel, 109
Bashoff, Jaclyn, 146
Basile, Mary-Beth, 187
Baskin, Ellen, 125
Basner, Glen, 130
Bassick, Michael, 201
Bastian, René, 81

Basulto, David, 99
Basulto, Loren, 99
Bateman, Jason, 63
Bauch, Mark, 173
Bauman, Beau, 88
Bauman, Beau, 253
Baumgard, Caroline, 123
Bay, Michael, 208
Bay, Michael, 79
Bean, Henry, 138
Beaumont, Sidney, 213
Beck, Lauren, 213
Becker, Michael, 156
Becker, Wolfgang, 276
Becker, Walt, 266
Beckner, Amanda, 197
Beddor, Frank, 76
Bedell, Austin, 258
Bedusa, Susan, 56
Beers, Betsy, 229
Beery, Noah, 123
Bekmambetov, Timur, 79
Belgrad, Doug, 101
Bell, Dave, 111
Bellisario, Donald, 81
Bellisario, David, 81
Bello, Steven, 274
Benaroya, Michael, 81
Bender, Lawrence, 171
Bender, Chris, 82
Benson, Alison, 211
Benveniste, Racheline, 267
Berenson, Matt, 230
Berg, Peter, 129
Berger, Albert, 87
Berger, Liz, 171
Berger, Dan, 199
Bergman, Debra, 101
Bergthold, Lara, 61
Berk, Rachel, 194
Berk, Jason, 82
Berkowitz, Dan, 191
Berlanti, Greg, 82
Berliner, Mark, 76
Berman, Bruce, 263
Bernardi, David, 233
Bernsein, Nancy, 117
Bernstein, Carolyn, 219
Bernstein, Larry, 117
Berstein, Armyan, 80
Berta, Maritza, 221

Besman, Michael, 77
Bespalov, Sergei, 65
Bespalov, Marina, 65
Best, Otis, 132
Bianco, James, 56
Biel, Jessica, 160
Biggar, Maggie, 134
Bilgrad, Aaron, 123
Bill, Tony, 78
Binder, Mike, 241
Binder, Jack, 147
Binder, Jack, 241
Birkemoe, Tamara, 133
Birnbaum, Roger, 236
Birzneck, Art, 84
Bitzelberger, Rick, 159
Bixler, Kelli, 84
Black, Todd, 126
Black, Ryan, 147
Black, Jack, 120
Blackman, David, 171
Blank, Matthew, 230
Blasband Page, Kat, 243
Bleiberg, Ehud, 85
Bliss, Tom, 239
Bliss, Howard, 258
Block, Bill, 212
Bloom, Jeremy, 126
Bloom, Scott, 73
Blum, Adam, 201
Blum, Jason, 86
Blumenthal, Jason, 126
Blumenthal, Gail, 221
Bobker, Daniel, 86
Bochco, Steven, 237
Bodde, Margaret, 231
Bogner, Jonathan, 87
Bogner, Oliver, 86
Bohrer, Gillian, 240
Bolotin, Nate, 277
Bolt, Jeremy, 156
Bonacci, Tara, 143
Boorstein, Joan, 230
Borden, Bill, 243
Border, W. K., 192
Boros, Stuart, 114
Botwick, Terry, 52
Boughn, Lacy, 249
Bowen, Marty, 244
Bowers, Amanda, 275
Bowland, Jeff, 103

Bowles, Eamonn, 177
Bozell, Jennifer, 199
Bozotti, Filippo, 74
Bradford, Elizabeth, 194
Bradley, Paul, 183
Bradman, Michael, 88
Brady, Matthew, 190
Brand, Russell, 88
Brandstein, Jonathan, 182
Branson, Toni, 121
Brar, René, 238
Bratman, Josh, 184
Braun, Dan, 240
Braun, Josh, 240
Braunstein, Howard, 161
Brazzini, Valentina, 245
Bregman, Anthony, 173
Breiman, Eric, 106
Brener, Richard, 193
Brennan, Shane, 81
Brennan, Tracie, 67
Breton, Brooke, 155
Brewer Pennekamp, Ginny, 164
Brezner, Larry, 182
Brickhouse, Louanne, 90
Brin, Courtney, 218
Brion, Trent, 271
Broadbent, Graham, 86
Broccoli, Barbara, 108
Brodie, Tyler, 262
Brody, Jeb, 133
Brooker, Barry, 147
Brooks, Elena, 54
Brooks, James, 145
Brooks, Paul, 143
Brooks, Ryan, 259
Brookwell, Rick, 145
Broome, David, 54
Brosnan, Pierce, 160
Brotman, Arden, 224
Brown, Kevin, 171
Brown, Nicole, 178
Brown, Sam, 193
Brown, Stephen, 256
Brown, Todd, 277
Browning, Ben, 269
Bruckheimer, Jerry, 162
Brucks, Ashley, 203
Brunt, Daniel, 222
Buck, Cailey, 165
Buder, Emily, 203

Buelow, David, 124
Buffel-Matusow, Carissa, 136
Buirgy, Suzanne, 116
Bullock, Sandra, 134
Bulochnikov, Stella, 145
Buman, Lia, 130
Burdick, Geoff, 173
Burg, Mark, 257
Burger, Lee, 220
Burk, Bryan, 76
Burke, James, 124
Burke, Steve, 191
Burke, Dina, 78
Burke, Mary, 268
Burke, Jim, 61
Burleigh, Steve, 91
Burnett, Rob, 276
Burns, Alexander, 107
Burr, Kristin, 90
Burton, Tim, 252
Bush, Eli, 226
Butler, Gerard, 140
Butler, Alex, 63
Butler, Brad, 182
Caleb, Stephanie, 62
Callan, Adam, 116
Calley, John, 163
Callif, Dustin, 252
Cameron, Elaine, 151
Cameron, James, 173
Camp, Dee, 69
Camp, Steven, 113
Camp, Colleen, 100
Campbell, Tom, 275
Campos, Antonio, 87
Canavesio, Giancarlo, 178
Cannon, Cam, 150
Cannon, Vivian, 198
Cantillon, Elizabeth, 101
Caplan, David, 57
Cappucino, Mac, 263
Cardona, Richard, 63
Carey, Joey, 240
Carey, Anne, 227
Carlton, Peter, 267
Carmichael, Jamie, 102
Carolla, Adam, 161
Carreras, Jennifer, 256
Carroll, Casey A., 239
Carroll, Ryan, 90
Carter, Susie, 143

Cartsonis, Susan, 238
Casey, Jim, 167
Casey, David, 189
Cassidy, Shaun, 229
Castaldo, Mark, 113
Cates, Valerie, 214
Catmull, Ed, 207
Catron, Justin, 84
Cavalier, Liz, 76
Cawood, Ben, 116
C. Dickerman, Samuel, 101
Celani, Renato, 224
Celea, Alexandru, 176
Ceryak, Mark, 146
Cestone, Maria, 275
Chaffin, Stokely, 238
Chaiken, Jennifer, 58
Chaiken, Jennifer, 95
Chait, Marcus, 138
Chartier, Nicolas, 264
Chartoff, Robert, 95
Chase, Debra, 180
Chasin, Liza, 274
Cheadle, Don, 104
Chen, Angelina, 124
Cheng, John, 214
Chernin, Peter, 95
Chestna, Tamara, 171
Cheung, Vince, 220
Chilnick, Jeremy, 268
Chindamo, Frank, 138
Chotzen, Yvonne, 96
Chouinard, Sandra, 136
Choun, Chris, 161
Christeas, Julie, 218
Christensen, Tove, 133
Christensen, Eric J., 130
Christensen, Hayden, 133
Christiansen, Robert, 97
Chu, Li-Wei, 205
Chu, Patrick, 130
Chubb, Caldecot, 97
Church, Alexandra, 103
Chvatal, Cynthia, 153
Ciardi, Mark, 182
Clanagan, Jeff, 100
Clark, David, 278
Clark, Bill, 70
Clarke, Noel, 260
Clausi, Catherine, 242
Clear, Michael, 85

Clifford, Jeffrey, 153
Clifford, Ryan, 277
Clooney, George, 234
Clymore, Jacob, 154
Codikow, Stacy, 210
Cohan, Matthew, 79
Cohen, Andy, 145
Cohen, Kate, 239
Cohen, Jonathan, 76
Cohen, Howard, 221
Cohen, Bruce, 89
Cohen, Rob, 219
Cohen, Todd, 219
Cohn, Lee, 97
Cohn, Shannon McCoy, 178
Coker, Brett, 217
Colbert, Mary, 195
Cole, Alex, 122
Cole, Kai, 81
Coleman, Jonathan, 149
Colleton, Sara, 100
Collet-Serra, Jaume, 197
Collette, Scott, 133
Colpaert, Carl, 98
Colson, Christian, 100
Colucci-Zieger, Michele, 280
Colvin, Henrietta, 93
Colvin-Goulding, Suzanne, 92
Comerford, John, 203
Compere, Shakim, 132
Condito, Sandra, 202
Connell, Katie, 189
Connolly, Michael, 176
Connors, Michael, 131
Conrady, Jeremy, 249
Conroy, Toby, 199
Cook, Dane, 241
Cook, Chris, 176
Cooke, Drew, 115
Cooley, Aaron, 163
Cooper, Kimberly, 256
Cooper, Bob, 169
Cooper, Melissa, 161
Coote, Greg, 117
Coote, Greg, 170
Coppola, Francis, 70
Corcoran, Karen, 231
Cornwell, Stephen, 159
Corral, Pete, 101
Corriere, Konni, 168
Cort, Robert, 221

Cortes, Lisa, 172
Cortese, Nicki, 269
Corwin, Charlie, 198
Costa Reis, Ricardo, 214
Costa Reis, Rui, 214
Costner, Kevin, 253
Cowan, Gabe, 192
Cowan, Cindy, 97
Cowan, Chris, 82
Cowen, Rich, 195
Cowie, Robin, 151
Cowles, Chris, 114
Cox, Courtney, 103
Cray, Laura, 178
Crean, Kelly, 104
Creighton, Collin, 250
Crews, Terry, 57
Cristall, Erin, 90
Crocket, David, 142
Crofford, Keith, 62
Cronin, Mark, 57
Crooks, Jeffrey, 80
Crow, Christine, 195
Crown, Daniel, 215
Cruise, Tom, 259
Crystal, Billy, 127
Cube, Ice, 106
Cubit, Orlando, 181
Cullota, Jeff, 110
Culpepper, Clint, 226
Culpepper, Lindsay, 202
Cunningham, Ryan, 176
Cunningham, Sean, 105
Cunningham, Carolynne, 272
Curling, Chris, 279
Curtis, Bonnie, 186
Curtis, Cliff, 259
Cusack, John, 193
Cuthrell, Elizabeth, 126
Cutler, Jill, 273
Cutler, R.J., 61
Dahlia, B, 203
Daily, Patrick, 162
Dakss, Jon, 191
Dal Farra, Brice, 79
Dal Farra, Claude, 79
Damaschke, Bill, 116
D'Amico, Kirk, 190
Damon, Mark, 133
Dang, Binh, 237
Daniels, Lee, 172

Dante, Joe, 215
d'Arbeloff, Eric, 221
Darian, Craig, 254
Dark, Dylan, 95
Darobont, Frank, 110
Dauman, Philippe, 263
Davey, Chris, 183
David, Alan, 64
David, Kerry, 175
David, Lorena, 221
David, Erin, 163
Davidson, Boaz, 185
Davidson, Boaz, 195
Davies, Michael, 122
Davis, Jonathan, 256
Davis, Warren, 136
Davis, John, 111
Davis, Kira, 58
Davis-Dyer, Diana, 147
Davison, Doug, 212
Day, Rob, 123
Debbs, James, 72
de Braconier, Matthew, 245
Deege, Robert, 158
De Fillipo, Dan, 207
DeJoie, Julie, 229
Delaney, Tim, 230
De Laurentiis, Martha, 114
Del Deo, Adam, 124
DeLeon, Bobby, 159
D'Elia, Christopher, 115
D'Elia, Matt, 69
De Line, Donald, 112
del Toro, Guillermo, 186
DeLuca, Doug, 161
De Luca, Michael, 184
De Maio, Lorenzo, 114
Dembrowski, Christi, 158
Dembrun Sciavicco, Melissa, 154
De Niro, Robert, 253
Dennis, Chris, 258
Dennison, Kimberly, 213
Densham, Nevin, 254
Densham, Pen, 254
DePaolo, Joey, 125
Depp, Johnny, 158
DeRoss, Matt, 72
De Souza, Paul, 138
Detharidge, Jake, 271
de Toro, Guillermo, 192
Devine, Brian, 141

DeVito, Danny, 162
Devlin, Dean, 121
Diamant, Moshe, 231
Diamant, Illana, 231
DiAntonio, A.J., 107
Diaz, Philippe, 98
DiBona, Vin, 264
Di Bona, Cara, 264
di Bonaventura, Lorenzo, 113
di Bonaventura, Lorenzo, 113
DiCanio, Jerry, 192
Dick Hackett, Isa, 121
Dickie, Chris, 123
Diesel, Vin, 197
Diffley, Ida, 118
Diggins, Chip, 223
Diggs, Taye, 199
Dillon, Caroline, 218
Di Loreto, Dante, 223
Dinerstein, Ross, 210
Dinerstein, David, 171
Di Novi, Denise, 114
Dion, Garrick, 87
Dirksen, Jennah, 74
Disco, Michael, 193
Disharoon, Scott, 124
Distenfeld, David, 71
Dodd, Ted, 256
Dodds, Robert, 277
Dodson, Neal, 81
Donen, Joshua, 90
Donkers, Melanie, 129
Donley, Scott, 111
Donner, Richard, 115
Donnermeyer, Nicholas, 85
Donovan, Virginia, 207
Doran, Lindsay, 251
Dornig, Kristin, 210
Douglas, Terry, 53
Douglas, Michael, 138
Doumanian, Jean, 162
Downey, Susan, 243
Downey, Robert, 243
Drachkovitch, Stephanie, 56
Drachkovitch, Rasha, 56
Driver, Foster, 101
Drogin, Marcy, 181
Dubovsky, Dana, 69
Ducksworth, Sheila, 119
Dudelson, James, 243
Dudelson, Robert, 243

Duff, Timothy, 218
Dugdale, Rick, 108
Duncan, David Y., 89
Dungan, Sebastian, 58
Dunlap, Lindsay, 123
Duplass, Jay, 117
Duplass, Mark, 117
Duran, Venecia, 220
Durkin, Sean, 87
Dynner, Susan, 60
Eakle, Alison, 229
East, Guy, 126
Eastwood, Clint, 177
Eaton, Andrew, 219
Eberle-Adams, Kristy, 150
Edmonds, Kenneth, 119
Edmonds, Tracey, 119
Effron, Zac, 194
Egan, James, 271
Egan, Kalen, 121
Egoyan, Atom, 120
Ehrlich, Scott, 63
Eick, David, 111
Eigen, Sam, 230
Eisenberg, Arianna, 62
Ekins, Susan, 162
El-Hajoui, Omar, 91
Elliot, Jamie, 152
Elliot, Mike, 92
Elliott, Kiel, 151
Ellis, Suzann, 80
Ellis, Kylie, 213
Ellison, David, 233
Ellison, Megan, 71
Elman, Lawrence, 68
Elseman, Erik, 143
Emerson, Brady, 214
Emerson, Chris, 126
Emery, Stephen, 99
Emmerich, Ute, 94
Emmerich, Roland, 94
Emmerich, Toby, 193
Emmrich, Alicia, 196
Engelson, Trevor, 257
Englebardt, Sam, 112
Ensweiler, Aaron, 178
Ensweiler, Aaron, 154
Epstein, Brad, 202
Epstein, Stefanie, 237
Erman, Alish, 215
Esberg, Sarah, 208

Eskelsen, Peter, 271
Esparza, Moctesuma, 182
Estrada, Kimberly, 233
Evans, Marc, 203
Evans, Charles, 60
Evans, Marc D., 159
Eveleth, Brent, 213
Everett, Megan, 128
Ewart, Bill, 188
Ewing, Michael, 91
Eyre, Mike, 184
Ezhuthachan, Aditya, 201
Faigenblum, David, 102
Faillace, Maria, 94
Faivre, Bertrand, 245
Falbo, Mike, 189
Falconer, Douglas, 128
Falk, Brian, 245
Farrell, Joseph, 128
Farrell, Rebecca, 264
Farrelly, Bobby, 103
Farrelly, Peter, 103
Faust, Blye Pagon, 222
Feder, Steven, 85
Federico, TJ, 218
Fee, Edward, 113
Feltheimer, Jon, 174
Felts, Jason, 264
Fernandez, Robert, 189
Ferrall, Nicholas, 236
Ferrell, Will, 140
Ferrell, Lisa, 261
Ferro, Rita, 249
Fessenden, Larry, 142
Feuer, Zachary, 278
Fichman, Niv, 219
Fickman, Andy, 198
Field, Ted, 212
Field, Gwen, 232
Fields, Adam, 61
Fierberg, Andrew, 265
Filo, David, 277
Fineman, Eric, 101
Finerman, Wendy, 270
Fiorentino, Marc, 155
Fireman, Dan, 74
Firestone, Karen, 207
Fischel, Andrew, 267
Fischer, Eric, 119
Fisher, Lucy, 217
Fitzgerald, Michael, 161

Fitzgibbon, Mo, 266
Flanagan, Brian, 112
Flavin, Michael, 237
Fleder, Gary, 187
Floren, Clay, 132
Flores, Craig, 264
Floyd Johnson, Chas, 81
Forbes, Bonnie, 134
Forbes, Brett, 134
Foreman, Zev, 264
Forsythe, Jessica, 107
Foster, Karen, 116
Foster, Gary, 169
Fowler, Elizabeth, 99
Fox, John, 111
Fox, Kevin, 215
Fragner, Lisa, 86
Frakes, Kevin Scott, 201
Frakes, Randall, 123
Franchot, Pascal, 128
Francis, Alex, 181
Francis, Alex, 276
Franco, James, 212
Frank, Scott, 125
Frank, Paul, 211
Franke, Kyle, 277
Franklin, DeVon, 101
Franks, Jessica, 252
Franks, Jessica, 191
Freedman, Steve, 256
Freeling, Isa, 160
Freeman, Morgan, 219
Freeman, Scott, 90
Freeman, Matt, 180
Freis, Jon, 104
French, Gary, 60
French Isaac, Margaret, 159
Frey, Derek, 252
Freyer, Glen, 75
Fried, Robert, 137
Friedman, Elizabeth Zox, 225
Friedman, Brent, 121
Friedman, Rob, 240
Friendly, David, 137
Fries, Charles, 97
Fugardi, Dan, 80
Furer, Ken, 87
Furst, Bryan, 138
Furst, Sean, 138
Fuselier, Oliver, 252
Fyzee, Arish, 210

Gabler, Elizabeth, 135
Gabrawy, Mike, 73
Gabriel, Larry, 208
Gaglio, Florent, 106
Gainor, Glenn, 227
Galinsky, Dana, 94
Gallagher, Patrick, 262
Gallant, K.R., 139
Gallant, Michael, 139
Gallo, Bradley, 254
Gambino, David, 243
Gamble, Timothy, 251
Ganis, Sidney, 199
Gannon, Matthew, 64
Ganz, Tony, 274
Garavente, Jim, 63
Garcia, Andy, 98
Garcia, Alex, 172
Gardner, Bradley, 255
Gargano, Jennifer, 133
Garrett, Geoff, 105
Garth, Matthew, 89
Gartner, Alex, 75
Gatien, Jen, 111
Gatta, Joe, 216
Gatti-Pascual, Soledad, 245
Gauer, Luane, 169
Geary, Nathaniel, 229
Geiger, Boris, 271
Gelber, Danielle, 273
Geller, Aaron, 209
Gellert, Laurence, 270
Genier, Joe, 92
Gerber, Bill, 141
Giannetti, Andrea, 101
Giarraputo, Jack, 150
Gibgot, Jennifer, 196
Gibson, Mel, 155
Gienapp, Bill, 237
Gilbert, Gary, 141
Gill, Mark, 195
Gillian, Lisa, 216
Gilula, Stephen, 135
Gitlin, Mimi, 142
Gitlin, Richard, 142
Gittes, Harry, 142
Given, Andy, 101
Gladstein, Richard, 129
Glascoe, Jon, 107
Gluck, Will, 196
Glushon, Gary, 200

Godfrey, Wyck, 244
Goff, Gina, 143
Golchan, Frederic, 136
Gold, Alicia, 59
Gold, Eric L., 246
Gold, Jeremy, 123
Goldberg, T.S., 122
Goldberg, Amanda, 178
Goldberg, Dana, 233
Goldberg, Jason, 166
Goldberg, Cara, 90
Goldberg, Leonard, 178
Goldberg, David, 123
Goldberg, Keith, 110
Goldenberg, Josh, 165
Goldenring, Jane, 144
Goldman, Ethan, 268
Goldschein, Gil, 90
Goldsman, Akiva, 269
Goldsmith-Thomas, Elaine, 144
Goldsmith-Vein, Ellen, 246
Goldstein, Steve, 258
Goldstein, Gary, 246
Goldstein, Charlie, 182
Goldstein, Julie, 124
Goldstein, Leonard, 128
Goldworm, Adam, 72
Goldwyn, John, 163
Golighter, Tristan, 245
Golin, Steve, 72
Gonzales, Bobby, 114
Goodman, Ilyssa, 246
Goodman, Rosser, 166
Goodwin, Joy, 208
Gorai, Tom, 228
Gordon, Stuart, 216
Gordon, Mark, 248
Gorn, Phil, 274
Gorton, Jen, 230
Gosch, Jeremy, 137
Gosch, Monika, 137
Gottlieb, Bill, 144
Gou, Jeffrey, 95
Gough, Alfred, 185
Graham, Craig, 213
Grais, Michael, 184
Grammar, Kelsey, 145
Granger, Amelia, 274
Granger, Don, 259
Grass, Ben, 212
Gray, Hunter, 262

Gray, Hunter, 74
Gray, Malcolm, 233
Greco, John, 90
Green, Jessica, 246
Green, David, 223
Green, Adam, 73
Greenberg, Randy, 246
Greenblatt, Amanda, 84
Greenfield, Luke, 271
Greenspan, Alison, 114
Greenwald, Robert, 221
Gregory, Scott, 255
Gregory, Shannon, 233
Greisman, Alan, 217
Griffin, Tony, 184
Grodnik, Daniel, 181
Gross, Mary, 148
Grossbard, Beth, 83
Grossman, Gary, 270
Grosso, Nikki, 162
Grosso, Sonny, 148
Gubelmann, Bingo, 202
Guber, Peter, 177
Gugenheim, D.J., 158
Guiney, Ed, 121
Gunn, Jon, 175
Gunn, Andrew, 149
Gurthie, Grant, 213
Gutch, Robin, 268
Gutman, Mitchell, 174
Gwartz, Jennifer, 173
Haber, Ben, 166
Hack, Shelley, 234
Hacker, Jenny, 92
Haffner, Craig, 145
Hahn, Kristin, 118
Haight, Adam, 229
Hale, Gregg, 151
Halfon, Lianne, 190
Hall, Stewart, 175
Hall, Meredith, 191
Hall, Carter, 73
Hall, Nancy Mosher, 64
Hall, Stephanie, 105
Hall, Jessica, 86
Halper, Jenny, 181
Halperin, Dan, 125
Halpern, Ron, 239
Hamada, Walter, 193
Hamilton, Gary, 73
Hamilton, Dave, 123

Hamilton, Strathford, 254
Hamilton, Marcy Levitas, 254
Hamm, Nick, 187
Hammer, Wolfgang, 94
Hamori, Andras, 149
Hamrick, Shari, 66
Han, Howard, 254
Hanks, Tom, 208
Hanks, Poppy, 55
Hansen, Carter, 262
Harding, Richard, 233
Hargreave, Erica, 63
Hargrove, Suzanne, 78
Harlin, Renny, 185
Harms, Tim, 57
Harris, Lynn, 267
Haswell-Tannenbaum, Kim, 242
Hatanaka, Gregory, 97
Hausfater, Jere, 65
Hawk, Ron, 210
Hawk, Tony, 59
Hayes, Kelly, 266
Hayes, Sean, 151
Hayman, Tara, 195
Hays, Julianna, 244
Hazzard, Chris, 235
Headington, Tim, 130
Heaton, Patricia, 135
Hecht, Albie, 275
Hecht, Duffy, 247
Hedblom, Brett, 104
Heder, Dan, 146
Heder, Doug, 146
Heder, Jon, 146
Hedlund, Alex, 172
Hefferon, Michael, 213
Heffner, Daniel, 228
Hegyes, Stephen, 89
Heineman, Alex, 232
Helfant, Michael, 255
Heller, Rich, 92
Heller, Jack, 91
Henderson, Kate, 277
Henigman, Kris, 261
Henson, Brian, 248
Henze, Chris, 242
Herbert, Mark, 268
Herbert, Mark, 267
Hertzberg, Paul, 98
Herz, Adam, 244
Herz, Michael, 255

Heslov, Grant, 234
Heston, Fraser, 63
Hetzel, Eric, 221
Hevert, Jeff, 124
Heyman, Dahlia, 275
Heyman, John, 275
Heyman, David, 153
Hicks, Heather, 168
Higgin, David, 235
Higgins, Angelique, 170
Higgins, Bob, 273
Higgins, David, 170
Hikaka, Kimberly, 93
Hildebrand, Jodi, 196
Hill, John, 80
Hilton Monroe, Jennifer, 172
Hinojosa, David, 167
Hipps, Joe, 182
Hirigoyen, Christina, 182
Hirsch, Saryl, 224
Hirschorn, Michael, 160
Hively, Chad, 80
Ho, Jennifer, 141
Hobbs, Rebecca, 129
Hoberman, David, 178
Hobson, Jeanne, 90
Hochman Nash, Marney, 185
Hock, Trey, 244
Hoffman, Phillip, 103
Hoffman, Gary, 140
Hoffman, Peter, 228
Hogan, Justin, 166
Holderman, Bill, 272
Holland, Gil, 247
Homan, Eric, 136
Honor, Dana, 256
Honovic, Matthew, 147
Hoon, Samir, 210
Hopwood, David, 76
Hori, Takeo, 72
Horowitz, Jordan, 141
Horowitz, Mark, 81
Horwitz, Andy, 75
Householter, David, 189
Howard, Max, 127
Howard, Ron, 156
Howell, Lynette, 120
Howsam, Erik, 113
Huang, Joan, 95
Huck, Lori, 190
Hughes, Patrick, 154

Hughes, Mary Ann, 249
Hunt, David, 135
Hurd, Gale, 261
Husney, Evan, 64
Huston, Anjelica, 146
Hyde, John, 217
Hyman, Wendy, 229
Ianno, Dominic, 158
Ichise, Takashige, 200
Igbokwe, Pearlena, 191
Iger, Robert, 249
Imani Cameron, Kisha, 102
Ingle, Farrell, 280
Irwin, John, 160
Isaacs, Stanley, 52
Iso, Christine, 200
Israel, Jesse, 158
Israelson, Ally, 248
Istock, Steven, 92
Ivory, James, 183
Iwanyk, Basil, 251
Iwashina, Kevin, 210
Iwerks, Leslie, 172
Jablin, Burton, 153
Jacks, James, 136
Jackson, Ian, 128
Jackson, Alex, 182
Jackson, Peter, 272
Jackson, Calvin "C-Note", 195
Jackson, Samuel, 260
Jacobs, Andrew, 75
Jacobs, Katie, 152
Jacobs, John, 234
Jacobson, Danny, 159
Jacobson, David, 170
Jacobson, Nina, 101
Jacobson, Ross, 55
Jaffe, Michael, 161
Jaffe, Toby, 198
Jaglom, Henry, 213
James, Freddy, 153
Jan Savy, Lisa, 279
Janzen, Matthew, 174
Jarrett, Jennifer, 57
Jarzynski, Kevin, 76
Jeffries, Janet, 171
Jenckes, Joe, 81
Jenkins, Andy, 151
Jenkins, Jeff, 90
Jenner, William, 96
Jennings, Christina, 228

Jennings, Heather, 220
Jesuele, Neil, 183
Jewison, Norman, 278
Jewison, Michael, 278
J. Gaeta, Michael, 139
Jimenez, Javier, 186
J. Labarowski, Todd, 116
Johnsen, Polly, 209
Johnso, William D., 112
Johnson, Ryan, 262
Johnson, Broderick, 65
Johnson, Keith, 148
Johnson, Sarah, 179
Johnson, Mark, 146
Johnson, Brianna, 119
Johnson, Curt, 157
Johnson, Tom, 132
Johnson Redlich, Sarah, 275
Johnston, Stephen, 144
Johnston, Tammy, 122
Johnston, Andrea, 193
Jolivette, Vince, 212
Jones, Steven Lee, 80
Jones, Jina, 174
Jones, Justine, 153
Jones, Larry W., 255
Jones, Michelle, 80
Jones, David, 170
Jones, Gary, 167
Jordan, Ashley, 83
Jose, Kim, 121
Josefsberg, Lisa, 94
Josephson, Eliad, 214
Josephson, Barry, 164
Joung, Jinny, 164
Joyce, Sheena, 59
Judah, Jay, 139
Judkins, Toni, 255
Justice, Hardy, 181
Juul, Niels, 94
Kadin, Jonathan, 101
Kadison, Zak, 84
Kahane, Nathan, 178
Kahn, Harvey, 137
Kahn, Jenette, 116
Kalfus, Bryan, 226
Kalins, Dayna, 237
Kamen, Jon, 213
Kane-Ritsch, Julie, 246
Kaplan, Aaron, 165
Kaplan, Mitchell, 248

Kaplan, Aaron, 165
Karp, Amie, 117
Karpen, Andrew, 133
Karsh, Jonathan, 217
Kar-wai, Wong, 163
Karz, Mike, 165
Kassen, Adam, 165
Kassen, Mark, 165
Kasunich, Gregory, 104
Kathryn Ellis, Riley, 135
Katz, Lisa, 256
Katz, Aaron, 199
Katz, Campbell, 180
Katz, Marty, 180
Katz, Jon, 119
Katz, Ara, 74
Katzenberg, Jeffrey, 116
Kaufman, Lloyd, 255
Kavanaugh-Jones, Brian, 156
Keaney, Tom, 276
Keathley, Brian, 112
Kellam, Laura, 143
Keller, J.A., 122
Kelley, John C., 81
Kellison, Daniel, 161
Kelly, Jessica, 92
Kelly Kosek, Jane, 172
Kennedy, Steve, 108
Kennedy, Kathleen, 175
Kent, Alainee, 215
Keppler, Stacy, 196
Kerchner, Rob, 92
Kern, Bert, 271
Kerner, Jordan, 166
Kerr, Alex, 259
Kessell, Brad, 143
Kestin, Ketura, 228
Kilot, Jason, 198
Kim, Kari, 275
Kim, Gerry, 72
Kim, Bob, 83
Kimmel, Sidney, 230
Kimmel, Jimmy, 161
King, Graham, 130
King, Jon, 144
King, Julian, 69
King, Jonathan, 204
King, Graham, 142
King, Chris W., 66
Kipperman, Perri, 168
Kirton, Mona, 106

Kittle, T.L., 215
Kjarval, Keith, 258
Klaus, Brandon, 249
Klausner, Isaac, 244
Klausner, Isaac, 244
Klein, Howard, 55
Klein, Marci, 191
Klein, Michael, 115
Kleinbart, Philip, 221
Kleinberg, Elliot, 259
Klekowski, Glenn, 80
Kline, Wayne, 128
Klipstein, Alexandria, 136
Koffeman, Jason, 210
Koffler, Pamela, 167
Koh, David, 240
Kohan, David, 168
Kohn, Sharon, 213
Kohn, Benji, 202
Kokourina, Anna, 135
Kolbert, Katherine, 192
Kolbrenner, Adam, 176
Kolodner, Eva, 224
Komarnicki, Todd, 149
Konstantopoulos, Eva, 138
Koop, Christopher, 133
Kopeloff, Eric, 145
Kosinski, Geyer, 182
Koskoff, Emma, 231
Koslow, Rory, 170
Kostbar, Elana, 130
Kostbar, Eben, 130
Koster, Iren, 231
Kramer, Clare, 112
Kramer, Jonathan, 220
Kramer, Jeffrey, 165
Krane, Jonathan, 168
Kranzler, Eric, 129
Krasnoff, Russ, 168
Krauss, Jonathan, 85
Kreinik, Danielle, 251
Krieger, Steven, 58
Krieger, Lee Toland, 58
Krofft, Marty, 169
Krofft, Sid, 169
Kruger, Ehren, 86
Krupinski, Dana, 155
Kryszek, Raphael, 158
Kubena, Kent, 251
Kubicek, Victor, 247
Kuenert, Fred, 136

Kuhn, Tom, 269
Kujawski, Peter, 133
Kulchak, Kelly, 242
Kultzer, Robert, 102
Kulukundis, Cassandra, 259
Kunath, Pamela, 226
Kunkle, Brent, 142
Kupisk, Michael, 65
Kurily, Jake, 75
Kurtzman, Alex, 168
Kuser, Chris, 116
Kushner, Alwyn, 164
Kushner, Donald, 164
Kutcher, Ashton, 166
Kwapis, Ken, 157
Kwatinetz, Jeff, 211
Kyle, Brenda, 60
Lacey, Julie, 229
Lacroix, Hubert, 92
Laguette, Alejandro, 227
Laiblin, Kristel, 239
Lam, Justin, 193
Lambert, Scott, 129
Lambert, Michael, 112
Lambert, Matt, 174
Landau, Jon, 173
Lane, Matt, 82
Lange, Cassidy, 184
Langhoff, Stephanie, 117
Langlais, Rudy, 80
Lantos, Robert, 228
Laren, Dawn, 189
LaSalle, Lillian, 242
Lasseter, John, 208
Lasseter, John, 90
Latham, Taylor, 115
Latifah, Queen, 132
Latsis, Paris, 53
Latt, Brian, 252
Latt, David, 256
Lattaker-Johnson, Robyn, 83
Laub, David, 199
Lauder, Karen, 60
Lauren, Andrew, 70
Lavagnino, Tom, 140
Law, Josie, 224
Lawrence, Robert, 221
Lawson, Joseph, 245
Lawson, Peter, 251
Lazar, Andrew, 176
League, Tim, 64

Lear, Norman, 61
LeBoff, Jared, 179
Lebow, Amanda, 199
Lee, Tonya Lewis, 252
Lee, Stan, 209
Lee, Spike, 56
Lee, Kane, 161
Lee, Linda, 140
Lee, Erica, 251
Lee, Rob, 79
Leibowitz, Richard, 258
Leitman, Max, 77
Leo, Anton, 92
Lerner, Steven, 153
Lerner, Avi, 185
Lerner, Alex, 165
Leslie, Laura, 121
Lessans, Gregory, 244
Lester, Mark, 69
Letterman, David, 276
Leventhal, Jessica, 89
Levin, Daniel, 208
Levine, Russell, 223
Levine, Judi, 240
Levine, Stephanie, 252
Levine, Jackie, 156
Levine, Dan, 53
Levinson, Dan, 189
Levinson, Barry, 77
Levitt, Zane, 279
Levitt, Alfred, 245
Levy, Dani, 276
Levy, Robert L., 243
Levy, Shawn, 53
Levy, Brian, 193
Levy, Lawrence, 94
Levy-Hinte, Jeffrey, 72
Lewin, Ben, 240
L'Heureux, Stephen, 235
Liang, Josie, 130
Lichtenstein, Demian, 125
Liddell, Mickey, 171
Lieberman, Hal, 247
Lieberman, Todd, 178
Liggins, Alfred, 255
Liman, Doug, 155
Lin, Dan, 173
Lin, Justin, 206
Linde, David, 171
Lingg, Kathy, 76
Link, Julie, 217

Linnen, Nik, 88
Lista, Blanca, 248
Little, Greg, 225
Littlefield, Warren, 248
Litto, George, 140
Lobell, Mike, 185
Loeb, Allen, 225
Loos, Rob, 280
Lopez, Lucia, 181
Lopez, Jennifer, 195
Lopez, James, 226
Lorenz, Carsten, 186
Lorenz, Robert, 177
Loughlin, Sean, 123
Love, Sandi, 122
Love, NIck, 263
Lowe, Andrew, 121
Lowell, Richard, 276
Lowry, Hunt, 222
Lubinsky, Yvette, 190
Lucas, George, 175
Ludlow, Graham, 101
Lui, Cybill, 71
Luisi, Michael, 276
Luker, Kyle, 247
Lundberg, Robert, 170
Lunsford, Loris, 166
Luong, David, 59
Lupovitz, Dan, 109
Lurie, Christina, 265
Lynn, Julie, 186
Lynne, Michael, 258
Mabrito, Robin, 216
Macauley, Scott, 133
Macdonald, Andrew, 115
MacDonald, Laurie, 204
MacFarlane, Seth, 139
MacVicar, Caroline, 241
Macy, Trevor, 159
Maggini, Tia, 164
Magiday, Lee, 121
Magielnicki, Matt, 107
Mahdessian, Armen, 203
Maher, Michael, 269
Maisel, Ileen, 68
Malkovich, John, 190
Malmberg, Fredrik, 203
Mancini, Val, 143
Mancuso, Frank, 87
Mangano, Chris, 206
Maniscalco, Mia, 117

Mankoff, Douglas, 118
Mann, Thea, 103
Mann, Andrew, 260
Mann, Michael, 134
Manpearl, David, 193
Mao, Joan, 249
Maran, Rachel, 242
Marashlian, Paul, 73
Marchand, Xavier, 67
Marciano, Nathalie, 54
Marcus, Jay, 127
Margolies, Rob, 114
Mark, Laurence, 171
Marken, Dave, 207
Marker, Riva, 215
Marmor, Jennifer, 105
Marmur, Ori, 198
Marshall, Garry, 153
Marshall, Frank, 166
Marshall, Penny, 204
Marshall, Amanda, 69
Marshall, Nic, 181
Martin, Nic, 118
Martinez, Phillipe, 78
Marx, Hilary, 163
Mashouf, Manny, 73
Mashouf, Karim, 73
Masi, Anthony, 180
Matsushima, Arata, 243
Matthews, Gina, 174
Matthews, Jessica, 198
Mattoo, Priyanka, 120
Matusow, Kevin J, 136
Matz, Zachary, 131
Mauceri, Marc, 131
Maull, Judit, 150
Maurer, Joshua, 99
Mauvernay, Nicolas, 139
May, Robert, 227
Maynard, Jeff, 114
Mazur, Paula, 248
McCachen, Kyle, 89
McCall, Jasa, 253
McCormick, Kelly, 231
McCormick, Kevin, 170
McCoy, Mike, 77
McCreary, Lori, 219
McDermott, Dan, 113
McDonnell, Ed, 179
McEwen, Scott, 92
McFadzean, David, 272

McGonigal, Aoife, 128
McGrath, Jill, 247
McGrath, Tom, 117
McGuire Turner, Josh, 257
McGurn, Edward, 206
McHugh, Peter, 246
McInnes, Campbell, 158
McIntyre, Angela, 137
McKay, Douglas, 206
McKelheer, Joseph, 130
McKeown, Allan, 66
McLaughlin, Josh, 133
McLeroy, Val, 125
McMinn, Robert, 169
McNall, Bruce, 68
McNamara, James, 202
McNeill, Katie, 120
McQuarn, Michael, 59
McVicar, Cherise, 90
Mechanic, Bill, 201
Medjuck, Joe, 188
Medwid, Lisa, 163
Mehlitz, Marco, 135
Mehlitz, Marco, 169
Meidel, Greg, 256
Meier, Seth William, 91
Meisinger, Robyn, 176
Melamede, Yael, 224
Meledandri, Christopher, 155
Melnick, Jeff, 120
Meltzer, Maxwell, 269
Meltzer, Howard, 255
Mencer, Ron, 254
Menchel, Michael J., 257
Mendelsohn, Michael, 205
Mercer, Tracy, 219
Mercer, William, 242
Merlob, Michael, 54
Meron, Neil, 239
Merritt, Madison, 161
Messina, Michael, 192
Metzger, Tory, 171
Meyboon, Jan Peter, 229
Meyer, Ron, 259
Meyer, Nicholas, 230
Meyer, Sophie, 118
Meyer, Barry, 266
Meyer, Sarah, 232
Miano, Andrew, 112
Michael, Emanuel, 258
Michael, Terence, 52

Michaels, John, 70
Middlemas, Rick, 131
Middlemas, Morgan, 131
Migliavacca, Luciana, 183
Mihailovich, Vera, 134
Mikutowicz, Mark, 230
Milam, Matthew, 233
Milano, Alyssa, 206
Milchan, Arnon, 193
Millar, Miles, 185
Millbern, David, 217
Miller, Mark, 227
Miller, Craig, 274
Miller, Chris, 132
Miller, Jimmy, 189
Miller, Richard, 148
Miller, Warren, 268
Miller, Troy, 107
Miller, Jeffrey, 167
Mills, Josh, 113
Milton, Merideth, 240
Mimran, David, 186
Minghella, Hannah, 101
Mirosevic, Chris, 158
Misher, Kevin, 186
Missel, Renee, 218
Mitchell, Shuaib, 195
Mitchell, Jonathan, 65
Mitchell, Tyler, 169
Mittman, Andrew, 82
Mok, Ken, 52
Moll, James, 66
Monahan, William, 153
Moncrief, Andrew, 188
Mond, Josh, 87
Montanio, Ben, 220
Moody, Thomas, 62
Moore, Bryan, 134
Moore, Joanne, 264
Moore, Chris, 153
Moore, Matt, 55
Moore, Jeffrey, 268
Moore, Caroline, 109
Moos, Adam, 101
Moosa, Corey, 80
Moran, Patrick, 60
Moreland, Robert, 261
Morelli, Paulo, 196
Morewitz, A.J., 135
Morri, Kirk, 192
Morris, Jim, 207

Morrisesy, Michael, 88
Morton, Jeff, 162
Morton, Nick, 271
M. Osborne, Barrie, 123
Moses, Kim, 225
Moses, Lynne, 73
Moses, Ben, 72
Moses, Patrick, 198
Mostow, Jonathan, 278
Mower, Mark, 189
M Penotti, John, 147
M. Srtner, Robert, 265
Mueller, Benito, 78
Mullen, Kelly, 148
Mullen, Sean, 131
Munsch, Lauren, 79
Murata, Todd, 90
Murphy, Sara, 103
Murphy, Katie, 234
Murphy, Ryan, 223
Murray, Jonathan, 90
Mutchnick, Max, 168
Mutrux, Gail, 211
M. Wood, Jenny, 122
Nader, Louis, 253
Nardelli, Michael, 242
Nathan-Kazis, Saul, 162
Nathanson, Michael, 197
Navarro, Guillermo, 186
Nayar, Deepak, 167
Neal, Cory, 73
Neal, Larissa, 161
Nelson, Lee, 124
Nemeroff, Terry, 279
Nemeth, Stephen, 219
Nemoy, Carole, 106
Nesbitt, Nicholas, 86
Netter, Gil, 141
Netter, Jason, 167
Neuhaus, Adam, 213
Newman, Michael R., 222
Newman, Greg, 110
Newman, Gary, 256
Newman, Eric, 239
Newman, Vincent, 264
Newman, Joshua, 107
Niblo, Allan, 263
Nicholson, Mark, 239
Nicholson-Salke, Jennifer, 191
Nicklaus, Kevin, 250
Nield, Rebecca, 89

Nieves Gordon, Jennifer, 88
Nishioka, Melinda, 160
Noble, Dale, 154
Norkin, Susan, 167
Norton, Emma, 121
Norton, Edward, 99
Norton, Deborah, 256
Norwicki, Stefan, 240
Nozemack, Joe, 100
Nunnari, Gianni, 154
Nutter, David, 140
Nyberg, Tracy, 244
Oakes, Jon, 87
Oakes, Simon, 149
Obst, Lynda, 175
Ocean Hall, Colleen, 198
Ockman, Aaron, 192
O'Connor, Rachel, 101
O'Connor, Mark, 146
Odell, Ben, 202
Oglesby, Marsha, 89
O'Hara, Robin, 133
O'Keefe, Terence, 261
Oldman, Gary, 227
Oliver, Brian, 105
Olmos, Edward, 196
Olschan, Rachel, 121
Olsen, Mark, 165
Olsson Shear, Samantha, 167
Oppenheim, Daniel, 273
Oppenheim, A.D., 273
Oppenheimer, Joe, 79
Orci, Roberto, 168
Orlovsky, Alex, 262
Orlovsky, Alex, 74
Ormond, Julia, 157
Ornston, David E., 224
Osbrink, Chris, 91
Osowski, Pamela, 275
Ostroff, Daniel, 108
Ott, Alex, 104
Oxley, Simon, 183
Palermo, John, 200
Palmer, Amanda, 265
Palmer, Linda, 223
Panay, Andrew, 201
Panitch, Sanford, 135
Paolo Zerilli, Pier, 183
Papadopoulos, Phaedon, 262
Papandrea, Bruna, 200
Papavasiliou, Chris, 203

Paquette, Eric, 227
Parcero, Charmaine, 60
Parker, Christopher, 204
Parker, Hutch, 154
Parker, Gregory, 204
Parker, Jennifer, 94
Parker, Sarah, 211
Parkes, Walter, 204
Parry, Heather, 150
Pascal, Amy, 101
Patel, Palak, 223
Paternot, Stephan, 201
Patricof, Jamie, 120
Paul, Steven, 106
Paulson, Daniel, 108
Paulson Weber, Lindsey, 77
Paura, Catherine, 128
Payne, Judd, 272
Payne, Alexander, 61
Pearl, Steven, 225
Pecorin, Clay, 257
Penn, Zak, 278
Pennell, Mark, 80
Perini, Jennifer, 126
Perkins, Bill, 174
Perkins, Keith, 174
Permut, David, 206
Perr, Jason, 60
Perrin, Jacques, 139
Perrone, Sean, 165
Persitz, Daniel, 151
Pestano, Meryl, 114
Peters, Josh, 130
Peters, David, 188
Petersen, William, 153
Peterson, Christy, 106
Peterson, Clark, 239
Petrie, Dorothea, 116
Petrie, June, 116
Petrie,, Daniel, 108
Petrocelli, Patrick, 165
Pettit, Lauren, 186
Peyron, Nils, 85
Phelan, Shauna, 262
Phillips, Todd, 147
Phillips, Alissa, 184
Phok, Peter, 143
Piché, Billy, 53
Pierson, Joseph, 107
Pilcher, Lydia, 98
Piller, Shawn, 207

Pincus, Josh, 85
Pinkney, Rose Catherine, 255
Pinvidic, Brandt, 56
Pirie, Iain, 53
Pitt, Brad, 208
Pitt, Lou, 249
Plapinger, Alex, 188
Platt, Marc, 179
Platt, Dave, 70
Polhemus, Jib, 232
Polis, Michael, 273
Pollak, Jay, 77
Pollock, Tom, 188
Pollok, Stuart, 158
Pollok, Stuart, 224
Polone, Gavin, 204
Polsky, Alan, 209
Polsky, Gabe, 209
Polstein, Claire, 164
Polvino, Marisa, 239
Pope, Jennifer, 62
Pope, Katherine, 95
Pope, David, 108
Porter, Darryl, 209
Portillo, Ralph E., 152
Portman, Natalie, 150
Portnoy, John, 260
Postlewaite, Ashley, 218
Poul, Alan, 87
Powell, Crystal, 120
Pozo, Santiago, 73
Presburger, Paul, 202
Presley, Brain, 136
Press, Terry, 94
Pressman, Edward, 119
Preston, Rupert, 263
Preston Bosari, Jennifer, 172
Priess, Don, 143
Principato, Peter, 211
Prior, Rachael, 83
Prisand, Scott, 103
Pritchard, Robert, 184
Pritzker, Gigi, 196
Prokop, Paul, 79
Pugliese, Charles, 110
Purcell, David, 235
Purple, Michelle, 160
Putman, Fred, 111
Putman, Ross, 158
Putney, Troy, 80
Quinto, Zachary, 80

Quirk, Bradley, 205
Quod, Mark, 245
Rack, Will, 53
Rader, Rhoades, 152
Radmin, Linne, 249
Raffe, Alex, 251
Raimi, Sam, 218
Raimi, Sam, 90
Raimi, Sam, 141
Rajski, Peggy, 206
Ramey, Sarah, 119
Randall, Gary, 146
Rapke, Jack, 156
Rappaport, Daniel, 129
Rasberry, Amber, 55
Ratner, Brett, 214
Rattray, Celine, 181
Rawlings, Marshall, 68
Raymond, Patrick, 171
Rayne, Allison, 54
Reading, Austin, 174
Reading, Julie, 174
Ready, David, 113
Redfearn, Catherine, 272
Redford, Robert, 272
Redlin, Christine, 113
Reed, Patricia, 222
Register, Sam, 266
Reich, Allon, 115
Reiner, Sarah, 192
Reiner, Rob, 93
Reiner, Rob, 217
Reitman, Ivan, 188
Rembert, Grey, 166
Reses, Jacqueline, 277
Reymann, Michael, 143
Reynolds, Matthew, 93
Rhimes, Shonda, 229
Rhodehamel, Angela, 59
Rhodes, Jessica, 85
Rice, Cindi, 125
Rich, Richard, 104
Richards, Steve, 109
Richardson, James, 263
Richardson, Mike, 110
Riche, Peter, 220
Riche, Alan, 220
Richey, Cooper, 174
Richman, Adam, 116
Rifkin, Arnold, 96
Rigberg, Glenn, 159

Rinehart, Steven, 126
Rini, Christmas, 75
Rionda Del Castro, Richard, 150
Rionda Del Castro, Patricia, 150
Rios, Tiana, 195
Ripp, Adam, 105
Risher, Sara, 96
Rivele, Stephen J., 71
Rizor, Joel, 226
Rizzotti, Patrick, 134
Roach, Jay, 126
Robbins, Isen, 215
Roberts, Julia, 216
Roberts, Mark, 55
Roberts, J.B., 242
Roberts, Mark, 221
Robertson, Amy, 245
Robertson, John, 231
Robertson, Phil, 279
Robin, Michael, 229
Robinov, Jeff, 267
Robinson, Dave, 121
Robinson, Scott, 136
Robinson, Doug, 150
Robinson, Danielle, 140
Robinson, Marcello, 58
Robinson, Jacob, 112
Robinson, Sanders, 274
Rock, Bobby, 118
Rogow, Stan, 121
Roiff, Michael, 194
Roker, Al, 67
Romano, Anthony, 149
Roman-Rockhold, Laura, 132
Romero, Richard, 161
Rona, Andrew, 109
Roodman, Joel, 145
Roos, Fred, 138
Rose, Alexandra, 66
Rose, Philip, 216
Rose, Jacobus, 234
Rosenberg, Tom, 169
Rosenberg, Billy, 53
Rosenberg, Jacob, 78
Rosenberg, Michael, 124
Rosenblatt, Bart, 100
Rosenblum, Bruce, 266
Rosenblum, John, 125
Rosenbush, Barry, 243
Rosenfelt, Karen, 241
Rosenthal, Rick, 271

Rosenthal, Jane, 253
Roskin, Marc, 121
Ross, Mark, 94
Ross, Damon, 117
Rossel, Alec, 214
Roston, Sam, 157
Roth, Joe, 223
Roth, J.D., 56
Roth, Wendy, 160
Roth, Peter, 267
Rothman, Noah, 257
Rowan, Kelly, 101
Rowinski, Lisbeth, 127
Rowley, Joshua, 96
R. Rosenzweig, Alison, 139
Rubinstein, Richard, 192
Ruddy, Albert, 99
Rudin, Scott, 226
Ruffman, Paul Michael, 258
Ruskin, Morris, 230
Russell, Dylan, 238
Rutare, Micho, 245
Ryan, Ann, 140
Ryan, Barry, 268
Ryan, Shawn, 185
Ryan, Daniela, 78
Saab, Sam, 128
Saavedra, Craig, 237
Sabatine, Teresa, 147
Sacks, David O., 222
Sacks, Alan, 65
Saffer, Wendy, 228
Saffran, Michael, 198
Saffran, Michael, 161
Safran, Peter, 249
Safran, Keri, 198
Sakai, Richard, 145
Salas, Rossana, 140
Salas, Carlos, 140
Salciccioli, Nate, 112
Salsano, SallyAnn, 56
Salvatore, Richard, 224
Samuelson, Marc, 224
Samuelson, Peter, 224
Sánchez, Eduardo, 151
Sanchini, Rae, 173
Sander, Ian, 225
Sanders, Scott, 226
Sandler, Adam, 150
Sanitsky, Larry, 225
Saria, Sudhanshu, 205

Sarkar, Sam, 159
Satchu, Asif, 182
Satre-Meloy, Liam, 209
Saunder, David, 151
Savage, Stephanie, 128
Savage, Stephanie, 128
Savitch, Annette, 150
Savjani, Anish, 131
Saxon, Ed, 119
Sayler, Joeanna, 80
Schaeffer, Paul, 177
Schamus, James, 133
Scharbo, Grant, 174
Schechter, Dan, 218
Schechter-Garcia, Ivana, 95
Scheinkman, Dan, 247
Scheinman, Andrew, 93
Scherma, Frank, 212
Schiff, Devon, 187
Schlamme, Thomas, 229
Schlessel, Peter, 130
Schmidt, Aaron, 170
Schmidt, Tore, 211
Schneeweiss, Barbara, 250
Schneider, Steven, 222
Schnider, Daniel, 105
Schoof, Aimee, 215
Schorr, Robin, 214
Schrader, Wes, 107
Schreiber, Michael, 243
Schreiber, Nina, 242
Schumacher, Jon, 54
Schumacher, Joel, 163
Schur, Jordan, 186
Schwartz, Paula Mae, 96
Schwartz, Loren, 226
Schwartz, Lizzie, 189
Schwartz, Richard, 196
Schwartz, Robert, 227
Schwartz, Roger, 96
Schwartz, Steve, 96
Schwartz, Rick, 200
Schwartz, Jonathan, 241
Schwartz, John, 212
Schwarzman, Teddy, 84
Schwatz, Josh, 128
Sciavicco, Jason, 154
Scorsese, Martin, 231
Scott, Nicholas, 57
Scott, Andy, 94
Scott, Ridley, 226

Seagal, Steven, 237
Segal, Peter, 91
Segan, Lloyd, 207
Seifert-Speck, Anna, 123
Selbert, Fred, 136
Selby, Jack, 157
Seyyid, Jubba, 255
Shader, Josh, 244
Shaffner, Tyrrell, 137
Shah, Ash, 232
Shah, Anand, 129
Shainberg, Steven, 265
Shamberg, Michael, 115
Shane, Michel, 149
Shankman, Adam, 196
Shapiro, Leonard, 118
Shapiro, James Emanuel, 64
Share, Jillan, 172
Sharma, Neetu, 261
Shaw, Tony, 93
Shawkat, Tony, 78
Sheehan, Vincent, 209
Sheehan, Anita, 209
Sheehan, Trace, 210
Sheehy, Ginger, 268
Shenkler, Craig, 237
Shepard, Sarah, 269
Shephard, Greer, 229
Shepherd, Scott, 207
Shepherd, John, 105
Sheppard, Janet, 203
Sher, Stacey, 115
Sherman, Sidney, 222
Shestack, Jonathan, 164
Shetty, Pavun, 95
Shieh, Aimee, 132
Shikiar, Dave, 226
Shore, Martin, 235
Short, Trevor, 185
Shub, Alex, 94
Shukla, Ameet, 115
Shulman, Michael, 237
Shultz, Steven, 62
Siebel, Jennifer, 142
Siegal, Rebecca, 234
Siegel, Alan, 140
Siegel, Adam, 179
Sighvatsson, Joni, 201
Signer, Matthew, 114
Silver, Joel, 109
Silver, Jeffrey, 84

Silver, Joel, 232
Silver, Casey, 93
SIlver, Nikki, 252
Silverberg, Evan, 258
Silverman, Greg, 267
Silvers, Tracey, 231
Simon, Chuck, 236
Simon, Andrea, 70
Simonds, Robert, 222
Simons, Ron, 232
Simpson, Joe, 202
Sinclair, Nigel, 236
Sinclair, Nigel, 126
Singer, Bryan, 76
Singleton, Joan, 59
Singleton, Ralph, 59
Sinovoi, Maxwell, 233
Sirkis, Steve, 57
Skapars, Tom, 220
Skiena, Matt, 263
Skinner, David, 228
Skodras, Jimmy, 156
Skouras, Marielle, 75
Skura, Chris, 275
Sladek, Daniel, 108
Sladek, Tom, 199
Sloane, Lindsay, 155
Small, Allison, 203
Smiley, Stu, 102
Smith, James, 118
Smith, Sara, 248
Smith, Russell, 190
Smith, Jonah, 251
Smith, Molly, 54
Smith, Ben, 93
Smith, Arthur, 75
Smith, Will, 199
Smith, Paul, 94
Smith, Lucas, 124
Smithson, Carol, 227
Snyder, Robyn, 180
Soisson, Joel, 192
Sola, Juan, 197
Solomon, Susan, 211
Sonnier, Dallas, 91
Sorrentino, Scott, 208
Sosnoff, Jason, 77
Spade, Christina, 230
Sparks, Jewell, 271
Spaulding, Andrew, 118
Spellman, Andy, 74

Spencer, Jim, 263
Sperling, Andrea, 241
Sperry, Stephane, 173
Spevak, Albert, 68
Spielberg, Steven, 68
Spielberg, Steven, 117
Spigel, Arthur, 74
Spigel, Artur, 58
Spink, J.C., 82
Sprecher, Samantha, 127
Spring, James, 118
Spry, Stan, 217
Spurlock, Morgan, 268
Staman, Jessica, 118
Stamos, John, 236
Stanford, Halle, 248
Star, Darren, 110
Stark, Austin, 202
Starke, David A, 256
Starkey, Steve, 155
Starrett, J.W., 67
Startz, Jane, 161
St. Clair, Beau, 160
Stearn, Andrew, 164
Steiger, Jett, 244
Stein, Bob, 213
Stein, Robert, 254
Steindorff, Scott, 238
Steingart, Jon, 74
Stempel, Jennifer, 165
Stenson, Mike, 162
Stepanek, Sheila, 205
Stephens, Norman, 228
Stephenson, Marc, 229
Sterling, Danielle, 210
Stern, Jay, 223
Stern, James, 124
Stern, Sandy, 233
Sterns, David, 168
Stewart, Jennifer, 92
Stiller, Ben, 216
Stillman, Ben, 84
Stipe, Michael, 233
Stoff, Erwin, 55
Stone, Scott G., 157
Stone, Bridget, 218
Stone, Scott, 238
Stonebraker, Lori, 205
Storm, Christina Lee, 60
Stratton, Dene, 184
Strauss, Scott, 226

Stroh, Shahar, 188
Stuber, Scott, 85
Studin, Zachary, 171
Styler, Trudie, 181
Styler, Trudie, 276
Suits, John, 192
Sullenger, Betsy, 198
Sullivan, Timothy, 280
Sumner, Anita, 181
Sumner, Anita, 277
Supnik, Debbie, 270
Swetnam, John, 176
Symons, Sam, 93
Szew, Fernando, 180
Tabarrok, Nicholas, 109
Tang, Michael, 172
Tannenbaum, Eric, 243
Tapert, Robert, 218
Tarpinian, Gary, 189
Tauber, Jim, 230
Tavel, Connie, 134
Taylor, Camille, 105
Taylor, Gregg, 116
Taylor, Grazka, 146
Taylor, Michael, 184
Teitel, Robert, 237
Tenenbaum, Nancy, 191
Tennenbaum, Andrew, 132
Testerman, Isaac, 112
Thai, Thyrale, 197
Thomas, Jeremy, 215
Thomas, Rhodri, 159
Thomas, Nigel, 181
Thomas, Tony, 273
Thomas, Kelly, 187
Thompson, Virginia, 262
Thompson, Barnaby, 118
Thompson, John, 195
Thompson, April Yvette, 232
Thompson, Alfred Rubin, 57
Thorton, Kayla, 205
Thrasher, Lisa, 210
Tiddes, Mike, 268
Tillman, Jr., George, 237
Timmons, Whitney, 182
Tirola, Douglas, 56
Tisch, Steve, 126
Tisch, Steve, 249
Tischler-Blue, Victory, 224
Tisdale, Ashley, 85
Tisdale, Jennifer, 85

Tish, David, 125
Tobin, John, 123
Todd, Norman, 158
Todd, Suzanne, 244
Toffler, Van, 263
Tolan, Peter, 129
Tomita, Sandra, 246
Tonino, Robert, 187
Topping, Jenno, 95
Tornell, Lisa, 253
Toukan, Ali, 206
Tovell, Eric, 265
Trotiner, Glen, 91
Trowbridge, Chelsey, 199
Truesdell, Ember, 132
Tryon, Sol, 178
Tseng, Mimi, 193
Ts'o, Pauline, 220
Tsujihara, Kevin, 267
Tucker, Matt, 205
Tull, Thomas, 172
Turner, Evan, 265
Turner, Bryan, 183
Tyree, Michael, 209
Ufland, Mary Jane, 257
Ufland, Harry, 257
Ullmann, Lisa, 273
Ungar, Gary, 127
Unterman, Zac, 234
Urbanski, Douglas, 227
Urdang, Leslie, 197
Urrutia, David, 126
Vachon, Christine, 167
Vahradian, Mark, 113
Vaisman, Eddie, 55
Valente, Renee, 218
Van Citters, Darrell, 218
VanCleave, Darren, 149
van den Houten, Andrew, 187
VanDerKloot, William, 261
Van Steemberg, Peter, 177
Van Vliet, Michael, 251
Vatan, Roxana, 217
Ventura, Josie, 191
Verbinski, Gore, 85
Vertue, Beryl, 151
Vertue, Sue, 151
Vertue, Debbie, 151
Vicente, Joana, 198
Victor, Mark, 179
Vignola, Charlie, 162

Vincent, Samantha, 197
Vinson, Tripp, 103
Viola, Mary, 274
von Trier, Lars, 279
Von Zerneck, Frank, 265
Voorhees, Tucker, 211
Wachsberger, Patrick, 240
Wade, Todd, 223
Wadlow, Jeff, 253
Wagner, Paula, 95
Wagner, Adam, 61
Wagner, Todd, 54
Walden, Dana, 256
Waldron, Michael, 107
Walker, Jeremy Kipp, 269
Walton, Trevor, 92
Waltrip, Kim, 167
Wang, Edward, 142
Wang, Jason, 243
Ward, Ron, 184
Ward, Jeffrey James, 113
Warner, Cass, 267
Warren, Suzanne, 201
Watson, Luke, 190
Watson, Peter, 215
Watson, John, 254
Watts, Emma, 256
Watts, Liz, 209
Waugh, Scott, 77
Wayans, Keenan, 268
Wayans, Marlon, 269
Wayans, Shawn, 269
W. Balsiger, David, 147
Weathersby, Nadine, 175
Weathersby, Joshua, 175
Weathersby, Cassius, 175
Weaver, Matthew, 103
Weaver, Brooklyn, 124
Webb, Scott, 276
Weber, Benjamin, 240
Wechsler, Nick, 194
Wedge, Chris, 86
Wee, Billy, 150
Wegner, Steven, 65
Weiant, Ted, 111
Weide, Robert, 271
Weinberg, Jason, 260
Weinberg, Michael, 123
Weiner, Shay, 54
Weiner, Jeffrey, 93
Weinstein, Bob, 114

Weinstein, Bob, 250
Weinstein, Harvey, 250
Weinstock, Charles, 269
Weintraub, Jerry, 162
Weintraub, David, 238
Weintraub, Jackie, 270
Weintraub, Fred, 269
Weiss, Bruce, 160
Weistein, Larry, 219
Weitz, Chris, 112
Weller, Robb, 270
Weller, Wendy, 117
Welling, Tom, 252
Wells, John, 164
Welsh, Berry, 253
Werber, Clifford, 99
Werdin, Russell, 257
Werner, Tom, 144
Wertlieb, Stan, 147
Wessler, Charles B., 270
West, Ron, 242
West, Simon, 232
West, Palmer, 251
Weston, Ann, 148
Whedon, Joss, 81
Wheeler, Kris, 238
White, Morgan, 91
White, Marla A., 129
White, Courtney, 153
Whitehill, Sally, 260
Wick, Douglas, 216
Wickham, Athena, 77
Wiczyk, Modi, 182
Wieneke, Todd, 110
Wigram, Lionel, 271
Wigutow, Dan, 109
Wike, Jeffrey, 117
Wilcox, Stephanie, 87
WIlkes, Justin, 213
Wilkinson, Christopher, 71
Williams, Steven, 93
Williams, Brittany, 183
Williams, Tucker, 103
Williams, Matt, 272
Williams, Mark, 207
Williams, Debbie, 123
Williams, Janice, 148
Williams, Pamela, 170
Williams, Mike, 120
Williams, Ryan, 261
Williams, John, 261

Williamson, Shawn, 89
Williamson, Kevin, 199
Willingham, Kathryn, 162
Wilson, Kim, 92
Wilson, Brad, 152
Wilson, Don, 144
Wilson, Michael, 108
Wimer, Michael, 129
Winer, Harry, 234
Winfrey, Oprah, 150
Winfrey, Oprah, 200
Winikoff, Cami, 235
Winkler, Irwin, 272
Winkler, Charles, 273
Winkler, David, 272
Winslow Wehrenfennig, Seanne, 173
Winstone, Simon, 216
Winter, Ralph, 52
Winterbottom, Michael, 219
Wise, Robert, 57
Wiseman, Len, 233
Wishman, Seymour, 131

Witherspoon, Reese, 200
Witt, Paul, 273
Woertz, Gregory, 194
Wolf, Dick, 273
Wolfe, Steven, 235
Wolfman, Marv, 274
Wolper, Mark, 250
Wong, Max, 207
Wood, Patrick, 207
Woodrow, Christopher, 275
Worthen Brooks, David, 135
Wright, Richard, 169
Wright, Michelle, 274
Wuerfel, Ryan, 77
W. Walker, Robert, 266
Wyman, Brad, 164
Yan, Luo, 231
Yang, Janet, 179
Yang, Emmeline, 72
Yari, Bob, 277
Yarincik, John, 118
Yeldham, Rebecca, 63
Yellen, Mark, 180

Yorn, Rick, 188
Young, Jill, 248
Young, Clayton, 81
Young, Jim, 71
Zackham, Justin, 257
Zadan, Craig, 239
Zakin, Michael, 70
Zakk, George, 71
Zanuck, Harrison, 250
Zanuck, Lili Fini, 250
Zanuck, Dean, 279
Zappa, Ahmet, 187
Zemeckis, Leslie, 279
Zemeckis, Robert, 155
Zenga, Bo, 88
Ziskin, Andy, 138
Znak, Natalka, 280
Zotnowski, Robert D., 166
Zucker, David, 226
Zucker, Janet, 280
Zucker, Jerry, 280
Zupan, Lisa, 270
Zweibel, Alan, 231

Index by Submission Policy

Accepts query letter from produced or represented writers

3311 Productions, 55
Aldamisa Films, 65
Atlas Media Corporation, 75
Bayonne Entertainment, 79
Beth Grossbard Productions, 83
Clifford Werber Productions, 99
Constantin Film, 102
Darius Films Incorporated, 109
Dark Castle Entertainment, 109
DeerJen Films, 111
Delve Films, 112
Endemol Entertainment, 123
Exclusive Media, 126
Fox Digital Studios, 135
Gigantic Pictures, 141
Grindstone Entertainment Group, 147
Jackhole Productions, 161
Lakeshore Entertainment, 169
Liquid Theory, 174
Mandalay Pictures, 177
Midnight Sun Pictures, 185
Mimran Schur Pictures, 186
Relativity Media, LLC, 217
Renart Films, 218
Roadside Attractions, 220
Salvatore/Ornston Productions, 224
Score Productions, Inc., 225
Submarine Entertainment, 240
TV One LLC, 255
Verisimilitude, 262
W!ldbrain Entertainment, Inc., 273

Accepts query letter from unproduced, unrepresented writers

10 by 10 Entertainment, 52
25/7 Productions, 53
2929 Productions, 54
3 Arts Entertainment, 55
72 Productions, 58
Aberration Films, 60
Act III Productions, 61
Adam Fields Productions, 61
AEI - Atchity Entertainment International, Inc., 62
Ahimsa Films, 63
Airmont Pictures, 64
Alex Rose Productions, 66
Alianza Films International, 66
American Work Inc., 69
Anchor Bay Films, 70
Andrea Simon Entertainment, 70
Animus Films, 71
Argonaut Pictures, 73
Article19 Films, 74
Artists Public Domain, 74
Barnstorm Films, 78
Basra Entertainment, 78
Bauer Martinez Studios, 78
Bee Holder Productions, 80
Belladonna Productions, 81
Berlanti Television, 82
Bix Pix Entertainment, 84
Black Bear Pictures, 84
Black Sheep Entertainment, 84
Blumhouse Productions, 86
Bobker/Krugar Films, 86
Bona Fide Productions, 87
Boz Productions, 88
Brandman Productions, 88
Brooklyn Films, 89
Burleigh Filmworks, 90
Burnside Entertainment, Inc., 91
Caliber Media Company, 91
Chaiken Films, 94
Cinema Ephoch, 97
CineMagic Entertainment, 97
Cinema Libre Studio, 98
Cineville, 98
Circle of Confusion, 98
Class 5 Films, 99
Colleen Camp Productions, 100
Color Force, 100
Colossal Entertainment, 101
Comedy Arts Studios, 102
Completion Films, 102

Concept Entertainment, 102
Content Media Corporation PLC, 102
Contrafilm, 102
Cooper's Town Productions, 103
Crescendo Productions, 104
Crossroads Films, 105
CubeVision, 106
Daniel Ostroff Productions, 108
Daniel Petrie Jr. & Company, 108
Dan Wingutow Productions, 109
Darren Star Productions, 110
David Eick Productions, 111
Desert Wind Films, 113
DMG Entertainment, 114
Dreambridge Films, 116
Electric Dynamite, 120
EM Media, 123
Equilibrium Media Company, 125
E-Squared, 126
Exile Entertainment, 127
Eye on the Ball, 127
Fastback Pictures, 128
FilmNation Entertainment, 130
Film Science, 131
Filmsmith Productions, 131
Floren Shieh Productions, 132
Forest Park Pictures, 133
Fortis Films, 134
Frelaine, 136
Fried Films, 137
Friendly Films, 137
Front Street Pictures, 137
Fun Little Films, 138
Furthur Films, 138
Fusion Films, 139
Gaeta Rosenzweig Films, 139
George Litto Productions, 140
Gittes, Inc., 142
Goldsmith-Thomas Productions, 144
Good Humor Television, 144
Gray Angel Productions, 146
Hasbro, Inc./Hasbro Films, 151
Haxan Films, 151
HDNet Films, 152
Hemisphere Entertainment, 152
High Horse Films, 153
High Integrity Productions, 153
Horizon Entertainment, 154
Indie Genius Productions, 157
Jane Startz Productions, 161
Jean Doumanian Productions, 161

Jerry Bruckheimer Films, 162
Jersey Films, 162
John Wells Productions, 163
Junction Films, 164
Juniper Place Productions, 164
Kassen Brothers Productions, 165
Killer Films, 167
Kim and Jim Productions, 167
Kintop Pictures, 167
Krasnoff Foster Entertainment, 168
Landscape Entertainment, 169
Laura Ziskin Productions, 170
Laurence Mark Productions, 170
Lawrence Bender Productions, 171
Little Engine, 174
Lleju Productions, 174
Madrik Multimedia, 176
Mandy Films, 178
Manifest Film Company, 178
Maple Shade Films, 179
Marc Platt Productions, 179
MBST Entertainment, 182
Media Talent Group, 182
Midd Kidd Productions, 185
Mike Lobell Productions, 185
Millar/Gough Ink, 185
Mojo Films, 187
Monsterfoot Productions, 187
Montecito Pictures, 188
Montone/Yorn (Unnamed Yorn Production
    Company), 188
Morgan Creek Productions, 188
Mosaic/ Mosaic Media Group, 189
New School Media, LLC, 193
Nubia Filmworks LLC, 195
Oops Doughnuts Productions, 197
Original Film, 198
O'Taye Productions, 199
Overbrook Entertainment, 199
Palermo Productions, 200
Parkes/MacDonald Productions, 204
Permut Presentations, 206
Piller/Segan/Shepherd, 207
Pipeline Entertainment Inc., 207
Platform Entertainment, 208
Pretty Matches Productions, 210
Principato-Young Entertainment, 211
Random House Studio, 214
Rat Entertainment, 214
RCR Pictures, 214
Red Hen Productions, 216

Reiner/Greisman, 217
Remember Dreaming, LLC, 217
Renaissance Pictures, 218
Riche Productions, 220
Robert Cort Productions, 221
Robert Lawrence Productions, 221
Room 101, Inc., 222
Roth Films, 222
Scott Rudin Productions, 226
Scott Sanders Productions, 226
Screen Door Entertainment, 226
SE8 Group, 227
Shaun Cassidy Productions, 229
Silver Pictures, 232
Simon West Productions, 232
Simsie Films/ Media Savant Pictures, 232
Singe Cell Pictures, 232
Sky One, 234
Steven Bochco Productions, 237
Tamara Asseyev Production, 242
T&C Pictures, 243
The Gold Company, 246
The Goodman Company, 246
The Pitt Group, 248
The Steve Tisch Company, 249
Tornell Productions, 252
Turtleback Productions, Inc., 255
Twisted Pictures, 257
Unified Pictures, 258
Universal Cable Productions, 259
Universal Studios, 259
Universal Television, 259
Untitled Entertainment, 260
Varsity Pictures, 262
Velocity Pictures, 262
Vérité Films, 262
VH1, 263
Vin di Bona Productions, 264
Warren Miller Entertainment, 268
Weinstock Productions, 269
Wessler Entertainment, 270
Wigram Productions, 271
Winkler Films, 272
World Film Services, Inc., 275
Yahoo!, 277
Zachary Feuer Films, 278
Zanuck Independent, 278
Zieger Productions, 279
Zucker Productions, 280

Accepts query letter from unproduced, unrepresented writers via email

100% Entertainment, 52
100% Terrycloth, 52
1821 Pictures, 53
26 Films, 54
3 Ball Productions, 55
51 Minds Entertainment, 57
5ive Smooth Stones Productions, 57
72nd Street Productions, 57
777 Group, 58
8790 Pictures, Inc., 58
8th Wonder Entertainment, 59
900 Films, 59
9.14 Pictures, 59
Acappella Pictures, 60
Accelerated Entertainment LLC, 60
A.C. Lyles Productions, Inc., 61
Agamemnon Films, 63
Agility Studios, 63
Ahimsa Media, 63
Alexander/Mitchell Productions, 65
Allan McKeown Presents, 66
Alloy Entertainment, 67
American Moving Pictures, 69
Angelworld Entertainment Ltd., 70
Anonymous Content, 71
Arclight Films, 73
A. Smith & Company Productions, 75
Automatic Pictures, 76
BCDF Pictures, 79
Bellwether Pictures, 81
Benaroya Pictures, 81
Bernero Productions, 82
Big Foot Entertainment, Ltd., 83
Bleiberg Entertainment, 85
Boy Wonder Productions, 88
Broken Camera Productions, 89
Capital Arts Entertainment, 92
Chockstone Pictures, 96
Clear Pictures Entertainment, 99
Creanspeak Productions, LLC, 104
Crest Animation Productions, Inc., 104
Cross Creek Pictures, 105
Crystal Lake Entertainment, Inc., 105
Crystal Sky Pictures, LLC, 105
Curb Entertainment, 106
Cyan Pictures, 106
Cypress Films, Inc., 107

Cypress Point Productions, 107
Dan Lupovitz Productions, 108
Dave Bell Associates, 110
Deed Films, 111
Defiance Entertainment, 111
Double Nickel Entertainment, 115
D. Petrie Productions, Inc., 116
Duplass Brothers Productions, 117
Eclectic Pictures, 118
Edward Saxon Productions, 119
Efish Entertainment, Inc., 119
Electric City Entertainment, 120
Electric Farm Entertainment, 121
Electric Shepherd Productions, LLC, 121
Elevate Entertainment, 122
Elkins Entertainment, 122
Ember Entertainment Group, 122
Envision Media Arts, 124
Epic Level Entertainment, LTD., 125
Epigram Entertainment, 125
Epiphany Pictures, Inc., 125
Farrell Paura Productions, 128
Five By Eight Productions, 131
Flavor Unit Entertainment, 132
Forensic Films, 133
Foresight Unlimited, 133
Forget Me Not Productions, 133
Forward Entertainment, 134
Frederator Studios, 135
Fred Kuenert Productions, 136
FR Productions, 137
Furst Films, 138
Galatee Films, 139
Gallant Entertainment, 139
Gary Hoffman Productions, 139
Genext Films, 140
Genrebend Productions, 140
Gilbert Films, 141
Gitlin Productions, 142
Glass Eye Pix, 142
Goff-Kellam Productions, 143
Go Girl Media, 143
Goldenring Productions, 144
Gotham Entertainment Group, 144
Grade A Entertainment, 145
Greasy Entertainment, 146
Greenstreet Films, 147
Greentrees Films, 147
Grosso Jacobson Communications Corp., 147
Guardian Entertainment, LTD, 148
H2O Motion Pictures, 149

Hannibal Pictures, 150
Impact Pictures, 156
Indomitable Entertainment, 157
Informant Media, 159
Ironworks Productions, 160
Jet Tone Productions, 163
KGB Films, 166
Kinetic Filmworks, 167
Krofft Pictures, 169
Launchpad Productions, 170
Lee Daniels Entertainment, 172
Londine Productions, 174
Lucky Crow Films, 175
Mad Horse Films, 176
Mandate Pictures, 177
Mark Victor Productions, 179
Mark Yellen Production, 179
Marty Katz Productions, 180
MarVista Entertainment, 180
Mass Hysteria Entertainment, 180
Matador Pictures, 181
Maya Entertainment Group, 181
Merchant Ivory Productions, 183
Michael Grais Productions, 184
Michael Taylor Productions, 184
Millennium Films, 185
Mockingbird Pictures, 186
Momentum Entertainment Group, 187
Montage Entertainment, 187
Moonstone Entertainment, 188
Morningstar Entertainment, 188
Moshag Productions, 189
Nancy Tenenbaum Films, 190
Neo Art & Logic, 192
New Artists Alliance, 192
New Crime Productions, 192
Night and Day Pictures, 194
Olympus Pictures, 197
Ombra Films, 197
One Race Films, 197
Open City Films, 198
Outerbank Entertainment, 199
Out of the Blue Entertainment, 199
Pandemonium, 201
Papa Joe Entertainment, 202
Paradigm Studio, 203
Parkway Productions, 204
Pathe Pictures, 205
Patriot Pictures, 205
Peace By Peace Productions, 205
Phoenix Pictures, 206

POW! Entertainment, 209
Power Up, 210
Prospect Park, 211
Pure Grass Films, LTD., 211
Quadrant Pictures, 212
Rainbow Film Company/ Rainbow Releasing, 213
Rainmaker Films Inc., 213
Rainstorm Entertainment, INC., 213
Redfield Productions, 215
Regent Entertainment, 217
Rehab Entertainment, 217
Renee Missel Management, 218
Renee Valente Productions, 218
Renegade Animation, Inc., 218
Rhino Films, 219
Rice & Beans Productions, 220
Rubicon Entertainment, 223
Salty Features, 224
Sander/Moses Productions, 225
Shadowcatcher Entertainment, 228
Shoe Money Productions, 229
Silly Robin Productions, 231
Silver Dream Productions, 231
Silver/Koster Productions, 231
Sinovoi Entertainment, 233
Smart Entertainment, 234
Smash Media Films, 234
Sneak Preview Entertainment, 234
Solipsist Films, 235
St. Amos Productions, 236
Starry Night Entertainment, 236
Steamroller Productions, Inc., 237
Stefanie Epstein Productions, 237
Stokely Chaffin Productions, 238
StoneBrook Entertainment, 238
Stone & Company Entertainment, 238
Story and Film, 238
Strike Entertainment, 239
Such Much Films, 240
SuperFinger Entertainment, 241
Taurus Entertainment Company, 243
Terra Firma Films, 244
The American Film Company, 244
The Goldstein Company, 246
The Greenberg Group, 246
The Hal Lieberman Company, 247
The Hecht Company, 247
The Radmin Company, 249
Thousand Words, 250
Tonik Productions, 252
Tool of North America, 252
Tower of Babble Entertainment, 253
TV Land, 255
T.V. Repair, 255
Two Ton Films, 257
Vanguard Productions, 261
Vanquish Motion Pictures, 261
Vincent Newman Entertainment, 263
Vulcan Productions, 265
Walden Media, 265
Walker/Fitzgibbon TV & Film Production, 265
Warp Films, 267
Wendy Finerman Productions, 270
Wolfmill Entertainment, 274
York Square Productions, 278
Zephyr Films, 279
Zodiak USA, 280

Accepts scripts from produced or represented writers

Ambush Entertainment, 69
An Olive Branch Productions, Inc., 71
Atmosphere Entertainment MM, LLC, 76
Bad Hat Harry Productions, 76
Birch Tree Entertainment, 83
Blacklight Transmedia, 84
Castle Rock Entertainment, 93
Catapult Films Inc., 93
Celador Entertainment, 94
Centropolis Entertainment, 94
Chartoff Productions, 95
Chernin Entertainment, 95
Cheyenne Enterprises LLC, 95
Chicagofilms, 96
Chickflicks, 96
Chotzen/Jenner Productions, 96
Chris/Rose Productions, 96
Chuck Fries Productions, Inc., 97
Cindy Cowan Entertainment, 97
Cine Mosaic, 98
Cloud Eight Films, 100
CODE Entertainment, 100
Colleton Company, 100
Conundrum Entertainment, 103
Davis Entertainment, 111
Depth of Field, 112
Dinovi Pictures, 114
Edmonds Entertainment, 119
Fake Empire Features, 127
Fake Empire Television, 127

Flower Films Inc., 132
Gross-Weston Productions, 148
Hughes Capital Entertainment, 154
Hutch Parker Entertainment, 154
Industry Entertainment, 158
Jaffe/Braunstein Films, 161
Kaplan/Perrone Entertainment, 165
Larrikin Entertainment, 170
Ninjas Runnin' Wild Productions, 194
Parker Entertainment Group, 204
Recorded Picture Company, 214
Roughhouse, 223
Skydance Productions, 233
Team Todd, 244
The Badham Company, 245
Voltage Productions, 264
Weller/Grossman Productions, 270

Accepts scripts from unproduced, unrepresented writers

59th Street Films, 57
American World Pictures, 69
American Zoetrope, 69
Andrew Lauren Productions, 70
Aperture Entertainment, 72
Ars Nova, 74
Asylum Entertainment, 75
Ballyhoo, Inc., 77
BBC Films, 79
Bogner Entertainment Inc., 86
Camelot Entertainment Group, 91
Dobre Films, 115
Fresh & Smoked, 137
Katalyst Films, 166
Mad Hatter Entertainment, 176
QED International, 212
SimonSays Entertainment, 232
Sogno Productions, 235
Troma Entertainment, 255
TwinStar Entertainment, 256
Unstoppable, 259
Wonderphil Productions, 274
Zentropa Entertainment, 279

Accepts scripts from unproduced, unrepresented writers via email

MasiMedia, 180

Sixth Sense Productions, Inc., 233
Underground Films, 257

Does not accept any unsolicited material

1019 Entertainment, 52
19 Entertainment, 53
21 Laps Entertainment, 53
2S Films, 54
2Waytraffic - A Sony Pictures Entertainment
    Company, 54
34th Street Films, 55
40 Acres & A Mule Filmworks, Inc., 56
44 Blue Productions, Inc., 56
495 Productions, 56
4th Row Films, 56
7ATE9 Entertainment, 58
8:38 Productions, 58
Aardman Animations, 59
Abandon Interactive Entertainment, 60
ABC Studios, 60
Actual Reality Pictures, 61
Adelstein Productions, 61
Ad Hominem Enterprises, 61
Adult Swim, 62
A&E Network, 62
After Dark Films, 62
Aggregate Films, 63
Alamo Drafthouse Films, 64
Alan Barnette Productions, 64
Alan David Management, 64
Alan Sacks Productions, 64
Alchemy Entertainment, 65
Alcon Entertainment, LLC, 65
A-Line Pictures, 66
Allentown Productions, 66
Alliance Films, 67
Aloe Entertainment, 67
Al Roker Productions, 67
Alta Loma Entertainment, 67
Alturas Films, 67
A-Mark Entertainment, 68
Ambassador Entertainment, Inc., 68
Amber Entertainment, 68
Amblin Entertainment, 68
Annapurna Pictures, 71
Antidote Films, 72
Apatow Productions, 72
Appleseed Entertainment, 72

Arenas Entertainment, 73
ArieScope Pictures, 73
Artfire Films, 74
Atlas Entertainment (Production Branch of Mosaic), 75
Bad Robot, 76
Baldwin Entertainment Group, LTD., 77
Baltimore Pictures, 77
Barry Films, 78
Bay Films, 78
Bazelevs Productions, 79
Beacon Pictures, 79
Bedford Falls Company, 80
Before The Door Pictures, 80
Belisarius Productions, 81
Benderspink, 82
Berk/Lane Entertainment, 82
BermanBraun, 82
BET Networks, 83
Big Talk Productions, 83
Biscayne Pictures, 84
BlindWink Productions, 85
Blondie Girl Productions, 85
Bluegrass Films, 85
Blue Print Pictures, 86
Blue Sky Studios, 86
Boku Films, 87
Bold Films, 87
Borderline Films, 87
Boss Media, 87
Boxing Cat Productions, 88
Branded Films, 88
Brightlight Pictures, 88
Bruce Cohen Productions, 89
Buckaroo Entertainment, 89
Buena Vista Home Entertainment, 90
Buena Vista Television, 90
Bunim-Murray Productions, 90
Callahan Filmworks, 91
Canadian Broadcasting Company (CBC), 92
Capacity Pictures, 92
Captivate Entertainment, 92
Carnival Films, 93
Casey Silver Productions, 93
CBS Films, 94
Cherry Sky Films, 95
Chestnut Ridge Productions, 95
ChubbCo Film Co., 97
Cineson Entertainment, 98
CineTelFilms, 98
City Entertainment, 99

Clarity Pictures, LLC, 99
Clearview Productions, 99
Closed On Mondays Entertainment, 100
CodeBlack Entertainment, 100
Columbia Pictures, 101
Coquette Productions, 103
Corner Store Entertainment, 103
Crave Films, 104
Crime Scene Pictures, 104
Crucial Films, 105
Dakota Pictures, 107
Daniel L. Paulson Productions, 107
Daniel Sladek Entertainment Corporation, 108
Danjaq Productions, 108
Dark Horse Entertainment, 109
Darko Entertainment, 110
Dark Sky Films, 110
Darkwoods Productions, 110
De Line Pictures, 112
Demarest Films, 112
Destiny Pictures, 113
Di Bonaventura Pictures, 113
Di Bonaventura Pictures Television, 113
Different Duck Films, 113
Dimension Films, 114
Dino De Laurentiis Company, 114
DNA Films, 115
Donners' Company, 115
Double Feature Films, 115
DreamWorks Animation, 116
DreamWorks Studios, 117
Dune Entertainment, 117
Ealing Studios, 117
Echo Bridge Entertainment, 118
Echo Films, 118
Echo Lake Entertainment, 118
Eden Rock Media, Inc., 119
Edward R. Pressman Film Corporation, 119
Ego Film Arts, 120
Eighth Square Entertainment, 120
Electric Entertainment, 120
Element Pictures, 121
Elephant Eye Films, 121
Elixir Films, 122
Embassy Row, LLC, 122
Emerald City Productions, Inc., 123
Endgame Entertainment, 123
Energy Entertainment, 124
Entertainment One Group, 124
entitled entertainment, 124
Escape Artists, 125

Evenstart Films, 126
Everyman Pictures, 126
Exodus Film Group, 127
Face Productions, 127
Falconer Pictures, 128
Fastnet Films, 128
Fedora Entertainment, 129
Film 360, 129
Film 44, 129
FilmColony, 129
FilmDistrict, 129
Film Harvest, 130
First Run Features, 131
Five Smooth Stone Productions, 131
Flashpoint Entertainment, 131
Focus Features, 132
Fortress Features, 134
Forward Pass, 134
FourBoys Films, 134
Fox 2000 Pictures, 135
Fox International Productions (FIP), 135
Fox Searchlight Pictures, 135
Frederic Golchan Productions, 136
Freedom Films, 136
Fuller Films, 138
FuseFrame, 138
Fuzzy Door Productions, 139
Gary Sanchez Productions, 140
Gerard Butler Alan Siegel Entertainment / Evil Twins, 140
Gerber Pictures, 140
Ghost House Pictures, 141
Gil Adler Productions, 141
Gil Netter Productions, 141
Girls Club Entertainment, 142
GK Films, 142
Glory Road Productions, 143
Gold Circle Entertainment, 143
Goldcrest Films, 144
Gorilla Pictures, 144
Gracie Films, 145
Grammnet Productions, 145
Grand Canal Film Works, 145
Grand Productions, 146
Gran Via Productions, 146
Grazka Taylor Productions, 146
Green Hat Films, 146
Grizzly Adams Productions, 147
Groundswell Productions, 148
Gunn Films, 148
Guy Walks Into A Bar, 149

Hammer Films, 149
Handpicked Films, 149
Handsomecharlie Films, 150
Happy Madison Productions, 150
Harpo Films, Inc., 150
Hartswood Films, 150
Hazy Mills Productions, 151
HBO Films & Miniseries, 152
Heavy Duty Entertainment, 152
Heel & Toe Productions, 152
Henceforth Pictures, 152
Henderson Productions, 153
Heyday Films, 153
HGTV, 153
Hollywood Gang Productions, 154
Home Box Office (HBO), 154
Hyde Park Entertainment, 155
Hypnotic, 155
Icon Productions, 155
Illumination Entertainment, 155
ImageMovers, 155
Imagine Entertainment, 156
IM Global, 156
Imprint Entertainment, 156
In Cahoots, 156
Incognito Pictures, 157
Indian Paintbrush, 157
Indican Productions, 157
Ineffable Pictures, 158
Inferno Entertainment, 158
Infinitum Nihil, 158
Ink Factory, 159
INPHENATE, 159
Intrepid Pictures, 159
Irish Dreamtime, 160
Iron Ocean Films, 160
Irwin Entertainment, 160
Ish Entertainment, 160
Ithaca Pictures, 161
Jeff Morton Productions, 162
Jerry Weintraub Productions, 162
Joel Schumacher Productions, 163
John Calley Productions, 163
John Goldwyn Productions, 163
Jon Shestack Productions, 164
Josephson Entertainment, 164
Kapital Entertainment, 165
Karz Entertainment, 165
Kennedy/Marshall Company, 166
Kerner Entertainment Company, 166
Kickstart Productions, 166

KippSter Entertainment, 168
Komut Entertainment, 168
K/O Paper Products, 168
Krane Media, LLC., 168
Lago Film GmbH, 169
Langley Park Productions, 169
Lava Bear Films, 171
LD Entertainment, 171
Legendary Pictures, 172
Leslie Iwerks Productions, 172
Liaison Films, 172
Lightstorm Entertainment, 173
Likely Story, 173
Lin Pictures, 173
Lionsgate, 173
Lucasfilm Ltd., 175
Lynda Obst Productions, 175
M8 Entertainment, Inc., 175
Mad Chance Productions, 176
Madhouse Entertainment, 176
Magnet Releasing, 177
Malpaso Productions, 177
Mandalay Television, 177
Mandeville Films, 178
Martin Chase Productions, 180
Maven Pictures, 181
Maximum Films & Management, 181
Mayhem Pictures, 182
Media Rights Capital, 182
Medusa Film, 183
Melee Entertainment, 183
Merv Griffin Entertainment, 183
Metro-Goldwyn Meyer (MGM), 184
Michael De Luca Productions, 184
Mirada, 186
Miranda Entertainment, 186
Misher Films, 186
Modercine, 187
Moxie Pictures, 189
MRB Productions, 189
Mr. Mudd, 190
Myriad Pictures, 190
NALA Investments, 190
NBC Productions, 191
NBC Studios, 191
NBCUniversal Television Distribution, 191
Necropia Entertainment, 192
New Amsterdam Entertainment, 192
New Line Cinema, 193
New Wave Entertainment, 193
Nick Wechsler Productions, 194

North By Northwest Entertainment, 194
Nova Pictures, 195
Nu Image Films, 195
Nuyorican Productions, 195
O2 Filmes, 196
OddLot Entertainment, 196
Offspring Entertainment, 196
Olive Bridge Entertainment, 196
Olmos Productions Inc., 196
O.N.C., 197
Open Road Films, 198
Original Media, 198
Oscilloscope Pictures, 199
Overnight Productions, 200
OWN: Oprah Winfrey Network, 200
OZLA Pictures Inc., 200
Pacifica International Film & TV Corporation, 200
Pacific Standard, 200
PalmStar Entertainment, 201
Palomar Pictures, 201
Panay Films, 201
Pantelion Films, 201
Panther Films, 202
Paper Street Films, 202
Paradox Entertainment, 203
Parallel Media, 203
Paramount Pictures, 203
Pariah, 203
Participant Media, 204
Partizan Entertainment, 204
PCH Film, 205
Peace Arch Entertainment, 205
Peggy Rajski Productions, 206
Perfect Storm Entertainment, 206
Pink Slip Pictures, 207
Pixar, 207
Plan B Entertainment, 208
Platinum Dunes, 208
Playtone Productions, 208
Plum Pictures, 208
Polsky Films, 208
Polymorphic Pictures, 209
PorterGeller Entertainment, 209
Practical Pictures, 210
Preferred Content, 210
Pretty Pictures, 211
Protozoa Pictures, 211
Rabbit Bandini Productions, 212
Radar Pictures, 212
@Radical Media, 212
Rainmaker Entertainment, 213

RCR Media Group, 214
Red Crown Productions, 215
Red Giant Media, 215
Red Granite Pictures, 215
Red Hour Films, 216
Red Om Films, Inc., 216
Red Planet Pictures, 216
Red Wagon Entertainment, 216
Reveille, LLC/ Shine International, 218
Revelations Entertainment, 219
Revolution Films, 219
Rhombus Media, Inc., 219
Rhythm & Hues Studios, 220
River Road Entertainment, 220
Robert Greenwald Productions, 221
Roberts/David Films Inc., 221
Robert Simonds Company, 221
Rocklin/ Faust, 222
Room 9 Entertainment, LLC, 222
Rosa Entertainment, 222
Roserock Films, 222
Route One Films, 223
Ryan Murphy Productions, 223
Saltire Entertainment, 224
Samuelson Productions Limited, 224
Sandbar Pictures, 224
Sanitsky Company, 225
Scarlet Fire Entertainment, 225
Scott Free Productions, 225
Screen Gems, 226
Second and 10th Inc., 227
Seismic Pictures, 227
SenArt Films, 227
Seraphim Films, 227
Serendipity Point Films, 227
Serendipity Productions, Inc., 228
Seven Arts Pictures, 228
Shaftesbury Films, 228
Sheep Noir Films, 229
Shephard/Robin Company, 229
Shondaland, 229
Shoreline Entertainment, 230
Showtime Networks, 230
Sidney Kimmel Entertainment, 230
Sierra/ Affinity, 230
Signature Pictures, 231
Sikelia Productions, 231
Silver Nitrate Entertainment, 232
Sketch Films, 233
Skylark Entertainment, Inc., 233
Smokehouse Pictures, 234

Sobini Films, 235
Social Capital Films, 235
S Pictures, Inc., 236
Spitfire Pictures, 236
Spyglass Entertainment, 236
Stage 6 Films, 236
State Street Pictures, 237
Stone Village Pictures, 238
Storefront Pictures, 238
Storyline Entertainment, 239
Straight Up Films, 239
StudioCanal, 239
Summit Entertainment, 240
Sundial Pictures, 240
Sunlight Productions, 241
Sunswept Entertainment, 241
Suntaur Entertainment, 241
Super Crispy Entertainment, 241
Sweet 180, 242
Taggart Productions, 242
Tagline Pictures, 242
Tannenbaum Company, 242
Tapestry Films, Inc., 243
Team Downey, 243
Temple Hill Entertainment, 244
The Asylum, 245
The AV Club, 245
The Bureau, 245
The Gotham Group, 246
The Group Entertainment, 246
The Halcyon Company, 247
The Hatchery, 247
The Jim Henson Company, 247
The Littlefield Company, 248
The Mark Gordon Company, 248
The Mazur/Kaplan Company, 248
The Safran Company, 249
The Walt Disney Company, 249
The Weinstein Company, 249
The Wolper Organization, 250
The Zanuck Company, 250
Three Strange Angels, Inc., 251
Thunderbird Films, 251
Thunder Road Pictures, 251
Tim Burton Productions, 251
Tom Welling Productions, 252
Trancas International Films, Inc., 253
Treehouse Films, 253
Tribeca Films, 253
TriCoast Studios, 254
Tricor Entertainment, 254

Trilogy Entertainment Group, 254
Troika Pictures, 254
Twentieth Century Fox Film Corporation, 256
Twentieth Century Fox Television, 256
Twentieth Television, 256
Ufland Productions, 257
Union Entertainment, 258
Unique Features, 258
United Artists, 259
Upload Films, 260
UppiTV, 260
USA Network, 260
Valhalla Motion Pictures, 260
Vanderkloot Film & Television, 261
Vanguard Films + Animation, 261
Vertebra Films, 262
Vertigo Films, 263
Viacom Inc., 263
Village Roadshow Pictures, 263
Virgin Produced, 264
Von Zerneck Sertner Films, 264
Vox3 Films, 265
Walt Becker Productions, 266
Warner Bros. Television Group, 266
Warner Brothers Animation, 266
Warner Brothers Entertainment Inc., 266
Warner Brothers Home Entertainment, 266
Warner Brothers Pictures, 267
Warner Horizon Television, 267
Warner Sisters Productions, 267
Warp X, 268
Warrior Poets, 268
Wayans Brothers Entertainment, 268

Wayfare Entertainment Ventures LLC, 269
Weed Road Productions, 269
Weintraub/Kuhn Productions, 269
We TV Network, 270
Whitewater Films, 270
Whyaduck Productions Inc., 271
WideAwake, Inc., 271
Wild at Heart Films, 271
Wildwood Enterprises, Inc., 272
Wind Dancer Films, 272
Wingnut Films Ltd., 272
Winsome Productions, 273
Witt-Thomas Productions, 273
Wolf Films, Inc., 273
Wonderland Sound and Vision, 274
Working Title Films, 274
World of Wonder Productions, 275
Worldview Entertainment, Inc., 275
Worldwide Biggies, 275
Worldwide Pants Inc., 276
WWE Studios, 276
X Filme Creative Pool, 276
Xingu Films Ltd., 276
XIX Entertainment, 277
XYZ Films, 277
Yari Film Group, 277
Yorktown Productions, 278
YourFace Goes Here Entertainment, 278
Zak Penn's Company, 278
Zemeckis/Nemeroff Films, 279
Zeta Entertainment, 279
Zing Productions, Inc., 280